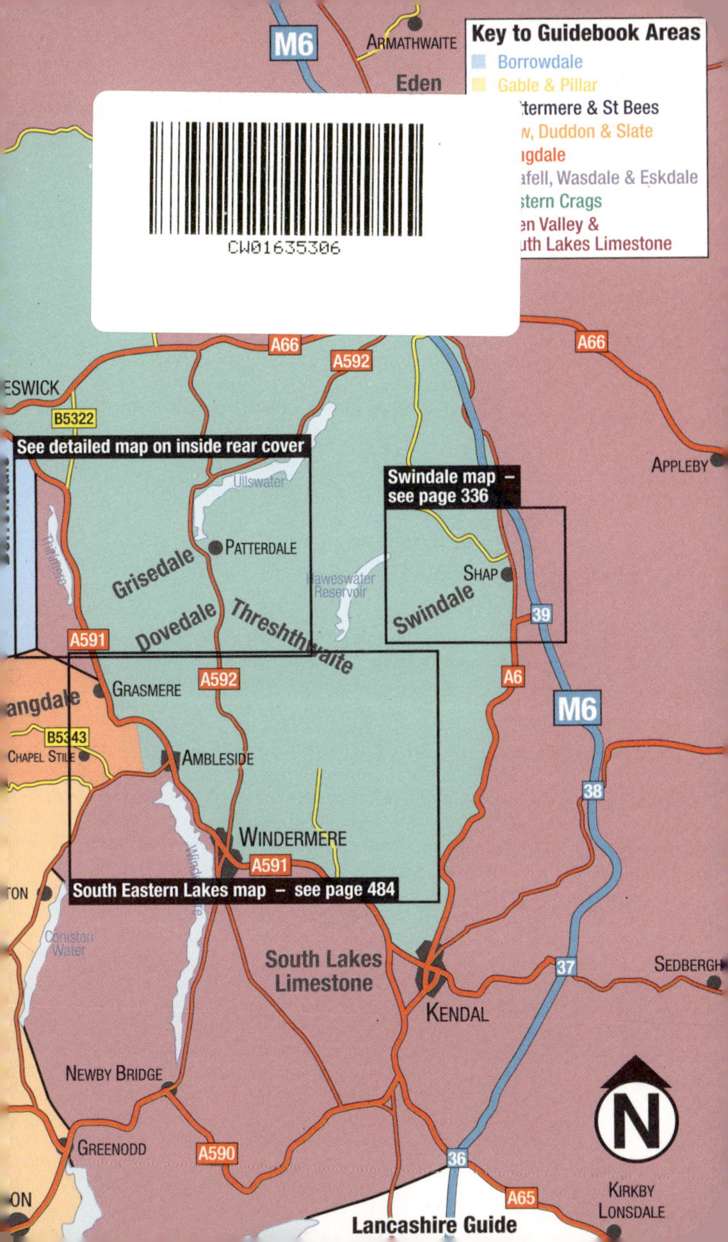

Key to Guidebook Areas
Borrowdale
Gable & Pillar
ttermere & St Bees
v, Duddon & Slate
ngdale
afell, Wasdale & Eskdale
stern Crags
en Valley &
uth Lakes Limestone
CW01635306
M6
Armathwaite
Eden
A66
A592
ESWICK
B5322
See detailed map on inside rear cover
Ullswater
Thirlmere
Patterdale
Grisedale
Dovedale
Threshthwaite
Haweswater Reservoir
Swindale map – see page 336
Shap
Swindale
39
Appleby
A591
A592
A6
angdale
Grasmere
B5343
Chapel Stile
Ambleside
38
Windermere
A591
South Eastern Lakes map – see page 484
TON
Coniston Water
South Lakes Limestone
Kendal
37
Sedbergh
Newby Bridge
Greenodd
A590
36
A65
ON
Kirkby Lonsdale
N
Lancashire Guide

£18

Eastern Crags

FRCC GUIDE

Published by
the Fell and Rock Climbing Club
of the English Lake District

276.

E18

Climbing Guides to
the English Lake District

Eastern Crags

by A Davis
and N Wharton

Photodiagrams &
Picture Research by
PC Rigby
(Photographs Editor)

Maps by
A Phizacklea (Diagrams Editor)

Edited by
SJH Reid

FRCC GUIDE

Published by
the Fell and Rock Climbing Club
of the English Lake District

Peter Hodgkiss. **Photo**: Bob Aitken

Dedication

This guide book is dedicated to the late Peter Hodgkiss, co-founder of the specialist mountaineering publishers, the Ernest Press, and printer extrordinaire of so many of the recent FRCC guidebooks. A stickler for quality, it is in no small measure due to Peter that the FRCC climbing guides are viewed as leaders in their field.

1907 – 2010

The FRCC and Rock Climbing Guides to the English Lake District

Pete Whillance on the first ascent of **Grand Prix** (E3), Raven Crag, Thresthwaite Cove.
Photo: Pete Botterill

The formation of the **Fell and Rock Climbing Club** was proposed at Coniston in 1906 at the instigation of Edward Scantlebury and Alan Craig, two of a "coterie of keen young mountaineers living on the southern confines of the English Lake District". Before the end of the year the club had over 40 members enrolled and was officially founded in 1907 when Ashley Abraham accepted the office of President. The first Club Journal was produced that same year and many new climbs were reported therein and in further annual volumes.

The Club published its first rock climbing guidebook in 1922 (Doe Crag by George Bower) and since that date has produced a continuous series of definitive guidebooks to Lake District rock climbing. These guidebooks are written and published by volunteers who update the text and check new climbs, many of which have been, and continue to be, pioneered by Club members.

The Club now has over 1200 members and owns several club huts both in the Lake District and elsewhere. Membership has always been open to applicants of either sex who can demonstrate an ongoing interest and enthusiasm for climbing in the Lake District. Enquiries regarding the FRCC and its guidebooks should be addressed to the current Club Secretary or Guidebooks Editor, whose addresses are available from the Club's website at www.frcc.co.uk or from the BMC.

Previous Editions
Eastern Crags:

1938 CJ Astley Cooper, E Wood-Johnston
1959 H Drasdo
1967 H Drasdo, NJ Soper
1969 H Drasdo, NJ Soper
1979 EM Grindley, GN Higginson
1987 J Earl, A Griffiths, R Smith
1992 A Davis, T Price

British Library Cataloguing in Publication Data
Davis, A.
Eastern Crags. – [9th Series] –
(Climbing Guides to the English Lake District) –
(FRCC Guide)

ISBN 978-0-85028-051-7

Front Cover: Dave Birkett all fired up on the first ascent of **Up Hellya** (E8), Dove Crag.
Photo: Alastair Lee

Frontispiece: A century ago, climbers strike a dramatic pose for the postcard trade on the flank of **Sharp Edge, Blencathra**, an area without known rock climbs, nor indeed it would seem, belaying techniques.
Photo: Abraham Collection

Designed and typeset by **Vertebrate Publishing**, Sheffield, a division of **Vertebrate Graphics**. www.v-publishing.co.uk

Distributed by Cordee, Leicester. www.cordee.co.uk

Printed in China through Colorcraft Ltd, Hong Kong. www.colorcraft.com.hk

Published by The Fell and Rock Climbing Club of the English Lake District Limited
Industrial and Provident Societies Registration: 30506 R

All rights reserved. No part of this publication may be reproduced or transmitted in any form or by any means, electronic or mechanical, including photocopy, recording, or any information storage and retrieval system, without permission in writing from the FRCC.

Contents

Thirlmere 45

Above: Mark Greenbank and Russell Dicks getting stuck into a slice of **American Pie** (E2), Lower Swirl Crag. **Photo:** Tony Greenbank

Introduction

This guidebook is the fourth volume in a new series of definitive climbing guides to the Lake District, one of the most popular climbing areas in the British Isles. This guide deals with the eastern half of that area. It is published by the Fell and Rock Climbing Club of the English Lake District, the club that has been responsible for producing definitive guides to the area since 1922. It is intended that the full Ninth Series will eventually comprise:

1. *Lake District Winter Climbs*
   (published in conjunction with Cicerone Press)
2. *Gable & Pillar*
3. *Buttermere & St Bees*
4. *Eastern Crags*
5. *Eden Valley & South Lakes Limestone*
6. *Langdale*
7. *Dow & Slate*
8. *Duddon & Eskdale*
9. *Scafell & Wasdale*
10. *Borrowdale*
11. *Lake District Rock* (Selected Climbs)

"The busy Kendal to Keswick artery through the Lake District and its continuation along the north shore of Bassenthwaite Lake towards Carlisle, cuts the National Park and its mountains into two approximately equal portions, and the layman might assume, if he was sufficiently interested, that it does much the same for the rock climbs of the district," wrote Harry Griffin in his article on being promoted to the giddy heights of Eastern Crags guidebook writer's assistant, '*Innocents in the East*' in the 1955 FRCC Journal. He went on to add, "Climbers, however, know differently. West of the main road, with its double-decker buses, caravan sites and flourishing ice cream trade, there are listed, in half-a-dozen stout guide books, between six and seven hundred rock climbs, and many more routes still await official recognition. In the neglected eastern area, however –

a reasonably hilly area which contains the Helvellyn range, Skiddaw, Blencathra, Fairfield, High Street and many more elevated sections of the countryside – the climbs are easily contained in one modest section at the end of the old Dow Crag and Langdale guide, published in 1938. Even including obscure routes which have since proved unidentifiable the grand total is – or was – the miserable one of thirty-eight. No doubt there are geological reasons why there should be more rock climbs west of Dunmail Raise than east of it but it seems strange that there should be as many as seventeen times more."

Over half a century on and it seems little has changed except the numbers, but those numbers now mean that, ***Eastern Crags***, long lumped in with Buttermere on the rather flimsy grounds that it was "all of northern Lakeland without Borrowdale" finally warrants its own guidebook again.

Colour photos have been used for crag diagrams, and virtually every crag has been covered in this way, no easy task on complex multi-pitch crags such as Dove Crag and Raven Crag, Thirlmere. The writers and their assistants, photographers and the Photographs Editor are to be congratulated on the outstanding collection of photodiagrams that has resulted.

Since the last guide, numerous micro routes have been recorded, many of them of dubious worth. In an effort to keep this volume to a size and weight which one might consider taking along, at least to the crag, if not up the route, many such climbs, and indeed whole crags where warranted, have been consigned to the archive on the Fell and Rock website. With rather more reluctance, one good venue, Whelter Crags, where access is currently banned on conservation grounds and there seems no hope of it being regained in the immediate future, has also been placed there – it is hoped this latter measure is only temporary.

Continuing his 1955 article, Harry Griffin went on to say, "If you care to look for it there is, in fact, any amount of rock amongst the eastern fells, although some of these crags may only be reached by walking, which may not suit everyone. There are also several beautiful and, so far, almost deserted valleys, comparatively free of tracks, orange peel and litter. At the moment you can climb on these crags without the need for queueing, watch buzzards soaring undisturbed or bathe in the pools without considering the proprieties – an idyllic state of affairs..." One could almost say the same today.

Stephen Reid (Editor), March 2011

Right: Lakeland saga: Al Davis and Eric Parker take on **Beowulf** (VS), Scrubby Crag.
Photo: Ron Kenyon

General Notes

Terminology

A *wall* ranges from almost vertical to slightly overhanging. A *slab* is less than vertical. A *glacis* is a very easy-angled slab. An *arête* is a sharply-angled rib or ridge. Climbs and pitches are measured in metres (m). The terms *gill* and *ghyll* (meaning stream or gully) are interchangeable. *Fell* is the Lakeland word for hill.

Grades

The standard British double-grade system is used for all except bolted routes and boulder problems. On first acquaintance this may be puzzling to visitors from overseas used to climbs having a single grade, but in fact it is relatively simple and once understood provides a great deal of information about the climbs. By far the majority of climbs in this guide require the use of leader-placed natural protection and on any route given an adjectival grade a full rack suitable to the climb being attempted should be carried. Grades are very personal, being influenced by an individual's stature and physique, their willingness to climb above protection, and their preference for a particular style of climbing.

Adjectival Grades

These give the overall grade of the climb in good weather conditions, taking into account such factors as technical difficulty, rock quality and protection. The grades are: Moderate, Difficult, Very Difficult, Mild Severe, Severe, Hard Severe, Mild Very Severe, Very Severe, Hard Very Severe, Extremely Severe, with the standard abbreviations being used in the text. The Extremely Severe grade is open ended and is currently divided into E1, E2, through to E11, though the hardest climb described in this book is E9.

Plus and Minus Grades

Adjectival grades have been further subdivided by use of a minus sign (-) to indicate routes that are considered easy for the grade, and a plus sign (+) for those thought to be hard. This system replaces the traditional graded list and needless to say, just like a graded list, it is completely subjective.

Technical Grades

These are included for each pitch of 4a and above on routes of VS and above. This grade is an attempt to assess the pure technical difficulty encountered on each pitch and once again is open-ended. The grades to date are: 4a, 4b, 4c, 5a, 5b, 5c, 6a, 6b, 6c, 7a.

UK Adjectival Grade	UK Technical Grade (approx)	UIAA (alpine) Grade	European Equivalent	USA Equivalent	Australian Equivalent
Moderate		I, II	1	5.1, 5.2	4, 5
Difficult		II, III	1, 2, 2+	5.2, 5.3	5, 6, 7
Very Difficult		III, III+	2, 2+, 3–	5.2, 5.3, 5.4	6, 7, 8
Hard Very Difficult		III+, IV, IV+	2+, 3–, 3, 3+	5.4, 5.5, 5.6	8, 9, 10
Mild Severe		IV, IV+	3–, 3, 3+	5.5, 5.6	10, 11
Severe		IV, IV+, V–	3, 3+, 4	5.5, 5.6, 5.7	10, 11, 12
Hard Severe		IV+, V–, V	3, 3+, 4, 4+	5.6, 5.7	12, 13
Mild Very Severe	4a, 4b, 4c	IV+, V–, V	3+, 4, 4+	5.6, 5.7	12, 13, 14
Very Severe	4a, 4b, 4c	V–, V, V+	4, 4+, 5	5.7, 5.8	13, 14, 15
Hard Very Severe	4c, 5a, 5b	V+, VI-, VI	4+, 5, 5+, 6a	5.8, 5.9	15, 16, 17, 18
E1	5a, 5b, 5c	VI, VI+	5+, 6a, 6a+	5.9, 5.10a	18, 19, 20
E2	5b, 5c, 6a	VI+, VII–, VII	6a+, 6b, 6b+	5.10b, 5.10c	19, 20, 21
E3	5c, 6a	VII, VII+	6b, 6b+, 6c	5.10d, 5.11a, 5.11b	20, 21, 22
E4	6a, 6b	VII+, VIII–, VIII	6c, 6c+, 7a	5.11b, 5.11c, 5.11d	22, 23
E5	6a, 6b 6c	VIII, VIII+, IX–	7a, 7a+, 7b	5.11d, 5.12a, 5.12b	23, 24, 25
E6	6b, 6c	IX–, IX, IX+	7b, 7b+, 7c, 7c+	5.12b, 5.12c, 5.12d, 5.13a	25, 26, 27, 28
E7	6c, 7a	IX+, X–, X	7c+, 8a, 8a+	5.13a, 5.13b, 5.13c	28, 29, 30
E8	6c, 7a	X, X+	8a+, 8b, 8b+	5.13c, 5.13d, 5.14a	30, 31, 32
E9	7a, 7b	XI-, X+	8b+, 8c, 8c+	5.14a, 5.14b, 5.14c	30, 31, 32

French Grades

Fully bolt-protected 'sport' routes are given French grades overall. These grades, prefixed with an 'F', are comparable with the standard French/Spanish grades of 4, 5, 6a, 6b, 6c, 7a, 7b, 7c, and 8a. They are further subdivided with a (+) symbol. In this guide there are very few sport routes.

French Grades have also been given to some routes of E6 and above in addition to their UK grades as an extra assistance to those contemplating such climbs. These climbs are not sport climbs, nor is any encouragement to bolt them intended.

Boulder Problems

These notes are intended for those new to bouldering - regulars already understand the subtle nuances of the dark art.

The V grade system, developed in Hueco by John Sherman ('Verm' to his mates, hence the V) has been employed. This takes into account the physical challenge of the overall difficulty and not the technicality of the hardest move. Sustained traverse problems will thus often be technically easier for the given V grade. Fear and danger are not accounted for so that a decent crash mat and an alert spotter are invaluable.

For trad climbers new to bouldering, the problems can seem frustratingly perplexing at first as even the easiest problems are technically difficult. Direct comparison with trad grades is difficult; on V0 problems moves of 5a/5b can be expected, V1 to V2 and you can expect something around the 5b/5c/6a mark, V3 to V4 you can expect 6a/6b moves and after that it just gets hard.

Aid, Bolts and In Situ Protection

Only a few routes still require the use of artificial assistance and this is indicated in the description where appropriate. Aid reductions continue to be made; routes are described and graded according to the most free style in which they are known to have been climbed.

The placing of bolts is a subject which has aroused much emotive discussion during recent years. In the interest of care and concern for crags and the mountain environment, and a belief that British climbing in general should continue with the principle of leader-placed removable protection, the FRCC are generally in accord with the guidelines on the use of bolts for the protection of routes as set out by the BMC. It is agreed that in the Lake District bolts are only acceptable on certain quarried crags and some agreed limestone and sandstone outcrops. Climbers are asked to adhere to this policy and refrain from the temptation to place bolts on any natural crags.

Retro-bolting has taken place on a number of routes in the Lake District but only after consultation with the first ascentionist of that route. In order to avoid any conflict, please ensure that this policy is maintained.

A number of route descriptions in this guide contain references to in situ protection including pegs, slings, bolts and wires. The history of these frequently dates back to the first ascent. There can be no guarantee that the fixed gear mentioned will still be in place when you climb the route or, more importantly, if it is there, that it will be of any use. It is well known that in situ gear will deteriorate to a fraction of its original holding power due to the elements. This can occur in a matter of months rather than years, particularly where wires or hard steel blade pegs are concerned. Therefore it is for the individual climber to assess the reliability of any in situ protection encountered. Bolts are not infallible and have been known to fail in the past. The Cumbria Bolt Fund was set up in 2008 to replace the more dodgy Cumbrian bolts, some of which are over twenty years old and of dubious safety. See www.cumbriaboltfund.com for more information.

Fixed abseil points may be found on some crags. These should be thoroughly inspected before use and, if found to be doubtful, backed up with new equipment.

Stars and Quality

The star system of indicating the quality of a climb has been established for many years in Britain and climbers have long come to expect a three star route to be something extra special, not just in terms of the particular area being described, but vis-à-vis other climbs in the Great Britain as a whole. Whilst the original aim of this practice was laudable, giving only a handful of climbs three star status has brought its problems. Three star routes attract queues and queues create polish whilst nearby almost as good two star climbs that could do with a bit of traffic often languish in obscurity and become lichenous, and so on down the scale. To remedy this many more stars have been used in this guide than in the previous edition and they are now intended to indicate quality on a much broader scale, viz:

★★★	Good climbing, on good, mainly clean rock, with purpose to the line.
★★	Mostly the above.
★	Some good climbing and a permutation of the other two factors.
	Of interest to mainly to regular visitors to the crag.

It will be seen that a three star route no longer needs to be one of the best in the country, though it will provide an entertaining (and possibly adventurous) outing. This represents a substantial change in the starring policy and has been adopted in FRCC guides since 1999.

It is particularly difficult to rate new or unrepeated routes. Therefore, these have been given "hollow" stars as a provisional assessment. Feedback would be welcome.

Unrepeated Routes

Climbs that are thought not to have been repeated, have their grades suffixed by a '?'. Feedback on these routes would be appreciated.

FRCC Routes Archive

In order to keep the size of this guide to something that will fit in your pocket on multipitch climbs, poor or overgrown routes, and in some cases whole crags, have not been described. However, to preserve a complete history of climbing in the area, and to discourage unnecessary gardening activity, their descriptions have been preserved for posterity in the Rock Climbing section of the FRCC website, www.frcc.co.uk.

New Routes and Corrections

To aid writers of future guidebooks, please post comments, corrections, and details of all new climbs on the FRCC website www.frcc.co.uk. Several "New Routes books" exist in the area, including the Log Books in FRCC huts. However, these may not be checked regularly and first ascensionists are urged to also record their route on the website above or it may be missed. Please provide all relevant details in the usual format including grades, dates, first ascensionists and style of ascent.

Location of Crags

The location of each crag is indicated by its national grid reference. Beware those crags where the name on the map may be some way from the grid reference shown, and those where the climbers' name for a crag or other feature is different from that on the map - such instances are detailed in the text. The aspect of the main faces has been included to aid the choice of crags. The altitude given is based on a mean sea level of zero. The terms 'true left' and 'true right' are used to describe the position of a crag in a valley or gill relative to the direction of flow of the stream. The terms 'left' and 'right', unless otherwise stated, mean as the climber faces the climb.

Maps

Ordnance Survey Explorer Series 1:25000 maps that cover the large area described in this guide are OL4 (The English Lake District - North-West Area), OL5 (The English Lake District - North-East Area), OL7 (The English Lake District - South-East Area). Harvey also produce an excellent set of Lake District maps at this scale (their Super Walker series), but the climber is perhaps better served by their collaborative map with the British Mountaineering Council, Lake District at 1:40000. At 1:50000, the Ordnance Survey's Landranger maps numbers 90 and 97 cover the area in this guide.

Photodiagrams Key

- (green 1) Moderate to Hard Severe
- (blue 1) MVS to E1
- (red 1) E2 to E4
- (black 1) E5 and above
- (V1) Variation
- 1 Boulder Problem
- Belay
- (A) Abseil
- Fixed lower off
- Footpath
- Scramble/descent
- Caution required
- Danger

Photodiagrams

Full colour photodiagrams of almost every crag and buttress covered have been included. The amount of work required to produce these, particularly on high remote crags, has been immense, requiring many visits and the climbing of almost every route. However it is possible that some small errors remain and if in doubt it is probably better to rely on the written description rather than the photodiagram. The symbols used should be fairly self explanatory.

Photographs

The Editor has little sympathy for those who criticise photographs in climbing guides yet don't carry a camera themselves. Tracking down good climbing photographs for guidebooks is always a difficult task and the FRCC Guidebook Committee would like to express their gratitude to all those who submitted photographs for consideration. To those whose photographs were not selected this time, please do not be discouraged, and please keep snapping away and sending them in to the Guidebook Photographs Editor, whose address, together with details of current guidebook work being undertaken, is available from the Club's website at www.frcc.co.uk.

Safety Advice

Climbing is a dangerous pastime that can seriously damage your health! Details of climbs recorded in this guidebook, together with their grades, reference to in situ or natural protection, and locations, are made in good faith having been compiled from first ascent or past descriptions, checked and substantiated where possible with consensus comments.

Unfortunately climbs can change; holds fall off, rock becomes dirty, in situ gear deteriorates or disappears. Even a minor alteration can have a dramatic effect on the grade or seriousness of a route. It is therefore essential that climbers judge the condition of any route before committing themselves.

The contents of this guidebook are believed to be correct. However, neither the FRCC nor its members and their friends involved with its production can be held responsible for any omissions or mistakes, nor liable for any personal or third party injuries or damage, howsoever caused, arising from its use. In this claims-conscious age, climbers are recommended to obtain suitable insurance cover. The BMC now provides third party liability cover for members and members of affiliated clubs.

Campsites, Bunkhouses, Camping Barns and Club Huts

Within the Lake District there are numerous camping barns, bunkhouses and campsites. To find out more about these contact details are given on page 418. There are also many climbing club huts, most of which are available to non-club members - contact the BMC for a list.

Wild Camping

Wild camping (ie camping outside of a proper campsite) is generally allowed on the fells above the 300 metre contour as long as one is above the final (intake) wall and not within 100 metres of habitation. Any campsite used should be left as it was found and all litter cleared.

Right: Al Wilson powering his way up **Vlad the Impaler** (E7), Dove Crag. **Photo:** Steve Crowe

Geological Notes

by Dave Bodecott

The rocks of the eastern Lake District, between Thirlmere, Ullswater, Swindale and Kirkstone Pass, form the crags of greatest interest in the area. This is the volcanic belt, part of the Borrowdale Volcanic Group, formed 460–450 Ma (million years ago), and there are spectacular and varied volcanic sequences in this area that form high friction slabs and walls. These will be memorable to anyone who has climbed the lonely wall of Bloodhound on Gouther Crag, formed by an 80–180 metre thick pyroclastic breccia ejected from an explosive volcano. There are columnar jointed andesitic (fine grained) lava flows, possible pillow lavas (formed under water) and volcanic ash units on some of the high crags of the area.

Flanking the volcanic belt, and north of the A66, are the less interesting Ordovician Skiddaw Slates (490-460 Ma) of the Skiddaw-Blencathra massif. These areas are generally without rock climbing interest apart from outcrops on Carrock Fell of gabbro (an intrusive igneous rock formed from molten magma around 450 Ma). South of Kirkstone Pass, the Silurian shales of the Windermere group form the low ground (without climbing interest) below Kentmere.

These volcanic and slate belts are intruded by various granites such as the Shap granite and the Threlkeld microgranite (450 Ma) – these are climbable when bolted as at Bramcrag Quarry, St. John's in the Vale, but otherwise do not form natural crags. The Carrock Fell gabbro intrusion however does form a variety of natural crags and good bouldering. Student geologists should note that smashing holds away with geological hammers is not welcome, as the beautiful weathered surfaces are part of our heritage, and often key holds for someone's boulder problem!

Some time after the Borrowdale Volcanic period, the area was uplifted by the Caledonian mountain-building phase (about 400 Ma). The Mell Fell conglomerate of Devonian age (370 Ma, or possibly Early Carboniferous, ca 350 Ma) is the erosional product of this uplift, but apart from forming conical hills in the Ullswater area, no climbing crags developed on these rocks. Major fault lines like the Coniston fault, St Johns and Thirlmere fault line and the Deepdale Hause fault developed.

These have been re-activated during later tectonic phases often leading to poor rock near the fault zones on some crags, e.g. Ferrous Buttress - a real adventure on Iron Crag.

The main Quaternary glaciation (the Ice Age) was from 26,000–10,000 years ago and led to many of the present-day landforms including most of the familiar hills of the Lake District. Some crags such as Mart Crag and parts of Castle Rock South, Gouther and Swirl Crags are strongly affected by glacial erosion leading to rounded tops, forming so-called "roches moutonées".

Finally, these earthquakes have been recorded: 1786-7, 1867, 1885, 1901, 1911, 1979/1980, 1988. That is once every 28 years on average, so climbers beware!

Acknowledgements
British Geological Survey.
www.bgs.ac.uk
Cumberland Geological Society.
www.cumberland-geol-soc.org.uk
Dr. Andrew Bell, Open University.

Above: Upper Grisedale valley with Eagle Crag in the centre. **Photo:** Eric Shaw

Access & Conservation

by Simon Webb & Peter Davies

Access

Access to the crags described in this guide will be taken for granted by the majority of users but in fact in some cases it may have been achieved only through years of patient negotiation. Fortunately, the National Trust, Forestry Commission, United Utilities, or other private owners who are broadly sympathetic to climbers, own most of the crags described. In a few cases however, the situation remains delicate and increasing numbers of climbers are only likely to make it more so. Here is an area in which we can all help, not only by cherishing this region in the manner it deserves, parking thoughtfully, co-operating with farmers and landowners, following the country code, observing bird restrictions, picking up litter at crags and so on, but by ensuring that others do the same. Outsiders look on climbers as a group and inconsiderate behaviour by a few will be seen, rightly or wrongly, as a reflection upon us all. The onus is on all of us to make certain that it doesn't happen in the first place.

Bird Restrictions

Four species of bird nesting on the crags described in this guidebook are of particular note - these are the **peregrine, raven, ring ouzel** and **golden eagle**. All use crags as nesting sites as a strategy to avoid predators. In addition, ground-nesting upland **waders** (such as curlew and golden plover) frequent the Far Eastern Fells of the Lake District.

Peregrine and Raven

Many climbers will be familiar with the iconic birds of the Cumbrian uplands, peregrines and ravens.

Photo: RSPB

Peregrines are stocky, broad-winged birds of prey, which swoop at lightning speed from above onto unfortunate medium sized birds such as pigeons. Their call is a piercing shriek, which if they are disturbed will be repeated for long periods. They nearly always nest on coastal cliffs or inland crags but their nest will not be obvious - just a shallow depression in the soil or grass. White bird droppings can sometimes mark the location but could equally just be a roost or perching site. Cumbria has an exceptionally high density of nesting peregrine with some 60 pairs breeding in a good year. This core population is important in conservation terms as birds from here will spread out and re-colonise other areas in the UK.

Photo: RSPB

Ravens are very large black birds, much bigger and more thick set than a crow. Their calls are a distinctive "cronk" and "pruck-pruck". Also distinctive is their acrobatic flights with tumbling and inverted flying characteristic. The birds seem to delight in this and appear to be playing in the air. Ravens nests are large piles of twigs, often on a crag.

Both raven and peregrine are vulnerable to disturbance but the peregrine receives stronger (Schedule 1) legal protection on account of the shooting, poisoning, egg and chick theft that they have been subjected to over the years. Voluntary **Bird Restrictions** to protect both birds are put in place annually on various crags across Cumbria (raven: 15th February to 31st May, peregrine: 1st March to 30th June). Crags that have been restricted regularly in the past are indicated in the text. Usually restricted crags will be signed, but this may not always be the case and all climbers should acquaint themselves with the latest known details which can be found on the BMC website at www.thebmc.co.uk or on the FRCC website at www.frcc.co.uk. It may be that only some parts of the crag are restricted, so other routes can be climbed. If this is the case it will be indicated on the signs. These bird restrictions generally only apply to the more popular crags but this does not mean that it is acceptable to climb on all other crags in the nesting season. On crags where there are no formal restrictions you will need to keep an eye out for birds and nests and make judgements about your impact. Where birds have not nested in any particular year, the ban may be lifted early.

It is important that climbers follow some basic guidance in order to prevent disturbance as well as to make sure they are not breaking the law. Apart from possible prosecution, the police may arrest you and confiscate your climbing equipment as evidence to present at your trial - which may take a long time to come to court! The law states that it is an offence to intentionally or recklessly disturb a Schedule 1 bird at, on, or near the nest. It is also an offence to recklessly or intentionally disturb dependent fledged young. These fledglings are young birds that have just moved away from the nest but are still dependent to some extent on their parents for food and protection.

As you walk into the crag keep a look out for peregrines and other birds. Peregrines in particular may be calling as they fly about the area. When you arrive they may be disturbed but this is a normal response. Try and move out of their line of sight as quickly as you can and then wait and see if they settle down. Try to spot where they originate. This will enable you to decide whether there is a nest site that is being used near the route that you are hoping to do. The birds will probably be disturbed if they can see you so don't climb next to the nest but find a route that is not within their line of sight instead. If you do this, and the crucial early period of egg incubation is past, then you might find that the birds calm down quickly and climbing will not move them off the nest. However, if the birds continue to appear aggressive and agitated and are staying away from the nest, to continue climbing will cause damaging disturbance by keeping the parents off the nest for too long. In such circumstances you should find another climb either on another part of the crag further away from the nest or even on another crag.

There are no hard and fast rules to determine when you might be too close as so much depends upon the tolerance of the individual bird. If the crag is very popular with climbers, then any nesting birds may be habituated to climbers' presence. Such peregrines may be able to accept climbing in quite close proximity, as long as it is around the other side of an arête or on a separate buttress. But you can always be sure that climbing very close or directly onto the nest will cause damaging disturbance. At crags in remote areas where there is little climbing activity, birds may be disturbed even at some distance. Of particular importance is the line of sight. The best policy is to err upon the side of caution and if in any doubt retreat. For this reason it is not possible to set firm guidelines about how far away you need to be to avoid disturbance or whether you will be breaking the law or not.

There is increasing conservation concern about the ring ouzel. **Photo:** RSPB

Ring Ouzel

The ring ouzel is closely related to the blackbird and looks similar. Adult males are all black except for a white crescent on the breast and a yellow bill. The male sings its loud and mournful song from trees or rocks, although if disturbed near the nest they make a harsh "chack chack" call. The female is similar but duller, and young birds often lack the breast crescent. The ring ouzel is migratory, spending winter in Spain and Africa, but breeds in the Lake District in gullies, rocky areas or scree slopes above the 250-metre contour line. They usually nest in mature heather or occasionally under bracken, but very often on rock ledges or steep slopes laying several eggs in a neat cup-shaped nest. More than half the UK population of ring ouzels have been lost between 1988 and 1999 and this has led to its recent (2002) red listing as a bird of conservation concern. It is thus extremely important that crags with heather or bilberry covered ledges are safeguarded from crag clean ups or gardening. If you encounter a chack-chack call from the bird it would be sensible to retreat and help this threatened bird maintain breeding success in Cumbria.

Golden Eagle

The golden eagle (also Schedule 1) is dark brown with a paler red-brown head, a long tail and a wingspan of more than 2 metres. The Haweswater valley has long been the only English outpost for these magnificent birds. Eagles spend much of their time perched rather than flying, and spotting them against the fell side is a difficult task. Currently (2011) there is no female eagle at Haweswater and this means the male spends his springtimes valiantly displaying in the sky above Mardale Head in the hope of attracting a new mate. Golden eagles are therefore no-longer breeding in the Lakes but the territory they occupy has supported eagles for many years and it is clearly good enough for breeding success.

Breeding Waders

The blanket bogs and heather moorlands of the valleys of Swindale, Mosedale and Mardale, are known for their breeding wader populations. Curlews, golden plover, and dunlin breed here, together with red grouse. These birds, which are almost absent from the central and western Lake District, are ground nesting and are sensitive to disturbance. Advice to climbers is simple: do not take a dog to the crag in these areas during spring and early summer, but if you must, then keep it on a short lead.

Rare Plants, the Climber and "Gardening"

The most impressive English examples of upland vegetation are found amongst the high fells of the Lake District and North Pennines where there is steep craggy ground that sheep can't reach, with specialised soils and climatic conditions that are favoured by upland plants. In the valleys and the lowlands, agriculture has led to a loss of ecological diversity, with grasslands ploughed up and fertilised and natural vegetation only surviving on the crags. Although we often think of the fells and mountains as natural or wild, the vegetation is in general highly modified and man is responsible. In particular the impact of increased sheep numbers over the past fifty years has led to a huge reduction in the area of heathland vegetation in Cumbria. Crag vegetation is therefore particularly important as it provides a reservoir of rare flora that can re-colonise the uplands now that conservation organisations are negotiating lower sheep numbers. But for now, only climbers experience and enjoy these stands of wild plants, which have been lost or degraded elsewhere.

Bilberry is one of the plants that dominate the Lake District heathlands.
Photo: Jean Johnston

Juniper clings to the crags and steep slopes.
Photo: Simon Webb

Climbers will also notice that there are more trees on the crags than on gentler fell-sides. Sheep are once again the culprits and only on the steeper slopes (or where grazing pressure is very low) can trees get beyond the seedling stage. Some of the Lake District upland trees are rare and specialised - juniper is probably the most well known of these. A scrubby evergreen and rather prickly native conifer, its berries smell strongly of gin when they are purple and ripe. A specialist dwarf type of juniper inhabits the crags above 500 metres. A more natural landscape would have a greater woodland cover and junipers and willows would grow high on the open fells.

The vegetation described below needs protection across its whole range. It really is so rare and vulnerable that it is vitally important to conserve any fragments that are left. What follows describes the most extensive and richest areas that we know about but if a place is not mentioned it does not mean that it is unimportant nor that it does not matter.

The Eastern Fells of the Lake District are dominated by the Helvellyn and High Street mountain ranges whose high mountain crags are exceptional. They contain the best assemblage of rare arctic-alpine plants in England. Saxifrages, downy willow, alpine saw-wort, moss campion and cinquefoils adorn the high north-east facing coves. These plants thrive in cold dry winters and are threatened by climate change. Tarn Crag, Falcon Crag, Hutaple Crag, Greenhow End, Scrubby Crag, Hart Crag and the southern edge of Dove Crag are the richest botanically, but most of the outcrops on the Helvellyn, Fairfield and High Street ranges contribute to the conservation importance of this area. It would be an ecological disaster if these stunning examples of rich upland vegetation were lost or damaged due to the activity of climbers. Winter and summer climbing can impact on these fragile plant communities, which are extremely vulnerable to "gardening" or winter

Moss campion. **Photo:** Jean Johnston

Alpine cinquefoil. **Photo:** Jean Johnston

climbing in poor conditions. In the valleys below, lakeshores are often cloaked with rich woodlands full of fern banks, ancient trees and twisted junipers. In the Northern Fells, on the eastern fringes of the Skiddaw massif, lies Carrock Fell. Here vegetation is heathland with a colourful mixture of ling, bell heather and bilberry. The natural crags here are set amongst blocky broken fellside, which is the favoured haunt of ring ouzel and peregrine.

The Law on Wild Plants and Birds

Natural vegetation and birds are an important part of our heritage and Government has enacted strict laws to protect them. These laws apply to both landowners and those enjoying outdoor recreation. This legal framework is part of the UK's national and international obligations towards conservation.

Much of the upland landscape is within Sites of Special Scientific Interest (SSSIs). Although there is much of interest to conserve outside these sites, SSSIs do form the central core of the statutory conservation system in the UK. This wildlife law doesn't just give powers to designate and protect special sites, it also provide for many positive initiatives to conserve our wildlife including mechanisms for grants, management agreements, action plans as well as open access provision.

In general terms all wild birds and their nests and eggs are protected by law with heavy penalties (a fine of up to £5000 and/or six months' imprisonment) for disturbance.

Natural vegetation is also protected by legislation both within SSSIs and beyond. Reckless damage to an SSSI carries severe penalties with a £20,000 maximum fine. In addition to general protection many of the rarer plants and animals receive additional protection.

These laws are tough but if you take time to find out about the birds and natural vegetation it is unlikely that there will be conflicts. Following the code of conduct is always a better alternative to court cases or permanent climbing bans.

Code of Conduct

Climbers (and others involved in outdoor recreation) are not generally responsible for the decline in the extent and quality of wildlife habitats in the UK. However the nature of the sport is that it takes you to the most sensitive parts of the landscape, to the refuges unaffected by grazing pressure and to the places best suited to rare plants and nesting birds. Climbers need to be aware that they are going to these special places and must take extra care not to damage or disturb them.

Take care not to damage the crag flora. Route preparation (or gardening) is a significant threat to rare upland vegetation. If new route preparation will result in the destruction of upland vegetation or bird habitat then it should not go ahead. Gone are the days when it was acceptable to dig routes out of the hillsides, the environmental price is far too high. More detail on this subject can be found in the ***Lake District Green Climbing Guide*** (BMC, 2006).

Any trees growing above the 600 metre contour are likely to be really important ecologically or a rare species or both - these are not good places for runners, belays, lower-offs or abseils. On lowland crags trees are equally important - they may be rare whitebeams or ancient yews and they were there centuries before climbers.

Adhere to the negotiated restrictions to protect nesting birds. These protect the birds from disturbance and the climber from accidentally breaking the law. If you experience obvious 'alarm calling birds' then retreat from the area, even if there is no bird ban in place. In some locations (see above) ground-nesting waders are extremely vulnerable to disturbance by dogs in spring or summer. Please do not let your dog threaten successful bird breeding. A short lead will happily resolve the conflict.

Conclusions

Climbers (in both summer and winter) can play an important role in protecting the natural environment. The best places for climbing are often the most important locations of natural vegetation, home to rare plants trees and ferns and they also provide nesting locations for a range of vulnerable bird species. These places are sensitive and climbers must take extra care to minimise their impact. Climbing and nature conservation can happily co-exist if the code of conduct described above is followed.

Simon Webb (Natural England, www.naturalengland.org.uk) &
Peter Davies (Cumbria Bird Club, www.cumbriabirdclub.org.uk)

Acknowledgements

The Eastern Fells of the Lakes are home to some of the more obscure lumps of rocky hillside which climbers have chosen to excavate over the years only for subsequent climbers to ignore. The authors are therefore indebted to a number of friends who have given up days, when they could have been better employed, to visit neglected classics. Thanks go to Jim Arnold, Kate Arnold, Gary Baum, Brian Davison, Dominic Donnini, Alan Dougherty, Colin Downer, John Ellerton, Jonathan Farnsworth, Steve Goodwin, Al Hewison, Dave Hollows, Ron Kenyon, Chris King, Mick Lovatt (The Perfect Man), Paul O'Reilly, Eric Parker, Steve Prior, Steve Scott, Tim Whiteley, Cherrie Whiteley, Johnny Wilson and Stuart Wood - not only the loudest retailer in Cumbria, but also a great partner on the crag. Thanks in particular are due to Mary-Grace Brown who has uncomplainingly checked out more esoteric gems than any California girl deserves.

A special mention must go to James and Kerrie Bumby who wrote the Longsleddale section of the guide, with the assistance of Shaw Brown on Nether Crag, and to Max Biden who has sorted out the long-standing historic and descriptive anomalies of Calf Howe Crag. Also to Eric Shaw who has produced an excellent set of photographs for the photodiagrams. This was carried out with great patience and effort to arrive at the crag in just the right lighting conditions.

Many other climbers gave freely of their time and experience with advice and information. Most remain anonymous as their advice was culled at the crag in passing but thanks go to Johnny Adams, Bill Birkett, Martin Bagness, Dave Birkett, Duncan Booth, Steve Broatch, Greg Chapman, Barry Clarke, Steve Crowe, Jim Fotheringham, Chris Gore who allowed himself to be dragged away from his sport-climbing, Rick Graham, Tony Greenbank, Alan Greig, Tony Marr, Al Phizacklea, Colin Read, Stephen Reid, Trevor Suddaby, Matt de Vaal, Tom Walkington, Mike Weeks and Al Wilson.

And a massive thank you from the whole of the climbing community to the boys of the "North Lakes Job Club" under the leadership of Al Wilson who spent hours cleaning some of our best hard crags and replacing old fixed gear and tat. If ever you meet these lads in the pub - buy them a pint, they deserve it!

Thanks are also due to the families of the authors, to Al's son John,

Al Davis
Photo: John Trengrove

Nick Wharton
Photo: Flora Wharton

his literacy consultant, who helped sort out the nuances of the English language and Nick's daughter Flora who helped check numerous approach descriptions as well posing for photos. Finally, special thanks to our wives Linda (Al) and Karen (Nick), who have happily tolerated our absence for days on end and most evenings. They may see a little more of us in future.

Al Davis, Nick Wharton 2011

Editorial

As with most guidebooks, this one is late – for which the Editor accepts his fair share of the blame, though the excellent winter ice climbing of 2009/10 was also culpable. It has been a mammoth task though, for this guide covers half the Lake District, and the authors and their assistants are to be congratulated on their perseverance in checking so many lesser known climbs on seldom visited crags. This guide though is based on that of all the previous guidebook writers whose contributions are acknowledged in the previous editions list on page vi.

Phil Rigby deserves an official FRCC gold medal for the number of hours he has laboured to produce all the photodiagrams – these are not only a real aid to locating climbs but also a tremendous source of inspiration. Phil has also tracked down and collected together a host of fascinating historical photographs and a superb collection of action shots to get us all itching to climb in the Eastern Crags. Al Phizacklea's maps and hand drawn bird's eye views, such a major feature of FRCC guides, once again delight the eye and get us to the crags with the minimum of losing our way. Eric Shaw has gone the extra mile to supply crag photos for many diagrams. Al Wilson, Al Phizacklea, Nick Wharton and Steve Crowe also contributed many excellent photos which involved a lot of work setting up abseils etc. A special thank you too to Neil Allinson, Bill Birkett, Andy Birtwistle, Tony Greenbank, Ron Kenyon, Alastair Lee (for the fine cover shot), Karl Lunt, Ian Roper, Paul Ross, Jack Soper, Ken Wilson and Peter Smith (FRCC Archivist) for help with many historical pictures, and, in addition, we once again express our gratitude to the Abraham family for allowing us free use of the wonderful photographic record of George and Ashley Abraham.

Numerous other climbers have contributed photographs; some of these are professionals who would normally charge for their work but have been happy to forgo their usual fee to support a good cause –

the continuance of club-published definitive guidebooks: their names are recorded in the text and we are grateful to them all. We would encourage all climbers to consider carrying (and using!) a camera when they climb in the Lakes - good results can be sent to the Photographs Editor who can be contacted via the FRCC website.

We are grateful to Simon Webb and Peter Davies for the section on access and conservation, a reminder that there are other things that appreciate the crags even more than climbers. The geological section was written by Dave Bodecott, and Ron Kenyon has compiled all the information sections at the rear of the book with the exception of the advice on mountain accidents which was written by Dr John Ellerton, and the crag guide which was the work of Max Biden. I would also like to thank John Robinson (FRCC President during the two years that this guide was in preparation) for his unstinting enthusiasm and encouragement, and John Moore (current FRCC President) for continuing that support. The jedious tob of proo ferading was greatly assisted by Max Biden with additional help from Sally Baxendale, Al Davis, Ron Kenyon, Nick Wharton and Alan Wilson, so any mistakes are their fault. Vertebrate Graphics, and in particular Jane Beagley, have once again done wonders with the layout and, following the sad death of Peter Hodgkiss, Colorcraft have taken on the role of printer, converting the whole mass of computer gobbledygook into the useful guidebook that you now hold in your hand.

Stephen Reid, 2011

Above: Sunset from Castle Rock. **Photo:** Ron Kenyon

Historical

Eastern Crags

1890 – 1959

The eastern fells of Lakeland, grassy and rounded for the most part, lonely and rather remote, have, until comparatively recent years, been written off as fell-walking country only. Most climbers hurrying, during the last half-century, to Scafell, Gable or Langdale have hardly given them a glance, but now their eyes have been opened to a cluster of entirely new climbing grounds. For these neglected eastern fells do, in fact, run to rock – fine crags which stand bare and bold on the hillside, often tucked away in north-east corners, uncairned, unscratched and only reached by considerable walking.

Rock-climbing on these fells has been, for the most part, a post-war development. Previously the climbs, few in number, occupied a modest section – styled 'Outlying Crags' – at the end of the Dow Crag and Langdale Guide published in 1938. Even including obscure routes which have since proved unidentifiable the grand total was only 38 but the present guide lists four times that number. The original guide included about one dozen climbs in the Severe or Very Severe category whereas the present publication contains no less than 48 Severes and 38 Very Severes, some of which are among the hardest routes in Lakeland. One precipice, Raven Crag, Thirlmere, yielded 'nothing worthy of description as a climb' in the original work, but today the same crag boasts eight hard routes of considerable character.

Although the development of the eastern fells as climbing country is of comparatively recent date, and still continues, the first climbs were done during the very beginnings of the sport, and characteristically the Abrahams were in the lead. Although subsequently H Westmorland and EW Hodge both laid separate claims to its first ascent, Sandbed Ghyll in St. John's in the Vale was first climbed by the redoubtable Keswick brothers in the early 1890s. They followed this exploration with the first ascent of Dollywaggon

Left: Alan Austin and Jack Soper on an early exploration of Raven Crag, Thresthwaite Cove.
Photo: Rosemary Soper

Gully*, and, in 1896, in company with John Wilson Robinson, they overcame the steep, crumbling rock of Iron Crag Chimney, Shoulthwaite – a remarkable tour de force which has been comparatively rarely repeated.

Fifty years before even the Abrahams there is evidence of a sporting attempt on 'the Eagle's Crag' in Grisedale by Edward Rose (later Rev.) 'an experienced cragsman,' accompanied by George Butler (later Canon). Matthew Arnold and AH Clough were also in the party, which was climbing Helvellyn, but not on the climb. Half-way up a hold gave way – it was a juniper bush – and Butler might have crashed to the screes had his shooting jacket not caught on a sharp, projecting corner. He subsequently extricated himself and surmounted the mauvais pas by hooking his walking-stick, a Kendal hazel, on to a jutting rock overhead.

But for more serious climbing, after the Abrahams, we must leap forward to 1910 when Horace Westmorland, then a young man of 24, was exploring the area. Away back in 1897, Westmorland, with his father, met John Wilson Robinson, Haskett-Smith, Ellis Carr and Geoffrey Hastings who had just failed in an attempt on the big gully on Dollywaggon Pike. The following year, again with his father, the boy got about 20 feet up the great pitch and, twelve years later, he was able to lead his two cousins, John Mounsey and Arthur North in the first ascent of the whole climb.

A few days later Westmorland led the same party up the upper part of the route on Dove Crag, which was led throughout 27 years later and, under the impression it was a new route, given the name Wing Ridge. In acknowledgment of Westmorland's contributions to climbing in this as well as in other areas this route has since been renamed Westmorland's Route.

The next area in the eastern fells to be explored by rock climbers was the rocky face of Buckbarrow in Longsleddale – an interesting development as the late Maurice Linnell, who was later to become such a brilliant cragsman, was involved in all the early climbs more than 30 years ago. Indeed, Linnell's very first climb, with JD Best as leader, was the first ascent of Dandle Buttress on this crag.

A redoubtable explorer of the eastern crags about this time and in fact right up to the Second World War was Mabel M Barker who was active (with Graham Macphee) on the South Crag of Castle Rock of Triermain, in Dovedale (with CR Wilson) and on Carrock Fell. But these explorations were mainly flanking attacks on major crags and some of the resultant climbs, although pleasing, tended to be artificial.

A leader in one of these early Dovedale assaults was Jim Birkett, a pioneer of some of the hardest routes in many parts of Lakeland. Birkett's new routes in the eastern fells extend over 17 years (The Tarsus to Kestrel

---

* The Abrahams climbed it in 1910 and for many years this was believed to have been the first ascent. However, recent historical research by Mike Cocker has revealed that it had been climbed in 1896 by Wilberforce, N Tribe and J Robinson.

Above: Pictured after their first ascent of **Overhanging Bastion**, Castle Rock on 1st April, 1939, from left, Len Muscroft, Jim Birkett and Charlie Wilson. **Photo:** Bill Birkett Collection

Wall) and include two major steps forward – Overhanging Bastion (1939), one of the finest climbs in this area, and Harlot's Face (1949) – both on the extremely steep North Crag of Castle Rock of Triermain. This local climber emerges as probably the biggest figure in the exploration of this area.

An important new climb made in the months before the Second World War was Hangover, a route which boldly tackled the overhanging face of Dove Crag, one of the steepest crags in Lakeland. The leader was JW Haggas – he also led the first ascent of the Gordian Knot in Langdale – and although there are now many harder climbs in the eastern fells this frontal assault on an intimidating, almost unknown crag must rank as an exceptionally bold piece of exploration.

The post-war exploration started with new climbs by JS Williams and CR Wilson on low, steep crags in Swindale, in effect a new climbing ground, and this search for new valleys, let alone new crags, was to be the pattern of exploration for the next few years. After exploration of a new crag in Dovedale – Black Crag – A Gregory moved into a completely new valley, Deepdale, and to him must go the credit for the discovery of this fine, craggy dale as a climbing ground. In the main Gregory climbed the more obvious routes and left the development of the area to two Preston climbers, JC Duckworth and G Batty, and others, who went straight on to major crags, like Hutaple and Scrubby, without knowing of any previous exploration. Their contribution to new climbing in eastern Lakeland was considerable.

The vanguard of the Bradford assault on the eastern crags in the persons of Harold Drasdo, the author of this guide, and D Hopkin, produced The Barbican on Castle Rock and this Yorkshire leadership of some of the hardest routes in this section was to continue with great vigour until the present day. Drasdo later made North Crag Eliminate on the Castle Rock and

he was also on the first ascent of the first climb on Raven Crag, Thirlmere. Earlier climbers had judged this crag too formidable to be tackled, but much harder routes on these two fearsome crags were to follow. Don Whillans and Joe Brown made their contribution here. Scrubby, Hutaple and Falcon Crags have also yielded hard new climbs. Appropriately enough, a young Keswick climber, Paul Ross, has put up what was possibly the hardest ever lead in this area – the original finish of Thirlmere Eliminate.

But the emphasis has not only been on exceptional severity. Eagle Crag in Grisedale was found to yield a number of interesting routes and recently the Sheffield University Mountaineering Club, from their base at Ruthwaite Lodge, have been exploring, with considerable success, the Grisedale cliffs in particular. Even now the eastern fells have not been exhausted. New climbs may still be found – perhaps not climbs like Hangover or the Eliminates – but pleasant routes for the average climber in slightly different country. For the eastern fells still retain their own, rather lonely, charm.

AH Griffin, 1959

1959 – 1969

The area covered by this guide is extensive and diversified, and in order to project a true historical record it is essential to indicate that the area has two distinct climbing grounds, each demanding its own technique and philosophy, and each having its own special rate of development. Conveniently, the mass of Helvellyn divides the two. To the west are the accessible roadside crags of Castle Rock and Raven Crag, Thirlmere, superb crags, comparable in scale and standards to the Llanberis cliffs. Here the climber can leave the car and arrive at the crag with his courage still intact to perform great feats to the accompaniment of the hubbub of the main road traffic below.

It is different in the east: the effort of the long and steep approach walk gnaws insidiously at the climber's courage and the crags are big and lonely and serious.

Castle Rock will always be a popular crag and development has been continuous since 1939 when Jim Birkett breached the defences of the North Crag by climbing Overhanging Bastion. Paul Ross, Geoff Oliver and Chris Bonington are notable for having continued the exploration; the crag now has such a network of routes that further activity must surely be curtailed. It seems inevitable that historical prediction must be proved wrong, and the final sentences of Harry Griffin's Historical Notes are no exception to this rule; many routes have been found to equal the Eliminates and Hangover in difficulty and quality alike. The very fine Eliminate Girdle by Paul Ross and

Left: Sobrenada (VS), Eagle Crag, Grisedale. Quite likely a photo of the first ascent in 1957.
Photo: Mike James collection

Geoff Oliver usurps and destroys the Gossard, not the best of Birkett's routes while Agony provides one of the finest pitches in the area.

Across the valley is the intimidating Raven Crag. In 1964 Martin Boysen, Chris Bonington and Mike Thompson discovered two routes of exceptional quality. The Medlar takes a malevolent and improbable line into the huge bottomless groove that bisects the great cave. The ascent of this route, like the routes which were being climbed on Dove about that time, shows a thoroughly modern approach to problems, which even ten years earlier would have been unthinkable. The line of the Medlar is fierce and its ascent must rank as one of the major achievements of the decade. Totalitarian, although lacking the ferocity of the Medlar, is both elegant and strenuous, and is surprisingly sustained at its standard.

In the east, the men of the fifties had worked well, and had left few natural lines for those that were to follow. Hutaple was so completely climbed that, apart from the minor flanking line of Exhaustion, the crag is even now as Drasdo left it. Not quite so Scrubby: Deflected Route was an attempt to climb the huge shallow groove to the right of Grendel, but Drasdo could not find the key to start the groove from below and had to traverse out of Grendel – hence his deflection. Soper found the true start, made an independent finish and re-named this fine route Hrothgar. An earlier visit had produced the elegant Beowulf, and in 1961, the girdle was shared with O Woolcock.

For almost a decade the mighty Dove Crag sat in inviolate splendour boasting the challenge of Dovedale Groove, which was climbed as early as 1953 by Joe Brown and Don Whillans. While ordinary mortals thought that the potential of Dove had been realized, others knew differently: Whillans returned to Dove in 1960 and climbed Extol. The ferocity of its line, the extreme and sustained technical difficulties, the long run-outs and the overpowering atmosphere of the place all combine to make Extol the most serious undertaking in an area that is not without its share of serious climbs. This was an outstanding lead by a brilliant climber, hard and uncompromising. It has been said that on the first ascent, on account of the long run-out, both leader and second were climbing extreme rock simultaneously. But the play was not yet over. In 1962 Pete Crew and Barry Ingle came out of Wales, put an end to the myth of Dovedale Groove's inaccessibility, and then went on, with typical impudence, to create the even harder Hiraeth. E Metcalfe and Jack Soper climbed Entity on the Gully face of the crag. Although of a similar standard to Hangover, it lacks the character of that fine climb.

In the charming and friendly Grisedale valley several of the long-standing problems were being solved in the early sixties by the Sheffield group operating from Ruthwaite Lodge. It is natural that Eagle Crag should emerge as the most popular crag in the Ullswater area and, no doubt, much of its attraction stems from the fine crop of routes produced by this group.

Longsleddale has long been the domain of the Kendal climbers. In the early sixties a fresh assault was made on Buckbarrow Crag, but apart from Minotaur, climbed by Ian Roper, nothing noteworthy emerged.

Ignored by earlier generations, the potential of Rainsborrow Crag was realised simultaneously, but quite independently, by two teams, KI Meldrum with N Rogers and Neil Allinson with Soper, each team thinking that the secret of the crag was theirs alone. Inevitably the two groups met, and although a pact of silence was agreed, Rogers recruited Roper to his team. Rainsborrow now boasts several top-class routes and further scope remains.

When Soper was asked to revise the 1959 guide, it was realized that there was a dearth of roadside climbs in the Ullswater area. It was decided to amend the situation. Allinson, who lives in the heart of the area, began a systematic search for crags and lines; this resulted in one or two good routes, and several which were not so good. The Girdle of Gowbarrow and three of the routes on Thrang Crag are perhaps the best. Of the routes found in the immediate vicinity of Patterdale, Draconic Groove and Nurglar make up in difficulty what they certainly lack in charm.

These two climbs could well illustrate the pattern of the future. Technical standards are rising. Dove's last defences have yet to be breached, but the accent will surely be on shorter, less inviting crags with which the area abounds. Crags will be climbed because they exist and not because they are attractive. Men in ten years's time will walk long distances to climb vicious little routes on crags which we pass by. This is as it should be. Exploration must go on, and what is acceptable to us was certainly not acceptable to our predecessors.

N Allinson, January, 1969

1970 – 1987

During the first part of this period little major development took place on the Eastern Crags. The notable exceptions were the Girdle of Dove Crag by John Adams and Colin Read in 1971 and although using much aid it was an impressive performance that was not freed until Bill Birkett's ascent in 1985**; Empire by Keith Myhill and Eric Jones in 1973 using two points of aid, subsequently freed by Jeff Lamb in 1974; and the good and surprisingly neglected Heorot on Scrubby Crag by Bob Hutchinson and John Earl, also in 1974.

Things started to "hot-up" in 1976 with Martin Berzins and Ed Cleasby joining forces to climb the serious Problem Child on Dove Crag (later improved by the addition of pitches 2 and 3 by Lamb and Pete Botterill in

** It has since transpired that this ascent was not of the complete climb, though it did free the aided sections.

1979), and Botterill and Pete Whillance putting up Explosion, a deceptively steep route up the right edge of North Buttress. Raven Crag, Thirlmere saw two new routes: the brilliant, classic The Gates of Delirium by Botterill and Steve Clegg and the hard and serious Creation by the same team. In July, C Brown and Birkett added Redex to Raven Crag, Threshthwaite Cove but unbelievably did not come back, leaving the development of what was to become one of the major crags of the area to others.

1977 resulted in further fine climbs on Raven Crag, Thirlmere: Close to the Edge by Clegg and Botterill, First Circle by Bob and Martin Berzins and the superb Peels of Laughter by Pete Livesey and Pete Gomersall, which repulsed a number of good leaders in its early days. The same team then went on to free Blitz of its aid to produce Blitzkreig, another fine and strenuous route out of the cave. Over on Castle Rock, Gomersall added the popular Ted Cheasby. On Dove Crag, Dave Armstrong and Whillance added the steep and bold Aurora, and Thrang Crags were investigated by Earl and Hutchinson, resulting in Jude the Obscure, Wilderness and Locust.

Early in 1978, Lamb, Botterill and J Taylor ascended the very steep rock left of Dovedale Groove to give Ommadawn. Two eliminate style routes were added on Castle Rock: White Dwarf by Birkett and Ken Forsyth, and Ecstasy by Cleasby, B Wright and Rob Matheson. On Gouther Crag, Hutchinson and Earl climbed the superb slab route Bloodhound. The most significant activity however was again on Raven Crag, Thirlmere with Livesey and Gomersall adding both Polytruk, a technical and poorly protected wall climb, and Das Kapital, which goes directly out of the cave to give possibly the hardest route in the Lakes at that time.

In 1979 Relayer was added on Raven Crag, Thirlmere by Lamb, the Berzins brothers and Botterill.

In 1980, Cleasby and Matheson added First Republic to Castle Rock, meanwhile Rick Graham and Birkett were exploring North Buttress on Dove Crag, producing the superb Fear and Fascination and Broken Arrow which although taking an excellent line is unfortunately somewhat marred by the use of aid. The potential of Raven Crag, Threshthwaite Cove was now realized by Whillance who added GTX in company with Ray Parker and Grand Prix with Bob Berzins and Botterill. The outlying crags were also receiving attention with Castration Crack, Vasectomy and Times of Stress all being added to Gouther Crag by Whillance and Botterill.

Whillance started 1981 where he had left off the previous year, with the superb Top Gear on Raven Crag, Threshthwaite Cove accompanied by Armstrong, thereafter Lamb and Botterill completed the first phase of development of the crag with an excellent string of routes: Overdrive, Running on Empty, Boy Racer, High Performance and Lap of Honour.

Left: Jeff Lamb on the first ascent of **High Performance** (E5), Raven Crag, Thresthwaite Cove.
Photo: Pete Botterill

Whillance then turned his attention to Iron Crag, discovering good rock on the left-hand buttress and producing six new routes in the process: Granolithic Groove and Solidarity with Loxham, Steel Band, Marble Staircase, Hiddenite and Black Gold with Armstrong. Birkett, Graham and Dave Lyle added the excellent Asolo to Dove Crag and Birkett and Graham also produced the free version of North Buttress. Thrang Crags received attention from a number of teams resulting in seven new routes, the best of which, Desperate Remedies and Far from the Madding Crowd belonging to Whillance and Armstrong. Child in Time and All the way from America were added to Sandbed Ghyll Crag by Paul Cornforth and John White.

In 1982 and 1983 there was some activity on the minor crags but the only routes of real significance were Fast and Furious on Dove Crag by Graham, Lyle and Birkett and the impressive and strenuous Committal Chamber on Iron Crag by Graham and Colin Downer.

The development of the minor crags continued in 1984 with Armstrong and Whillance playing the lead roles on Lower Swirl Crag. Thackmell Crag was dug out by Chris Dale and friends and G Derbyshire and company were responsible for the new routes on Mart Crag. Sandbed Ghyll was becoming more than a minor crag with four new routes by Armstrong and Whillance. The major route however was the excellent Liquid Engineering on Raven Crag, Threshwaite Cove by Phil Rigby and Al Murray.

In 1985, under the pretence of writing the new guide book, John Earl and Bob Smith did a number of new routes on Thrang Crags and Raven Crag, Threshthwaite Cove, the best of them being Stern Test, a bold route up the impressive arête on Upper Thrang, and Cabriolet, a problematical roof problem on Raven. In Thirlmere, The Gates of Delirium and Close to the Edge each received hard direct starts by Doug Dinwoodie accompanied by C. McLean and C. Ord respectively.

Guidebook writer Bob Smith checking out **Raven Crag**, Keldas for the 1987 edition of Eastern Crags. **Photo:** Andy Birtwistle

1986 saw three more new routes on Sandbed Ghyll: Ape Factor and Monkey Business by Armstrong and John Williams, and Caged by Smith and Earl. The discovery of new crags continued, Tony Greenbank started the frenzied activity late in the year on Erne Crag and Dave Bates and Tom Walkington were mainly responsible for the development of the ferocious Iving Crag enlisting the services of Tony Mitchell for the very hard Shaken not Stirred. The high points,

Right: Bill Birkett on the first ascent of **Asolo** (E3) in 1981. **Photo:** Bill Birkett Photo Library

however, were undoubtedly Smith and Earl's ascent of the excellent and very hard Internal Combustion up the centre of the 'Shield' on Raven Crag, Threshthwaite Cove and Dougie Hall's very steep and impressive Western Union, which crosses Committal Chamber on Iron Crag.

During the period since the last guide the development of hard free climbs has continued, some on the existing major crags of the area, but many on the newer smaller crags. The length of routes and the number of pitches is now generally considered to be of less importance than the quality and sustained nature of the climbing. Bolts have not been used and long may this continue, for if it does not, this will surely be the demise of Lakeland climbing as we know it. We must not allow these crags to be turned into outdoor climbing walls.

This guide contains many of the best crags and the finest routes in the area which are set in some of the most impressive, beautiful and tranquil surroundings. Please respect them, we owe that to those who follow.

JW Earl, 1987

1987 – 1992

Climbing development since the last guide has produced a mix of routes ranging from the sublime to the ridiculous. Some outstanding routes, equal to the hardest and best in the Lake District, have been made on the major crags, particularly the North Buttress of Dove Crag. Meanwhile the development of ever smaller and more obscure crags continues. A third strand of development has been the creation of bolt protected routes on quarried rock. Elsewhere a few gaps have been plugged but spaces for worthwhile new routes are becoming limited.

The first development in 1988 was that of Calf Howe Crag in Kentmere by J and K Daly. While the routes are not significant the history of the crag is instructive. Climbs were made here in the 1960s and a typescript guide produced but not widely circulated. The crag was rediscovered in the 1970s by David Craig but once again the routes were forgotten. In 1988 therefore, some of the routes were being climbed for the third time, although of course there were harder additions. One wonders how often this scenario has been repeated on other crags.

The most significant development of the year was undoubtedly Martin Berzins' return to the North Buttress of Dove Crag to begin a single minded and determined assault that was to extend over the next few years. His first target was to remove the two remaining aid points from his attempt a decade earlier to free climb the North Buttress aid route. The result, Bucket City, was a superb pitch and a worthy companion to Rick Graham's two big routes – Fast and Furious and Fear and Fascination – which in the next couple of years were at last to receive the acclaim they had always deserved. Rick Graham quickly responded to the attack on his territory with the strenuous Yorkshire Pudding.

In Swindale, Gouther Crag saw a flurry of activity, and two eliminate routes. Bob Wightman's Bloodletting took a direct line up the Bloodhound slab to give a fine, albeit escapable, climb. Steve Reid's The Fells! The Fells! was flawed by high side (top?) runners and possibly awaits a true ascent. Elsewhere Stuart Miller developed the very esoteric but accessible Shawbank Crag.

In 1989 Berzins returned to Dove Crag with Al Manson to produce Beyond the Pail, the very bold second pitch of which probably still awaits repetition. The bold trend continued with Mark Radtke's ascent of Phoenix in Obsidian on Iron Crag. Less bold, but very hard, was Paul Cornforth's Mindscape on Iving Crag. Three E6's had been added to the area on very varied crags in the space of a month.

In Swindale, Al Phizacklea squeezed a contrived line up the right side of the Bloodhound slab, to produce Bloodpoisoning. It was well-named because its controversial peg can be clipped from Bloodhound. On Rydal Cave J Metcalfe and Iain (Wilf) Williamson produced String of Burls, a bolt protected excursion across the lip of the cave. A mini controversy erupted when Chris Dale chopped one of the bolts claiming it devalued his earlier route Scary Monsters from which the bolt could be clipped.

The following year saw the development of Kirkstone Crag by Steve Reid and Tony and Mark Greenbank. New routeing on this tiny but very accessible crag is typical of one branch of development recurring throughout the area.

Once again the most significant developments were taking place on Dove Crag. Berzins teamed up with Neil Foster in a concerted campaign to fill the remaining gaps on the North Buttress. The first visit saw Berzins tackling the intimidating line of Pail Face while Foster found a spectacular finish to Explosion up the obvious hanging arête on its left. The following weekend Foster claimed a fine variation finish to Fast and Furious. Berzins meanwhile, set about cleaning the stupendous faultline which crosses the most overhanging part of the buttress from Fear and Fascination to the stance on Asolo. This line was to be the object of Berzins' obsession for the next couple of weeks. Finally, driven by raging paranoia that someone was about to steal his prize, he succeeded on a damp day at the end of August and named the route Vlad the Impailer.

Odd pickings were to be found elsewhere. Dave Kay and John Campbell twice braved the walk to Hutaple Crag to produce Waiting for Laura and Late Back for Laura. Most surprising of all, Stuart Miller found the obvious and excellent line of The Watchtower on Castle Rock. Most parts of this had been climbed before but they had never been linked together.

The quest for ever more obscure pieces of rock continued in 1991 with development on two new buttresses near Sandbed Ghyll and the truly esoteric Goat Crag and Smaithwaite Crags. The tiny Shundraw Quarry

was developed, (with some bolts); Paul Cornforth's Lemon Dixon and Pete Botterill's Short Circuit both make up in ferocity what they lack in length.

Meanwhile back on the real crags, Ron Kenyon and Steve Reid ventured to Hutaple to climb the fine slab pitch of Scallywag. Route of the year however, was undoubtedly Berzins' and Foster's Bucket Dynasty on Dove Crag which climbed the improbable looking wall below Vlad the Impailer. Steve Meyers also earned himself a place in history by making the first free ascent of the original North Buttress route. Also on Dove Crag, Mike Miller found an unlikely line out of the Priest's Hole cave above the North Buttress.

Acting on a tip off from Tony Greenbank, Paul Ross imported his son from the States to develop Heirloom Crag. The pick of the routes were Family Affair and Bloodline with the brutal crack of Like Father Like Son perpetuating a family speciality. Greenbank also lost out on the central grooveline to Rick Graham. Ross later returned with Pete Lockey to produce Reunion 35 years after their ascent of Post Mortem.

Most activity this year however, took place in Bramcrag Quarry. This owed more to its proximity to the road than to its quality. Al Phizacklea with John Holden had the pick of the routes, including Marine's Slab, Eastern Promise, Coup d'État and Barrow Boys' Day Out. Content with his contribution Phizacklea left the quarry in peace to allow others to find the remaining lines. Foremost among these was Ron Kenyon who has produced nine routes to date. Although many routes in the quarry now have bolts most were originally led with only dubious protection.

The hunger for new routes therefore continues unabated. The supply of virgin rock must be finite but it would take a brave man to say when it will run out. New routes are still being found by climbing harder or by climbing further afield or by climbing shorter routes or, it has to be said, by climbing routes up vegetated rock that would be far better left alone. Time as usual will judge the relative merits of these trends in both the quality of the routes and the ethics of their production.

A Davis, T Price, February 1992

1992 – 2010

New routes have continued to be discovered throughout the Eastern Crags area in the 18 years since the last guide. Chief and most significant of these are a series of major routes of the highest quality on the prime crags. As a counterpoint, ever more obscure and tiny buttresses have been developed and subsequently ignored though some worthwhile gems deserve popularity. A much better use of time has been the recent trend

Left: Mick Lovatt on the first ascent of **Meltdown** (E7), Low Raven Crag, Grasmere in 1997. **Photo:** Steve Wilcox

of re-cleaning and equipping existing neglected classic routes which then regain deserved popularity.

Following publication of the last guide in 1992, the first major new route climbed was to be a highly significant milestone in Lakes climbing. Dave Birkett's ascent of If 6 was 9 on Iron Crag was a terminally bold undertaking and at E9 was as hard as any route in the country at the time. Despite the attentions of numerous talented climbers, it had to wait 17 years before Dave McLeod claimed the second ascent.

In the same year, John Shepherd and Karl Lunt developed the excellent Nab Crag in Wythburn producing five routes which deserve popularity. The following year a similar discovery, Goat Crag in the Shoulthwaite valley, was developed by Colin Downer and Eve Prickett with contributions from Paul Ross, Pete Lockey, Dave Birkett and Paul Cornforth. This is an accessible and potentially excellent crag which has been neglected – a recurrent theme throughout this period. Another significant contribution of the year was Glen Sutcliffe's appropriately named Pumping Iron (E7) on Iron Crag.

The next major route was Nick Wharton's ascent of the bold Road Rage (E7) on Raven Crag, Threshthwaite in 1995, named after the driving antics of his climbing partner, Dom Donnini. He was under some pressure to complete the route that evening as a very strong team led by Twid Turner was also climbing on the crag at the time. This route had to wait a mere 10 years for a repeat by Duncan Booth. In the same year, Ian Weetman and Dave Birkett began the further development of Mart Crag with the imaginatively named Route Twelve and Route Thirteen. Two years later, Rick Graham, Ted Rogers and Bill Birkett completed development with thirteen excellent routes on this fine crag which despite its easy access and quality rock has been unjustly neglected. Also at this time, Mick Lovatt and Tim Whiteley developed Low Raven Crag, Grasmere producing the very bold Meltdown (E7) as their highlight.

During this period, two strands of development were evident. Difficult eliminates were squeezed into small buttresses of excellent rock as with Adam Hocking and Pete Botterill's activities on Lower Swirl Crag or Phil Rigby and Paul Carling's contributions to the Castration Crack area of Gouther Crag. Meanwhile, at a more amenable level, surprisingly independent lines on established crags were being developed. Tony Marr began work on Eagle Crag and had A Grand Day Out, so grand that he has continued to make regular contributions to this fine crag up to the present day, producing an excellent series of routes.

In 1999, Nick Dixon accepted the "challenge for the future" thrown down by the previous guidebook, visiting the obscure Birks Crag, Haweswater to climb Groove Central (E6).

The following year saw Tom Walkington develop the obvious Yew Crag South, work that he completed late the following year when foot and mouth relented to allow access to the fells. Nine years later, oblivious to Tom's activities, Colin Downer "discovered" the same crag producing a new series of routes taking similar though different lines. The guidebook writer has done his best to sort out the resulting muddle.

2002 was significant for two activities at opposite ends of the climbing spectrum. Barry Clarke arrived in the area and produced his first new route. For the next five years Barry roamed far (very far) and wide across the area producing a large number of minor routes. No obscure craglet was safe from Barry's forensic gaze during this period. Though much of his activities have been assigned to the FRCC website archive, some worthwhile discoveries were made. Of much more significance was James McHaffie's Fear of Failure (E8) on Dove Crag – a hard bold route which initially freed old aided climbing before making a harrowing traverse across the top wall.

This route heralded the following year's "Summer of Dove". The North Buttress received attention from a team whose main activists were Chris Hope, Al Wilson, Duncan Booth, Steve Crowe and Karin Magog. In a stunning summer of activity, as well as numerous repeat ascents, six superb hard new routes were climbed on this awesome buttress. The season's activities continued with Duncan Booth's ascent of Imminent Arrival (E4) on Iron Crag and then the brilliant The Second Coming (E6) which he extended with The Infestation Finish (E7) to produce a magnificent hard route up Raven Crag. Karl Telfer top-roped and then summoned up the courage to lead the very bold slim pillar left of Triermain Eliminate to produce Die Another Day (E7), Castle Rock's most difficult and serious route. Finally, Duncan Booth rounded off the year by tackling the much-eyed open groove above Sostenuto on Gouther Crag. Many had looked at this line but were repulsed

Above: Lakelander Colin Downer keeping cool, calm and collected on **Mr Angry** (E1), Bram Crag Quarry, one of several fine new routes he was involved in there in 2009. **Photo:** Lesley Nicholson

by the complete lack of gear. Relentless Rage (E7) was the result.

Following this year of frenzied and highly significant activity on the major crags, the following years saw major developments dry up and a return to a succession of developments on minor and obscure crags. A more worrying trend was the neglect of once popular crags. The rise in popularity of bouldering and the consistently wet summers we have endured have led many crags to disappear beneath a carpet of moss and lichen. To reverse this trend, the activities of "The North Lakes Job Club", a Keswick based group of enthusiasts led by Al Wilson, who have retro-cleaned existing classic routes, are to be hugely welcomed and applauded. The altruistic hard work of reviving quality climbs is infinitely preferable to first ascentionists unearthing worthless routes from crags destined for obscurity.

Major routes have been few recently. In 2004, Andy Mitchell produced Liquid Wall (E8), a harder variation on Liquid Engineering on Raven Crag Threshthwaite. The next route of significance did not appear until 2008 with Al Wilson's ascent of The Iron Man (E7) on Iron Crag which gave a more aesthetic start line to the upper part of Pumping Iron. Details of the latter route were texted immediately which led to two repeat ascents within 4 hours of the first ascent.

The following year Nick Wharton, during work on the guidebook, produced the bold Amabilite (E4), filling an all-too-obvious gap on Iron Crag, while Mark Greenbank used his charm with Lady Driver (E5) on Raven Crag, Threshthwaite. Meanwhile Colin Downer visited the highly accessible and sadly neglected Bramcrag Quarry armed only with a bolt gun and produced five excellent routes.

It is appropriate that the climber who kicked off activities in 1992 and has dominated the Lakes' climbing scene throughout this period should produce the final significant route in the area. Typically, Dave Birkett found an area of rock which had been totally overlooked. Up Hellya, weighing in at E8, climbed the steep and not wholly secure wall left of Inaccessible Gully on Dove Crag. This was 72 years after his grandfather Jim Birkett produced his first new route, The Tarsus, up the right wall of this same gully.

For the future, no doubt careful study of the photodiagrams will reveal gaps to be exploited but perhaps prospective new routers could ensure they operate with discrimination and concern for the precious ecosystems supported by the more esoteric buttresses to be found in this area.

The Eastern Crags have a wonderful mix of some of the best and most challenging routes in the Lakes but also quiet crags in remote settings where climbers of all standards can enjoy their day undisturbed in a wild mountain setting.

Al Davis, February 2011

Left: Mark Greenbank on the first ascent of **Lady Driver** (E5), Raven Crag, Thresthwaite Cove in 2009. **Photo:** Ross Cowie

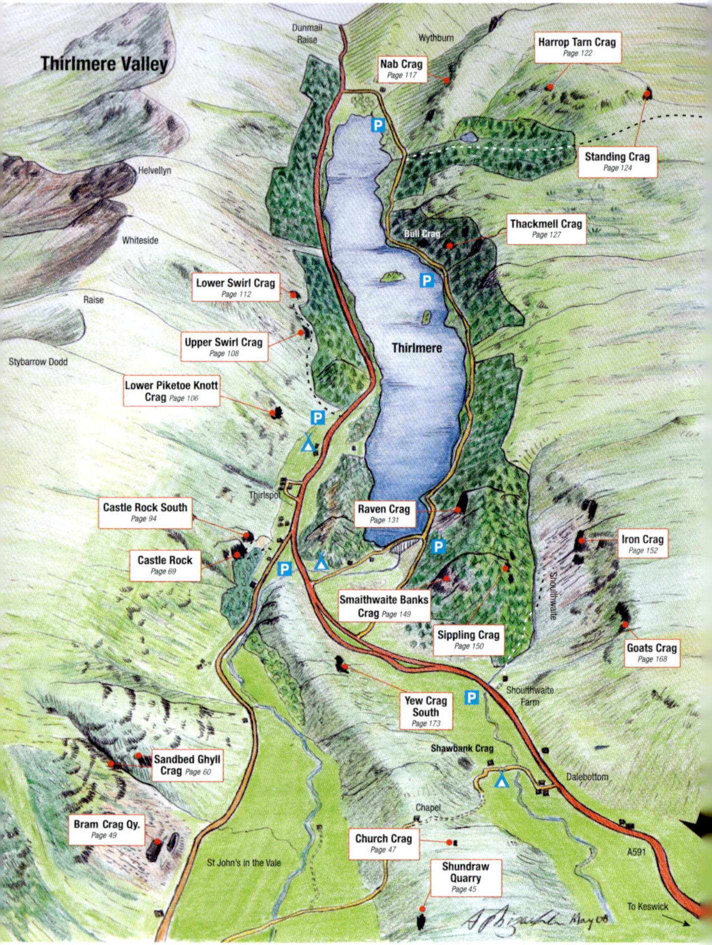
Thirlmere Valley
Dunmail Raise
Wythburn
Nab Crag
Page 117
Harrop Tarn Crag
Page 122
Standing Crag
Page 124
Helvellyn
Whiteside
Thackmell Crag
Page 127
Bull Crag
Lower Swirl Crag
Page 112
Raise
Upper Swirl Crag
Page 108
Thirlmere
Stybarrow Dodd
Lower Piketoe Knott Crag Page 106
Thirlspot
Castle Rock South
Page 94
Raven Crag
Page 131
Iron Crag
Page 152
Castle Rock
Page 69
Shoulthwaite
Smaithwaite Banks Crag Page 149
Sippling Crag
Page 150
Goats Crag
Page 168
Yew Crag South
Page 173
Shoulthwaite Farm
Shawbank Crag
Sandbed Ghyll Crag Page 60
Dalebottom
Chapel
Bram Crag Qy.
Page 49
Church Crag
Page 47
A591
Shundraw Quarry
Page 45
St John's in the Vale
To Keswick

Thirlmere

The Thirlmere valley is the main thoroughfare between the North and the South Lakes. It contains a wealth of excellent climbing of all standards.

The main crags are grouped at the northern end of Thirlmere about 8 kilometres from Keswick. The biggest cliffs, ***Castle Rock of Triermain*** and ***Raven Crag***, face each other across the valley, ***Castle Rock*** on the eastern side above the southern part of the Vale of St John, ***Raven Crag*** on the western side above the Thirlmere dam. ***Iron Crag*** is tucked away in a side valley on the western side of Shoulthwaite Gill. In addition, there are numerous smaller crags which provide a wide variety of excellent climbing.

All the cliffs are easily accessible from the various main roads. They are comparatively low lying and the west and south-facing crags dry quickly.

Shundraw Quarry

Grid Reference: **NY 307 237** Altitude: **180m**
Faces: **East** Approach: **3 mins**

A tiny quarry of flaky volcanic rock with an impressively steep wall. Its proximity to the road compensates for its obvious shortcomings.

Approach:

One hundred metres north of Shundraw Farm a gate marked 'Private' leads to a second gate. The quarry is just above.

The routes are described from **left** to **right**.

Shundraw Quarry

1	Shundraw Slab	E1
2	Carol's Delight	E1
3	Bold As Brass	E1
4	Marc One	HVS
5	Short Circuit	E5
6	Lemon Dixon	E6 *

1 **Shundraw Slab**	23m	E1		1991

Start 2 metres left of the tree at the centre of a slim overgrown slab which is very mossy and probably unclimbable in its present state.

(5b). Climb directly up the filthy slab and take the left arête. Gain the slabby wall and climb directly up the centre of the slab to the top.

2 **Carol's Delight**	23m	E1		1991

Start at the left side of the tree.

(5b). Climb the open groove and pass the overhang above on its left. Climb the vertical crack and the steep wall on the right of a large flake.

3 **Bold as Brass**	10m	E1		1991

Start 2 metres right of the tree below a diamond-shaped block.
An unprotected contrived problem.

(5a). Gain the block and continue directly above trending slightly rightwards (avoiding the ramp) to a big ledge.

4 **Marc One**	13m	HVS		1991

Start at the left end of the ramp 4 metres right of the tree.

(5a). Climb up on big flaky holds to a ledge beneath a bulge. Step left and follow the thin crack to a big ledge and easy scrambling.

5 **Short Circuit**	20m	E5		1991

Start as for *Lemon Dixon*.

(6b). Climb the crack to the first bolt. Traverse left (No. 3 Flexible Friend) and upwards along the cracked break to finish up a short groove.

6 **Lemon Dixon**	15m	E6 {7b+}	★	1991

Start at a crack in the right side of the steep wall with two bolt runners.

(6c). Climb the crack.

Church Crag

Grid Reference: **NY 305 227** Altitude: **240m**
Faces: **East** Approach: **5 mins**

A tiny quick drying crag of excellent rock with good incut holds and natural protection which is ideal for beginners. The crag is situated in a lovely location with stunning views. There are some belay bolts in place on top of the crag.

Approach:

Park at St. John's in the Vale Church and cross a stile into the field to the north. The crag is visible about 200 metres away. The crag is divided into two small buttresses by a left-slanting gully.

The climbs are described from left to right.

1 **Cottontail**	12m	VD		1993

Start at the left side of the buttress at a grassy bay.

Follow the left-slanting blocky ramp line moving straight up through the overlap and then step out left to finish up a vegetated mossy rib.

2 **Carrick's Climb**	12m	D		1997

A very pleasant climb. Start, as for ***Cottontail***, one metre left of the lowest point of the crag at a grassy bay.

Climb directly up over overlaps until forced right to join *Confidence*. Where *Confidence* traverses right, move leftwards and then continue direct to the top through overlaps and finish up a rib.

3 **Confidence**	12m	D	★	1992

Start at the lowest point of the buttress at the left side of a smooth wall.

Climb the rib and the wall above to a bulge. Step up right to a groove and finish up this by its right rib.

Church Crag

1	Cottontail	VD
2	Carrick's Climb	D
3	Confidence	D *
4	Roger Rabbit	VS *
5	Graveyard Gully	M
6	Pandamania	VD
7	Flopsy	MVS
8	Easter Bunny	HVD

Photo: Al Davis

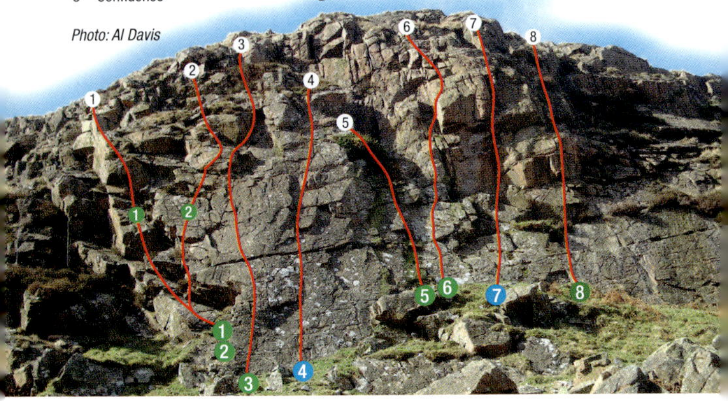

4	**Roger Rabbit**	12m	VS	★	1993

(4b). Climb boldly up the centre of the slab just right of *Confidence*.

5	**Graveyard Gully**	12m	M		1993

The central gully is very grassy and is best avoided.

6	**Pandamania**	12m	VD		1992

Start just right of *Graveyard Gully*, at the left side of an overhung slab.

Climb the slab to a chimney-groove which is entered with difficulty. Climb the groove moving rightwards at its top and then back left.

7	**Flopsy**	12m	MVS		1993

Start one metre right of *Pandamania*.

(4b). Climb up to the bulge and gain the slim groove on the right with difficulty. Easier climbing leads to the top.

8	**Easter Bunny**	12m	VD+		1993

Start just right again at the right-hand side of the buttress.

Climb up to a tiny niche below a bulge. Move left on good sharp holds and make a long reach to easier ground.

Easter Bunny Twin Chimney Variation VD+ 1997

Instead of moving left on good holds, finish by stepping up right via twin chimneys to the same point then more easily to the top.

Divine Cross	35m	VD		1996

A complete traverse of the crag from right to left.

Start up *Easter Bunny*, cross under the bulge of *Flopsy*, pass under the V-grooves of *Pandamania*, traverse leftwards across the slabs of *Roger Rabbit* onto *Confidence* and finish up the rising traverse of *Cottontail*. It was first done in reverse, starting up *Confidence* and finishing up *Easter Bunny*, and is almost as good that way - two routes for the price of one!

Bram Crag Quarry

Grid Reference:	**NY 320 219**	Altitude:	**200m**
Faces:	**West**	Approach:	**5 mins**

This quarry of fine-grained micro granite is found at the foot of Sandbed Ghyll in St. John's in the Vale, 3 kilometres south of Threlkeld. First impressions can be off-putting with areas of apparently tottering blocks though closer examination reveals some areas of good solid clean rock with excellent friction.

The quarry is close to the road and catches the afternoon sun. The better routes are protected to an extent by bolts or pegs and are reasonably user friendly, but a rack is still required. However, most routes rely on natural protection and are serious undertakings. Large Friends are often useful in shot-holes. Climbers should err on the side of caution as the rock is not totally trustworthy and there are some large unstable areas, though these are obvious and easily avoided. The resident family of goats which used to wander across the highly unstable scree above the quarry appear to have moved on to pastures new so that the fusillades of rocks they used to unleash on the unwary are no more, though a helmet is still recommended.

Despite the health warnings above, there are some excellent routes in this quarry.

The climbs lie on two levels. The *Lower Quarry* is separated from the *Upper Tier* by a broad terrace. The *Upper Tier* is topped by a band of extremely dangerous scree and the routes here should be **descended** by abseil.

Approach:

Cars can be parked just south of the quarry in a small lay-by. Do not block the quarry entrance as this is still being used.

For the *Lower Quarry*, follow the quarry road round the first bend where an obvious track leads right.

The *Upper Tier* is reached by following the quarry road. At a fork, follow the right branch into the quarry. Scramble up the back left side of the quarry to a narrow grassy ridge leading to the terrace below the upper quarry.

Bram Crag Quarry Lower

1	Marine's Slab	HVS *
V1	Captain Pugwash	HVS
2	Seconds Away	VS
V2	Variation	HVS
3	Baptismal Vows	E1
4	Nappyrash	HVS
5	Life Begins at Forty	E1

Lower Quarry

The wall has an obvious quartz band at 3 metres. This is a very wet fault-line that blocks access to much of the wall. The first two routes start at a dry pillar below the main central corner. The routes are described from **right** to **left**.

1	**Marine's Slab**	30m	HVS	★	1991

A good route up the attractive slab which is reasonably well-protected by two bolts and small wires.

(5a). Climb the pillar on sloping holds (bolt) to a ledge. Trend right on steps to below a thin crack-line in the slab. Follow this (bolt) for 15 metres to a small ledge on the left and step right to finish.

v1 ***Captain Pugwash*** HVS 1991

(5a). From the first bolt climb up and right to the flake in the centre of the slab. Finish back left, 1.5 metres right of the final bolt on *Marine's Slab*.

2 **Seconds Away**	30m	VS		1991

The obvious corner. Care is needed with the rock.

(4c). Climb the pillar on sloping holds to a ledge as for *Marine's Slab*. Continue cautiously up the corner for 10 metres then step out left onto the semi-detached pillar to finish easily.

Variation HVS 1991

(5a). Instead of stepping left, swing right on a sloping ledge and finish up a shallow scoop in the headwall.

3 **Baptismal Vows**	30m	E1		1991

Start 5 metres left of the pillar of *Marine's Slab* at a sharp nose. Awkward to start if wet.

(5b). Surmount the nose to gain a ledge. Move up left to the base of a groove and climb this with interest. At the top of the groove, move over a small overlap to gain the final slab.

4 **Nappyrash**	30m	HVS		1991

Start at a cracked nose of brown rock 12 metres left of *Marine's Slab*. A difficult start leads to poorly-protected but easy climbing.

(5b). Climb the nose on fissile rock (bolt) to the break. Move up right to gain a good hold just left of a V-groove. Move up and left to easier ledges. Ascend the corner above then move right at an overlap to gain and climb the final slab.

5 **Life Begins at Forty**	30m	E1		1991

Very loose and serious – should have been called "Life Could End at Forty"! It takes the obvious V-groove which starts about 5 metres above the ground, 17 metres left of *Marine's Slab*. Start below and right of the groove.

(5b). Ascend fragile rock to a break then climb the groove (2 bolts) in spectacular fashion. Follow a crack-line leftwards to a cracked corner and climb this and a short slab to the top.

To the left of the *Lower Quarry* is a steep bank. Just left of the top of the bank is an obvious gangway slanting up to the left.

Beyond The Fringe	10m	VS		1991

(4b). Climb the arête to the left of the gangway using sloping holds.

Moggy's Meander	10m	VD		1991

Start 10 metres left of *Beyond the Fringe* at an obvious weakness.

An awkward start leads to pleasant but unprotected climbing leftwards up slabby rock.

Bram Crag Quarry Upper Tier

1	St John's Ambulance	VS
2	Goodbye Mr Major!	HVS
3	Barrow Boys' Day Out	E1 *
4	Vale of Secrecy	E1
5	Brothers in Arms	E2
6	Blencathra Badger	E1
7	Sorry, No Bolts	E1
8	Farewell to Adventure?	E1 *
9	Good Luck Mr Blair!	E1
10	Tyke's Teeter Direct	E2
11	Tyke's Teeter	E1 *
12	On the Edge	VS

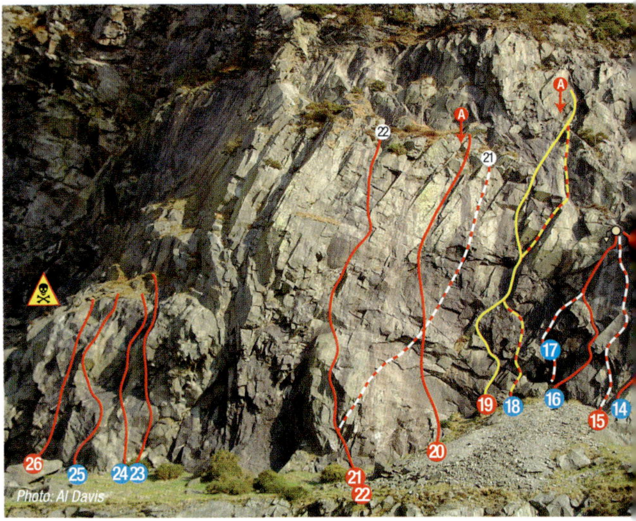

Upper Tier

The routes here are described from **right** to **left**.

The right-hand side of the *Upper Tier* is very broken and has a small waterfall spilling over it. About 80 metres along the terrace, rightwards from the narrow grassy access ridge, is a clean rounded pillar with an obvious corner towards the top. There is an abseil chain at the top of this pillar. It will be found 2 metres above the top of the final groove of *St. John's Ambulance* and *Barrow Boys' Day Out*. You may have to unearth it from beneath the dead gorse but it's there – honest!

The following five routes climb the pillar.

1	St. John's Ambulance	33m	VS		1991

A bold lead for the grade. It starts at a sloping groove to the right of the pillar. (4b). Follow the groove to its top, step delicately left and climb the unprotected upper corner to a bolt and chain belay.

13	Bambino Bolero	MVS	20	The History Boys	E2 ***
14	Take It or Leave It	HVS	21	Coup d'État	E3 **
15	Bonne Chance	E2 *	22	Eastern Promise	E2 **
16	Mr Angry	E1 *	23	The Quarryman	HVS
17	Bon Courage	E1 *	24	Hound-dog	HVS
18	Bobby Dazzler	E1 ***	25	Twilight	MVS
19	Dapper Dan	E2 **	26	Last Dash	E2

2	**Goodbye Mr Major!**	31m	HVS		1997

A good route which starts 4 metres left of ***St. John's Ambulance*** at a rounded bulge at the lowest part of the buttress.

(5a). Gain a ledge at 3 metres either direct or by a groove on the left. Follow darker-coloured dike rock to a ledge then ascend the centre of the shield (protection from the bolt on *Barrow Boys' Day Out*) to gain the ramp of *Barrow Boys' Day Out*. Cross the ramp and climb a groove to join *Vale of Secrecy* (bolt hidden low down) and follow this to the chain belay.

3	**Barrow Boys' Day Out**	33m	E1	★	1991

Good open climbing. Start at a rounded rib just left of a shot-hole and about 10 metres left of the previous route.

(5b). Climb the rib to a bolt. Step right and move up to the obvious slim ramp. Follow this and the corner above to a chain belay.

4	**Vale of Secrecy**	30m	E1		1991

Slightly harder than *Barrow Boys' Day Out* but the difficulties are all avoidable.

(5b). Climb *Barrow Boys' Day Out* to the first bolt and continue steeply right to a groove and ledge. Climb a slim groove and keep on the left of the rib to the top and the chain belay.

5	**Brothers in Arms**	30m	E2		1992

A series of variations on *Vale of Secrecy*. Start just left of *Barrow Boys' Day Out* at a black-streaked wall.

(5b). Climb the black-streaked wall to a grassy ledge. Follow the ledge on a rightwards-trending traverse to below the overhang. Surmount the overhang and climb a direct line up to the steep cracked slab. Ascend the slab directly to the top and belay at the belay chain.

6	**Blencathra Badger**	30m	E1		1991

This route climbs the water-worn slabs 6 metres left of *Barrow Boys' Day Out*. There is no protection and the belays at the top are very poor. Moreover, the slabs are dirty and the climbing feels insecure. If that doesn't put you off, then:

(5a). Climb the slabs directly to a difficult finish with no protection.

7	**Sorry, No Bolts**	25m	E1		1991

Beyond the water-worn slabs is a recessed area of small brown-streaked slabs. Start 12 metres left of the water-worn slabs of *Blencathra Badger* and just right of the brown streaks, below a sloping corner. Unprotected.

(5a). Climb the smooth corner (crux) to a right-trending ramp. Follow this then climb directly up pleasant slabs above. Trend left at the top to an abseil point (as for *Bambino Bolero*).

8	**Farewell to Adventure?**	20m	E1	★	1992

Climbs the front of the buttress just left of *Sorry, No Bolts*.

(5b). Either start up the corner, or the slab to its left, to surmount a steep broken wall. Move right then left to below an overlap which is surmounted to gain a ledge. Pass the overlap above on the right and finish up a short groove to the abseil point.

9	**Good Luck Mr Blair!**	20m	E1		1997

Start 2 metres left of *Farewell to Adventure*. The lack of protection low down adds some spice.

(5a). Ascend the wall to the left of *Farewell to Adventure* just right of the arête (Friend 2/2.5 below overlap) to gain a good ledge (bolt on right). Move along the gangway to the left and follow the arête to the top and the abseil point.

10 **Tyke's Teeter Direct**	20m	E2		1993

This route starts 2 metres right of the left-slanting groove of *Tyke's Teeter*.

(6a). Climb directly up to the second bolt of *Tyke's Teeter*. Move up leftwards to the third bolt and climb the arête to the top of the ramp. Scramble up the rightwards-facing corner/groove to the abseil point.

11 **Tyke's Teeter**	23m	E1	★	1991

Enjoyable but difficult slab climbing. Start 23 metres left of the water-worn slabs of *Blencathra Badger* at a left-leaning gangway just right of a prominent rib.

(5c). Follow the gangway leftwards for 3 metres. Step rightwards on to the slab and move up (crux) into a scoop. Move up leftwards, then rightwards up a wall, using a shot-hole, to a grassy bay. Above is an obvious overlap with a bolt just over the lip on the left. Surmount the pinnacles, overcome the overlap on its left, and continue to the abseil point.

12 **On the Edge**	23m	VS		1991

Start 25 metres left of the water-worn slabs of *Blencathra Badger* at a prominent rib which forms the right side of a right-slanting ramp system. Pleasant but poorly-protected climbing.

(4b). Climb up just right of the toe of the rib into a scoop which leads to the arête. Follow the arête to the bolt then climb the arête direct, or the groove above the bolt, to the abseil point.

13 **Bambino Bolero**	25m	MVS		1991

This takes the obvious ramp system on the right of the large overhangs.

(4b). Climb up then move right into the main ramp system. Continue pleasantly to a ledge then up a slim groove to a belay ledge and abseil point.

Immediately left of the large overhangs a scree-filled bay leads up to the crag. A number of routes start at this bay and the first four of these lead to a ledge and abseil point at 20 metres.

14 **Take It or Leave It**	20m	HVS		1991

Start at a short arête on the right of the bay and left of the prominent overhangs above *Bambino Bolero*.

(5a). Climb a short slab and arête to a bulge. Surmount this and go up to a ledge. Gain a crack between the wall and a dubious looking block and layback with high anxiety to a ledge and chain belay.

15 **Bonne Chance**	18m	E2	★	2009

Start at the right side of the scree fan just below a square cut overhang and just left of *Take it or Leave It*.

(6a). Climb the short wall (bolt). Difficult moves up and left gain a hanging groove. Follow this to vertical shot-hole (bolt). Intricate moves keeping left of the shot-hole lead to a bay and chain belay.

16 **Mr Angry**	18m	E1	★	2009

Start just right of the large block at an obvious slab 2 metres right of *Bon Courage*.

(5c). Follow the slab to an overlap. Make a difficult pull over (it's a bit of a sweater!) to gain the upper slab then trend left (bolt). Above is a suspect-looking block (apparently sound). Use this, moving right into the obvious bay as for *Bon Courage*.

17 **Bon Courage**	18m	E1	★	2009

Start in a corner at a large block.

(5c). Climb the groove (bolt). Difficult moves leftwards (bolt) lead to the upper slab (bolt). Follow this, trending rightwards to a small ledge (bolt). Above is a suspect-looking but apparently sound block. Use this, moving right into the obvious bay. Chain belay.

18 **Bobby Dazzler**	30m	E1	★★★	2009

An excellent and very enjoyable route. Start at the top left of the scree slope at a large flake.

(5a). Climb the flake to a bolt on the right and move up to a block (bolt). Step left into a fine groove and follow this to the top. Pull out right onto a rib (bolt) and climb the slab aiming for the large block. Step right and pull into the bay and chain belay.

19 **Dapper Dan**	30m	E2	★★	2009

Start at the top left of the scree slope at a large flake, as for *Bobby Dazzler*.

(5c). From the left side of the large flake pull into a niche (bolt). Awkward moves up lead to another bolt. Move right into the groove of *Bobby Dazzler* and follow this for 3 metres until a hard move gains a hanging groove on the left. Move easily up this to join the slab on *Bobby Dazzler* and up to the small bay and chain belay.

20 **The History Boys**	30m	E2	★★★	2010

Continually interesting climbing taking a direct line up the cliff with adequate protection from bolts and wires. Start 3 metres right of *Coup d'État* and just left of some gorse bushes.

(5c). Climb easily to ledges and attain a standing position on the left end of the flake (bolt). Pull directly over the roof using the shot-hole (and avoiding the suspect block on *Coup d'État*). Climb the groove and slab to a projecting block. Move right to a bolt and pull out left to a ledge (bolt). Climb the groove (Friend 1) to the lower off.

21 **Coup d'État**	36m	E3	★★	1991

A pleasant route which is marred by a doubtful block on the first overlap. Start at the little groove on the left of the rounded foot of the slabs which lie at the left end of the *Upper Tier*.

(6a). Climb up the little groove, step right onto the slab and continue to a small ledge. Traverse right using a doubtful block and pull over the overlap to a shot-hole. Climb to a peg and move right (crux – fortunately protected by a bolt) to below a second overhang. Pull over this to good holds and finish directly up the groove. Bolt and chain abseil point on the left.

22 **Eastern Promise**	35m	E2	★★	1991

A good climb with the crux protected by small wires. Start at the little groove as for *Coup d'État*.

(5c). Climb the little groove to its top then swing right using a shot-hole and move up to a small ledge (junction with *Coup d'État*). Continue straight up (crux) to reach a grassy ledge. Climb up for about 5 metres to a good Friend slot then trend left below the shallow grooves to reach a headwall. Pull over this past a peg to a belay. Bolt and chain abseil point on the right.

The next four routes are found at the left end of the terrace before it bends round to the clean sweep of slab just before the narrow grassy access ridge. A fan of scree abuts the crag at this point. **They all take the same area of rock leading to poor belays and a dangerous descent to the left and cannot be recommended. You have been warned!**

23 **The Quarryman**	15m	HVS		1997

Start 12 metres left of *Coup d'État* at a black-streaked bulge on the right side of a large scooped recess.

(5a). Climb the black-streaked bulge and gain the corner. Climb directly to the spike belay at the top.

24 **Hound-dog**	15m	HVS		1997

Start one metre left of *The Quarryman* at a small slab leading to a scooped recess.

(5b). Climb up 3 metres to join *Twilight* at the bottom of the recess. Move directly up on the right side of the large recess to gain the niche (crux) then climb directly up to the spike belay.

25 **Twilight**	15m	MVS		1997

Start at a right-leaning groove which leads up to a scooped recess.

(4b). Climb the rightward-leaning groove to gain the bottom of a large recess and move diagonally left to a shot-hole. Climb directly up on big flaky holds to the top and a large belay spike on the right.

Bram Crag Wall Area

27	Wai Lord	7b+*
28	Bram Crag Wall	7a **
29	Middle Earth	7b *
30	Michelangelo	6b **

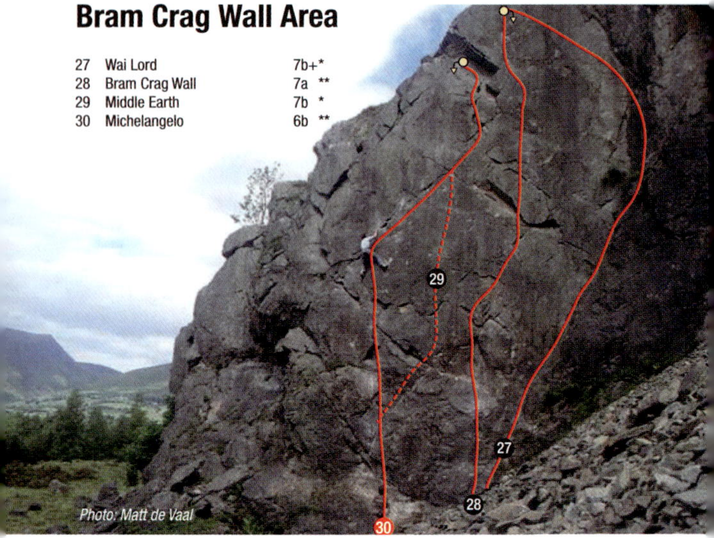

Photo: Matt de Vaal

26 **Last Dash**	15m	E2		1997

This route starts 3 metres left of ***Twilight*** and climbs the corner direct.

(5c). Start at the bottom of the corner and layback to a bridging position. Levitate up the corner to the top on little edges. Belay on the spike on the right.

One hundred metres to the left is an attractive south-facing slabby wall. This is to the left of the narrow grassy access ridge and beyond the old buildings in the upper part of the quarry workings.

27 **Wai Lord**	19m	F7b+	★	

Start at the ramp right of ***Bram Crag Wall*** and follow the obvious curving line with desperate moves to gain the lower off (if you're lucky!).

28 **Bram Crag Wall**	19m	F7a	★★	2010

Start at the large flake leaning against the centre of the wall.

Great moves up the steep slab lead to a rest at a large block. Climb over this and the steeper wall above to a rest at the niche lower off of ***Michelangelo***. Step back right and make thin and excellent moves (crux) to finish at a lower off. 9 bolts.

Above: Matt de Vaal ponders his next move on the first ascent of **Bram Crag Wall** (F7a). **Photo:** Colin Downer

29 **Middle Earth**	16m	F7b	★	2010

A direct route up the shield between *Michelangelo* and *Bram Crag Wall*. Start as for *Michelangelo*.

From the first bolt, step right and attack the shield to a stopper move. Stand here for a while looking for holds that aren't there (crux), then climb the next bit without them. Once the blank section is crossed continue to join the top of *Michelangelo* and follow this to the niche. 7 bolts.

30 **Michelangelo**	16m	F6b	★★	2010

Start beneath the obvious rising crack on the left, 3 metres left of *Bram Crag Wall*.

Climb the short wall to gain a huge flake. Climb the flake on its right to gain the crack above. Difficult but never desperate moves rightwards across the crack lead to a niche and lower off. 8 bolts.

Bramcrag (NY 321 219) is situated immediately above *Bram Crag Quarry* at the top of a scree slope. It is steep and seamed with fine-looking groove lines but the routes are not recommended due to loose rock.

Sandbed Ghyll (NY 322 218) is the earliest recorded climb (1890) in the Eastern Crags. The gill gives a worthwhile and entertaining scramble with two Difficult pitches. It is harder, but no less enjoyable, in wet conditions and is at its finest when the beck is frozen. Often an ice pitch forms on the steep ground on the right after the exit from the ravine.

Ghyll Buttress (NY 322 216) is the undercut crag 200 metres up *Sandbed Ghyll* on its south side. Four routes have been climbed but have never become popular.

Sandbed Ghyll Crag

Grid Reference:	**NY 322 215**	Altitude:	**390m**
Faces:	**North-West**	Approach:	**15 mins**

This is the steep crag high on the fellside immediately south of *Sandbed Ghyll*. The routes, although comparatively short, are technically demanding and on excellent rock. The crag has been sadly neglected despite its obvious attractions and the routes are currently rather dirty though most are still climbable. The approach walk is painfully steep but mercifully short.

In the centre of the crag is a fine prominent corner (*Little Taff*) to the left of which is a steep slab capped by a body length roof. The area below the roof seeps after wet weather but this can be checked from the road. To the right of *Little Taff* are two lesser corners with bulging walls between them.

Sandbed Ghyll overview

Sandbed Ghyll Crag

1	Powder Monkey	E2	
2	Damp Powder	S	
3	Gorilla	VS	
4	Ape Factor	E4	*
5	Caged	E3	
6	Monkey Business	E4	*
7	Chimp Dach	E4	*
8	Walk Under Ladders	E1	**
9	Little Taff	HS	
10	All the Way From America	HVS	

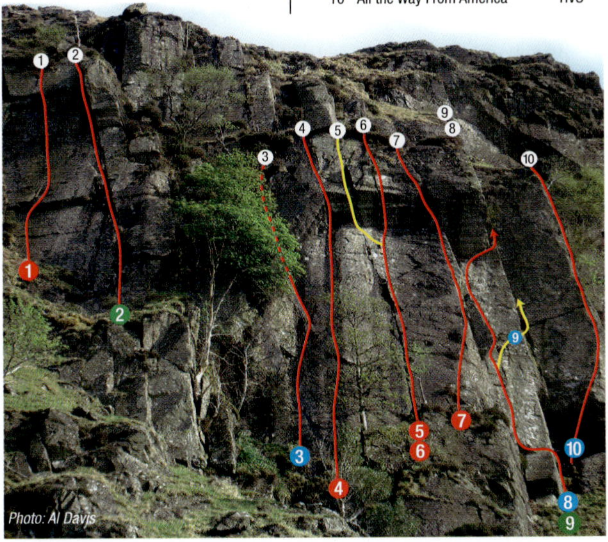

Approach:

Park in the lay-by directly below the crag and trot lightly up the vertical fellside.

The best **descent** is to the right-hand side down along a traverse line past an obvious tree.

The climbs are described from **left** to **right**.

1	Powder Monkey	20m	E2		1991

At the left end of the crag is an obvious filthy slab. This is 15 metres left of the big roof and at the same level.

(5c). Climb up over the overhang at its left-hand side (or more directly just right) and follow a thin crack to a niche. Continue up the crack and exit right on a grass ledge.

2 **Damp Powder**	23m	S		1993

Climbs the obvious leaning corner to the right of *Powder Monkey*.

1 20m. Start directly below the corner and climb some cracks to the top of the corner. Step out right to the grassy ledge.

2 3m. The route can be finished up the little wall above. Step down and right (directly below the leaning block on top) go up and exit to the right of the block. Belays can be found behind the perched block but better ones are 15 - 20m back; threads behind a half-buried boulder.

The next five routes ascend the left-hand buttress which has a steep slab capped by a prominent roof.

3 **Gorilla**	30m	VS		1984

Takes the stepped grooves at the left end of the smooth wall. Start on the ledge below the groove. Often wet.

(4c). Climb the slabby grooves to a ledge 4 metres below the line of overhangs. Traverse left, pull up and follow the black slab to the top.

4 **Ape Factor**	30m	E4	★	1986

Start from the ledge behind the sycamore tree 3 metres right of the corner.

(6b). Climb directly up the black streak in the slab to a step in the overhang. Pull up left round the bulge and climb the slab above to finish beside the large hanging block at the top.

5 **Caged**	30m	E3		1986

Takes the weakness through the roof between *Ape Factor* and *Monkey Business*. Start as for *Monkey Business*.

(6a). Climb the wide crack of *Monkey Business* to the roof, move left and from an undercling reach over the roof to a finger lock; better holds follow.

6 **Monkey Business**	30m	E4	★	1986

Start from the ledge at the rowan tree below the wide crack in the slab.

(6b). Follow the wide crack to below a thin crack in the overhang. Climb this and the continuation crack above.

7 **Chimp Dach**	30m	E4	★	1984

Start from the right-hand end of the ledge.

(6b). Climb the arête following the right-hand edge of the wall to the roof. Climb the thin crack above to good holds.

Sandbed Ghyll Crag

Overview

6	Monkey Business	E4	*
7	Chimp Dach	E4	*
8	Walk Under Ladders	E1	**
9	Little Taff	HS	
v1	Direct start	HVS	
10	All the Way From America	HVS	
11	Doghouse	HVS	
12	Child In Time	E2	*
13	Pebble Dash	E5	*

Not all routes shown.

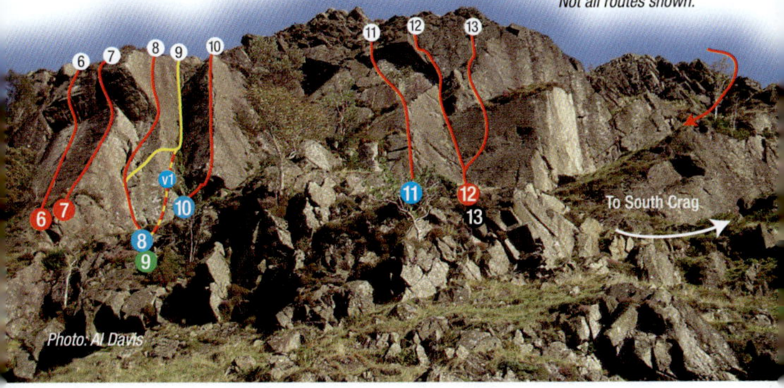

8 **Walk Under Ladders**	30m	E1	★★	1984

To the right of the smooth wall is a fine prominent corner. This excellent route takes the groove and wall to its left. Start under the large detached block 6 metres left of the base of the corner.

(5b). Move up onto the block and then up the wide groove to a ledge. Continue up the groove to about 2 metres below the roof where a line of holds lead right to the arête. Climb the wall on the right and then leftwards to the crack above the overhang. Follow the crack to where it fades then move left again. Up slightly right to finish.

9 **Little Taff**	33 m	HS		1962

This route tackles the fine but vegetated corner. Start under the large detached block as for *Walk Under Ladders*.

Move up onto the block. Go up the wide groove left of the corner for 9 metres until it is possible to traverse into the corner which is followed to the top.

v1 ***Direct Start*** HVS 1984

(5a). Climb the corner direct.

10 **All the Way From America**	33m	HVS		1981

The obvious arête right of *Little Taff* is poorly protected.

(5a). Starting left of the arête, go up to a good hold and swing right onto the arête proper. Follow this to the top.

11 **Doghouse**	35m	HVS		1991

Start up the left-bounding rib of the groove of *Child in Time*.

1 **15m** (5a). Climb the rib (poorly-protected) and move left at the top to a ledge.

2 **20m** (4c). Climb up to a heathery ledge on the left then straight up the steep wall moving right to finish.

12 **Child In Time**	33m	E2	★	1981

The corner/groove 20 metres right of *Little Taff*. It lies round to the right of a short wall and at the same level as *Little Taff*.

(5c). Climb the vegetated corner to a ledge below a hanging groove. Pull into this using the jamming crack (crux) and continue up the groove to the top.

13 **Pebble Dash**	33m	E5	★	1984

The bulging wall right of *Child In Time*.

1 **18m** (6b). Climb up the corner for a couple of metres and move rightwards to footholds on the wall. Continue up to a poor peg runner, pull round the bulge on the right and climb the slab above to a grass terrace. Belay to the left.

2 **15m** (5b). Climb the groove above to a small pedestal. Hand traverse to the right-hand end of the ledge, pull up and continue rightwards to the top.

Hit the Fan	33m	E4		1991

Start 5 metres right of the corner of *Child in Time* at the arête.

1 **18m** (5b). Move onto the arête via an obvious short groove. Climb the arête and belay at the right end of a large grass ledge.

2 **15m** (6a). Climb the smooth wall via a two finger pocket finishing directly at an obvious jug pocket just below the top. Bold and poorly protected.

Stingray	27m	E2	★	1984

The corner 10 metres right of *Child In Time*. The initial corner is serious for leader and second.

(5c). Climb the corner to the terrace and pull up the thin crack to a ledge on the right. Climb the slab above to the top.

Left: Ron Kenyon tempting fate on **Walk Under Ladders** (E1), Sandbed Ghyll Crag.
Photo: Stephen Reid

Sandbed Ghyll South Crag

1	Friendly Fire	VS
2	Lovely Boy	E1
3	Lovely Charter	E3
4	Citizen's Charter	MVS
5	Citizen's Fever	HVS
6	Jungle Fever	HVS

Photo: Al Davis

Sandbed South Crag

This attractive little buttress is reached by traversing 60 metres horizontally to the right from the lowest point of the main crag.

1	**Friendly Fire**	12m	VS		1991

(4c). Climb the steep wall at the extreme left-hand side of the buttress.

2	**Lovely Boy**	14m	E1		1991

(5b). Climb the obvious left-slanting crack-line.

3	**Lovely Charter**	20m	E3?		1993

(5c). An eliminate between *Lovely Boy* and *Citizen's Charter*.

4	**Citizen's Charter**	20m	MVS		1991

The central heather-choked crack-line.

5	**Citizen's Fever**	20m	HVS		1993

(5a). The wall between *Citizen's Charter* and *Jungle Fever*.

6	**Jungle Fever**	20m	HVS		1991

Start at a short arête at the right-hand end of the buttress.

(5a). Climb up to the overhang, then follow a crack and slab above.

Sandbed Ghyll

Lower South Crag

1 Call Up HVS
2 England Calling E3

Photo: Al Davis

Lower South Crag

This crag lies below and right of the main crag. The rock is quite good but the top of the crag is very loose in places and belays should be taken well back. The left end of the crag is marked by slabby broken grooves above a prominent yew tree.

The routes are described from **left** to **right**.

Call Girl	25m	VS		1992

Climbs a slim groove and ramp at the left end of the crag. Start 5 metres left of the yew tree at a large block beneath a slim groove.

(4c). Climb the groove to a tree. Trend up to the right and then more directly and steeply to finish.

1 **Call Up**	25m	HVS		1992

Twenty five metres around the crag to the right is a prominent cave. Start 10 metres left of the cave beneath a grooved arête.

(5a). Climb diagonally left and then pull up steeply into the right-facing groove which leads to the top.

2	**England Calling**	25m	E3		1992

Start 8 metres left of the cave at a small gorse bush below a smooth wall. (5c). Climb directly up the poorly-protected wall to a steeper wall. Trend left and up an easy rib.

	Call to Arms	25m	E3		1992

Start from the shallow cave and grassy bay at the right hand side of the crag. (5c). Gain and climb the obvious groove following a slim ramp leftwards at the top.

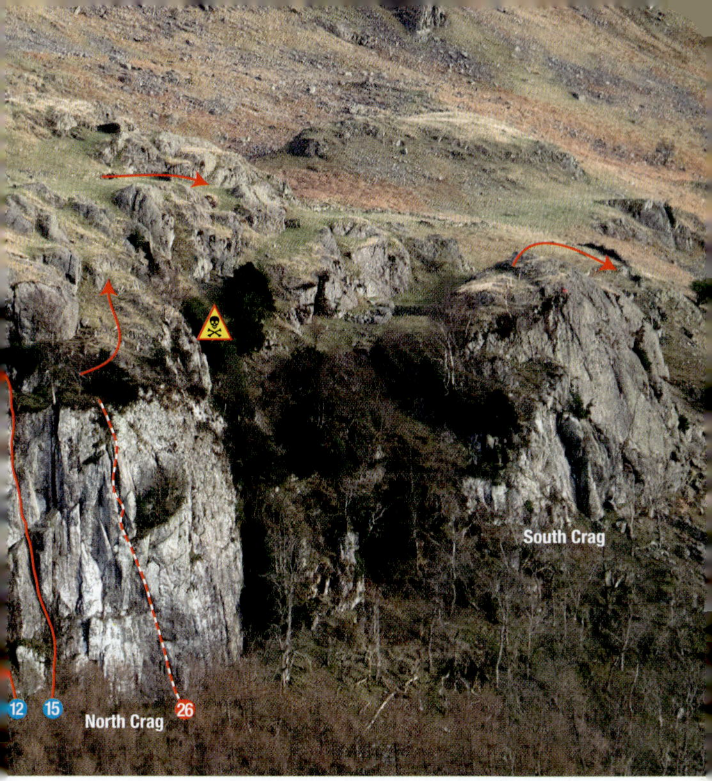

Castle Rock of Triermain

Grid Reference: **NY 321 197** Altitude: **275m**
Faces: **West to South** Approach: **10 mins**

Castle Rock is a magnificent crag on the lower slopes of Watson's Dodd and towering above St John's in the Vale. It catches the afternoon sun, has classic quality routes of all grades and is deservedly popular.

The crag can conveniently be divided into three distinct areas. From left to right these are *North Gully Wall*, *North Crag* and *South Crag*. *North Gully Wall* is a 30 metre face on the left side of the crag. It lies above the tree-filled *North Gully* which bounds *North Crag* on its left. *North Crag* is an impressive and slightly impending wall breached in its centre by the deep

V-groove of *May Day Cracks*. It is 75 metres high at its higher left-hand end and wooded along its base. To the right of the *North Crag* is some steep broken ground and then *South Crag* which is a clean compact dome about 35 metres high.

Approach:

Legburthwaite car park is situated directly beneath the crag. From here a footpath crosses the road and leads into a field via steps and a gate. To reach *North Crag*, follow the track which heads up to the top left corner of the field, cross the culvert and follow the track alongside the wall. To reach *South Crag*, break off right from the track and go steeply up to the top right corner of the field, cross the culvert and follow a path up through the wood to the crag.

North Gully Wall — West Facing

North Crag is bounded on its left by the vegetated and dirty *North Gully*. This wall forms the left wall of the gully.

A **Diamond Jubilee**	22m	E2		2007

Climbs the lower left wall starting near the foot of the diagonal ramp that leads into the dank gully. Start below a short prominent groove in the front of the wall. Most of the rock is good but some of the flakes tend to be a bit friable.

(5b). Climb a short dark groove (the right-hand one) and step left to a ledge under the prominent groove. Step up to the overhang, swing left onto a spike and pull hastily up to a larger spike. Climb diagonally left on good holds (keeping above a sloping ledge) to gain a smaller ledge by a rather unprotected move. Step right on good holds to finish.

The following two routes start further up *North Gully*. The routes are in a gloomy dank position and rather overgrown.

B **Castle Wall**	35m	MVS		1947

Start at the right end of a large slanting ledge where it meets the gully.

(4a). Climb up to another sloping ledge beside a holly. Follow the gangway leftwards for 6 metres and ascend the wall above over a series of bulges.

C **Flying Buttress**	30m	VS		1947

A neglected route. Start as for *Castle Wall* where the slanting ledge meets the gully.

(4b). Climb painfully past a holly to the second sloping ledge. Start up the corner-crack and traverse left to the arête. Move left under a bulge, pull over it and ascend directly to the top.

Castle Rock

North Crag Far Left Side

1 The Watchtower E2 **
2 The Barbican VS *
3 Matheson Avenue HVS *
4 Side of the Hill E1 **

Photo: Al Phizacklea

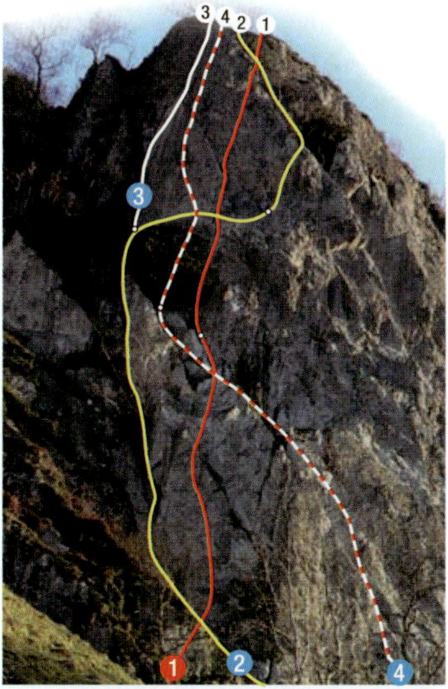

North Crag

West Facing

The *North Crag* of *Castle Rock* provides some of the finest middle grade climbing in the area. The rock is steep and juggy, though it provides rather flaky holds which can prove loose and should be treated with caution. Protection can be sparse outside the comfort of the crack and groove lines and many routes call for a bold approach.

A stone wall bounding the wood meets the crag near its left end and provides a convenient reference point.

The easiest **descent** is over the top of *South Crag* to the right. *North Gully* on the left provides a shorter but more serious and dirty descent.

The climbs are described from **left** to **right**.

1 **The Watchtower**	70m	E2	★★	1990

An interesting and very worthwhile route giving surprisingly independent climbing and a very exposed finish. Start from a small tree 10 metres left of the stone wall.

Castle Rock
North Crag Left Side
1 The Watchtower E2 **
2 The Barbican VS *
4 North Crag Eliminate E1 ***
5 Side of the Hill E1 **
6 First Republic E3 *
7 The Last Laugh E4 *
8 Crusader E3
9 Agony E2 **
v1 Agony Direct E2
10 Zig Zag VS **
11 Ecstasy E3 *
12 Overhanging Bastion VS ***
v2 Original start
13 Deliverance E1 **
14 Eliminator E3 *
15 May Day Cracks HVS ***
Not all routes marked.
Photo: Eric Shaw

1
2 4 5
5
6
7
8 9
8
9
10 11
10
11
11
10
12 13
13
V2
14 15
14
15

1 30m (5b). Climb the short wall rightwards to gain the gangway of *Barbican*. Starting from the left, climb the rib above trending right to the slab on *North Crag Eliminate*. Continue straight up over a bulge and slab to a perched block and belay.

2 40m (5c). A superb pitch. Climb past two bushes to below an overhanging corner just right of the yew tree on *North Crag Eliminate*. Layback up this strenuously and continue in the same line crossing the gangway of *North Crag Eliminate* and joining *The Last Laugh* to gain the top of the flake. From the right end of the flake, climb straight up then move left to good finishing holds in the shallow chimney – quite serious.

2 **The Barbican**	85m	VS	★	1951

After a dank start the route breaks onto the left side of the main face by an exposed traverse (steady second necessary). Start by a large ash just left of the stone wall.

1 27m (4b). Climb leftwards on a dirty slab (often wet) to gain a large corner which is climbed to an elm tree.

2 16m (4a). A heavily vegetated corner/chimney leads to a good ledge. Continue easily to a large ash.

3 14m (4c). From the tree, step onto the wall and traverse rightwards to the arête. Descend for 3 metres and make a delicate step right. Continue to a ledge and elm tree belay.

4 10m (4a). Climb up to a ledge on the right and ascend the steep wall to a recess with a yew.

5 18m. The tree-covered gangway on the left.

The next two routes start in a bay halfway up the crag. They are reached by climbing the first two pitches of *The Barbican* or *North Crag Eliminate*.

Prenotion	24m	MVS		1959

Climb the vegetated crack and groove at the back of the bay.

3 **Matheson Avenue**	24m	HVS	★	1965

A superb pitch. Start from a large ash some 4 metres above the yew on *North Crag Eliminate*.

(5a). Carefully avoiding two large loose blocks at the start, climb the excellent crack to the niche on *North Crag Eliminate*. Most now finish by a pull out right to reach easier ground (as for *North Crag Eliminate*).

Direct Finish E1 1977

(5b). Make a hard move into the steep groove directly above the niche (and just left of the finishing groove of *North Crag Eliminate*) and follow it to the top. Bold and rather dirty.

4 **North Crag Eliminate**	75m	E1	★★★	1952

A classic and popular route with good protection. Start at the large ash just left of the stone wall. After a scruffy start the route steadily improves.

> *"North Crag Eliminate's exposed corner – here, at least ten cigarettes were required before the crux was overcome".*
> Paul Ross, Castle Rock of Triemain, FRCC Journal 1961

1 33m (4b). Enter the corner/groove above the tree from the left (or direct at 5b) and climb it until it steepens. Follow the mossy slab on the left up to its edge then step up and move slightly right to reach a terrace. The continuation of the corner/groove can also be climbed direct with little increase in difficulty.

2 9m. Step left and bushwack behind a pinnacle to a yew.

3 9m (5a). Climb precariously up the much abused yew tree to gain holds above the overhang and swing across to the top of the gangway on the right. Move up to a balcony and elm tree belay.

4 24m (5b). Climb the narrowing gangway on the left and make a blind move left to reach a flake-crack and resting place at its top. Traverse left round the corner into a niche. Pull out right to reach easier ground.

5 **Side of the Hill**	70m	E1	★★	1974

This climb originally had three pitches but most teams start at the yew of *North Crag Eliminate* to enjoy the bold top pitch. The lower two have been re-cleaned but are still a bit grubby; they are described for those who want to savour the full experience.

Start as for *North Crag Eliminate* at a large ash just left of the stone wall.

1 25m (5b). Climb the steep crack direct to a narrow ledge at 4 metres. Traverse the footledge horizontally to its left-hand end and then make a rising traverse leftwards up slabs to a small cracked ledge on the arête. Climb the bulge above to pull out onto the ramp of *North Crag Eliminate* and follow its left arête leftwards into a scoop. Climb out of this to a belay at the foot of a short cracked corner overhung by brambles.

2 15m (5b). From the foot of the corner, step diagonally leftwards and gain the arête. Move up with difficulty to a resting place and then follow the blunt arête above, direct to a ledge behind the yew on *North Crag Eliminate*.

3. 30m (5a). Climb the yew to gain holds above the overhang. Move left and climb the slim corner-groove in the arête, crossing *North Crag Eliminate* just left of the flake, and continue direct to the top via a crack. Quite a bold lead.

The Gossard (VS, 130m, 1947) a poor girdle of only historic interest, traversed from left to right starting up *North Crag Eliminate*.

Above: Belinda James prepares to launch herself off the top of the yew and over the overhang on **North Crag Eliminate** (E1), Castle Rock of Triermain. **Photo:** Stephen Reid

6 **First Republic**	54m	E3	★	1980

A good top pitch which plugs the gap between *The Last Laugh* and *Overhanging Bastion*. Unfortunately it is all rather filthy at present. Start at the large ash tree just left of the stone wall.

1 27m (5c). A contrived and poorly-protected pitch. Climb the first few moves of *The Last Laugh*, then step left and climb directly up the slim pillar left of *The Last Laugh*. (A more direct start is to approach the pillar from the left and swing right onto the pillar.) Belay on the terrace.

2 27m (6a). Climb the wall, as for *Last Laugh*, to beneath the corner. Climb the groove on the right to a peg then continue diagonally left to the groove above *The Last Laugh* which is followed to the top. Yew tree belay.

7 **The Last Laugh**	65m	E4	★	1965

In the wall right of *North Crag Eliminate* is a thin rightward-facing corner which provides the very difficult second pitch. Start at the large ash tree just left of the stone wall.

Right: No pain, no gain. Steve Scott looking for a way up the main pitch of **Agony** (E2), Castle Rock of Triermain. **Photo:** Ron Kenyon

1 27m (5b). Climb straight up the wall on the right to a resting place beneath a thin corner (peg). Move up and use a good hold to gain the gangway on *Zig Zag*. Follow this to the terrace.

2 18m (6b). Climb the wall on the right to the foot of the prominent smooth and rightward-facing corner. Ascend this with difficulty and pull out to a ledge on the left. Traverse left for a couple of metres to reach the final stance on *North Crag Eliminate*.

3 20m (5b). Move halfway up the narrowing gangway on the left until a steep crack leads to the top right-hand corner of the large flake. Continue rightwards up the steep wall to the top.

8 **Crusader**	74m	E3		1994

Start as for *Agony*. A series of contrived variants.

1 30m (5a). Climb to the thin flake at 5 metres then go vertically up the cleaned wall to join *Zig Zag* at the bulge. Continue up *Zig Zag* to the left end of the terrace. Tree belay.

2 20m (6a). Up the clean wall on the right to a ledge below the *Last Laugh* crux. Traverse left for 3 metres and climb the shallow groove (peg runner) slanting left through the bulges (crux) direct to the tree belay on *North Crag Eliminate* pitch 3.

3 24m (5b). Continue up the gangway as for *North Crag Eliminate* pitch 4.

9 **Agony**	90m	E2	★★	1959

A brilliant though spooky wall climb with two bold exposed pitches. Start two metres right of the stone wall. Protection is poor on the first pitch and non-existent on the second. The lack of gear and the rattly flakes make for a memorable experience.

1 40 m (5a). Climb the mossy dirty wall without any protection to join *Zig Zag* at the break in the gangway. Traverse right for 6 metres to a thin bulging crack which is climbed to easier ground. Belay by a large ash tree.

2 36m (5a). A very bold pitch. From a shallow scoop directly above, move right to a blunt flake and up to a grass ledge. Step left round the arête and climb steeply up to a flake on the left. Make further steep moves back right to a scoop in the arête. Follow this more easily to the slab of *Zig Zag*. Belay below an open groove in the wall above.

3 14m (4a). Climb the groove.

v1 ***Agony Direct*** E2 1984

2 (5b). Instead of moving up right to the scoop climb directly up the steep wall. Very bold.

10 **Zig Zag**	100m	VS-	★★	1939

An interesting, varied and well-protected route giving a good introduction to the delights of the *North Crag*. It has some rattly flakes and the rock should be handled with caution. Start at a pedestal 10 metres right of the stone wall.

1 37m (4c). Climb easily to an ash by a leftward-slanting gangway. Follow the gangway to a large terrace.
2 15m. Walk to the right descending slightly and traverse a big flake to an ash.
3 24m (4c). Ascend the slab on the right and climb a steep crack and then a further crack moving onto the left wall to avoid debris from a collapsed ledge. Belay at the foot of the obvious large slab.
4 24m. Climb the centre of the big slab on the left.

11 **Ecstasy**	70m	E3	★	1978

Climbs the wall between the starts of *Agony* and *Overhanging Bastion* and finishes to the left of *Eliminator*. Start at the bottom of the gangway on *Zig Zag*.

1 33m (5b). Climb the wall up and left following roughly the line of *Zig Zag* past a deep pocket heading for a rising flake-line which leads to a large shattered spike. Pull rightwards through the bulges and move easily up to the *Zig Zag* traverse. Head up and right and make a tough move into a short rightwards-facing corner. Exit this left onto a large grassy ledge.
2 37m (5c). Climb the wall on the left, passing a good spike, to pull right onto the ramp of *Overhanging Bastion*. Climb the ramp for a couple of moves then traverse boldly across the steep wall on the right to a niche. Pull up and out right to an easier-angled wall. Climb this for 5 metres and then up a ramp to belays at the top.

12 **Overhanging Bastion**	82m	VS+	★★★	1939

The classic route of the crag, swaggering up the gangway which cuts the *North Crag* in such an obvious and exposed manner. The bold moves to start the gangway place the route at the upper limit of the grade. Start 15 metres right of the stone wall at the lowest point of the crag where an easy-angled slab leads to a steep wall with a clean crack on the left.

1 15m (4b). Climb the slab, traverse left to the crack and climb it to a belay beneath a steep corner on the right.
2 18m (4c). Ascend the wall for 5 metres and climb the corner to a leftward-slanting groove/gangway which leads to an ash with a large ledge behind it.
3 32m (5a). Ascend the slab on the left to the pinnacle (possible belay). From the top of the pinnacle step boldly onto the gangway and follow it much more easily to its top. Move down and left and climb steeply up dubious rattly flakes to a recess with a yew.
4 18m. The natural line continues up the tree covered gangway (as for the final pitch of *The Barbican*). Alternatively, as on the first ascent, climb out of the recess on the right and continue easily to the top.

Original Start 12m

Start 20 metres right of the stone wall beneath a strangled holly.

Climb up to the holly and pull round it to a large ledge. Move up to beneath a steep corner.

Direct Finish 25m

From the top of the gangway on pitch 3, climb the wall above. A poor alternative.

Overhanging Bastion/Zig Zag combination VS- ★★

Pitches 1 and 2 of *Overhanging Bastion* followed by pitches 3 and 4 of *Zig Zag* provide a superb direct way up the crag at an amenable grade with good protection and is especially suitable for nervous seconds.

13 **Deliverance**	71m	E1	★★	1994

A combination of eliminates giving a fine direct route up the crag. Pitch 3 makes an excellent HVS in its own right. Start as for *Overhanging Bastion*.

1 **14m (4b).** Climb the slab, traverse left to a crack and climb it to a good ledge.

2 **18m (5a).** Climb up to a spike on the left. Either move up left to join *Agony* then from the base of the groove make an improbable move right to a good hold and into a short groove, or climb the groove direct (5c), without runners in *Agony*. Climb the steep wall on the right on improving holds to belay as for *Overhanging Bastion*.

3 **25m (5a).** Step up right onto the foot of the easy-angled slab of *Zig Zag*, leave it immediately by a shallow groove leading to the flake on *Agony* and continue to a grass ledge. Climb the excellent corner/crack into the easier groove which joins the slab of *Zig Zag*. Cross the slab to belay as for *Agony*, below a yellow groove in the wall above.

4 **14m (4a).** Climb the groove (pitch 4 of *Agony*).

14 **Eliminator**	92m	E3	★	1969

Two good pitches of climbing though not exactly a natural line. The scary top pitch crosses the wall left of *Agony*. Start at a shallow groove beneath a vegetated ledge as for *May Day Cracks*.

1 **10m.** Ascend the groove to the ash as for *May Day Cracks*.

2 **35m (5a).** Climb the fine tapering unprotected rib on the left. The climbing is easy enough but very bold. Traverse some way left to belay on the large ledge behind the ever-popular ash tree.

3 **35m (5b).** Climb rightwards across the wall behind the ledge to the grass ledge as for *Agony*. Step back left round the arête and go

Left: Rob Keet just above the hard moves on the exposed gangway pitch of **Overhanging Bastion** (VS), Castle Rock. **Photo:** Keith Sharples

Castle Rock
North Crag Right Side
15 May Day Cracks HVS ***
v1 Wet Day Wander E1
16 Thilmere Eliminate E1 ***
17 Wild Wall E4
18 The Ultimate Eliminate E3
19 Rigor Mortis E2 ***
20 White Dwarf E4 *
21 The Ghost E3 **
v2 The Loop E2
22 Die Another Day E7 **
23 Harlot Face E1 ***
v3 Walsh's Blind Variant E2 **
24 Triermain Eliminate E2 ***
25 Where Monkeys Dare E5
26 Angel's Highway E1 **
27 Ted Cheasby E2 ***
v4 Ted Cheasby Direct E4 **
28 The Final Giggle E1 *
29 Wingnut E2 *
Photo: Eric Shaw

v1
18
19
22
24
23
v3
v4
25
15
16
18
19
20
21
22
24
26
23
24
25
26
27
28
29

diagonally leftwards with little in the way of protection to the foot of a right-facing corner which is climbed to the slab above. There is a most welcome peg just on the slab. Climb this for 5 metres and then up a ramp on the left to a block belay.
4 12 m (4b). Climb the wall above.

15 **May Day Cracks**	70m	HVS	★★★	1947

This fine climb takes a series of cracks which divide the high left part of the crag from the lower right-hand section. The start of the second pitch is often wet and is then much harder – leave it to dry out! The climb is sustained, well-protected and very worthwhile. Start at a shallow groove a few metres right of *Overhanging Bastion* which leads to a vegetated ledge. There is an obvious deep V-groove above.
1 10m. Ascend the groove to the ash tree.
2 36m (5a). Climb the chimney and V-groove above to join *Zig Zag*. Continue to a belay at the base of the obvious large slab.
3 24m. Climb the big slab on the left.

v1 ***Wet Day Wander*** E1 1984
(5a). An eliminate variation linking *May Day Cracks* with the arête on *Thirlmere Eliminate*.

16 **Thirlmere Eliminate**	55m	E1+	★★★	1955

An enjoyable (if you are going well!) and sustained climb up the ribs and corners to the right of *May Day Cracks*. Protection is only just adequate. Start below a 2-metre high perched flake, 4 metres right of *May Day Cracks*.
1 37m (4c). Climb onto the flake and continue up a corner to the left end of a long narrow ledge (possible belay). Traverse diagonally left into a corner and pull onto the arête. Follow the arête to a sloping ledge in an overhanging bay.
2 18m (5b). Climb the steep corner moving onto the right wall at the top. A bold pitch.

Original Finish E1
The original finish to the last pitch has been cleaned but is still rather green.
3 (5b). Climb the corner to above the overhang then a couple of moves are made up to the left edge. The difficulties ease and pleasant climbing up right brings you to the large birch tree at the top of the pitch.

17 **Wild Wall**	18m	E4		1989

Bold and very poorly protected. Start from the belay below the last pitch of *Thirlmere Eliminate*.
(6a). Climb the wall between the final pitches of *Thirlmere Eliminate* and *The Ultimate Eliminate*.

18 **The Ultimate Eliminate**	35m	E3		1979

Start from the long narrow ledge at the top of the first pitch of *Rigor Mortis*. A very serious climb which is bold and poorly-protected.

1 20m (5c). Climb the centre of the wall between *Thirlmere Eliminate* and *Rigor Mortis*. Belay in the overhanging bay.

2 15m (5c). Step right and follow the groove and crack in the arête to a ledge. Move right and climb a thin crack to the top.

19 **Rigor Mortis**	57m	E2	★★★	1959

A good and varied climb. The second pitch is bold and technical and the third pitch is very exposed. Start at a shallow corner just right of the perched flake of *Thirlmere Eliminate*.

1 15m (4c). Climb the wall to a small overhang in the corner. Swing right onto the front and follow a steep crack to the long narrow ledge.

2 20m (5c). A thin corner which peters out into a crack rises from the left end of the ledge. Climb the corner and crack to the top of the *White Cone*. Step up and traverse the steep little wall leftwards into a shallow scoop. Climb the scoop and belay in the bay of *Thirlmere Eliminate*.

3 22m (5a). Round the corner on the right a line of interrupted gangways provides a sensational passage ending with a swing round a rib into the final chimney of *Harlot Face*.

Last on the List	125m	HVS	★★	1991

A lower level and easier girdle than the *Eliminate Girdle*. It takes in some excellent pitches and provides a sustained and exposed way up the crag at a reasonable standard with the crux in the final few moves. Start as for *Rigor Mortis*.

1 15m (4c). Climb the wall to a small overhang in the corner. Swing right onto the front and follow a steep crack to a tree belay on a long narrow ledge (pitch 1 *Rigor Mortis*).

2 22m (4c). Traverse diagonally left into a corner and pull onto the arête. Follow the arête to a sloping ledge in an overhanging bay (as for *Thirlmere Eliminate*).

3 25m (4b). Step down left and traverse leftwards on narrow sloping ledges crossing *May Day Cracks* to pull up an undercut corner onto a large ledge (this is a belay on *Zig Zag* and *Overhanging Bastion*). Ascend the slab on the left to a pinnacle belay.

4 25m (5a). From the top of the pinnacle, step onto the gangway and follow it to its top (as for *Overhanging Bastion* pitch 3). Step left and descend the wall leftwards to a tree belay (pitch 4 of *Barbican* in reverse).

Overleaf: Brian Davison strikes a classic pose at the end of the gangway on **Rigor Mortis** (E2), Castle Rock. **Photo:** Keith Sharples

5 14m (4c). Step down and traverse delicately leftwards to the arête. Climb steeply up for 3 metres and move round the arête to a tree belay (pitch 3 of *Barbican* in reverse).
6 24m (5a). Move left to a superb rightward-curving crack on the left of the blank wall and follow it to the niche on North Crag Eliminate. Step right and climb the groove to the top (*Matheson Avenue*).

20 **White Dwarf**	30m	E4	★	1978

An eliminate route linking variations but providing a good direct way up the crag. It is very bold up the corner with poor protection where it matters. Start at the top of the first pitch of *Rigor Mortis*.

(6a). Climb the face of the *White Cone* and move into the obvious corner above its apex. Follow this to the gangways of *Rigor Mortis*. Finish up the bulging wall above.

21 **The Ghost**	30m	E3	★★	1964

A steep strenuous and committing route taking the impending groove right of the *White Cone*. The loss of a large block on the traverse has made the original line much harder.

Start at the top of the first pitch of *Rigor Mortis*.

(5c). Climb a short wall into the bottom of the groove to the right of the *White Cone*. Make hard moves right to gain the large flake and step left into a V-groove. Follow this groove to the end of the *Rigor Mortis* traverse. Climb the steep wall above moving leftwards.

v2 ***The Loop*** E2 1969

A variation which is more popular for those who cannot commit to the hard moves right.

(5b). Climb to the top of the *White Cone* and traverse right into the V-groove. Follow this to the *Rigor Mortis* traverse. Climb the steep wall above moving leftwards.

22 **Die Another Day**	47m	E7	★★	2003

Two hard and very bold pitches make for a serious undertaking up the pillar between the second pitches of *Triermain Eliminate* and *The Ghost* with a finish up the the rib above in a superb position.

1 12m (6b). The short and serious wall to the left of pitch 1 of *Harlot Face*.
2 35m (6b). Start behind the hawthorn on the long ledge below a thin crack-line. Climb the crack-line to a good jug on the right at about 5 metres (poor Black Diamond Microstopper 3 down left, good RP 1

Left: Crux moves on the original way on **The Ghost** (E3), Castle Rock. **Photo:** Al Phizacklea

high left). Continue up the crack-line to a downward-pointing spike. Reach high left and climb the bulge (crux) to easier rock and past two old pegs to a blocky ledge on the right. Step left and round onto the rib and climb past the *Rigor Mortis* traverse to the top. Tree and nut belay.

The following routes lead to a tree-covered ledge which gives a convenient abseil descent for those keen to avoid the easier top pitches.
The ledge above the first pitch of the following four routes may be more pleasantly (and safely) reached by climbing pitch 1 of *Rigor Mortis*.

23 **Harlot Face**	50m	E1	★★★	1949

A good climb with a short crux. Start 10 metres right of a 2 metre high perched flake at a line of shallow interrupted corners rising to the left.
1 15m (5a). Climb the line of corners to the long narrow ledge – rather serious.
2 15m (5b). Climb a short way up the overhanging corner at the right end of the ledge (as for *Triermain Eliminate*) until an escape can be made round the rib on the right. Continue steeply to a good resting place then up a corner to a tree-covered ledge.
3 20m (4c). Bridge up the open groove above.

v3 ***Walsh's Blind Variant*** 15m E2 ★★ ca1960
2 (5b). Step rightwards from the ledge and climb a thin crack to join *Harlot Face*. Climb the bulging wall rightwards to the trees.

Original Finish 22m
3 Walk leftwards through the crevasse and finish up the easy chimney.

24 **Triermain Eliminate**	49m	E2	★★★	1953

The main pitch provides strenuous but well-protected climbing. Start at a crack just right of the line of shallow interrupted corners rising to the left which are taken by *Harlot Face*.
1 16m (5a). Climb to a small ledge and go up a corner above to a long narrow ledge.
2 15m (5b). Ascend the overhanging corner at the right end of the ledge to a little chimney. Move up to a tree-covered ledge.
3 18m. Finish by the shallow groove above.

Left: Nick Wharton stretched out on **White Dwarf** (E4), Castle Rock. **Photo:** Ron Kenyon

25 **Where Monkeys Dare**	30m	E5		1987

A bold climb which takes a direct line up the wall between *Triermain Eliminate/Harlot Face* and *Ted Cheasby* as far as the tree-covered ledge.

(6b). Climb pitch 1 of *Triermain Eliminate* to a ledge at 8 metres (side runner 3 metres up *Triermain Eliminate* on the left). Climb directly up the inverted L-shaped groove to reach a good hold above its top when awkward moves lead to improving holds. Continue more easily past a sapling to a large block and straight up the steep wall above.

26 **Angel's Highway**	52m	E1	★★	1955

An exposed climb up the blunt rib at the right end of the *North Crag*. A very bold route. Start left of the rib as for *Triermain Eliminate* at a crack just right of a line of shallow interrupted corners.

1 36m (5a). Climb rightwards to a small ledge and traverse right to the overhanging corner of *Ted Cheasby*. Move to the right, crossing the exposed arête onto the face, and work back left up to a shallow groove. Climb the groove, passing a small tree, and traverse left to a big tree on the tree-covered ledge.

2 16m. Climb the wall above and continue up heathery rock.

27 **Ted Cheasby**	46m	E2+	★★★	1977

A strenuous and sustained crack and groove in the left side of the blunt rib of *Angel's Highway*. Start just to the left of the rib.

1 30m (5c). Climb directly up the thin crack past two peg runners and the groove above until a step right can be made above the bulge. Move back left and climb a shallow groove as for *Angel's Highway* to the belay on a tree-covered ledge.

2 16m. Climb the wall above, as for *Angel's Highway*.

v4 ***Direct Finish*** E4 ★★

A very good direct finish to *Ted Cheasby*.

(6a). Follow *Ted Cheasby* to the top of its crack but instead of stepping right above the bulge make a hard move up and left to sinking jugs. Follow the wall past a sapling and the groove on the right (as for *Ted Cheasby*) to a tree-covered ledge.

Gabriel	47m	E2		1977

A dirty route giving poorly-protected climbing. Start at the foot of the rib.

(5b). Climb a short crack to a broken flake and climb the wall above via a niche on widely spaced holds.

Eliminate Girdle	122m	E1+	★★★	1960

An excellent climb. The standard of difficulty is well maintained and some of the best pitches on the crag are included. Start 5 metres right of the rib at the stub of a tree, as for *The Final Giggle*. Pitch 1 is poorly-protected.

1 33m (5a). From the left end of the rock ledge above the tree, climb a shallow groove to a square overhang and pull out to the left. Make an ascending traverse leftwards into the groove of *Angel's Highway* and climb it, passing a small tree, until it is possible to move left to a large ledge. Go left behind a huge flake and belay below a chimney.

2 10m (5a). Step round the steep arête, cross a bottomless groove and follow interrupted gangways, descending slightly to the belay below the final pitch of *Thirlmere Eliminate* (pitch 3 of *Rigor Mortis* in reverse).

3 13m (4c). Climb the left wall of the corner until it is possible to pull round the rib on the left and traverse into *Zig Zag*. Descend the easy-angled slab on the left.

4 32m (5a). Ascend the slab on the left to the pinnacle. From its top step onto the gangway and follow it to its end. Move down and left and climb steeply to a recess with a yew (pitch 3 of *Overhanging Bastion*).

5 10m (4a). Descend the steep wall below until it is possible to move left to a recess and tree belays (pitch 4 *The Barbican* in reverse).

6 24m (5b). Move up to the top of the narrowing gangway on the left and make a blind move left to reach a flake-crack and resting place at its top. Traverse left round the corner into a niche. Pull out right to reach easier ground (pitch 4 *North Crag Eliminate*).

28 **The Final Giggle**	46m	E1+	★	1965

Takes the prominent brown groove and slab at the right end of the crag. Good climbing but spaced protection, especially on the crux. Start 5 metres right of the rib at the stub of a cut down tree below a prominent overhang at 3 metres.

1 30m (5b). From the left end of the ledge above the tree (Friend under the overhang), climb the shallow groove and step right to two peg runners. Climb the groove above then step right and climb the wall to a small tree. Traverse left to the tree-covered ledge.

2 16m. Steep but easier rocks lead to the top.

29 **Wingnut**	33m	E2	★	1979

Start at a shallow groove just right of *The Final Giggle*.

(5c). From the right-hand side of the ledge, climb the shallow groove to its top then step left on to the wall. Climb past a peg to easier ground.

Drag (E1, 1960), at the extreme right-hand end of the crag, was never popular and is thankfully now lost to tree-covered vegetation.

Castle Rock South Crag Left Side

1	Howler	E1 *
2	Chapel Cracks	VS
3	Eleven Hundred Miles	E4
4	Hope	E2
5	Scoop and Crack	HVS
6	Green Eggs and Ham	E2 **
7	Reward	E2

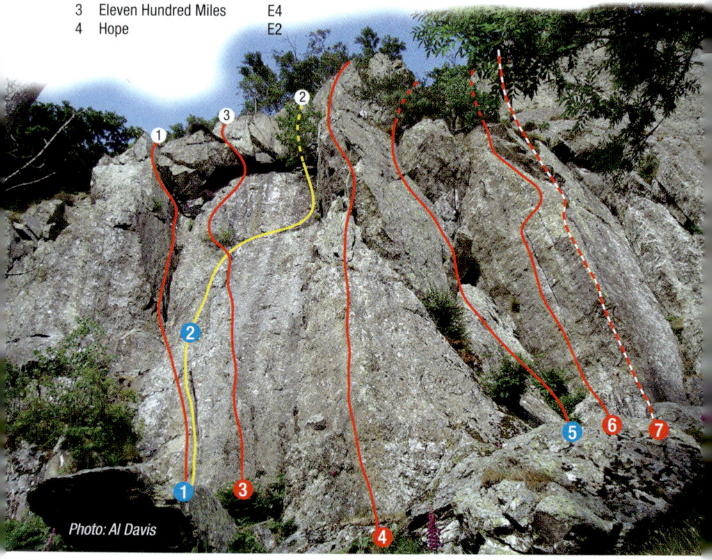

Photo: Al Davis

South Crag

South and West Facing

An open sunny aspect and good clean rock ensure the popularity of the *South Crag*. However, although there is a good selection of routes in the easier grades, protection is not always easy to arrange and it is not an ideal place for beginners learning to lead. Particular care is required in setting up belays at the top of the crag.

A stone wall runs up to the centre of the crag and this provides a convenient reference point for identifying the start of routes.

Descent is to the right.

The routes are described from **left** to **right**.

Most of the initial routes end on a grass ledge from where a short wall (upper section of pitch 2 of *Chapel Cracks*) gains the top.

1 Howler	30m	E1	★	1988

Start at the foot of a recessed wall capped by overhangs, 15 metres left of the stone wall.

(5b). Climb up leftwards to the slim right-facing corner on the left. Follow this up towards the large overhang and make interesting moves out left to gain the ledge on the arête. Finish boldly up a short groove.

2 Chapel Cracks	38m	VS		1947

Start as for *Howler* at the foot of a recessed wall capped by overhangs 15 metres left of the stone wall.

1 22m (4c). Climb up on the right of the trees and pull into a scoop at the base of the left-hand corner of *Howler*. Make a blind move right to a small sloping ledge in the middle of the wall. Move up and hand-traverse to the right-hand corner. Climb the corner to a ledge and belay on a holly.

2 16m. Climb the groove behind the holly and the scruffy wall above.

Alternative Start VS-

1 (4b). Climb the right-hand corner directly (if it's dry).

3 Eleven Hundred Miles	20m	E4		1990

This route takes the prominent overhanging wall above *Chapel Cracks*. Start just right of *Chapel Cracks*.

(6a). Climb directly to the traverse of *Chapel Cracks* following a vague crack-line. Technical moves lead out left then back right to gain the base of the final wall. Using a large flat hold on the right, lunge back left. Beware of loose rock under the overhang.

4 Hope	24m	E2		1986

The blunt arête between *Chapel Cracks* and *Scoop and Crack* provides the main interest of this bold route.

1 15m (5b). Climb the blunt arête to a grass ledge. Continue to the upper ledge and then up the overhanging rib to a tree belay.

2 9m (5a). Climb the steep wall just right of the tree to a short groove which leads to the top.

5 Scoop and Crack	31m	HVS+		1928

A very unbalanced route. Only the *Scoop* presents difficulty, and then some! Start at a corner 8 metres left of the stone wall.

1 15m. (5a). Climb the left wall passing a tree to a ledge. Climb the *Scoop* (which is really a short corner) with great difficulty and move right to a stance by a yew.

2 16m. The route originally traversed right and finished up what is now *Via Media* (from whence the *Crack* part of the name), however, to avoid traffic jams most people nowadays finish up pitch 2 of *Chapel Cracks*.

Castle Rock South Crag

1	Howler	E1	*
2	Chapel Cracks	VS	
3	Eleven Hundred Miles	E4	
4	Hope	E2	
5	Scoop and Crack	HVS	
6	Green Eggs and Ham	E2	**
7	Reward	E2	
8	Gazebo	HVS	***
v1	Gazebo Direct	HVS	***
9	Via Media	S	**
10	Romantically Challenged	E1	**
11	Direct Route	VS	**
12	Failed Romantic	E1	**
v2	Romantically Direct	E1	*
13	Kleine Rinne	VS	**
14	Yew Tree Climb	VD	**

15	Pinnacle Wall	E1
16	In Commemoration	E3
17	Gangway Climb	VD **
v3	Gangway Direct	VS
18	Wall Climb	S *

Photo: Al Phizacklea

6 **Green Eggs and Ham**	15m	E2	★★	1990

A well-protected crack with a bold slab above. Start as for *Scoop and Crack*, under a steep crack in the wall.

(5c). Climb the steep crack and where it fades, swing right onto the arête (junction with *Reward*). A few bold delicate moves up the ramp lead up left into a hanging groove which is followed to the tree.

7 **Reward**	39m	E2+		1978

The bold arête 7 metres left of the stone wall and just right of *Scoop and Crack*.

1 15m (5c). Start at the bottom of the undercut arête and climb to a good spike at 9 metres. Move onto the ramp then pull over an overlap into a short groove. Up this to a ledge and yew tree belay.

2 24m (5a). Move right and up the wall. After the second ledge make directly for an obvious scoop then straight for the top.

The fine wall above the dry stone wall provides the next few excellent climbs. The wall is climbable anywhere at about HVS/E1 so that many variations are possible. No more claims please.

8 **Gazebo**	38m	HVS-	★★★	1971

Superb climbing on good holds provides a most enjoyable route. Start at the foot of a big groove 5 metres left of the stone wall.

(4c). Climb the groove and exit right. Follow the crack of *Via Media* to just below the big ledge and then follow the rising traverse rightwards across to the centre of the wall which is climbed to the top.

v1 ***Gazebo Direct*** HVS ★★★

(5a). A bolder alternative for the full experience is to climb the wall direct from its base.

9 **Via Media**	38m	S+	★★	1945

A fine steep route with a hard crux. Start as for *Gazebo* at the foot of the big groove 5 metres left of the stone wall.

Cross the right wall of the groove to the rib and climb it. Climb the slabs and then the obvious crack on the left side of the steep wall. The crack is hard to enter. Prolong the enjoyment by finishing up the short wall on the right near the top.

Original Start

The right wall of the rib can be climbed though this is much harder.

Right: Martin Armitage reaching out on **Failed Romantic** (E1), Castle Rock.
Photo: Stephen Reid

Original Finish

An easier but inferior variation.

From the start of the slabs, climb to a tree on the left of a large ledge. Climb diagonally right from behind the tree to join the crack.

10 **Romantically Challenged**	36m	E1-	★★	2002

A left-hand variant on *Failed Romantic*. Start at the fence.

(5a). Climb the short groove containing a stunted yew then straight up the wall to a rightward-rising crack-line. Follow this but then leave it and climb directly up the left-hand side of the wall to join the last few moves of *Failed Romantic* and gain the ledge. Pull over the juggy sandwiched bulge above.

11 **Direct Route**	36m	VS+	★★	1930

A very good climb with an intimidating start. It begins 3 metres right of the stone wall.

(4b). Climb the steep wall for 6 metres (all very bold for the grade – just keep moving) and move leftwards and up to ledges. Climb the wall to a sentry box and follow the crack to a ledge. Climb the bulge and slab above.

12 **Failed Romantic**	36m	E1-	★★	1984

Very good climbing on small sharp holds. Rather bold. Start 4 metres right of the stone wall at a steep rib.

(5b). Climb the bold rib direct to a small ledge (or do what nearly everyone else does and gain the ledge more easily via *Direct Route* just to the left). Climb the wall above direct to the right end of a leftward-slanting crack and follow this to the top of *Direct Route*.

v2 ***Romantically Direct*** E1- ★ 2002

It is also possible to climb straight up from the start of the leftward-slanting crack and pull out rightwards to join *Kleine Rinne*.

13 **Kleine Rinne**	36m	VS	★★	1963

An excellent route. Start at the foot of a steep groove 5 metres right of the stone wall.

(4b). Climb the groove passing a small tree on its left. Climb the slab to its left edge below a steep groove in the wall above. Pull up into the groove and continue up the exposed wall to easier ground.

14 **Yew Tree Climb**	38m	VD+	★★	1928

Start at the inviting left-slanting wide slab as the crag turns a corner, 12 metres right of the stone wall. Rather bold for the grade at the start.

1 **26m.** Climb the slab on the left to just below an overhung corner. Climb the broken rib on the right to a ledge and yew tree then move left and up the slab to a wall.
2 **12m.** Climb the wall to the right of the crack and the slabs above.

15 **Pinnacle Wall**	30m	E1+		1978

Start at the lowest point of the crag between *Yew Tree Climb* and *Gangway Climb*. Unprotected.
1 **15m (5a).** Climb to the left of a small pinnacle just right of the start of *Yew Tree Climb*. Surmount a second pinnacle and climb a very direct line to a grassy belay ledge.
2 **15m.** Easy climbing leads to the top.

16 **In Commemoration**	30m	E3		1995

(5c). A poor filler-in taking a direct line through two small overlaps just left of the pinnacle. Cross *Gangway Climb* and finish more easily up the wall above. There is no protection until past the overlaps!

17 **Gangway Climb**	34m	VD+	★★	1928

A superb but serious second pitch with very poor protection where it matters. Start at the foot of a rib 3 metres to the left of the large blocks at the right-hand corner of the crag.
1 **9m.** Climb on to the ledge on the left and ascend the rib to a stance on the right.
2 **25m.** Climb the gangway on the left and continue up the slab above.

v3 ***Gangway Direct*** 22m VS+ 2007

Rather contrived but it provides pleasant though rather bold climbing at the grade.

(4b). Follow *Gangway Climb* to the blocks at the top of the first pitch. Reach left for good handholds on the left edge of the gangway and swing round left onto the face at a heather-filled crack. Now climb direct (as for *Commemoration*), through *Gangway Climb*, and up the bold lichen-speckled wall above to a ledge with a pinnacle at its left end. Finish direct.

18 **Wall Climb**	25m	S	★	1978

Start up and round to the right of the main crag on a ledge on top of the large blocks and below the large detached block on *Gangway Climb*.

Climb onto the block. Step right on to the wall and up the short steep corner/groove. Move straight up the slab to a slim groove with a slightly bulging entry which is climbed directly to a good belay ledge. Follow easy slabs to finish.

Castle Rock
South Crag Right Side

17	Gangway Climb	VD **
v1	Gangway Direct	VS
18	Wall Climb	S *
19	Lilith	HS *
20	Slab Climb	S **
21	Companion Way	MS *
22	No Name	M *

Photo: Al Davis

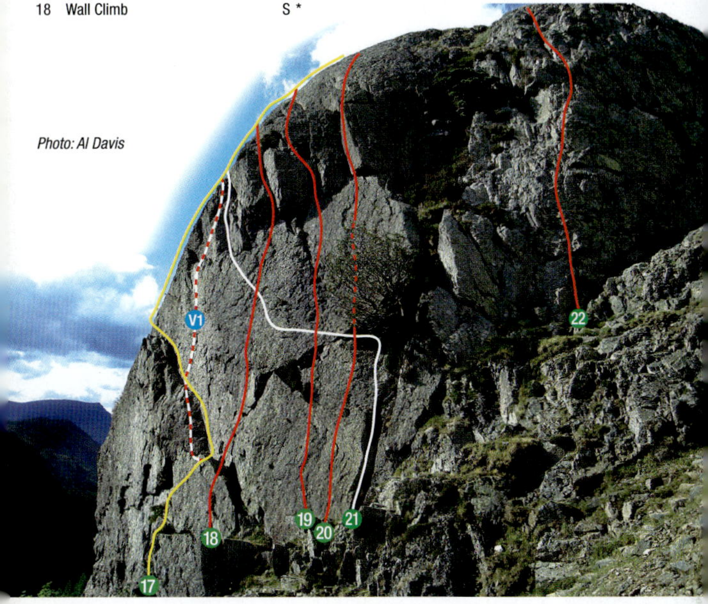

19 **Lilith**	25m	HS	★	2002

A pleasant alternative to ***Wall Climb*** and ***Slab Climb***. Start 2 metres right of ***Wall Climb***.

Ascend the slab and steep wall above. A hold does move on the steep wall but it is well-protected.

20 **Slab Climb**	25m	S+	★★	1928

A pleasant climb though the corner is bold and reachy. Start 3 metres right of ***Wall Climb*** and just left of a shallow chimney with a holly at its top.

Climb the slab to the foot of a short steep corner which is climbed direct. (The corner can be avoided by traversing right and climbing easier rocks above.) Easy slabs lead to the top.

Left: Chris King with not many runners on **Pinnacle Wall** (E1), Castle Rock.
Photo: Stephen Reid

21 **Companion Way**	28m	MS	★	1944

The easiest route on this little wall. Start just right of *Slab Climb* under the holly.

Climb a shallow chimney to the holly. Traverse left and up to a spike. Stand on the spike, climb up a little then traverse left again to finish up the leftmost groove on the headwall.

22 **No Name**	17m	M	★	

Start 3 metres left of a small stone wall at the upper right-hand side of the crag.

Climb the rough buttress on big holds.

Sursum Tuus	100m	E1-		2005

A left-to-right girdle. Surprisingly independent, low in the grade and not sustained. Care is needed to protect the second. Rather an antisocial route, so best avoided on bank holidays.

Start 10 metres left of *Chapel Cracks* at the left side of a multi-stemmed tree above which is a prow of rock.

1 12m (4a). Climb up the right side of the prow passing a stunted tree to reach a ledge. Climb the steep wall above to a sapling belay.

2 20m (5a). Traverse right and step up onto a platform. Gain and traverse rightwards along the slabby shelf into the corner of *Chapel Cracks*. Make an awkward move down to a ledge. Traverse straight across the wall on the right into the obvious corner. Move down and enter the chimney on the right which is climbed into a rock crevasse. Junction with *Scoop and Crack*.

3 12m (5b). Step right into the groove. Move right and up then pull round onto the steep slab of *Green Eggs and Ham*. Move right and climb a short steep wall to gain runners in the narrow groove above on the left (to protect the second). Traverse right across the top of a groove and pull out right to a belay (junction with *Gazebo*).

4 20m (4b). Move up and traverse right along a rock foot ledge to gain and climb a rightward-rising crack-line to the arête (junction with *Kleine Rinne*). Step round onto the slab and bridge across the top of the corner and pull out right to tree belays on *Yew Tree Climb*.

5 36m. Step right and up before making a slightly rising traverse rightwards across the wall to gain a spike runner just above the gangway on *Gangway Climb*. Traverse right across the wall to gain the top of the slabs and traverse these just beneath the steeper headwall to the foot of the short steep corner of *Slab Climb*. Move right and climb the pleasant clean wall rightwards to the top. From the foot of

Left: Mike Gullen and Dylan Carline enjoy the afternoon sun on **Lilith** (HS), Castle Rock.
Photo: John Holden

the short steep corner of *Slab Climb*, the traverse can be continued across a little vegetation onto the final rocks of *No Name*. Then continue to the extreme right edge of the crag!

Southern Traverse	72m	MVS		1944

A traverse of the crag from right to left. Start at the small stone wall at the upper right-hand side of the crag. A steady second is required. Another route designed to annoy the rest of the crag's occupants.

1 20m. Make a rising traverse left and move down to the remnants of a holly. Traverse left under the corner of *Slab Climb*, continuing left and up to a good stance above the corner of *Slab Climb*.

2 16m. Climb down the slabs to the left to a ledge with a yew and then descend the rib of *Yew Tree Climb* below the trees and cross the slabby scoop on *Yew Tree Climb*.

3 30m. (4b). Traverse left at the same level then descend for a move or two to a ledge. Step left, crossing *Direct Route*, then climb the slabs moving slightly leftwards to the foot of a crack (*Via Media*). Move along the ledge to the left to a big platform.

4 6m. Climb the wall behind the trees.

Back Castle Crag (NY 325 194) is clearly visible from the top of the *South Crag* of *Castle Rock* and is situated one kilometre up the fellside above. From *South Crag* it looks quite impressive but it is disappointing on closer acquaintance. Three poor routes have been climbed and forgotten.

Lower Piketoe Knott Crag

Grid Reference: **NY 319 170** Altitude: **300m**
Faces: **West** Approach: **5 mins**

This tiny crag is situated on the east side Thirlmere, up the hillside, just left of the toilet block and car park at the north end of the forest.

Approach:

From the car park for Swirl Forest Nature Trail, follow the footpath as for Helvellyn, cross a footbridge and go through a gate onto the open hillside. From the gate head north on the path for Stannah and Sticks Pass. After 100 metres, the crag can be seen 200 metres up the fellside. The crag can be identified by a corner in the centre with a small holly tree on the top.

Descend on either side.

The climbs are described from **left** to **right**.

Lower Piketoe Knott Crag

1	Lion Sheep	VS	4	Armo's Slab	VS
2	Morton's Boys	MVS	5	Cross Hands	MVS
3	Gary's Crack	S	6	Shake Hands	E1

Ilex Slab	12m	D		2004

Pleasant climbing. At the left of the crag is a slab leading up leftwards from the foot of a gully.

Climb this slab to the left of a holly to a spike belay.

Two Step Buttress	12m	HS		2004

Just left of the main routes lies a grotty gully. Left of this is a buttress split by a ledge. Start at the base of this below a V-corner.

Climb into the V, then step left and up to the ledge. Climb the bulging block above on its left side via a short arête, moving right onto a slab.

1 Lion Sheep	10m	VS		1996

4c). Start one metre left of *Morton's Boys* and climb the face on good holds.

2 Morton's Boys	10m	MVS		1996

(4a). The leftwards-slanting crack one metre left of *Gary's Crack*.

3 Gary's Crack	10m	S		1996

The most obvious crack.

Start 2 metres left of the corner and climb the crack to the top.

4 Armo's Slab	10m	VS		1996

Start one metre left of the corner and climb the face to the top.

5	**Cross Hands**	10m	MVS		1996

The obvious corner at the right side of the crag.

6	**Shake Hands**	9m	E1		1996

The slab to the right of the corner.

Swirl Crags

These crags are situated on the east side of Thirlmere, on the slopes of Helvellyn, and just above the tree line. Though short, the rock is good and they are a lovely place to climb on summer evenings. The *Lower Crag* in particular offers high quality climbing. The outlook is superb.

Approach:
From the car park for Swirl Forest Nature Trail (about one kilometre south of the King's Head, Thirlspot), follow the footpath as for Helvellyn, cross a footbridge and go through a gate onto the open hillside. From the gate follow the wall south along the hillside just above the forest. *Upper Swirl Crag* is about one kilometre from the gate and 100 metres above the wall; *Lower Swirl Crag* is about 1.5 kilometres from the gate, just above the forest wall where the wall drops down the hillside and just north of a stream.

Upper Swirl Crag

Grid Reference: **NY 322 163** Altitude: **400m**
Faces: **West** Approach: **10 mins**

The prominent crag seen when walking along the wall mysteriously shrinks as it is approached. The left-hand side is composed of a slab and the right-hand side is seamed by a number of steeper grooves.

Descend on either side.

The climbs are described from **left** to **right**.

Left-Hand Side

The climbs are tightly packed in on the slab.

1	**How Hard**	18m	S		1986

A poor route climbing the left-bounding rib of the slab. Start at a holly at the left side of the slab.

Right: Catherine Kenyon leading **Midge Wall** (HS), Upper Swirl Crag. **Photo:** Ron Kenyon

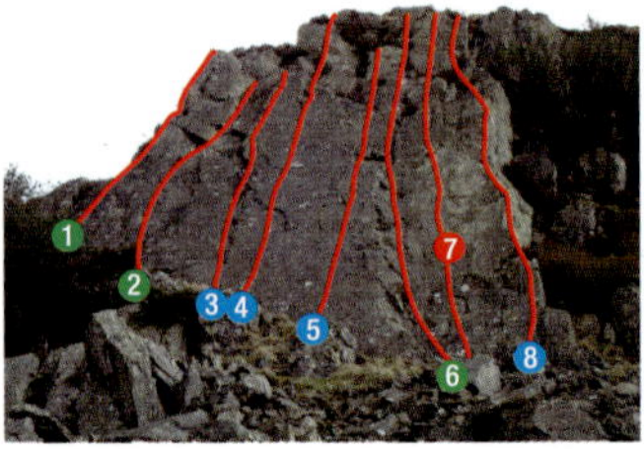

Upper Swirl Crag

Left-Hand Side

1	How Hard	S
2	Sunset	S
3	Tight Fit	VS
4	Two Sizes Too Big	E1 *
5	The First One	VS*
6	Midge Wall	HS*
7	The Race	E3
8	Midget's Slab	E1

Photo: Al Davis

2 **Sunset**	18m	S		1982

Start at the left of the slab below a groove.

Follow the groove to the top.

3 **Tight Fit**	20m	VS		1985

Start below the left end of a little overlap.

(5a). Climb to the left side of the overlap (delicate), then step right and up to climb a thin crack and easier ground above

4 **Two Sizes Too Big**	20m	E1	★	1987

Start right of *Tight Fit* below a little overlap. Unprotected until after the overlap.

(5b). Climb up the steep slab over the overlap passing a faint crack-line (crux) to gain a narrow ledge. Continue up a wider crack to a large ledge and finish up bulging rock above.

5 **The First One**	21m	VS	★	1984

Start just left of the groove towards the right of the slab.

(4b). Climb directly up the slab.

6 **Midge Wall**	21m	HS	★	1982

Climb the groove towards the right of the slab to gain ledges. Finish up the short rib above.

7 **The Race**	20m	E3		1991

The slab between *Midge Wall* and the arête is very bold, thin and unprotected. Blinkers are also obligatory.

(5c). Climb the slab, trending rightwards at the overlap.

8 **Midget's Slab**	20m	E1		1989

Bold unprotected climbing up the arête.

(5a). Climb the right arête of the slab moving left at the top to gain ledges and a broken arête above.

Upper Swirl Crag

3	Tight Fit	VS	
4	Two Sizes Too Big	E1	*
5	The First One	VS	*
6	Midge Wall	HS	*
8	Midget's Slab	E1	
9	La Habanera	HS	
10	Ballet Mecanique	VS	*
11	A Day at the Races	MS	
12	The Runs	HS	
13	C.C. Rider	HVS	*
14	Bobby Rascal	E2	
15	Horse and Farrier Special	VS	

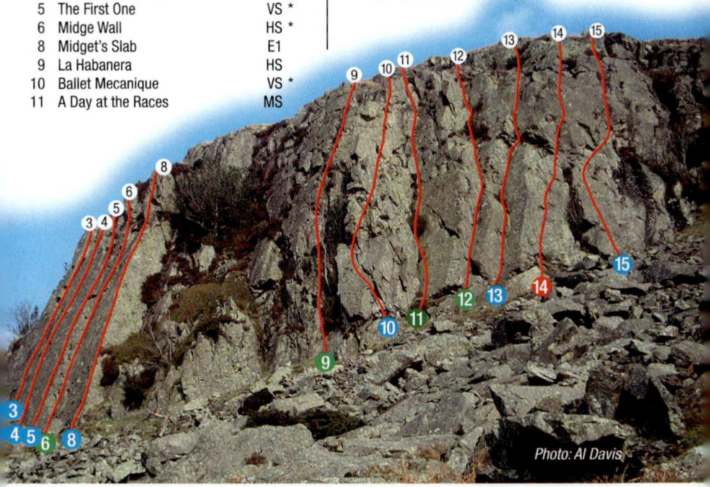

Photo: Al Davis

Right-Hand Side

The right-hand side of the crag consists of a large pillar with a number of clean grooves to its right.

9	**La Habanera**	23m	HS		1991

Climb dirty rock just to the left of the pillar. Follow a saw-toothed crack, trending rightwards over a bulge.

10	**Ballet Mecanique**	18m	VS	★	1991

(4c). Climb the overhanging slanted crack in the pillar to gain the face and climb this trending rightwards.

11	**A Day at the Races**	18m	MS		1982

Climb the V-groove on the right of the pillar finishing left at the top. Better than it looks.

12	**The Runs**	18m	HS		1982

Start just right of *A Day at the Races*.

(4c). Gain a hanging groove and follow this to the top. The first moves are the hardest.

13 **C.C. Rider**	18m	HVS	★	1984

The groove one metre right of *The Runs*.

(5a). Climb directly up the groove containing a sapling just right of *The Runs*.

14 **Bobby Rascal**	10m	E2		1995

Start just right of *C. C. Rider* at a rib left of a small tree

(5c). Climb the rib (very bold) just left of the tree to below a short groove in the headwall. Climb the groove and gain the crack above using a fabulous side jug. Follow vegetated crack to ledges and the top.

15 **Horse and Farrier Special**	10m	VS		1997

(4b). Climb the detached pillar just right of *Bobby Rascal* moving right to finish up a heathery groove.

Bimbo	14m	VD		1991

Climb the large detached block just right of a large tree. Follow a small arête, climb direct over an overhanging nose and trend left to finish up a corner.

The Knacker's Yard	18m	HS+	☆	2010

A pleasant pitch on good rock. Start 2 metres right of *Bimbo* at a thin crack up a clean slab.

Climb the steep slab just right of the crack to a grassy groove. Step boldly up and right onto a hanging slab and climb this to the top.

Middle Swirl Crag is the rather broken crag some 50 metres directly below *Upper Swirl Crag*. Its few poor routes hardly repay the effort involved.

Lower Swirl Crag

Grid Reference: **NY 321 159** Altitude: **330m**
Faces: **South-West** Approach: **15 mins**

On first acquaintance this appears to be a rather insignificant large boulder. This impression is correct. However, appearances can be deceptive and numerous routes have been squeezed in combining quality with brevity. The left-hand side is vegetated but the right-hand side presents a steep wall of excellent rock.

Approach:

The crag is approached by following the wall below *Upper Swirl Crag* southwards along the hillside then following the fence at the same level until it drops steeply below small rocky outcrops. The crag is around to

Lower Swirl Crag

1	Hot Dog	E2	*
2	Burger	E1	*
3	Swirled not Shaken	E3	*
4	American Pie	E2	**
5	Supertramp	E3	*
6	Frank	HVS	*
7	The American Cowboy	E4	*
8	Breakfast In America	E4	*
9	Rub Up, Push Up	E4	
10	Californian Weirdo	E2	**
11	American Express	E4	

Photos: Al Davis

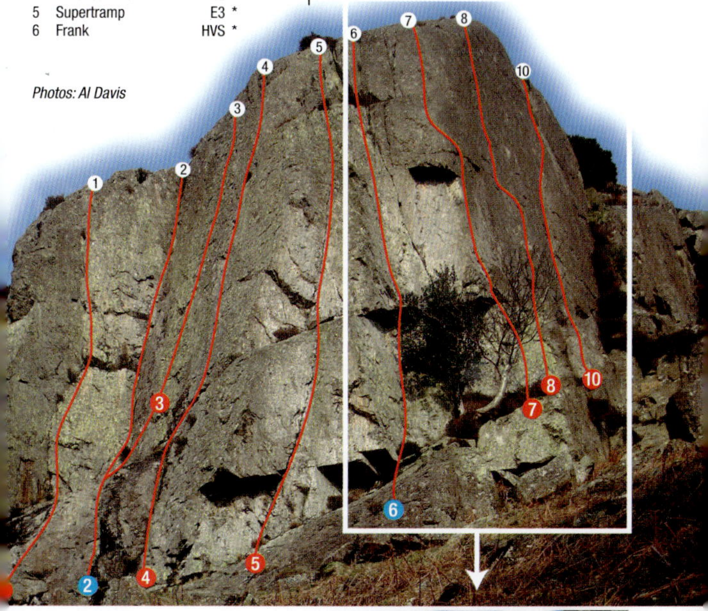

Side View

6	Frank	HVS	*
7	The American Cowboy	E4	*
8	Breakfast In America	E4	*
9	Rub Up, Push Up	E4	
10	Californian Weirdo	E2	**
11	American Express	E4	

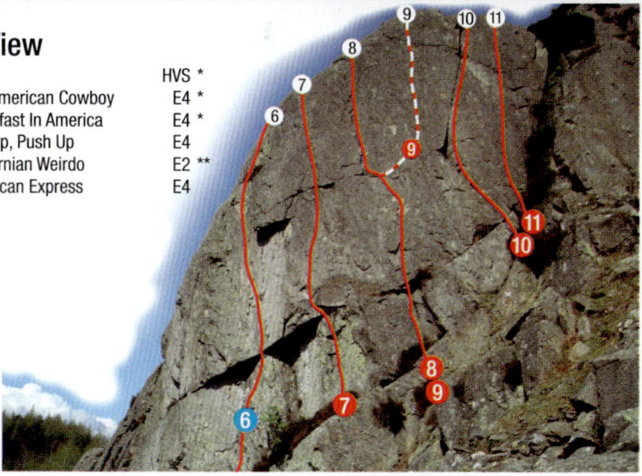

the right of these outcrops. The first feature encountered is a prominent short corner at the left of the crag (*Burger*).

Descent is easiest to the right.

The climbs are described from **left** to **right.**

Swirl Pinnacle	26m	D	★	1993

Five metres left of the corner of *Burger* and slightly lower is a steep mossy slab bounded on the left by a pinnacle. Start below the pinnacle at a holly by a huge flake.

Climb the right edge of the flake and step across to the right edge of the pinnacle. Climb this and the wall behind it. Pick the best way up rocky ribs to the top.

Swirligig	24m	VD+		1993

Start just right of *Swirl Pinnacle* at a steep mossy slab.

Climb the slab moving right and up to a large block on a ledge. Step right off the block onto the hanging arête to finish up this. (Poorly-protected on the upper section).

1 **Hot Dog**	24m	E2	★	1984

The left-hand groove in the twin-grooved corner at the left of the crag.

(5c). Climb the left-hand side of the slab and the corner to the top.

2 **Burger**	24m	E1	★	1984

The right-hand side of the obvious corner at the left of the crag. The long reach to enter the corner is hard for short climbers.

(5a). Climb the slab to below the corner which is followed to the top.

3 **Swirled not Shaken**	24m	E3	★	1989

The wall between *Burger* and *American Pie*. Start just right of *Burger's* corner.

(6a). Climb up right and stand on a flat-topped spike (2 peg runners). Climb straight up to a good jug. Rock up on an incut foothold to reach dinks. Step right and continue up right to an easy groove.

4 **American Pie**	24m	E2+	★★	1984

The thin crack in the wall right of *Burger*. Starting the crack is serious.

(5c). Climb up an easy groove on the right of the slab to the crack. Follow the crack to join the rib which is followed to the top.

5 **Supertramp**	21m	E3	★	1985

The thin crack up the blunt arête between *American Pie* and *Frank*.

(5c). Climb the thin crack to the ledge. Continue up the crack above to ledges and easy slabs.

6 **Frank**	21m	HVS+	★	1983

Start to the right of the prominent groove at a short slab below a groove with a holly tree in it.

(5a). Climb up to the groove which is ascended past the holly. Surmount a small overlap to gain a small ledge. Move up and left with difficulty and follow the ribbed slab to the top.

Two metres right of the holly and level with its top is a ledge. The next routes start from here.

7 **The American Cowboy**	18m	E4	★	1997

The rib to the left of *Breakfast in America*.

(6a). Make a hard bold start from the right to gain the rib and climb to a break at half-height (peg runner). Now pull up and left and then climb directly up the wall and slab to the top.

8 **Breakfast in America**	18m	E4	★	1984

The thin crack in the wall left of *Californian Weirdo*. Start from a ledge just left of that route. Very bold to start.

(6a). Use a broken flake to reach a thin break above (good skyhook). Move left to the base of the thin crack. Climb the crack then the flakes on the right wall. Return to the crack and up to the rib which leads to the top.

Rub up, Push up	18m	E4		1989

An eliminate which climbs the wall between the cracks of *Breakfast in America* and *Californian Weirdo*. Blinkers help but holds are needed on the parent routes.

(6a). Use a broken flake to reach a good hold in the break above (as for *Breakfast in America*). Reach right and use a hold in the crack of *Californian Weirdo* to gain the face above. Climb straight to the top on small holds.

9 **Californian Weirdo**	15m	E2+	★★	1983

Small but perfectly formed. Five metres right of the holly is a prominent right-slanting crack giving steep and strenuous climbing.

(5c). Start at the foot of the crack and move up left into a small pod. Leave the pod with difficulty and continue strenuously up the crack above on excellent holds.

American Express	12m	E4		1992

The wall right of *Californian Weirdo*.

(6a/b). Climb the wall direct with a small spike runner at two thirds height.

Swirlaround	50m	E4		1992

A left to right girdle starting as for *Burger*.

1 20m (5c). Climb *Burger* until level with a pair of pegs on the right wall (*Swirled not Shaken*). Traverse below these to the crack of *American Pie* and climb this to a good hold a metre below its ledge. Traverse right into the groove of *Frank* and a peg belay next to a prominent beak.

2 30m (6a). Swing round right on the beak to a horizontal crack and peg runner. Go right again to the base of the thin crack of *Breakfast in America* and climb this until it is possible to step right onto a broken flake. Pull up on a good flake, stand on it and reach right to the crack of *Californian Weirdo*. Move right again to a flake on the right wall. Stand on the flake to reach jugs leading to the top.

Nab Crag

Grid Reference: **NY 312 123** Altitude: **400m**
Faces: **South-East** Approach: **30 mins**

Nab Crag comprises two distinct buttresses. Seen from Steel End Farm near the foot of Dunmail Raise, the lower and easier buttress appears in profile as an isolated ridge on the northern slopes of the Wythburn Valley. A further clean steep buttress is obvious on the ridge to its right at a higher level.

Approach:

Park in Steel End car park at Stockhow Bridge where the Wyth Burn crosses the minor road running to the west of Thirlmere. A permissive path leads straight up the boggy valley.

Nab Crag Overview

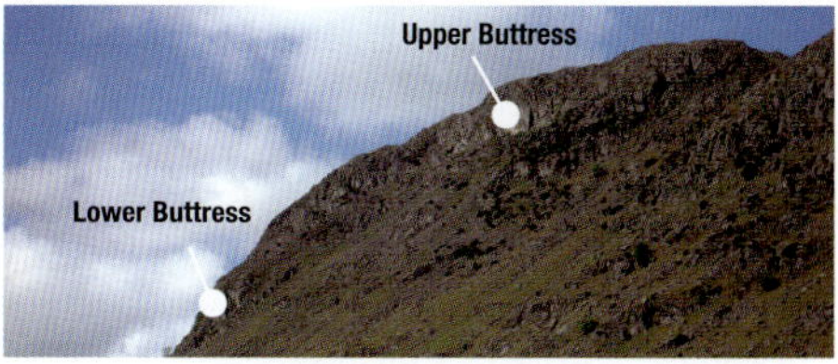

Photo: Al Davis

Left: California girl Mary Grace Brown eyes up **Californian Weirdo** (E2), Lower Swirl Crag.
Photo: Ron Kenyon

Nab Crag Lower Buttress

1	Crypt and Fingers	VD *
2	Forever Young	VS *
3	Central Rib Semi Direct	E1
4	Central Climb	VD
5	Sisters Ridge	D

Photo: Al Davis

Lower Buttress

Follow the path up the valley and make a rising traverse to the crag on the ridge.

The first five routes are located on the ridge area which consists of broken ridges of good quality rock.

The climbs are described from **left** to **right**.

1 **Crypt and Fingers Climb**	60m	VD+	★	1958

A disjointed route which makes good use of the left-hand buttress. The top pitch is a gem and crowns an enjoyable climb. Start at a groove at the left side of the left-hand buttress directly below a prominent arched niche – the *Crypt*.

1 25m. Climb a steep little cracked groove. Cracked slabs then lead to the *Crypt*. Traverse left out of the *Crypt* round the edge of the buttress and climb a grassy groove up to a heathery ledge on the ridge.

2 25m. Follow the ridge to the top.

3 10m. *The Fingers Pitch* lies on a buttress 10 metres to the left and at a slightly lower level. Descend to the foot of the buttress. The main pinnacle or *Finger* forms the front of the buttress. Climb the right-hand crack (hard to start) to the top of the main *Finger* and stride across the gap to finish. The left-hand crack may also be climbed at about the same standard.

2 **Forever Young**	20m	VS	★	2009

A route which makes good use of the available clean rock. Start 3 metres right of *Crypt and Fingers Climb* and 2 metres left of a large upstanding flake.

(5a). Use both cracks to move rightwards into the wide groove. Step left onto the rib and traverse leftwards below the obvious ramp to the left-hand arête and into the groove below the *Crypt*. Using good flake holds on the arête, move rightwards to an obvious flake and then more easily to the top. It is possible to traverse left from here onto easy ground.

Al Davis on the first ascent of **Forever Young**, Nab Crag. **Photo:** Stephen Goodwin

3 **Central Rib Semi-Direct**	20m	E1		1994

A poor climb which is dirty and badly protected. Begin 5 metres down and right of *Crypt and Fingers Climb* at a large upstanding flake.

(5a). Move diagonally right into an unpleasant gully and go up this for 2 metres. Traverse horizontally left into a scoop containing a dubious block. Move left again into a short groove and climb this to easier ground and a junction with *Central Climb* which is followed to the stance. It is possible to traverse left from here onto easy ground.

4 **Central Climb**	75m	VD		1994

A reasonable companion route to *Crypt and Fingers Climb* and of a similar nature. Start 8 metres down and right of that route at the foot of an easy-angled slab.

1. **15m.** Climb the slab just right of a horrible gully to an easy broken rib and step left off this to a belay behind two trees.
2. **12m.** Traverse horizontally left onto the buttress and into a clean groove which is followed to a grass stance and flake belay.
3. **8m.** Traverse horizontally right along a flake to enter a niche with difficulty. Exit from this to the right of a huge chockstone.
4. **30m.** Climb up rightwards and follow a direct line to finish to the right of a large flake.
5. **10m.** The final pitch lies on a buttress 10 metres to the left and at a slightly lower level. Descend to the foot of the buttress and go round to its left-hand side to a tree belay. Climb the off-width crack directly above the tree.

5	**Sisters Ridge**	50m	D		1958

The obvious ridge on the right.

Upper Buttress

The following excellent routes are located on the steep clean buttress on the skyline which can be seen clearly from the car park. They can be accessed from below, up the Wythburn valley, or perhaps more pleasantly, from the ridge above. Follow the road from the car park to the footpath at Stenkin. Take the path north onto the ridge and follow this south-west to the second small tarn which is 50 metres from the crag.The best access is by abseil or to the left of the crag.

Descend to the right, or by abseil.

The climbs are on the left-hand buttress and are described from **left** to **right**.

The central crack-line is taken by *Red Dwarf* and is an obvious reference point for the other routes.

1	**Starbug**	30m	E2	★	1992

Start 3 metres left of *Red Dwarf* at a small groove.

(5c). Climb the groove and step left into a leftward-slanting groove to a corner which is followed to a ledge. Climb a crack on the right.

2	**Mega Drive**	30m	E5	★★	1992

Start 2 metres left of *Red Dwarf* below a hanging groove.

(6a). Climb the leaning pillar to gain the groove. Go up this to a good flake at its top and make a hard move left into a faint corner. Follow this, exiting right, and climb the steep wall to a small overhang which is passed on the left. Belay in the groove.

3	**Red Dwarf**	30m	E1	★★★	1990

(5b). Gain and climb the central crack. The exit is awkward.

4	**Desert Storm**	30m	E1	★★	1992

Start 4 metres right of *Red Dwarf* below a steep groove in the lower wall.

(5b). Climb the wall and make an awkward step into the groove which is climbed to the ledge below a steep crack. Follow the crack into the corner above which is climbed to the top.

Nab Crag Upper Buttress

1	Starbug	E2 *
2	Mega Drive	E5 **
3	Red Dwarf	E1 ***
4	Desert Storm	E1 **
5	Hologram	E1 *
6	Histoplasmosis	E1 **

5 **Hologram**	35m	E1	★	1992

(5b). Follow *Desert Storm* to the ledge. Move right along the ledge for 2 metres to below a crack and climb this via a small but awkward roof to a ledge in the middle of the wall. Step right and climb the right-hand crack to the top.

6 **Histoplasmosis**	30m	E1	★★	1992

Start a few metres right of *Hologram* at a grass-choked rake with a small tree.

(5b). Climb easy rock then the bulging rib left of the rake to a slab and grass ledge above. From the right end of the ledge a thin crack leads to the top.

Birk Crag (NY 317 137) is situated at the southern end of Thirlmere on its western side opposite Wythburn and immediately south of Dob Ghyll. It is a small crag with a prominent arête which has been neglected in recent years so that its three routes are currently filthy.

Harrop Tarn Crag

1	Idle Vice	HS
2	Lucky Streaks	E2 *
3	Sea of Knobs	E6 *
4	Too Baldly Go	HVS **

Photo: Al Davis

Harrop Tarn Crag (Fairview Dome)

Grid Reference: **NY 307 134** Altitude: **400m**
Faces: **East** Approach: **25 mins**

An immaculate short wall giving some good climbing with a stunning view over Harrop Tarn towards Helvellyn. Well worth a morning visit followed by a picnic lunch at the tarn.

Approach:

From the Dobgill Bridge car park, follow the path up the hill to Harrop Tarn. Follow the bridleway on the right of the tarn for another 200 metres then bear left through the trees and above the bog to the deer fence. From the stile over the deer fence, the crag can be seen as a clean wall of rock on the hillside directly above left.

Descent is to the left.

The climbs are described from **left** to **right.**

1	**Idle Vice**	15m	HS		1999

Start at the bottom left of the crag as for *Lucky Streaks*.

Climb the shallow groove and step up to a ledge. Step back left into the corner and jam it to the top.

Above: Woodland on the edge of Harrop Tarn. **Photo:** Eric Shaw

2 **Lucky Streaks**	15m	E2	★	1997

A good route up the left edge of the wall. Start at the bottom left of the crag.

(5c). Follow the diagonal crack rightwards then straight up (Friend 0.5 in second break). Bold moves on small pockets lead to the pleasant easier top slab.

3 **Sea of Knobs**	15m	E6	★	1998

A bold and technical route up the middle of the wall.

(6b). Climb the shallow scoop in the centre on small edges and knobs to a break. Two hammered in wires have been left in place but are in a dubious condition.

4 **Too Baldly Go**	15m	HVS	★★	1998

A very good and well-protected route up the obvious crack in the right of the wall.

(5a). The crack – climb it.

Standing Crag

Grid Reference: **NY 297 135** Altitude: **560m**
Faces: **North** Approach: **1 hr**

A good crag in a fine position overlooking the broad col at the top of the track from Harrop Tarn to Watendlath. Viewed from the end of the fence at the foot of the crag, the main feature is a tapering slab above an overhang – the line of *Standing Slab*.

The climbs are described from **right** to **left**.

1 **Pokketz Lab**	18m	S	★	2007

Start 22 metres right of the fence below a clean slab. Good climbing with some tremendous pockets and adequate protection.

Move up to the centre of the low overlap and pull over onto the slab. Climb a short left-facing corner to a big flake then follow a slabby rib to the top. Scramble down left.

2 **Freddie Flintoff**	35m	E2	★	2004

The narrow open slab on the right of the crag just right of *D.K.W.*

(5b). Climb to a tiny spike at 8 metres (sling – the only protection). Stand on the spike (crux) then continue boldly. Finish up a steep crack just right of *D.K.W.*

3 **D.K.W.**	20m	HVS	★	1984

An excellent climb on superb rough rock with an unusual juxtaposition of clean rock for the left hand and mossy rock for the right. Start on the grass ledge above and right of the base of the crag.

(5a). Ascend grooves and open corners directly to the top. The climb gradually steepens to its crux.

4 **Fred Dibnah**	35m	E4		2004

The grooves just right of *Standing Slab*. The in situ wire protecting the crux is no longer in place and the climb is very mossy.

(5c). Monkey up the spike at the foot of the groove. Continue up the bold groove with a detour right onto a slab at 5 metres to get protection. Step back left then up to a ledge. Climb a bold slabby corner to a peg. Make a wild reach rightwards for a good hold, then go boldly up the headwall on flat holds.

Standing Crag

1	Pokketz Lab	S	*
2	Freddie Flintoff	E2	*
3	D.K.W.	HVS	*
4	Fred Dibnah	E4	
5	Standing Slab	MVS	*
6	Gritstone Dreamer	E2	
7	Standing Room Only	E2	
8	Standing Joke	VS	
9	Exhibition Rib	MVS	
10	One for the Road	E2	*

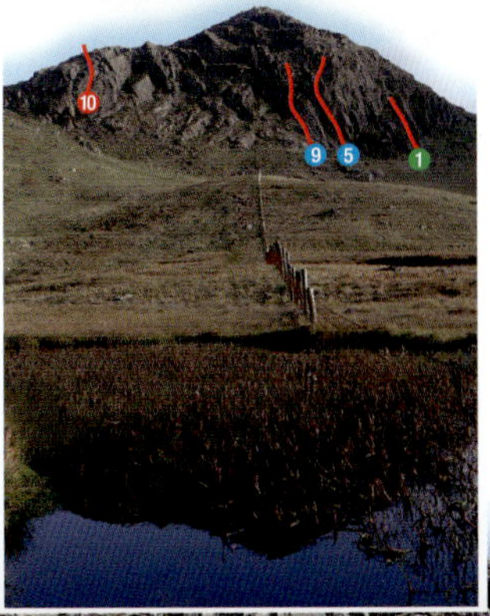

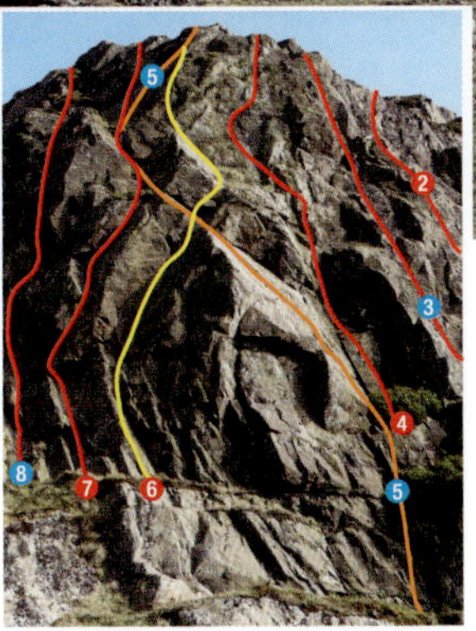

Photos: Al Phizacklea

5 **Standing Slab**	35m	MVS	★	1968

The main feature of the crag is a tapering slab above an overhang.

(4a). Climb up to a grass ledge to the right of the overhang. Move left onto the slab, climb it to its limit and pull round to the grass ledge on the left. Climb the groove above then follow a diagonal crack rightwards to the front of the buttress and so up to the top.

6 **Gritstone Dreamer**	35m	E2+		1998

Start to the left of *Standing Slab* at the left-hand side of the largest overhang.

(5c). Climb up and gain the slab above the overhang from the left. Follow the open groove rightwards with difficulty to a junction with *Standing Slab*. Pull out rightwards and climb very boldly up the wall via a committing mantelshelf move. Easier climbing leads to the top.

7 **Standing Room Only**	28m	E2		2007

Start on a grassy ledge below an open slabby corner 8 metres left of the prominent overhang.

(5b). Climb a slanting slab 2 metres right of the slabby corner to a chockstone runner. Pull right and climb the bulge to enter a hanging V-gangway with difficulty. Continue to a small overhang and a big undercut on the left then pull up rightwards to gain a grass ledge above the slab of *Standing Slab*. Climb the short groove above to a second ledge then take the slab above, left of the crack of *Standing Slab*, between two heather patches to the top.

8 **Standing Joke**	25m	VS		2007

Follows the open V-groove but gets mossy near the top just where the difficulties lie! Start as for *Standing Room Only*.

(4b). Climb the V-groove to just below the grass where a step right leads to a slanting groove. Pull up and out right to a short fist-wide crack and fight up this to an easier finish.

9 **Exhibition Rib**	23m	MVS		2007

Only the bottom half is good. Start 2 metres left of *Standing Joke*.

(4a). Start up the right-hand side of the lovely clean rib and then follow the arête to a ledge. The slabby mossy wall above leads delicately to the top.

10 **One For The Road**	12m	E2	★	2007

The tremendously rough slab 100 metres left of where the fence meets the crag – no protection at all.

(5a). Climb the slab 2 metres right of a heather patch to finish up the steep wall just left of the upper scoop.

A landslip stripped much (but sadly not all) of the vegetation from **Rough Crag (NY 314 154)** years ago. The exposed rock was pleasantly rough and pocketed but nature has reclaimed the hillside so that the crag is not recognisable. Three poor routes are thankfully lost. A recent landslip has exposed the rock once again but don't get too excited. **Bull Crag (NY 311 155)** is situated in the trees overlooking the road along the west side of Thirlmere. It is a mossy crag that never became popular so that the routes are indescribably filthy and overgrown.

Thackmell Crag

Grid Reference:	**NY 308 156**	Altitude:	**360m**
Faces:	**North-East**	Approach:	**10 mins**

The crag is situated above the road on the west side of Thirlmere. It offers a lovely wall of immaculate rock and is deserving of greater popularity.

Approach:

Follow the Launchy Gill trail from the lay-by. Follow wooden walkways across the gill, then take the faint track leading leftwards away from the gill across a shallow valley to reach a prominent perched boulder on the left of the track. The crag is just above through the trees and is best viewed from near the boulder.

Thackmell Crag

Photo: Al Davis

1	Siren	VS
2	Brave Ulysses	E3 *
3	Gulag Tour	MVS
4	Serious Sleeping	VS
7	Sasquatch	E1 *

The *Left-Hand Crag* can be seen as a prominent nose with a large overhang. The *Right-Hand Crag* is tucked away 30 metres to the right at the level of the overhangs.

Left-Hand Crag

The approach is obvious.

The best **descent** is down the left side.

1 **Siren**	45m	VS		1984

Start at the lowest point of the crag at the foot of the obvious rightward-trending slabs below the prominent overhangs. A poor mossy route.

1 33m (4c). Climb straight up the slab to the break in the overlap. Go leftwards over this then trend left up the slab to below the obvious corner. Traverse left to a large ledge and birch tree belay.

2 12m (4c). From the left-hand end of the ledge climb straight up the slab to a tree belay.

2 **Brave Ulysses**	43m	E3	★	1984

An exciting traverse between the roofs above *Siren*. Start as for *Siren*.

1 26m (4c). Climb *Siren* to a stance below the left-hand end of the overhangs.

2 15m (5c). Strenuous. Climb up to the roof and traverse rightwards between the roofs along an obvious crack-line to an ancient ring peg. Cross the wall on the right (crux) to the arête and continue up to a stance and belay below another overhang.

3 2m (5b). Possibly the shortest pitch ever described! Make one move over the overhang at the central weakness and belay well back on a pine tree.

Right-Hand Crag

Excellent pitches on good rock which have been rather neglected and are somewhat mossy at present. The crag is hidden from immediately below and is best viewed from the perched block. It is approached by following a vegetated right-slanting rake 25 metres right of *Siren* and 5 metres left of the lowest point of the steep hillside.

The best **descent** is on the right, though large trees on top provide convenient abseil anchors.

The climbs are described from **left** to **right**.

Thackmell Crag Right-Hand

4	Serious Sleeping	VS	
5	Sticky Jim	HVS	*
6	First Blood	HVS	*
7	Sasquatch	E1	*
8	Yowie	E1	**
9	Space Shuttle	E3	
10	Disappointment	MVS	*
11	Ken Rognon	E2	*

Photo: Al Davis

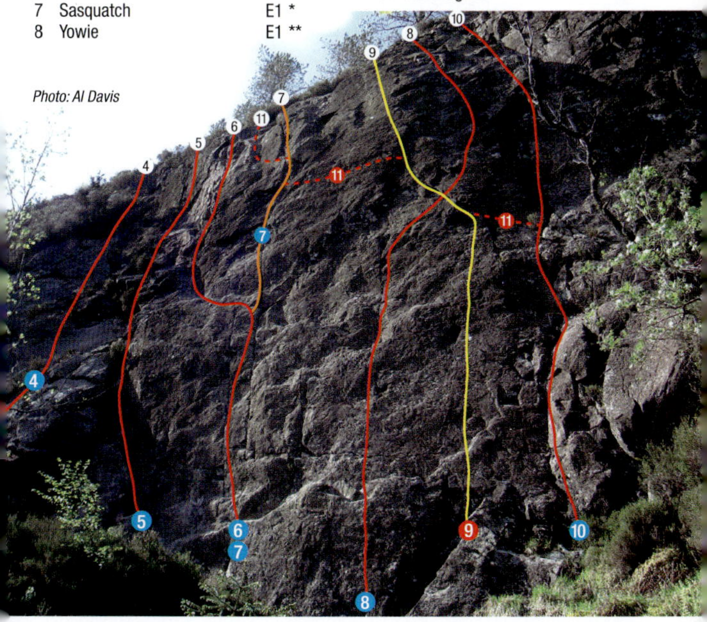

3 **Gulag Tour**	36m	MVS		1984

The obvious left-slanting ramps give pleasant climbing which is sadly disappearing due to neglect. Start near the top of the rake at the toe of the buttress.

(4b). Climb the two obvious ramps to a precariously perched loose block. Step leftwards over the block and climb the short corner and rib on the right for about 6 metres. Traverse left to a tree belay. Either finish up the vertical heather or abseil off the tree.

4 **Serious Sleeping**	45m	VS		1987

A route on good rock starting as for *Gulag Tour* at the toe of the buttress. Its mantle of moss is testament to its neglect.

(4c). Pull immediately and steeply right and trend right across a slab to below a steep groove to the right of an overhung triangular niche. Gain the groove and continue up the slab. Pleasant climbing leads to the top.

The remaining routes lie in a pleasant grassy bay 20 metres above and right and are well worth seeking out.

5 **Sticky Jim**	18m	HVS	★	1984

Start in the left corner of the bay at the foot of the obvious corner.

(5a). Climb the corner and the crack above.

6 **First Blood**	24m	HVS	★	1984

Start at the obvious crack-line 3 metres right of *Sticky Jim*.

(5a). Climb the crack-line for 5 metres (or climb the wall immediately on the left). Traverse 3 metres left into the blocky groove and climb this with a move right.

7 **Sasquatch**	21m	E1-	★	1984

Start as for *First Blood*.

(5b). Climb the obvious crack-line 3 metres right of *Sticky Jim* with some trying moves rightwards through an overlap.

8 **Yowie**	24m	E1-	★★	1984

An enjoyable wall climb which starts 2 metres right of *Sasquatch*.

(5b). Climb the vague crack-line in the centre of the wall (bold) to a good jug and runners. Make a hard move up and right and continue to the top.

9 **Space Shuttle**	24m	E3		1984

Start just right of *Yowie*. Rather contrived.

(6a). Climb the wall immediately right of an obvious pocket then up and right to the foot of a leftward-slanting crack. Climb this to join *Yowie* at the good jug. Continue strenuously leftwards until a thin line of quartz is reached. Move immediately right into a vague groove and continue straight up this to the top.

10 **Disappointment**	24m	MVS		1984

Start at the foot of the obvious crack and groove system at the right of the grassy bay.

(4b). Climb the cracks to a niche below an obvious corner. Bridge up the corner to easy ledges. A tree belay lies well back.

11 **Ken Rognon**	30m	E2	★	1995

A rising traverse taking a natural line across the crag. Start as for *Disappointment*.

(5c). Climb *Disappointment* for 8 metres until an obvious diagonal crack slants left across the steep wall on the left. Follow this to the huge jug on *Yowie*. Move up and left and make a very fingery traverse leftwards along a thin crack to step down with difficulty onto *Sasquatch* just under the overlap. Climb the crux of *Sasquatch* through the overlap but step left into the left-slanting groove which is followed to the top.

Raven Crag

Grid Reference: **NY 304 188** Altitude: **350m**
Faces: **East** Approach: **15 mins**

Raven Crag faces east overlooking the Thirlmere dam. The hillside around it is afforested as is the flat top of the crag. It is a steep and impressive place and although it provides one or two very good middle grade routes its main attraction is the number of excellent hard routes.

The most striking feature of the crag is a huge depression, the *Cave*, in the centre of the main face. On the left, the crag is bounded by a grass slope leading to a short shallow gully. To the right of the *Cave* there is an obvious right-angled corner with, on its right, a subsidiary buttress consisting of a series of walls. The crag is about 100 metres high. Due to the steep nature of the rock, routes such as *The Gates of Delirium*, *Close to the Edge* and *Das Kapital* stay surprisingly dry in wet spells of weather. The pegs on a number of routes were replaced in 2009.

Approach:

Cars can either be parked at the road junction where the road over the dam meets the road down the west side of the lake or at a lay-by 100 metres north towards Smaithwaite. Between the two parking places there is a public footpath which is followed up through the trees to a forestry track, which is in turn followed leftwards to a right-angled bend from where the crag is best viewed. Continue some 20 metres further up this track until a vague path off left contours beneath the crag.

The **descent** is on the right of the crag or from the various in situ abseil points on the crag.

The climbs are described from **right** to **left**.

A bird restriction may affect the crag in Spring.

Raven Crag Thirlmere

1	Polytruk	E4 *
2	The Apocrypha	VS
3	Anarchist	HS **
4	Creation	E5 **
5	Stir Crazy	E2
6	Empire	E3 ***
7	Totalitarian	E1 ***
8	Common Man	E2 *
9	Comunist Convert	VS **
v1	Direct Finish	HVS
10	Blitzkrieg	E4 ***
11	Das Kapital	E6 ***
12	The Gates of Delirium	E4 ***
13	The Second Coming	E6 ***
14	Infestation Finish	E7 ***
15	Close to the Edge	E3 ***
v2	Direct Start	E5
16	The Medlar	E4 ***
17	Relayer	E4 **
v3	Original Way	
18	Peels of Laughter	E5 ***

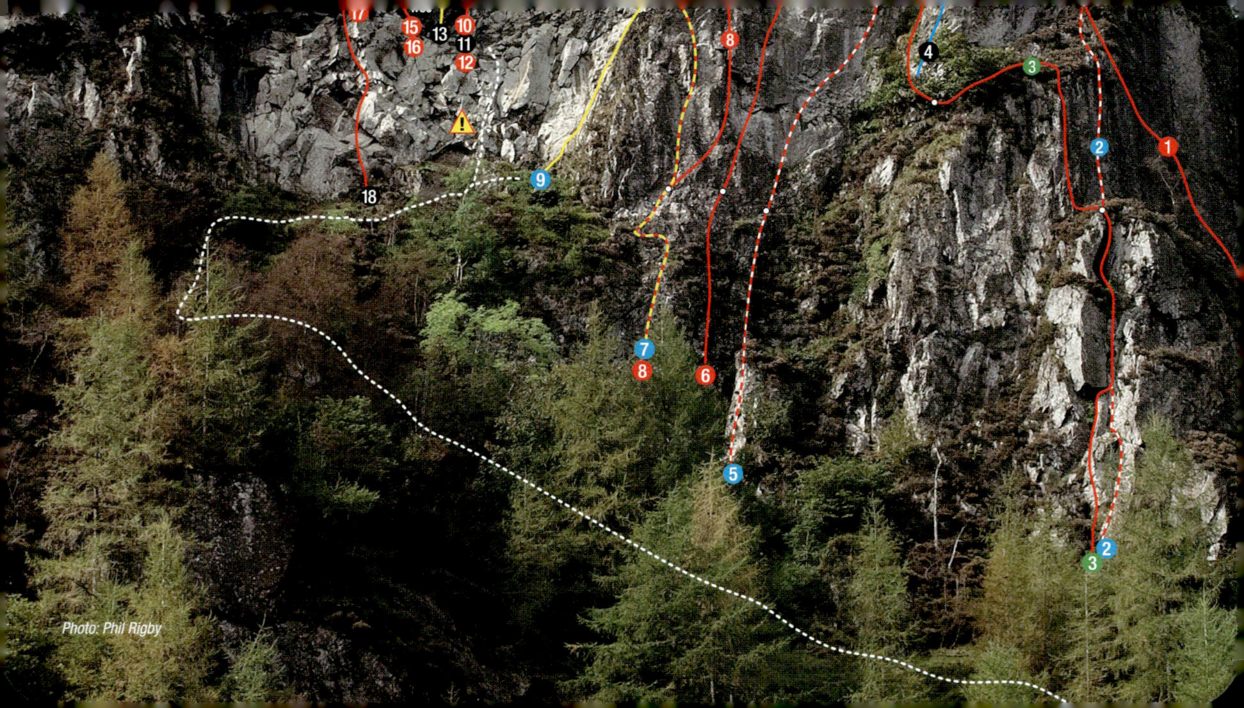

Photo: Phil Rigby

1 **Polytruk**	60m	E4	★	1978

Climbs directly up each of the stepped walls to the right of *Anarchist*. The top one provides excellent climbing but the first two pitches are rather poor and usually avoided. Scramble up to the left-hand side of the lowest wall.

1 26m (5c). Climb the short wall to the left end of a narrow grass terrace. Follow the obvious steep crack-line and wall above to a good ledge. A serious dirty pitch.

2 16m (5b). From the right-hand side of the next wall make a rising traverse leftwards to the top of pitch 1 of *Creation*.

3 8m (6b). Climb directly up the thin crack in the wall 5 metres right of *Creation* until at 7 metres a step right can be made to gain the foot of a short groove. Ascend this more easily to the top.

2 **The Apocrypha**	57m	VS		1967

Very much a minor variation on *Anarchist* and now dirty and overgrown. Start as for *Anarchist*.

1 30m (5a). Climb the right-hand groove to a junction with *Anarchist*. Follow this to the ledge.

2 18m (4a). Climb the wall, trending right to a ledge, and then climb the gangway on the left to a grass ledge.

3 9m. To the right is a chockstone-filled chimney. Climb the groove to the left of this, stepping right to the top.

3 **Anarchist**	77m	HS	★★	1953

The excellent pitch 3 justifies the vegetated ramblings on the lower pitches. It starts up the subsidiary right-hand buttress and finishes up the prominent right-angled corner to its left. Start 6 metres right of a dead larch tree at a little bulge directly beneath a square-cut overhang.

1 30m. Climb the grassy left-hand groove to the square-cut overhang. Move right and follow the groove and crack to a recess. Ascend the corner-crack and move out on the right wall to reach a ledge.

2 12m. Climb the steep wall starting just left of the highest point of the ledge. Bushwhack left to a large oak tree.

3 35m. Start up the left-hand side of the groove and climb the groove and corner-crack above. A superb pitch.

Genesis (S, 1952) follows the first two pitches that are now described as part of *Anarchist* and finishes up a chockstone chimney on the right.

4 **Creation**	33m	E5	★★	1976

A fine climb which is both hard and serious. Start at the oak tree at the

Left: Eve Prickett looking for the way on **Empire** (E3), Raven Crag, Thirlmere.
Photo: Andy Prickett

top of pitch 2 of *Anarchist*. The oak tree may be reached via a direct ascent but is best not.

1 24m (6a). Climb the left side of the arête to a groove (poor in situ peg runner out left) which is followed to the small overhang. Hard moves lead right and over the small overhang then up the wall to the belay at the top of *Anarchist*.

2 9m (6a). An awkward move up the wall above leads to the crack of *Totalitarian*.

5 **Stir Crazy**	70m	E2		1982

The main pitch follows a series of grooves between *Anarchist* and *Empire*. Start at the easy groove right of the start of *Totalitarian*.

1 18m. Climb the easy groove to a thread and peg belay or, much better, climb the first pitch of *Empire* to the same point.

2 33m (5b). Follow a rightward-sloping ramp to a short wall and pull over this onto easier ground. Follow a groove to a bulge and pull up steeply left into another groove which is followed direct to a pocket (good thread). Move left and up to a steep wall exiting left. Continue to a belay.

3 19m (5a). Climb diagonally left to a short groove which leads to a good flake-crack and swing left into the steep corner of *Communist Convert Direct Finish*.

6 **Empire**	63m	E3	★★★	1973

An excellent route up the wall left of Anarchist. The pegs were replaced in 2009. Above the usual arrival point at the crag is a shallow grassy bowl. Start at the top of this, just right of a large block just right of *Totalitarian*.

1 18m (5a). Move right and climb directly into a shallow groove. Continue straight up to the ledge system on the right. Thread and peg belay.

2 33m (5c). Go left into the niche and climb out of its right-hand side. Follow the ramp rightwards and climb up to a small ledge. Continue up the slab above to the obvious steep groove. Climb this and move left to reach *Communist Convert*. Continue rightwards to a good stance below the roof.

3 12m (6a). Climb up to the overlap and pull awkwardly onto the wall above (peg) and then up to the top. Abseil point in place.

7 **Totalitarian**	78m	E1+	★★★	1964

A magnificent climb crossing the smooth buttress right of the *Cave*. It is the outstanding route of its grade in the area. Above the usual arrival

Right: What's round the corner? Mark Johnston pondering the move around the front on the top pitch of **Totalitarian** (E1), Raven Crag, Thirlmere. **Photo:** Alan Wilson

point at the crag is a shallow grassy bowl. Start at the top of this at a large block. This is directly below the right-hand corner of the *Cave*.

1 18m (5a). From the block, move left round a rib and climb a shallow corner on the right. Step down to the left across a steep wall and climb up to a niche. Move up and right on good holds and continue to a good ledge and belay below an open groove to the right of the rib flanking the *Cave*. A bold pitch and quite a rude awakening!

2 20m (5b). Climb the groove. At the top, step up right and continue slightly rightwards to the belay below pitch 2 of *Communist Convert*.

3 22m (4b). Move diagonally right to an open groove, mantelshelf onto a small ledge and continue rightwards to a small rock ledge. Traverse right and upwards, step down into the crack of *Anarchist* and move up to a large ledge and spike belay on the right (all as for *Communist Convert*, pitch 2).

4 18m (5c). Step back left and climb the corner (peg) leading up to the roof and pull out right to the edge. Climb the crack above to the top.

8 **Common Man**	72m	E2	★	1977

An eliminate climb taking a direct route up the *Totalitarian* buttress. Start as for *Totalitarian*.

1 18m (5a). Pitch 1 of *Totalitarian*.

2 20m (5c). Traverse right from the stance and climb directly up the wall to the niche of *Empire*. Escape from the top left-hand corner of the niche using its left rib. Climb the crack and continue to a good stance.

3 16m (5b). Ascend the groove above to a ledge. Step up a couple of metres and move right round the rib. Climb up to another good stance.

4 18m (5b). Climb the wall behind the belay to a grass ledge at 12 metres. Traverse below the wall on the right for 3 metres and then steeply up the wall to the top.

The following routes start from the *Cave* area. To reach it, walk up the grass slope leading up to the left of the crag to a 5 metre crack behind a stout rowan tree. Climb the crack and scramble rightwards to a short wall below the *Cave*. *Communist Convert* starts here. To enter the *Cave* scramble up the leftward-sloping gangway, step right and ascend to the *Medlar* tree at the left side of the *Cave*.

9 **Communist Convert**	42m	VS	★★	1953

A left to right rising traverse across the *Totalitarian* buttress. A popular climb, the best at its grade, exposed and delicate on sound rock; a sheep among wolves. The crux is slow to dry. Start at the right-hand side of the short wall below the *Cave*.

1 15m (4a). Climb slabs and move right onto the nose.

2 27m (4b). Move diagonally right to an open groove, mantelshelf

Raven Crag
Cave area
10 Blitzkrieg E4 ***
11 Das Kapital E6 ***
12 The Gates of Delirium E4 ***
13 The Second Coming E6 ***
14 Infestation Finish E7 ***
15 Close to the Edge E3 ***
v2 Direct Start E5
16 The Medlar E4 ***
17 Relayer E4 **
v3 Original Way
18 Peels of Laughter E5 ***
A
V3
V2
Medlar tree
Photo: Phil Rigby

onto a small ledge and continue rightwards to a small rock ledge. Traverse right and upwards, step down into the crack of *Anarchist* and move up to a large ledge and spike belay on the right and a walk off rightwards.

v1 ***Direct Finish*** 40m HVS 1961

The square corner left of the big overhangs above the last pitch. The line is good but the rock is not above suspicion.

(5a). Climb to the small rock ledge on pitch 2 then cross the steep wall on the left to a grass ledge (possible poor belay). Climb up and right to enter the corner and follow it to the top.

The line of **Delphinus** (HVS, 1956) is marked by pegs in the right wall of the *Cave*. It has now been rendered obsolete by the loss of holds and its new neighbours.

10 **Blitzkrieg**	58m	E4	★★★	1977

A fine strenuous assault on the *Cave* headwall. The climbing is well-protected with a short technical crux section. Start in the back of the *Cave* right of the *Medlar* tree.

1 19m (5b). Climb the groove to a hole below the roof, swing right and traverse rightwards (peg runner) to a recess.

2 24m (6a). Traverse back left to a niche and climb the obvious flake to the overhang. Move left and up to the break through the overhang. Pull over this with difficulty to belay below the chimney, or maybe better to continue.

3 15m (5c). Climb the chimney and exit left. Move up and follow a line of flakes out left onto the wall. Follow this to the top. Abseil point in place.

11 **Das Kapital**	46m	E6	★★★	1978

A tremendous route with steep sustained climbing requiring total commitment. All the pegs and threads were replaced in 2009.

1 28m (6b). Climb the groove to the hole as for *Blitzkrieg* and follow the crack straight over the large roof above past two threads to a peg. Follow the intermittent crack until it is possible to swing right to the top of the flake of *Blitzkrieg*. Go back left and up *Blitzkrieg* for one metre and then traverse left for 3 metres, past two peg runners, to a shallow groove which is hard to enter and initially equally hard to ascend (peg runner) to the ledge. Move 2 metres left to a block belay.

2 18m (6b). Climb the crack above the belay to an overhang. Move right onto an undercut slab and follow this rightwards to a niche. Move up a couple of metres (in situ wire) and then step left to gain a thin crack. Climb the wall on the left of the crack to gain the final crack leading to the top.

12 **The Gates of Delirium**	57m	E4	★★★	1976

This brilliant classic takes the back of *The Cave* and then the groove system right of *The Medlar*. Start as for *Blitzkrieg*.

1 18m (6a). Climb the groove to the hole as for *Blitzkrieg*. Traverse left past two old peg runners then up leftwards to a foothold stance and peg belay in a groove.

2 21m (6a). Step up and right to attain a standing position in the groove above. Climb the groove pulling out left with difficulty and passing a sloping ledge to gain another ledge. Step right back above the groove and climb the wall above moving right to a grass stance. There is an abseil point here.

3 18m (6b). The route originally finished up the poor final corner-crack of *The Medlar* (4b) but the top pitch of *Relayer* is much more in keeping and is described here. From the abseil point, step left and scramble up to the foot of the headwall. Climb up 5 metres until it is possible to swing right across the overhanging wall to a good hold on the lip. Pull over and follow the slab to the top. A fantastic finish.

Direct Start 30m E5 1985

A bold variation climbing directly as far as the traverse. It is now incorporated into *The Second Coming*.

Above: Karin Magog on the first pitch traverse of the classic **The Gates of Delirium** (E4), Raven Crag, Thirlmere. **Photo:** Steve Crowe

13 **The Second Coming**	30m	E6	★★★	2003

A fantastic steep pitch which is pumpy to start and technical to finish.
(6b/c). Start up *The Gates of Delirium Direct*. Move out left and into the groove. Climb up this to a good slot. Make a further move up and then climb diagonally rightwards to an old peg beneath the bulge. Pull straight through the bulge above using a good undercut to a thin crack in a groove and climb to the top of this (good gear and a good rest). Move a little left, then up and back rightwards aiming for a stainless steel peg. Make technical moves past this and up awkwardly into the hard part on ***Das Kapital***, which is followed past another peg to a small sapling. Continue left to belay at the end of the *The Gates of Delirium* pitch 2.
From here it is possible to abseil off. However, if you need more and you have anything left in your arms, you will be tempted to fight your way up *The Infestation Finish*.

14 **Infestation Finish**	20m	E7	☆☆☆	2003

A useful hard finish to any of the routes on the lower wall.
(6c). Follow *Das Kapital* Pitch 2 up a short groove above the belay and step right onto a gangway. Move rightwards along this to two good incut jugs by a spike. From these, make some hard technical moves in a fantastic position up the steep headwall to a big flat hold. Move slightly right and up to a small triangular niche. Climb up a few moves before going left and up the centre of the slab to reach the top.

15 **Close to the Edge**	55m	E3	★★★	1977

This excellent route takes the slim groove between *The Medlar* corner and *The Gates of Delirium*. A good eliminate picking the easiest way up this section of the crag. The first two pitches are best done in one but this increases the grade to E4 due to the pump factor! Start as for *The Medlar*.

1 16m (5c). Follow *The Medlar* to the foot of the corner. Traverse right with difficulty across the overhung slab and pull round and up to the foothold stance and peg belays of *The Gates of Delirium*.
2 21m (5c). Step up and swing left to the left arête of the groove. Continue up the fine groove system to a large ledge. Abseil off or,
3 8m (4b). Move up left to the final corner-crack of *The Medlar* and climb it.

Left: Duncan Booth eyes up the moves ahead on the first ascent of **The Second Coming** (E6), Raven Crag, Thirlmere. **Photo:** Al Wilson

v2 ***Direct Start*** 15m E5 1985

Start as for *The Medlar*.

1 (6b). Climb up the groove of *The Medlar* to gain nut runners. Step down and move right onto the rib using a low layaway. Pull up the rib to gain a good letter-box hold then move up right to join *The Gates of Delirium* near the end of the traverse. Move left to the foothold stance.

16 **The Medlar**	51m	E4	★★★	1964

An excellent route with a very technical section up the open-book corner rising from the left side of the *Cave*. Start at the *Medlar* tree at the left side of the *Cave*.

1 27m (6a). Climb the curving grey-green wall immediately left of the tree to the overhang. Move left round the nose and pull up to a ledge at the foot of the corner. Bridge up the corner with increasing difficulty (awkward protection now the pegs have gone) until it is possible to make a hard move left to a jug. Continue traversing and then climb up to a good ledge. Abseil point in place.

2 24m (4b). Ascend to the recess and climb to a grass ledge. Climb the corner-crack to the top.

Above: Wes Hunter gets **Close to the Edge** (E3), Raven Crag, Thirlmere. **Photo:** Al Wilson

The Merger, (E2 1967) which has now been superseded by *Relayer* and *The First Circle*, climbed up left of the first pitch of *The Medlar* and then traversed under the roofs to finish up *Exodus*.

17 **Relayer**	54m	E4	★★	1979

Start just left of *The Medlar*.

1 36m (5c). Move up left of the arête and pull round right to *The Medlar*. Move up this to the ledge at the foot of the corner. Traverse left to the rib and follow a direct line to the traverse of *The Medlar*. Follow this leftwards to a possible stance and abseil point. Ascend to the recess and climb to a grass ledge.

2 24m (6b). From the right end of the ledge, climb up 5 metres until it is possible to swing right across the overhanging wall to a good hold on the lip. Pull over and follow the slab to the top.

v3 ***Original Way***

1 36m (5c). From where the rib meets the traverse of *The Medlar*, follow a direct line to the grass stance at the end of pitch 2 of *The Gates of Delirium* – all very dirty, unfortunately.

Medlayer	27m	E3	★★★	

(5c.) For a superb pitch, follow pitch 1 of *Relayer* up the rib to the second junction with *The Medlar* which is followed left to its abseil point.

18 **Peels of Laughter**	60m	E5	★★★	1977

A superb route combining thin wall climbing with a brutal roof. To the left of *The Medlar* is a steep wall capped by a large overhang. Start directly below the middle of this wall, 3 metres left of a sycamore.

1 36m (6b). Climb a very shallow loose groove to a large break. Pull leftwards off a block onto the steep wall using small holds. Step back right to the shallow scoop which is climbed to beneath the roof. Traverse left and surmount the roof with difficulty at the obvious weakness to a good hold. Continue more easily up the groove above to a block belay and abseil point (recommended!).

2 24m (4b). As for *The Medlar*, ascend to the recess and climb to a grass ledge, then climb the corner-crack to the top (or, better, do the top pitch of *Relayer*).

The grassy buttress immediately left of *Peels of Laughter* has been climbed by a wandering line, **Necropolis** (VS, 1953), leading to the top pitch of *The Medlar*. The following route crosses *Necropolis* and follows the lip of the roof above *The Cave*.

Lost in Space	61m	VS?		1991

An exposed route. A vegetated start and finish with an adventurous crossing of the *Cave* roof. It possibly awaits a second ascent. Climb steep grass to start at a short wall to the left of the *Cave*.

1 24m (4b). Traverse onto the face and round a bulge to a tiny pedestal stance on the edge of the *Cave* roof.

2 13m (5a). Make a rising traverse along the lip of the roof. At the end of the traverse a precarious and bold mantelshelf leads to a belay on the right.

3 24m (4b). Traverse left to a sloping ledge then scramble up left to a crack. Climb this or the wall on the right.

Two poor routes (**Exodus** MVS, 1952 and **Valedictory** HS, 1958) have disappeared into the vegetated hillside to the left.

The Raven Traverse	142m	VS	★★	1956

The original girdle. A very worthwhile expedition which crosses some impressive ground at a reasonable standard. Start as for *Anarchist*.

1–3 77m (4a). Climb *Anarchist*.

4 20m (4c). Reverse the crack for 2 metres, step left onto the wall and make a descending traverse to a small rock ledge. Cross the steep wall on the left to a grass ledge.

5 24m (4c). Ascend the little wall behind the belay and make an ascending traverse left to a small ledge below a V-groove. Step round to the left and then traverse ascending slightly following the interrupted ledges to pass above the *Cave* roof to a grass ledge.

6 21m (4b). Scramble across to the corner-crack of *The Medlar* and climb it.

The First Circle	108m	E3	★★	1977

An arduous crossing linking good existing pitches. Start 5 metres left of *Peels of Laughter*.

1 18m. Easy climbing up the ridge on the left leads to a cave with two small saplings.

2 30m (5c). Traverse right below the large overhangs of *Peels of Laughter* to a peg runner. Step down and round the rib to join *The Medlar*. Move up to the foot of the corner. Traverse right on the overhung slabs and pull up to the foothold and peg belay stance of *The Gates of Delirium*.

3 18m (5c). Reverse *The Gates of Delirium* to the hole and follow the fault right to a recess as for *Blitzkrieg*.

Left: Wes Hunter above the medlar tree on **Relayer** (E4), Raven Crag, Thirlmere.
Photo: Al Wilson

4 24m (4c). Climb up and rightwards to a ledge. Traverse along this and then down and across to join *Totalitarian*. Follow this to the ledge and belay.

5 18m (5c). Step back left and climb the corner (peg) leading up to the roof and pull out right to the edge. Climb the crack above to the top (pitch 4 of *Totalitarian*).

The following good routes lie on a small steep clean wall of good rock on the left of and just below the main crag.

Does Bob Smith Drink Shandy?	15m	E4	★	1989

(6a). Climb the shallow groove on the right and the arête above.

Time and a Word	14m	E4	★	1991

(6b). Climb the centre of the wall to the overhang. Use the groove to move onto the wall above to a good hold and protection. Climb the wall to the top.

Fragile	14m	E2	★	1991

(5c). Climb the black streak to the overhang then the thin crack and wall above.

Thrash around in the trees below and just to the north of *Raven Crag* and you might find the grotty diminutive **Lower Raven Crag** (NY 305 189) – then you'll wish you hadn't bothered.

Above: Thirlmere forest welcomes climbers! **Photo:** Al Wilson

Smaithwaite Banks Crag

Grid Reference: **NY 305 194** Altitude: **370m**
Faces: **East** Approach: **15 mins**

This three-tiered outcrop lies in a fine situation amongst verdant pines and large boulders and with splendid views down the length of Thirlmere. The routes are located on the *Upper Tier*. Some misguided souls have been climbing on the *Middle* and *Lower Tiers* but nature has taken its usual course in remedying such errors.

Approach:

Follow the forest road past ***Raven Crag***. At the second left-hand bend head to the right and under a broken buttress to an obvious slab. The climbs may need a brush but give pleasant climbing.

1 **Fingery Fun**	17m	E3		1991

The obvious clean slab. Almost worth the walk. Poorly protected.
(5c). Climb the thin rightwards-slanting crack on small flakes and layaways then move left to surmount the bulge.

2 **Graping Aches**	17m	E2		1991

Takes the right-hand side of the clean slab. Poorly protected.
(5b). Climb cracks and edges to the first break then move left to climb the crack in the bulge.

Sippling Crag

Grid Reference: **NY 301 195** Altitude: **350m**
Faces: **West** Approach: **30 mins**

Seen across the Shoulthwaite Valley from *Iron Crag*, this is the rather broken crag set amongst the trees. However, the buttress described provides excellent clean climbing.

Approach:

Take the track through Shoulthwaite Farm. Immediately after leaving the farm via a gate, follow a faint track rightwards uphill until it meets a forest road. Turn right and follow the forest road to a noticeboard which directs a fork right to Shoulthwaite Gill. Ignore this and continue up the main track round a zigzag left, then right at a second zigzag, ignoring a left fork. The crag is adjacent to the track 100 metres beyond the fork.

The buttress comprises two clean walls separated by a wide crack. Descent is via abseil from a large tree above the right hand buttress.

Sippling Crag

1	Sippling Groove	E2 *
2	Sippling Rivalry	VS *
3	Speeding for Fun	E1 *

Photo: Al Davis

1 **Sippling Groove**	20m	E2	★	2007

Good sustained climbing with diminishing protection up the inverted groove system. Start just left of the central crack.

(5b). Move into the base of the groove and ascend delicately to the half way ledge (peg). The upper wall is climbed direct to a finishing jug on the left to gain a ledge. Finish up the flake behind to a tree belay.

2 **Sippling Rivalry**	22m	VS	★	2007

An interesting and very worthwhile route on excellent rock with a well-protected crux. Start just right of the central crack.

(5a). Pull up the lower rocks to a ledge. Climb the left side of the wall to reach a small inverted V where a hard step left enables a jug to be reached. Finish easily behind to a tree belay.

3 **Speeding for Fun**	23m	E1	★	2007

Good but rather bold climbing.

(5a). Start up *Sippling Rivalry* to a small wire in the first bulge then move right to reach a good pocket (skyhook protection or reach right to a wide crack). Mantelshelf onto this (crux) and fix a nut out right before continuing up to a small niche/scoop. Easier climbing leads to the top.

North of *Sippling Crag* lies **The Benn (NY 303 208)** whose short climbs were apparently popular almost a century ago (1924) but haven't been seen since.

Above: Paul O'Reilly searching for good holds on **Solidarity** (E1), Iron Crag. **Photo:** Nick Wharton

Iron Crag

Grid Reference: **NY 297 193** Altitude: **350m**
Faces: **East** Approach: **40 mins**

Iron Crag stands on the western side of Shoulthwaite Ghyll just 2 kilometres from the main Keswick to Ambleside road (A591) at Roughow Bridge (this is at a long sweeping right-hand bend (coming from the south) a few hundred metres after the end of the dual-carriageway section of road).

Approach:

Cars can be parked in the lay-by on the east side of the road. Cross the main road and follow the track up to the farm and caravan/campsite. A permissive path leads between the farm buildings and through a gate into the wood. Follow the smaller path up the hill on the right until the main track is reached. Head right and follow the track to a gate on the right by the weir and bridge over the beck. Follow the beck up the valley until beneath the crag. The final slog up the hill is steep but mercifully short.
The crag comprises three buttresses. ***Left-Hand Buttress***, a steep wall high on the left has plenty of routes at the bottom of the extreme range plus a few harder ones. The rock is generally solid and clean, the lines pleasing and the climbing very worthwhile. The routes here keep the sun

Iron Crag Overview

Photo: Al Phizacklea

for a little longer as the buttress faces more south-east than the rest of the crag. *Central Buttress* is most impressive to look at, being 75 metres high, but is unfortunately composed of very loose and crumbly rock including some volcanic ash which appears to be explosive to the touch. It may nevertheless appeal to the unhinged. *Right-Hand Buttress* is a steep subsidiary buttress lower down on the right with the obvious horizontal break of *The Committal Chamber* at two thirds height. This buttress is home to one of the toughest collections of hard extremes in the region, all being incredibly steep and on good rock, giving lines of true classic status.

Left-Hand Buttress

The only safe **descent** is down the left-hand side.

The routes are described from **left** to **right**.

1 **Clearpoint**	36m	E3		1986

It's not that clear where it goes exactly! Climbs the steep area of rock and impressive arête on the left-hand side of the crag with some bold climbing on the first pitch and hard awkward moves to start the second. Start from a ledge at a small sapling above the little rocky ridge that runs up to the foot of the crag.

1 18m (5a). Climb a groove left of the sapling to a small overhang. Pull over leftwards and continue left to a small bulge which is overcome on good holds (this is not that obvious and once underneath the overhang it can be confusing as to where exactly you should be going). Go up to a large hollow flake; from the top of this, the groove above is followed to a ledge. Belay - or keep going.

2 18m (6a). Make a difficult move to get off the left end of the ledge and reach an obvious hand-jam right of the arête. Use this to gain a good hold above the overhang, pull over and follow the corner above more easily. Belay well back.

2 **Marshall Law**	42m	E1		1982

Takes the full length of the higher of the two obvious diagonal breaks slanting up to the right. Start on the ledge at the left end of the wall, just left of the small sapling at the loose looking break.

1 21m (5a). Follow the break rightwards to a belay on a ledge at the obvious groove. This is *Granolithic Groove*.

2 21m (5b). Continue rightwards along the obvious break with either hands or feet on the break - you figure out which! Keep going rightwards until it peters out at the grassy gully at the right end of the wall. Alternatively, for a much better finish, head up the top wall as for *The Steel Band*.

Iron Crag Left-Hand Buttress

1	Clearpoint	E3
2	Marshall Law	E1
3	The Steel Band	E2 **
4	Granolithic Groove	E1 **
5	Solidarity	E1 *
6	Kryptonite	E4 *
7	Marble Staircase	E4 ***
8	Amabilite	E4 **
9	Rust	MVS
10	Hiddenite	E2 ***
11	The Quest	E5 **
12	Black Gold	E5 **

Photo: Al Phizacklea

3
9
2
10
12
11
2
9
3
12
11
10

3 **The Steel Band**	45m	E2	★★	1981

Pleasant climbing using the lower of the two diagonal breaks. Low in the grade, though the top of pitch 2 requires a bold approach albeit on good holds. Start at the foot of a small greenish ramp just right of *Marshall Law*, above the rocky ridge.

1 17m (5a). Climb rightwards up the short green ramp, then straight up for 3 metres on good pockets until more good holds lead rightwards across a wall to a rib. Move right across the groove-line of *Granolithic Groove* and step down and right to a small ledge and belay in the next groove. This is the line of *Solidarity*.

2 28m (5b). Climb up right to the obvious horizontal break and follow this to the left-facing flake-crack on *Marble Staircase*. Step down and hand-traverse right to a sloping ledge. Good holds lead up the middle of a wall to the upper break and then directly up the wall above to the top. Not well-protected but a good hold always appears just when you want one!

4 **Granolithic Groove**	35m	E1	★★	1981

To the right of the previous wall is an obvious groove running almost the full height of the crag and which provides excellent climbing. Start from a ledge with a large block belay.

(5b). Climb the groove for 3 metres and then up the right-hand wall to the break. The steep groove and wall above lead to a cleaned rib which provides great climbing on positive holds to the top.

5 **Solidarity**	35m	E1	★	1981

Takes the next groove to the right starting at a small bush.

(5b). Climb a thin crack rightwards to a small overlap and pull up steeply into the groove. Follow this passing a small overhang to where it ends. Continue up a short wall and then finish up the short rib on the left as for *Granolithic Groove*.

Right: Nick Wharton on **Granolithic Groove** (E1), Iron Crag, Thirlmere.
Photo: Tim Whiteley
Left: Tim Whiteley steels himself for the next move on **The Steel Band** (E2), while Ron Kenyon admires the view.
Photo: Nick Wharton

6 **Kryptonite**	32m	E4+	★	1982

A worthwhile variation that takes the thin crack in the otherwise blank wall in the middle of the crag left of *Marble Staircase*. Quite tough! Start as for ***Solidarity***.

(6a). Climb a thin crack rightwards to a small overlap and then move right to a steep crack. Go up this until it is possible to move left to beneath the thin crack splitting a steep wall above the horizontal break. Follow the crack and the short section of wall above to the break beneath the overhang. This is where ***Marble Staircase*** comes in from the right. Surmount the overhang and follow the short groove above as for ***Marble Staircase***.

7 **Marble Staircase**	32m	E4-	★★★	1981

A fine climb that takes in the leftward-slanting flake-crack at half-height. Start below a steep corner/groove to the left of the obvious slanting gash of ***Rust***. The corner/groove slants rightwards steeply then kicks back left at an easier angle.

(6a). Climb the steep corner to reach jugs and a small ledge on the left. Climb straight up to regain the groove where it heads left at an easier angle, following it to a prominent horizontal break. Traverse right along the break for a few metres to the left-facing flake-crack. Go up this, then make delicate crux moves leftwards to reach the upper break below an overhang. Pull over into a short groove which leads to the top.

Above: Nick Wharton ready to pounce on the first ascent of **Amabilite** (E4), Iron Crag.
Photo: Tim Whiteley
Right: Mark Johnston on the groove moves of **Marble Staircase** (E4), Iron Crag.
Photo: Al Wilson

8 **Amabilite**	32m	E4	★★	2009

Good climbing with some significant run-outs between reasonable gear. Takes a fairly direct line right of *Marble Staircase*.

(6a). Climb the corner as for *Marble Staircase* then step right into the continuation groove. Move up and right making a mantelshelf onto a ledge. From the left side of the ledge, climb the wall above arriving at the niche on the horizontal break of *The Steel Band*. Make the first move right out of the niche but then gain a standing position in the break. Climb the wall above and left to reach the next break. Climb the wall directly above.

9 **Rust**	34m	MVS		1961

The prominent rightward-slanting chimney is loose and not recommended.

10 **Hiddenite**	32m	E2	★★★	1981

A fantastic route with a serious but easy start and a tricky but well-protected crux. It takes the green groove and wall right of the obvious slanting gash of *Rust*. Scramble up right over blocks until about 6 metres right of the groove behind a large detached flake.

(5c). Step up and traverse left along sloping ledges to below the green groove. This is unprotected but fairly straightforward. Go up the groove to an overhang and then move right to a faint groove in the wall. Climb the right wall to a thin horizontal break where good gear can be found. Now you need to figure out how you will reach the next holds at and above the small overhang. Once done, pull up and continue slightly leftwards to the top. A fantastic piece of climbing.

11 **The Quest**	26m	E5-	★★	1987

An excellent route giving sustained and fingery climbing up the arête right of *Hiddenite* directly below the prominent black groove in the upper wall. Start at ledges left of the large detached flake directly beneath the arête.

(6a). Move up onto the glacis and gain the obvious bracket above. Continuously difficult climbing past two peg runners leads to the base of the groove which is followed exiting left at the top to reach easier ground.

12 **Black Gold**	28m	E5	★★	1981

A good hard and sparsely-protected route up the orange wall and black curving groove on the right. Scramble up right over blocks to a tree belay.

(6a). Step onto the wall from the highest block left of the tree and pull up to a sloping ledge. Climb up rightwards to good holds and then traverse left across the wall to below the steep black groove. Climb this, as for *The Quest*, exiting left at the top to reach easier ground.

Left: Emma Twyford soaking up the atmosphere on **Hiddenite** (E2), Iron Crag.
Photo: Nick Wharton

Iron Crag Right-Hand Buttress

13	Cribin	HVS
14	The Committal Chamber	E5 ***
15	Imminent Arrival	E4 *
16	Pumping Iron	E7 *
17	Western Union	E6 ***
18	The Iron Man	E7 ***
19	If 6 was 9	E9 **
20	Phoenix in Obsidian	E7 ***

Photo: Nick Wharton

Central Buttress

This is separated from *Left-Hand Buttress* by the deep gash of **Iron Crag Chimney** (MS, 1896) which is extremely loose and should be avoided like the plague by all except those who weary of life. Two other poor routes, **Irony** (HS, 1957) and **Ferrous Buttress** (HVS, 1951), have been climbed to the right.

Right-Hand Buttress

The steep buttress below and right of *Central Buttress* is home to some very very hard test pieces. French grades are given for added insight into what to expect on the harder routes but are not intended to imply these are sport climbs – they are full-on trad adventure routes.

Descent is to the left.

13 **Cribin**	33m	HVS		1970

Very much a side-show to the main attractions further right. It takes the obvious line up the slabs on the left side of the buttress.

Climb the wet corner to gain the slab which is followed until a difficult move can be made onto the arête. Step up to a small ledge below a roof (peg runner). Climb up to the roof with difficulty and surmount the overhang until a steep corner is reached and climbed to the top.

14 **The Committal Chamber**	57m	E5	★★★	1983

An exposed and strenuous pitch which takes the obvious rising break across the crag from left to right. A tremendous outing across very steep ground giving an excellent insight into the nature of the other more direct routes on this part of the crag. Start at the left-hand end of the buttress at a short crack in a corner below and left of the yew tree.

1 12m (4c). Climb the corner to a belay in the yew tree.

2 24m (6a). Follow the crack to a good rest in a niche and step down right to a thread round a chockstone. From good jams, reach a good jug and make a series of committing and strenuous moves on jams and undercuts to reach the obvious sloping ledge. A well-protected pitch if you are strong enough to hang around.

3 21m (4c). Traverse right to the end of the ledge. Move up and keep moving right round the corner to a steep grassy finish. A better alternative is to finish up the *Phoenix in Obsidian* groove.

15 **Imminent Arrival**	40m	E4	★	2003

A direct line up the left side of the main part of the crag. There is a large yew tree just below half-height. Start below this, just to the left, between two smaller trees.

1 18m (5c). Climb poor rock to a shattered arête which leads to a ledge. Step right and belay at the yew tree.

2 22m (6a). From the belay step left and climb straight up a ragged blocky crack, passing a small tree and an even smaller sapling. Climb more steeply to the overhang and pull through this rightwards on good holds to stand in the base of a steep slim groove. Climb this to the top.

16 **Pumping Iron**	36m	E7 {F7b+}	★	1993

The original route up this part of the crag that takes the slanting black groove then the upper wall to the left of *Western Union*.

1 12m (5c). Climb pitch 1 of *The Committal Chamber* to belay at the yew tree.

2 24m (6c). Follow the break rightwards as for *The Committal Chamber* to a rest in the niche (junction with *Western Union*) and arrange protection (peg – new in 2008 – as for *The Iron Man*). Reverse back for 2-3 metres to below the overhanging black groove, take a deep breath, adjust your cap and follow this groove with considerable difficulty until it is possible to pull out right onto the wall. Tough moves up past a good peg and good hold lead to obvious undercuts, then on up to a small niche. Difficult moves left allow good holds to be reached. Finish up better holds.

17 **Western Union**	39m	E6 {F7c}	★★★	1986

An amazing direct line up steep and difficult ground taking the obvious corner-groove above the traverse of *The Committal Chamber*. Start below a grassy ledge at 5 metres, just right of the lower of two yews growing one above the other on the crag.

(6c). Go up to the grassy ledge, then climb a difficult wall, passing a peg runner, and move left into a sentry box. Climb this, then the crack above and wall on the right to meet the traverse of *The Committal Chamber* at the bottom of the groove. Get as much of a rest as possible in the niche, then launch up the groove to the top (5 peg runners – replaced 2008).

18 **The Iron Man**	36m	E7 {F7c}	★★★	2008

An awesome route, taking the true line up the wall to the left of *Western Union* and incorporating the top half of *Pumping Iron*.

(6c). Climb *Western Union* to the break. At the base of the thin groove is a flake which sports a peg. Climb boldly up the thin groove onto the head wall, one metre left of *Western Union*, before "out-there" moves left gain *Pumping Iron*. Follow this to the top.

Right: Andy Mitchell shows his mettle on **The Iron Man** (E7), Iron Crag. **Photo:** Al Wilson

19 **If 6 was 9**	40m	E9 {F8a+}	★★	1992

This impressive route tackles the all-too-obvious blank wall in the centre of the crag between *Western Union* and *Phoenix in Obsidian*. Start as for *Phoenix in Obsidian*.

(6c). Climb the initial wall (passing a peg runner) to a large ledge. Move left to below the left end of a small overlap. Climb directly, passing three peg runners on the way, to a junction with *The Committal Chamber* at the break. Finish up the steep V-groove above as for *Phoenix in Obsidian*.

20 **Phoenix in Obsidian**	40m	E7{F7b}	★★★	1989

A fairly direct line up the right-hand side of the buttress below the obvious overhang at two-thirds height. Beware of rope drag when climbing the final groove.

(6b). Climb the initial wall (passing a peg runner) to a large ledge. Climb up to two poor peg runners and then make some hard committing moves to gain a good hold (peg runner and wires). Move up into the niche. Swing right and make difficult moves to gain a good hold below the roof (Rock 5). Make a difficult traverse left and pull through the overhang at its narrowest point to gain the ledge below the groove. Climb the steep V-groove above.

Left: Dave MacLeod on the second ascent of **If 6 was 9** (E9), Iron Crag.
Photo: Claire MacLeod
Right: Hanging tat on **Iron Crag**.
Photo: Al Wilson

Goat Crag

Grid Reference: **NY 294 199** Altitude: **400m**
Faces: **East** Approach: **40 mins**

Goat Crag is the long cliff high above Shoulthwaite Farm.

Approach:

Zigzag through Shoulthwaite Farm until the path forks just after a gate. Follow the fainter right-hand path onto a forestry track which is followed rightwards. At a sign for a permissive footpath to Shoulthwaite Gill, turn right, leaving the forest, cross the gill and climb steeply to the crag. All of the climbs are located in the shorter steep Central Bay of walls and corners above the tumbled scree of large blocks which is gained by scrambling up from the left.

The crag is seamed with cracks and corners which provide steep satisfying climbing but also a good growing medium. The vegetation is currently winning but most of the routes are still climbable and worthwhile. The crag is owned by United Utilities and is a Site of Special Scientific Interest. The Authority are legally obliged to prevent damage and are concerned about the harm already done by cleaning. **Climbing continues to be permitted but if any further cleaning takes place the Authority may consider limiting access.**

Descent: a short distance to the right (looking up) of *Central Bay* a small spiky pinnacle can be seen below. Scramble down with care until behind the pinnacle and work down and along to the foot of the crag. Fixing an abseil enables a quicker, safer and more convenient descent.

The climbs are described from **left** to **right**.

1	**Hidden Agenda**	20m	E3		1993

The fine groove on the left-hand side of the steep wall.

(6a). Layback to the peg (Friend 2 below) and continue steeply up to a good ledge with a large suspect block. Cross the wall on the right (hidden Rock 5 at knee height) to good holds and small wires. Move up then left to finish by the wide crack.

2	**Shoulthwaite Crack**	20m	E1	★★	1993

The blatantly obvious crack in the left side of the wall.

(5b). Climb the fine crack - large Friends useful.

Goat Crag Overview

2	Shoulthwaite Crack	E1 **
16	The LA Way	E1

Goat Crag Left

1	Hidden Agenda	E3
2	Shoulthwaite Crack	E1 **
3	GCSE Escape	E2
4	Roraima	HVS

3 **GCSE Escape**	20m	E2		1993

Start from the grass ledge above and to the right of *Shoulthwaite Crack*. (5c). Follow the groove/crack system with a hard move at mid-height to gain a ledge.

4 **Roraima**	20m	HVS		1993

Start from the grass ledge above and to the right of *Shoulthwaite Crack*. (5a). Start as for *GCSE Escape* but move right onto the ledge then follow an obvious crack to a large block and the wide crack above.

5 **Thunder Dragons**	20m	E4		1993

Start from the grass ledge above and to the right of *Shoulthwaite Crack* just right of *Roraima*.

(6a). Gain the obvious large hold at 3 metres (first runners can be placed from here), stand up and quickly climb to a tricky pull onto a good ledge and an easy finish. Well-protected but very pumpy.

6 **Better Than Disneyworld**	20m	E1		1993

Start from the grass ledge to the left of *Grand Larceny* behind a small tree.

(5b). Climb the steep layback crack then the jamming crack to the top of the flake which is traversed left to a dirty finish above.

v1 ***Variation Finish*** 20m E1 1993

Instead of traversing the flake, step down rightwards onto the arête and climb the wall above (good wire, No.1 Stopper out left) to good finishing holds.

7 **Grand Larceny**	20m	HVS		1993

The route starts about 16 metres to the right *Shoulthwaite Crack* and takes the obvious groove capped by an overhang with a wide crack.

(5a). Climb the heathery groove then the overhanging crack using its right wall.

8 **Remission**	20m	E1	★★	1993

A little classic. Starts just to the right of the groove of *Grand Larceny,* up the hand-sized ferny crack with the remains of a tree stump near its top.

(5b). Climb the crack, which is steep and quite strenuous, to the roof, then finish via the overhung crack as for *Grand Larceny.*

9 **Lost World**	20m	E1	★★	1991

Starts 3 metres right of *Remission.*

(5b). Climb the fine flake-crack in the right side of the huge detached block in the centre of the upper mass.

The open vegetated groove has been climbed but the luxuriant eco-systems it supports are best left undisturbed.

10 **New Age Traveller**	20m	E1		1993

(5b). Start at the open vegetated groove, as for *Stegasaurus*, but follow the leftwards-trending line to an easy finish.

11 **Stegasaurus**	20m	S		1993

Start at the open vegetated groove.

Climb the steep heathery slab on the right to an exposed finish.

The next route starts round the corner to the right and 4 metres lower in a dip.

Buffalo Girls	20m	E2		1993

(5b). Start just left of *Jurassic Park* and follow the rightward-trending line on good holds. A steep pitch with adequate protection from small wires.

12 **Jurassic Park**	20m	E3		1993

Start at a green wall.

(5c). Climb the green wall in the middle of the crag on good holds to

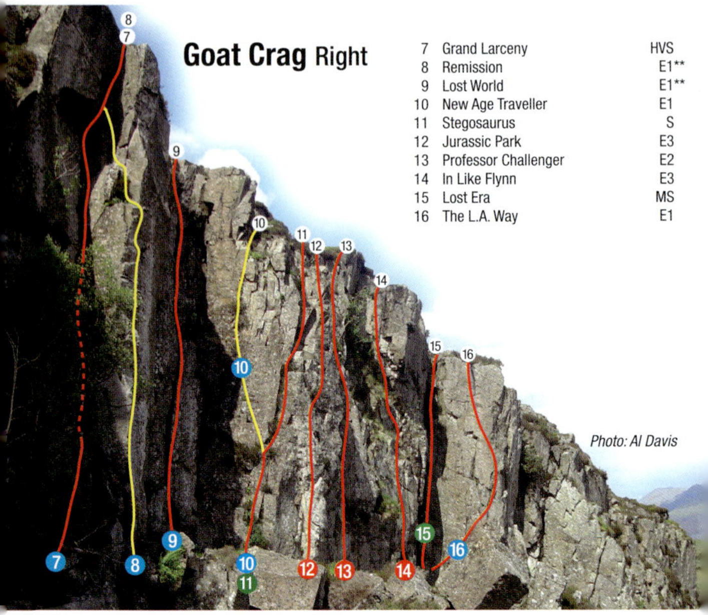

Photo: Al Davis

a bulge (wires on right and skyhook runner above the bulge). Attain the ledge above (long reach), move rightwards to a large block and then steeply up the pillar with another long reach to finish.

13 **Professor Challenger**	20m	E2		1993

Start just right of *Jurassic Park*.

(5c). Climb the steep stepped open groove on the right to a bulge at mid-height. Awkward moves up and left bring a good ledge to hand with a groove to finish. Strenuous but well-protected.

14 **In Like Flynn**	20m	E3		1993

This route climbs the short steep crack-line 5 metres left of *Lost Era*.

(5c). Climb steeply to a strenuous pull leftwards onto a good ledge. Go easily up and right across grassy ledges to the foot of a steep groove and finish up this. Belay a long way back.

15 **Lost Era**	20m	MS		1993

The prominent chimney near the right side of the alcove; all very traditional.

Climb the chimney and exit the top via the inside or outside.

16 **The L.A. Way**	21m	E1		1993

(5b). Start right of *Lost Era* and climb rightwards to the arête then left and straight up to finish.

The remaining crags lie to the north of the A591 dual carriageway. Unfortunately they are not as good as they appear when approaching from Keswick, but much worse are the few climbs claimed on the buttresses excavated to make the dual carriageway which have been filed appropriately!

Yew Crag comprises a number of buttresses. **North Buttress** is the largest but is very disappointing on close acquaintance. The routes are poorly protected undertakings on snappy flaky lichenous rock which no doubt excited their first ascentionists but are unlikely to do the same for anyone else.

Yew Crag – South Buttress

Grid Reference:	**NY 307 205**	Altitude:	**200m**
Faces:	**West**	Approach:	**10 mins**

This buttress is situated on the western side of High Rigg, close to the main Keswick to Ambleside Road (A591), 6 kilometres out of Keswick.

Approach:

Park in the lay-by on the east side of that road and walk 800 metres further along the road to a quarry from where a prominent buttress can be seen near the road. It faces west and is quick drying, especially on the left side of the crag.

Most of the routes are serious propositions due to friable rock and lack of reliable protection but despite this the climbing is very good. The routes described make the best use of the available rock: numerous small variations could be made but would be pointless.

Descent is to the right. An abseil point has been rigged on the large tree in the centre of the crag.

The climbs are described from **left** to **right**.

1 **Bin Laden**	30m	E1		2000

A serious and best avoided (loose after the crux) line up the left side of the crag. However, if you really must, start at a short groove just left of a small tree at 5 metres and just right of the broken vegetated part of the crag.

(5b). Climb up to a thin crack-line in the impending wall. Pull up to a sloping ledge (crux) then up leftwards towards vegetated rock.

Yew Crag South

1	Bin Laden	E1
2	Bombay Bambino	E2 *
3	Lakeland Spice	VS *
4	Two Bit Bombed Butty	E2
5	Help the Aged	E1 *
6	V.I.P.	E3
7	Bossman	E2 *
8	Peeping Tom	E1
9	Aristocrat	E1
10	Shameless	E1
11	Ruby Tuesday	E3 *
12	DJ Slate	E3
13	Grave Dodger	E1
14	Monarch	E2
15	Age Concern	E1
16	Nick's Brasher Boots	VS
17	Sweepstake	HS
v1	Sweepstake Corner	E1
18	Yew Crag Pinnacle	MVS
v2	Off Width Start	E1

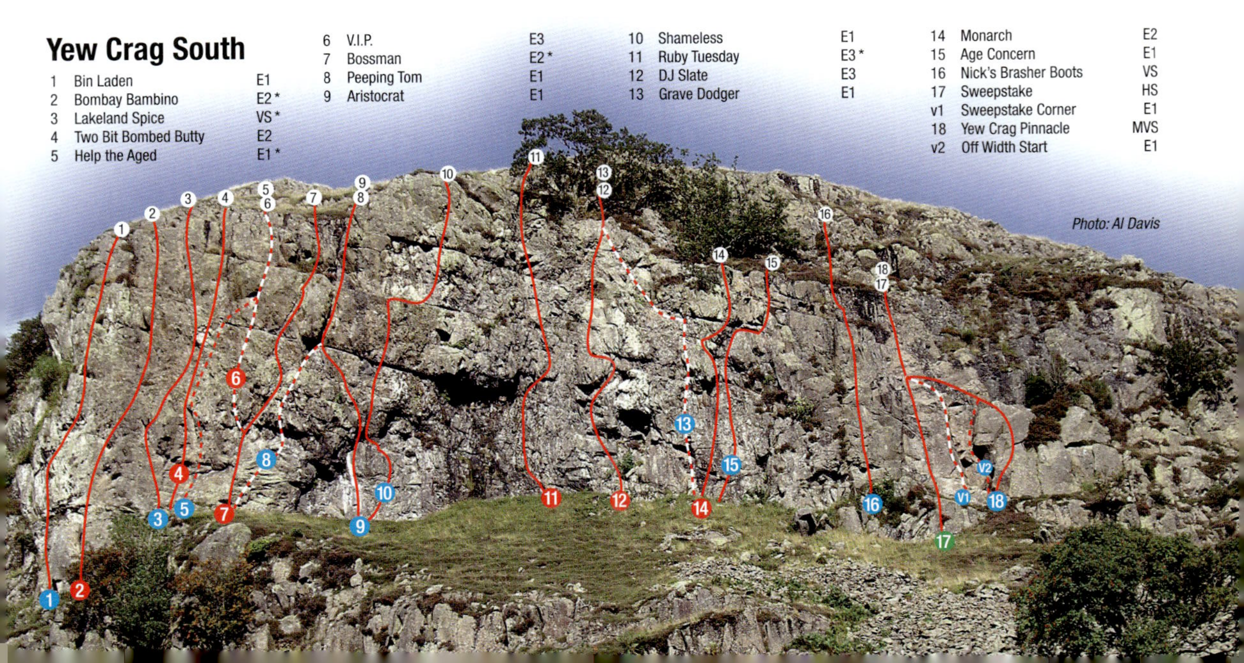

Photo: Al Davis

Climb up right on loose rock to a ledge with doubtful blocks then up past the blocks to good holds which are used to swing up right onto a rib. Climb up into a slab/corner which is followed to a final short wall.

2 **Bombay Bambino**	30m	E2	★	2009

Start at the lower left end of the crag at a large block. Very bold.

(5b). Climb the large crack for 4 metres to a ledge. Boldly follow the groove above where moves up and right lead towards the protruding blocks. Finish between the blocks.

3 **Lakeland Spice**	25m	VS	★	2009

Starts 4 metres right of ***Bombay Bambino*** on a high grass ledge. Excellent climbing.

(5a). Climb the easy ledges leftwards and up to a steep left-rising ramp. Follow the ramp to a pointed flake and make a long step right onto a large nose (crux). Now trend up and right 4 metres to a crack at a left-facing corner and follow this to the top.

President	25m	E2		2000

Start on the grass ledge, as for ***Lakeland Spice***, beneath a corner with a small triangular overhang.

(5b). Climb to overhang at 5 metres then pull up leftwards onto a steep section. Move straight up to big holds at 10 metres, and climb up leftwards to a steep wall (unprotected – as for ***Bombay Bambino***) which is topped by a sloping ledge and hidden incuts. Gain a standing position on the sloping ledge, then pull up right into a corner which leads to a large ledge. Continue up the easier wall above.

4 **Two Bit Bombed Butty**	25m	E2		1999

Start 2 metres right of ***Lakeland Spice*** below a steep right-facing corner. Poorly-protected.

(5b). Climb the corner (crux, with protection not obvious), step right when above the corner, and follow a vague groove/crack-line to the top (passing an unprotected corner at mid-height).

5 **Help the Aged**	20m	E1	★	2009

A good route. Start one metre right of ***Two Bit Bombed Butty*** below a slim groove containing an obvious fist crack.

(5b). Climb the groove direct to the fist-sized crack. A difficult move brings easier ground. Trend rightwards, heading for a short hanging groove, and go up this to the top.

6 **V.I.P.**	25m	E3		2000

An unbalanced route with a hard bold crux. Start 4 metres right of *Two Bit Bombed Butty* and 6 metres left of the obvious white streak.

(5c). Climb up to undercuts at 5 metres and make difficult moves up left (crux) to stand on a small ledge at 7 metres. Continue up to a short steep left-facing groove which is gained from the left. Climb the groove to gain a ledge and continue up the wall.

7 **Bossman**	25m	E2	★	2000

Good climbing with a bold crux. Start 6 metres left of the white streak, as for *V.I.P.*

(5b). Climb *V.I.P.* for 6 metres then gain the hanging slab on the right (crux). Move up right into a small groove and continue up to a ledge below a leaning corner-crack on the right which is climbed to gain a grassy ledge. Continue up a short undercut wall.

8 **Peeping Tom**	30m	E1		2009

Start 6 metres left of the white streak.

(5b). Cross the slab rightwards passing an undercut to beneath the overhang. Step across into the corner and pull over the bulge on good holds. Awkward moves lead to easier ground and a steep corner-crack leaning rightwards. Go up this to a ledge and an undercut wall and over this to the top.

9 **Aristocrat**	25m	E1		2000

Start at a steep corner-crack by a prominent white streak (beneath and left of the obvious overhang at 10 metres).

(5b). Climb the corner-crack then pull up left on to an undercut wall (big holds) to gain a small tree. Move up left then up right to enter a steep corner-crack which is climbed to a ledge. Continue up the undercut wall and and so to the top.

10 **Shameless**	30m	E1		2009

Start one metre right of the white streak. Two Friend 1s are useful.

(5b). Climb easily to a slab, bridge the groove and reach a large block. Traverse right and go up to the break. Pull over the bulge and make a long reach for a jug. Airy climbing leads to a large ledge. In front is a groove with a peg. From this, move right to a large block. Stand on the block then go straight up to a spike belay.

11 **Ruby Tuesday**	25m	E3	★	2009

A fine line that follows the obvious groove in the centre of the crag. Start 5 metres left of the tree stump at the right-hand edge of the overhang.

(5c). Climb direct to the thread passing an in situ peg on right.

Powerful moves lead to a good hold and runners. Pull over onto the ledge and enjoy pleasant climbing up a groove to a block belay.

Meritocrat (E4, 2001) is unprotected where it matters and has been superseded, following much cleaning, by *Ruby Tuesday*.

12 **DJ Slate**	25m	E3		2009

This route supersedes a previous route, **Lords** (E2, 2001), which used the trees for its starting moves. Two each of Friends 0 and 00 are helpful. Start just left of the tree stump.

(5c). Trend leftwards for 2 metres past a large pocket. Committing moves up and right gain a good side pull which leads to a roof. Move right to good wires then step into a groove with difficulty (crux). Follow the groove to a niche above and a large block. Easier ground rightwards leads onto a shared finish with *Grave Dodger*.

13 **Grave Dodger**	25m	E1		2009

Start 3 metres right of the tree stump at the right-bounding rib of a short V-groove.

(5b). Climb a rib to a good handhold. A difficult move (crux) gains a small pocket just left of a rib. Follow the groove until a traverse left leads to a large block, then the wall above to the tree.

Above: Colin Downer goes topless on **Shameless** (E1), Yew Crag. **Photo:** Martin Nicholson

14 **Monarch**	25m	E2		2001

Start 3 metres right of the tree stump as for *Grave Dodger*.

(5b). Climb a short rib and make thin moves on to a slab (protection awkward). Step right, then up to a steep open corner and climb up leftwards to a resting place. Move up, then step right on to a wall and follow good holds up to a rib on the right. Move right round the rib then up to the large tree (possible belay). Continue up the wall above the tree, or scramble up a leftward-slanting gangway.

15 **Age Concern**	20m	E1		2009

Start 4 metres right of the tree stump at a blunt rib.

(5b). A faint groove/corner followed by moves right lead to a good pocket. Move up to the overhung corner and gain the hanging slab above. Traverse right round a fin of rock to a good ledge and follow the groove above to the tree belay.

16 **Nick's Brasher Boots**	35m	VS		2000

Climbs the left side of the slabs. Start 12 metres right of *Monarch* and 2 metres right of blocks at the foot of the crag. Poorly protected.

(4b). Follow ledges and the clean slab directly. Near the top, move left on a ramp to gain a groove which is followed to a large ledge. Continue up the wall just right of the tree.

17 **Sweepstake**	18m	HS		2009

Start at the right end of the crag at a slab with a corner on its right.

(4c). Climb the slab direct to the top.

v1 ***Sweepstake Corner*** E1 5m 2009

Start at the obvious corner to the right of *Sweepstake*.

(5b). Climb the corner then finish up *Sweepstake*.

18 **Yew Crag Pinnacle**	20m	MVS		2009

(4b). Climb the front of the pillar/flake to the right of *Sweepstake Corner* via a short crack. From the top of the pillar, step onto the wall, traverse diagonally left and join *Sweepstake* to belay on a large block.

v2 ***Offwidth Start*** 4m E1 2009

(5b). Climb the offwidth on the left side of the pinnacle. Serious – no gear!

Shawbank Crag (NY 303 215) is a pleasantly situated small crag with some unattractive routes which are badly overgrown and are best left to wallow in obscurity.

The Northern Fells – Carrock Fell

North of Thirlmere, and north of the A66, lies the Skiddaw/Blencathra massif. It possesses little climbing of any sort but what there is is concentrated almost entirely on Carrock Fell.

Carrock Fell has in recent years become a very popular bouldering venue, with good reason - high quality problems on excellent rock in a lovely setting. However, Carrock Fell also provides some very pleasant routes on the same high quality rock, which is primarily gabbro. Its various crags and groups of rocks are best identified from the road before ascending the hillside.

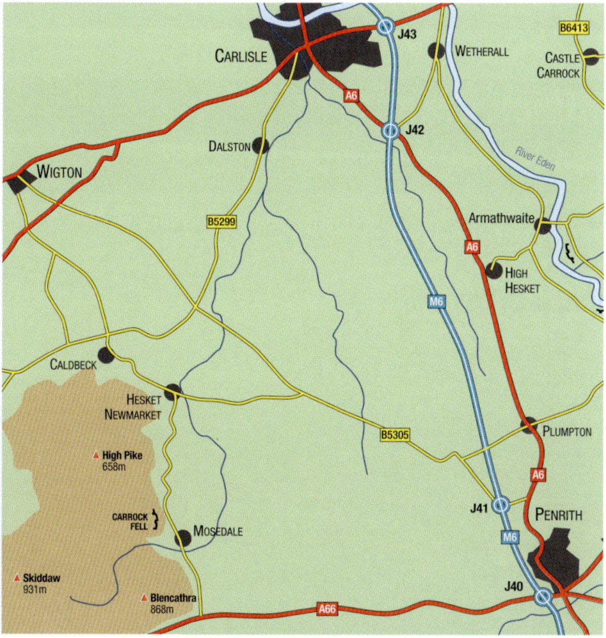

Carrock Fell

1 Black Crag
2 Snail Shell Crag
3 Weeping Wall
4 Slape Crags
5 Carrock Fell Boulders South
6 Juniper Crack
7 Carrock Fell Boulders North
8 Three Tier Climb
9 Twenty Metre Slab
10 Eighty Foot Slab
11 The Trough

Black Crag

Grid Reference: **NY 355 325** Altitude: **330m**
Faces: **East** Approach: **15 mins**

This is the very steep crag directly above the hamlet of Mosedale.

Black Crag Carrock Fell

1 Short and Brutal E5 **

Approach:
Park on the north side of the village and flog up the hillside above. It can also be gained by traversing left from *Snail Shell Crag*.

Short and Brutal	12m	E5	★★	2006

A minor classic. Well protected but very steep!
(6b). The obvious crack-line is climbed past the protruding block to easier ground.

Snail Shell Crag

Grid Reference: **NY 355 327** Altitude: **330m**
Faces: **East** Approach: **10 mins**

This lovely gabbro slab lies about 200 metres north of the hamlet of Mosedale. The easy-angled slabs are climbable almost anywhere – the lines described make best use of the rock.

Approach:
A holly and sycamore grow together about 45 metres above the road. The crag lies directly up the hillside above and is best gained by following the right-hand edge of the large scree run below it.

Snail Shell Crag

Descent is on the **left**.

The routes are described from **left** to **right**.

1	**Left Arête**	23m	D-		

Start behind a tree 5 metres left of the central gully.
Climb the easy-angled arête to the top. Poorly protected.

2	**The Scoop**	23m	MS		

Climb the scoop just left of *The Gully* trending leftwards. Poorly protected.

3	**The Gully**	25m	M+		

The obvious corner-gully is better than it looks. Finish straight up the slab above.

4	**Slabs Left**	25m	D+	★	

The slab just right of *The Gully*.

5	**Recess Route**	25m	D+	★★	

Start just left of some blocks and 3 metres right of *The Gully*.
Climb the obvious cracked groove. Either fork can be taken but the left one is often wet.

3	The Gully	M	8	Barker's Slab Direct	VS **
4	Slabs Left	D *	9	Right Crack	VD
5	Recess Route	D **	10	North Climb	MS
v1	Recess Route Direct	S **			
6	Rose Tree Route	VD **			
7	Barker's Slab	VD **			

v1 ***Recess Route Direct*** 25m S ★★ 2009

Follow *Recess Route* to the overlap at the fork in the cracks. Pull directly over this and pad straight up the delightful slab above.

6 **Rose Tree Route**	25m	VD-	★★	1934

Start at blocks below the slab.

Climb up to a narrow ledge then trend rightwards to a thin crack which leads to the top.

7 **Barker's Slab**	25m	VD	★★	

Start as for *Rose Tree Route* but climb diagonally rightwards immediately and follow the slim right-facing feature above.

8 **Barker's Slab Direct**	25m	VS-	★★	

Start just right of the blocks.

(4b). Make thin moves directly up the fine slab to a slight overlap then follow the ordinary route up the slim right-facing feature.

9 **Right Crack**	25m	VD		

Start 2 metres right of the blocks.

Climb a crack moving left at 4 metres and then straight up. It is also possible to traverse left at half-height to join the finish of *Barker's Slab Direct* at the same grade.

10 **North Climb**	25m	MS		1934

Start 12 metres right of the blocks.

Climb the slab passing to the right of a thorn bush. The finish is now overgrown.

Below *Snail Shell Crag* is a short mossy wall. This is the aptly named **Weeping Wall** which has a route of the same name (D, 1936) and some more recent additions of no better quality.

Slape Crags

Grid Reference: NY 355 329 Altitude: 300m
Faces: East Approach: 10 mins

These crags lie about 230 metres north of *Snail Shell Crag* at about the same level. This is a fine slab of excellent rock with some worthwhile pitches. It is at its best in Spring before bracken makes access difficult and trees obscure the crag.

Left: Sally Baxendale, feet sticking to the gabbro like glue, places the first runners on **Recess Route** (D), Snail Shell Crag. **Photo:** Stephen Reid

Approach:

From the road directly below using the *Undercut Boulder* (see photo on page 190) as a marker.

Descent: At the top, a scramble up for 3 metres brings you to a good thread belay and an easy walk off to the right.

A poor route has been claimed up rocks 90 metres to the left of the crag - this is not described.

	Slape Crags Arête	36m	VD		1933

A sadly neglected route and now very mossy. Start at the foot of the arête to the left of the slab.

1 10m. Climb the arête to a tree.

2 26m. Continue up the arête. Move left up a slab then back right by perched blocks to regain the arête which is followed to the top.

1	Bloodaxe	25m	E2-	★	

An excellent little route on perfect rock.

(5b). Starting at the middle of the slab, move left to a thin crack then climb directly to the top.

2	Scrubs Up Nicely	25m	E2	★	2005

(5b). Climb a direct line up the slab between *Bloodaxe* and *Slape Crags Direct*.

3	Slape Crags Direct	25m	VS+	★	1935

(4b). Climb up the right side of the slab following vague scoops to join the arête at the top. Good climbing but poorly protected.

Original Start: ***Lower Slape Crag*** VS+ 1935

(4c). Climb the centre of the smaller lower slab, moving left at the top. Traditionally described as "easier in tricounis" though in its present state even these wouldn't help much.

Moving 180 metres further north there is an obvious V-chimney topped by a juniper, **Juniper Crack** (S, 1932).

Right: Michael Kenyon stretches for a rugosity on **Bloodaxe** (E2), Slape Crag.
Photo: Ron Kenyon

Carrock Fell Boulders

The Eastern slope of Carrock Fell between Mosedale and Stone Ends Farm, below the line of the crags, is a huge boulder field.

The rock is gabbro offering superb friction, though it can be painfully rough on delicate finger tissue. The bouldering is outstanding and is at its best on Winter and Spring mornings before bracken and midges make life less pleasant. Landings can be poor in places so a mat and an attentive spotter are invaluable.

The area is complex and only a very small selection of the excellent problems on offer is described.

The two areas are easily indentified as they are close to the road. The adventurous will find excellent bouldering spread across the hillside above though the best is not always the most obvious. As usual, in addition to the problems shown, eliminates and sitting starts abound. There are friendly locals to show you the many variations and full details can be found at www.lakesbloc.co.uk or in *Lakes Bouldering* (Rockfax, 2006).

Approach:

Just north of Mosedale village, the boulders appear on the left of the road. The boulders described are at the northern end, about 1.2 kilometres north of the village. Park on the right by a grit bin. The first area is roadside, about 400 metres south. The second area, identified by three huge boulders, is just above the parking.

Carrock Fell Boulders Southern Group

1 Jake's Wall
2 Undercut Boulder
3 The Warm Ups
4 LIttle Groove Boulder
5 DuAL Boulder
6 Purple Slab
7 The Arêtes Boulder

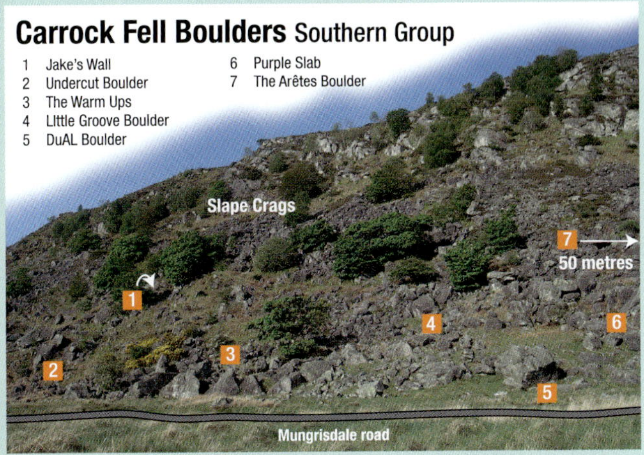

Carrock Fell Boulders Northern Group

8 Sitting Block
9 Low Boulder
10 Mushroom Boulder
11 Boardman's Boulder
12 Razor Wall
13 Flake Crack Boulder

Photo: Al Davis

"Three large boulders, A, B and C, south of the Sike and low down, are obvious, and the routes on them are now well scratched. C has a tantalising traverse, not yet fairly led. 'The Avenue' is a line of boulders parallel with the road. 'The Chapel Stone,' also near the road, is the most conspicuous of all the boulders and gives some easy routes".
Mabel Barker, 'Carrock Fell', FRCC Journal 1932

Opposite: Kate Arnold on **Boardman's Boulder**.
Photo: Jim Arnold

Carrock Fell Boulders Southern Group

† Sitting Start

1	Vesicle Graffiti	V3
2	No Pain, No Gain	V3
3	Via Dolorosa	V3

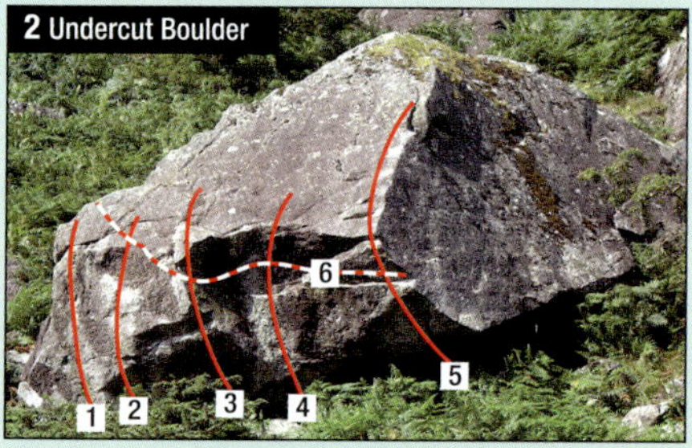

1	V1	
2	V2	
3	V2	
4	V2	
5	V2	
6	Surperb traverse	V1

1	Needle Arête	V0
2	Rising traverse	V0
3	Traverse	V1
4	Wall direct †	V
5	Frustration Slab	V

Carrock Fell Boulders Southern Group

4 Little Groove

1 Little Groove † V3
2 V3
3 Arête † V5
4 Right to Left traverse V7

† Sitting start

5 DuAL Boulder

1 The Sound of One Al Slapping
Left to Right traverse V2
There and back V3

6 Purple Slab

1 V3
2 V4

7 The Arêtes

1 The Arête V1
2 Crimpy Wall (no arête) V1
3 Arête left side V0
4 Arête right side † V0
5 Wall † V3

Carrock Fell Boulders Northern Group

1	Right to left traverse †	V2

† Sitting start

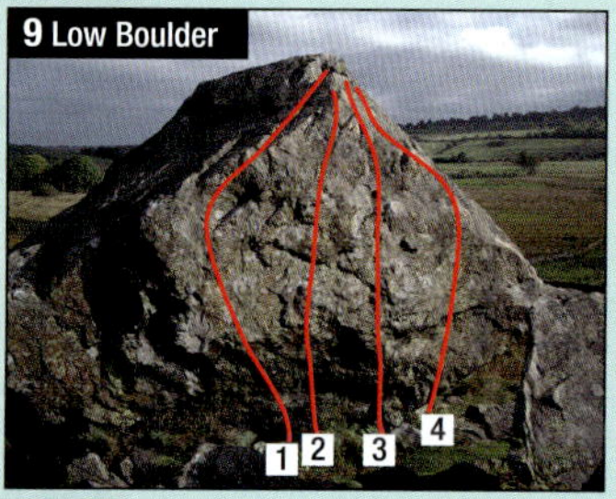

1	V2
2	V3
3	V2
4	V2

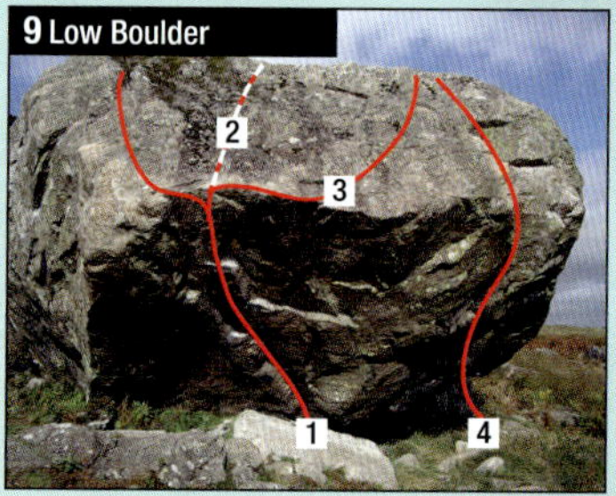

1	The Arête †	V8
2	Direct over the lip †	V3
3	Finish rightwards at lip †	V3
4	McHaffie's Crack	V4
	From sitting	V7

1		V1
2	From sitting	V2
3	The Little Groove †	V1
4	Mushroom Traverse R to L	V3
	L to R	V4
	There and back is an excellent workout.	

Carrock Fell Boulders Northern Group

11 Boardman's Boulder

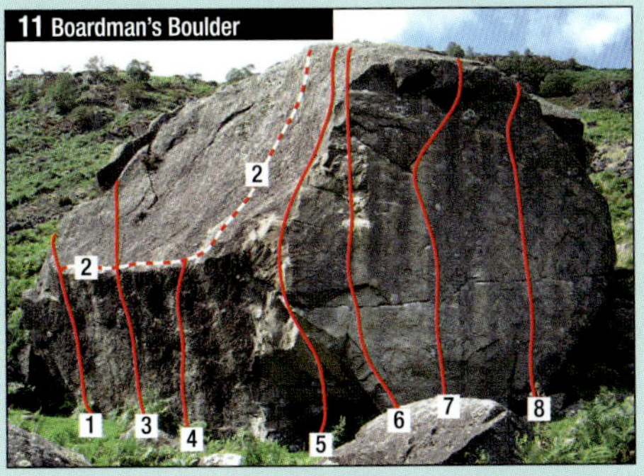

1 V0
2 Traverse the lip to big jug V6
3 V2
4 Move up and right to huge jug V1
5 Boardman's Arête V2
Sitting V7
6 V4
7 Rouse's Wall V5
8 V7

12 Flake Crack Boulder

1 Traverse the crack V0
2 V0
3 Popping with Conviction V3
4 With less conviction escapes left using the crack V2

13 Razor Wall

1 Left to right low traverse V2
Harder in reverse
2 Straight up V1

The Trough Area

Grid Reference: **NY 348 337** Altitude: **450m**
Faces: **East** Approach: **15 mins**

This lies to the north of the stream running down to Stone Ends Farm.

Just north of the stream is a series of tiny isolated outcrops. These are climbed by **Three Tier Climb** (S, 1931).

Twenty Metre Slab

Seventy metres up and left of *Eighty Foot Slab* is a slabby rib situated above a large scree slope and guarded at its base by a steep wall. The following imaginatively named climb makes pleasant use of the available rock.

Twenty Metre Slab	20m	VD		2007

Start just left of the lowest rocks.

Pull up a short steep wall and trend leftwards to reach a ledge. Continue up the pleasant slabby wall and rib to belay with care on the finishing terrace. A short slab just left of the top of the rib provides another short pitch of Mild Severe standard.

Eighty Foot Slab

The *Eighty Foot Slab*, the lowest outcrop on the fellside, lies directly above Stone Ends Farm and just above the start of the diagonal track up Carrock Fell. It gives pleasant climbing on clean rock but unfortunately there are no good belays at the top. A holly tree well back to the right could be used though it is guarded by a large juniper. Alternatively a second rope could be run up the hillside to a good tree directly above.

Descend by traversing horizontally rightwards past a rowan.

Eighty Foot Slab Left-Hand	14m	VD	Prior to 1932

The left-hand slab is climbed rightwards to finish up a fine rib. Lovely rock but protectionless.

The remaining routes are on the right-hand slab.

Smearing on Sunshine	25m	MVS		2006

Pleasant but lacking protection.

(4a). Follow a shallow groove just right of the central mossy scoop. Step right to avoid the rounded bulge and continue directly up slabby walls to the top, just left of *Eighty Foot Slab*.

Happy Feet HVS 2007
A direct start to *Smearing on Sunshine*.
(5c). Climb the thin crack in the centre of the slab to join the parent route at the rounded bulge.

Eighty Foot Slab	25m	VD	★	1927

Lovely climbing, but quite bold. Start at the right edge of the clean slab.
Climb to a heather ledge at 2 metres. Move up another two metres and make a delicate traverse leftwards to step onto the top of a bulge. Climb the easiest line up the slab above trending rightwards to the top. Alternatively, from the heather ledge, climb the rib direct.

Further north, and a long way up the hillside, lies the gully of **The Trough** (1927). A number of other routes hereabouts are largely and best buried, though the *The Trough* itself is worth excavating from the memory banks in a good freeze.

Virtually no other rock climbing exists in the Northern Fells. One route has been recorded on **Raven Crags (NY 362 308),** to the south of Carrock Fell, but the rock is very loose and continues to fall down without the assistance of climbers, and a climb has been claimed in **Dodd Wood Quarry (NY 240 268)** on Skiddaw.

Above: Sarah Bailey pads daintily up fine crystalline sunny rock on **Slabs Left** (D), Snail Shell Crag. **Photo:** Stephen Reid

Patterdale and Ullswater

This, the major valley of the Eastern Lake District, stretches from Kirkstone Pass to the north end of Ullswater. The A592 Ambleside to Penrith road runs the length of the valley and ensures easy access to the crags. The major side valleys of **Grisedale, Deepdale** and **Dovedale** are described separately. The remaining area boasts one major crag, *Raven Crag* in Threshthwaite Cove, with other limited climbing on esoteric crags in idyllic locations. The crags are described starting at Kirkstone Pass and working northwards up the western flank of the valley before returning southwards down the eastern flank.

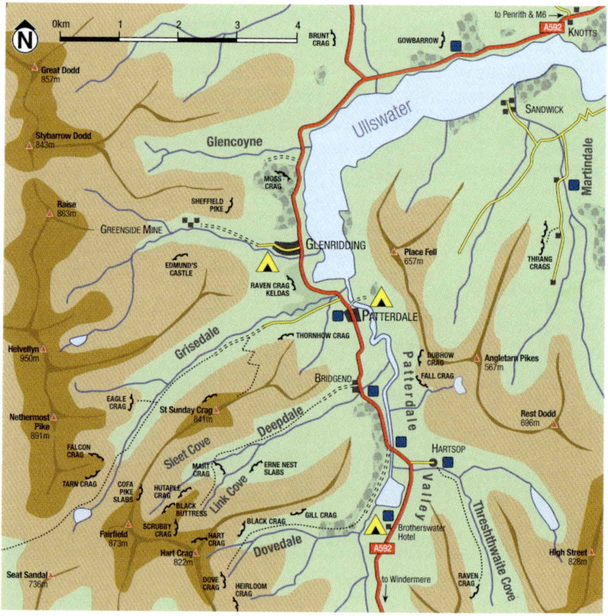

Kirkstone Crag

Grid Reference: **NY 402 090** Altitude: **400m**
Faces: **East** Approach: **3 mins**

Whilst this crag is small and slow to dry, the rock is excellent and its proximity to the road means it is a useful outcrop.

Approach:

From Kirkstone Pass summit, drive north down the pass for a kilometre to a small car park on the left: the crag lies directly above.

The climbs are described from **left** to **right**.

The central feature of the crag is an overhanging grooved arête which is taken by *The Great Game*. To the left of this is a deep corner taken by *Kirkstone Corner*. Ten metres left again is a short groove which is the start of *Miv*.

1 **Miv**	12m	M		1990

Climb the groove exiting to the right. Traverse horizontally right for 3 metres and then climb up to the top via a mossy scoop.

Kirkstone Crag

1	Miv	M
2	Willet, Won't It	MS
3	Mitchell's Route	E1
4	Kirkstone Corner	HS *
5	Legless Pigeon	HVS
6	The Raven	E5 *
v1	Direct Start	
7	The Great Game	E3
8	Red Pit Crack	HVS

Photo: Al Davis

2 **Willet, Won't It**	12m	MS		1990

Good juggy stuff! Start just right of *Miv*.

Climb leftwards up the steep wall to a bulge. Move over this to a ledge. Climb directly up the clean bulging wall above on good holds, just left of the scoop of *Miv*.

3 **Mitchell's Route**	12m	E1		1990

A steep and sustained pitch. Start just left of the left arête of *Kirkstone Corner*.

(5b). Climb the wall on large if occasionally dubious holds (slim tape runners useful) until a series of gymnastic moves gain a good hold over the small overhang. Either make another exciting move up rightwards or pull directly over the roof to easier ground.

4 **Kirkstone Corner**	12m	HS	★	1988

Though often wet, this is a fine little route.

Climb the corner on good holds moving right near the top.

5 **Legless Pigeon**	12m	HVS		1990

An exciting and exposed pitch. Start at the foot of *Kirkstone Corner*.

(5a). Climb diagonally rightwards on pockets to a ledge. Follow a short left-slanting groove and then up to the top.

6 **The Raven**	12m	E5	★	1990

A good sustained route up the blunt arête left of *The Great Game*. Start between *The Great Game* and *Kirkstone Corner* at a very shallow groove which peters out into a wall.

(6b). Climb the groove moving right to a jug. Continue up to an undercling and climb the overhanging wall to easier ground.

v1 ***Direct Start*** E5 1990

(6a). A dangerous start reaching the jug directly (and with the 6b bit still to come).

7 **The Great Game**	12m	E3		1990

(6a). Climb the sustained overhanging groove to a ledge on the left. Continue up the easier groove on the right.

8 **Red Pit Crack**	12m	HVS		1999

Start between *The Great Game* and *Resignation Route*.

(5b). Climb the damp crack to the overhang. Exit this on the left, step back right and climb the groove to the top, passing a large block on the left. Belay well back.

At the right end of the crag is a wide chimney. This is *Patterdale Chimney*.

Resignation Route	12m	HVS		1990

(4c). From the foot of *Patterdale Chimney* climb leftwards into a scoop. Make a hard step left and up to better holds. Continue diagonally leftwards to the top. (Poorly protected on the crux.)

Patterdale Chimney	10m	D		1990

Climb the chimney.

Well to the right of the main crag is a smaller buttress with a prominent cave and some further short routes.

Vulture's Flakes	10m	S		1991

Two metres left of the cave are two layered flakes.

Climb the flakes, wall and crack above.

Crusty Wall	10m	HVS		1990

(5a). From the cave move out left onto a rib and climb the wall.

Vulture's Claws	11m	E1		1991

Start two metres right of *Crusty Wall*.

(5a). Climb the lower thin crack traversing left then up.

Vulture's Crack	12m	VS		1991

(4b). Three metres right of the cave is a left-slanting crack - climb it.

Raven Crag, Keldas

Grid Reference: **NY 387 166** Altitude: **200m**
Faces: **East** Approach: **10 mins**

This limited little crag is close to Glenridding which may increase its appeal.

Approach:

Park in Glenridding and walk south along the road to St. Patrick's Boat Hire. A gate gives access to the fell and the crag is just above. The routes are on a short steep pale wall of excellent rock on the left side of the crag which is relatively clean. They start from the 'earth bergschrund' where a fallen tree created a ledge at the foot of the crag.

The routes are described from **left** to **right**.

Raven Crag Keldas

1 Songs from the Woods E2
2 Eastern Promise E1
3 Stigma HVS

Photo: Al Davis

1 **Songs from the Woods**	16m	E2		1986

Start at the left side of the wall below the obvious crack-line. A long reach is needed on the crux.

(5c). Follow the crack to below the overlap. Surmount this using a small incut on the left, just over the lip and then climb up rightwards to a tree belay.

2 **Eastern Promise**	15m	E1		1986

Start below the obvious wide crack just right of centre.

(5b). Climb the crack and enter the upper wider section with difficulty. Continue with further difficulty and finish up vegetation to a tree belay.

3 **Stigma**	15m	HVS		1986

Start just right of ***Eastern Promise*** at the right edge of the wall.

(5a). Climb the wall and thin crack to gain the right-hand crack above which leads to a wider groove. Finish up this on the right-hand side and then move left to the tree belay.

Two poor routes have been climbed up the repulsive area to the right.

Edmund's Castle

1	West Tower	MS
2	Machicoulis	VD*
3	East Tower	MS
4	Sallyport	D*
5	Ashlar	MVS*

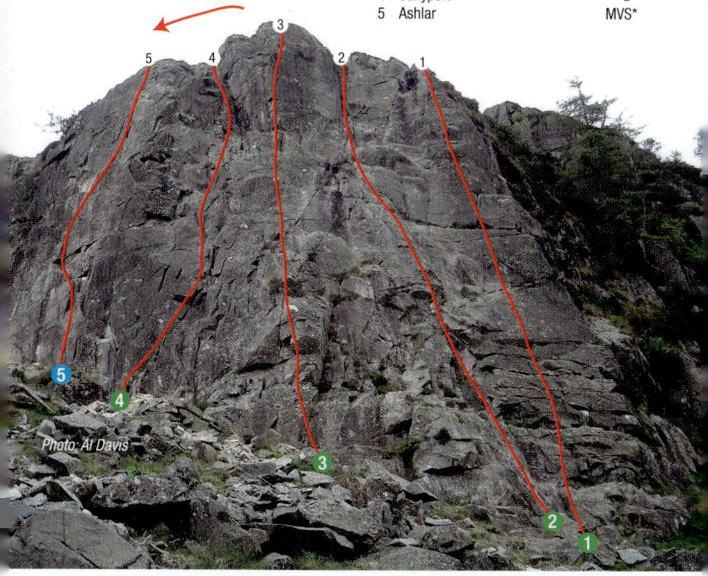

Edmund's Castle

Grid Reference: **NY 365 172**
Faces: **North**
Altitude: **400m**
Approach: **10 mins from Greenside Mine. 45 minutes from Glenridding.**

This small crag is of sound clean rough rock giving satisfyingly incut holds. An excellent beginner's crag though some routes are poorly protected. There are two ancient bolt belays on top.

Approach:

From Greenside Mine, the crag is clearly visible above the corner of the wood on the south side of the beck. Follow the track upstream to a bridge. Cross the beck and return downstream to the wood where a ruined wall leads directly up to the crag. From Glenridding, follow the high path on the south side of the valley to below the crag.

Descend to the left of the crag.

The climbs are described from **right** to **left**.

1 **West Tower**	23m	MS		1975

Start 3 metres right of the central groove.
Climb the buttress directly. An enjoyable pitch.

2 **Machicoulis**	23m	VD	★	1976

Start just right of the lowest point.
Climb the central groove to a ledge and finish up the corner above.

3 **East Tower**	23m	MS		1976

Start at the lowest point of the crag.
Climb the buttress just left of the central groove directly.

4 **Sallyport**	20m	D	★	1976

Start 7 metres left of the lowest point of the crag at a block.
Climb the blocky groove and the obvious corner above.

5 **Ashlar**	18m	MVS	★	1975

Start 11 metres left of the lowest point of the crag below a crack system.
(4b). Climb the central crack direct to the top.

A small crag high on **Sheffield Pike (NY 372 181)** has two routes recorded and the aptly named **Moss Crag (NY 384 184)**, hidden in Glencoyne Wood, has one unattractive climb.

Brunt Crag

Grid Reference: **NY 397 210**
Altitude: **300m**
Faces: **East**
Approach: **2 mins**

This tiny crag, situated only about 100 metres from the A5091 Ullswater to Dockray road, provides an idyllic situation for a pleasant family afternoon near the delightful pools of Aira Force Beck.

Approach:
Park in the roadside quarry. Walk a few metres down the hill to a field gate and go up to the crag behind the trees.

The routes are described from **right** to **left**.

Brunt Crag

1	Jack's Chimbley	VD
2	The Brunt	HVS
3	Picnic Groove	D
4	Drystone Gulch	D

Photo: Al Davis

1 **Jack's Chimbley**	10m	VD		1991

The obvious chimney on the right.

2 **The Brunt**	12m	HVS		1993

Good rough rock with adequate protection. Start 3 metres left of *Jack's Chimbley* at a pedestal.

(5a). Climb up onto a small ledge. Above is a line of flake holds leading up and rightwards across the steep wall. Follow these to reach the horizontal break with difficulty. Continue to the top on better holds.

3 **Picnic Groove**	10m	D		1991

Start at a blunt arête to the left of the chimney passing a block on its right side and finish up the crack.

Working Lunch HVS 1994

(5a). A pointless variation that tackles the overhang avoided by *Picnic Groove*. As the overhang is a detached block it is not recommended.

4 **Drystone Gulch**	10m	D		1991

Start one metre left of *Picnic Groove*.

Climb directly into a scoop then avoid poised blocks by moving right to a crack which leads to the top.

Ullswater

Upper Thrang Crag Page 216
Boredale
Farm Buttress
Roscombe Rigg
Steamer
Lower Thrang Crag Page 214
Martindale
Sandwick
P
Hallin Fell
Gowbarrow
Page 205
P
Howtown
Arthur's Pike
Ullswater Outward Bound School
Ullswater
To Penrith and M6
A592
Pooley Bridge
May 08

Gowbarrow

Grid Reference: **NY 414 205** Altitude: **245m**
Faces: **South-East** Approach: **10 mins**

Properly known as *Yew Crag*, this delightfully situated outcrop comprises three buttresses which stand above the road midway between Pooley Bridge and Patterdale. It has easy access, a sunny aspect and some pleasant routes. The rock requires care in places as there have been a series of rockfalls at the crag.

Approach:

Parking is possible in a small lay-by immediately below the crag. If this is full there are various other lake-side car parks available nearby. A path leads from the road to all three buttresses in turn. The path is in disrepair as its use by walkers has been discouraged by the National Trust due to the rockfalls.

Gowbarrow is a Site of Special Scientific Interest and is subject to a Code of Practice agreed between the National Trust, English Nature and the British Mountaineering Council. This relates to use by groups only; ordinary recreational climbers are not affected.

Gowbarrow

3	The Whistler	MVS	**
8	"It's a Good Job the Vulture's Got Long Wings!"	HVS	
9	Mike's Dilemma	MVS	
10	Gowbarrow Corner	S	
11	Gowbarrow Buttress	VS	
12	Susan	HVS	**
13	Birkett's Direct	E2	

Photo: Al Davis

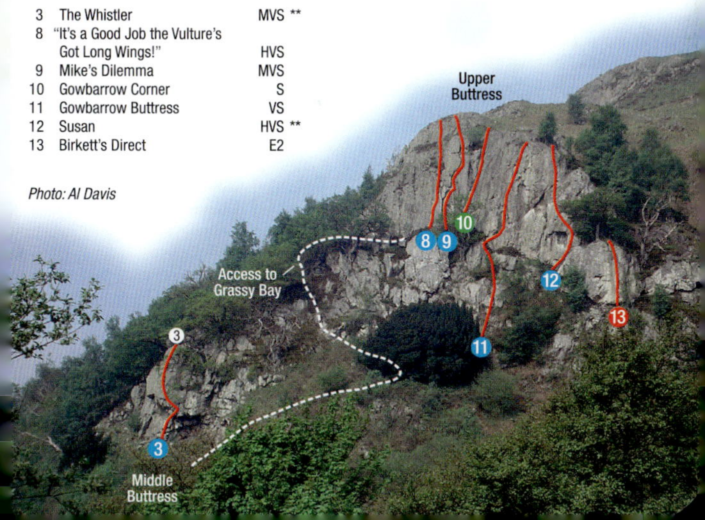

The Code of Practice is that:

1. Group use of the crag is confined to the *Lower Buttress*.
2. All belaying is to be from the bottom of the buttress.
3. Group movement is confined to the immediate area at the bottom of the buttress.
4. A group booking system is operated by Ullswater Outward Bound School to prevent overcrowding. Following rockfall in December 2005, the National Trust strongly recommend leaders of groups arrange an on-site briefing with Ullswater Outward Bound who are willing to share their experience and site specific risk assessments. Phone 017684 85000 (office hours) or 85001 (out of office hours).

Lower Buttress

A small outcrop just one minute from the road. As it is extensively used by groups some of the holds are very polished. There are four belay bolts at the top of the crag. The right side of this buttress has been the scene of large rockfalls in the very recent past. You have been warned!

From right to left the main climbs are as follows but many variations are possible:-

The right-hand groove and arête above (D).
The prominent crack up the middle of the face (D).
The thin crack just left of the prominent crack (VD).
The left-hand face starting at the bottom of the steps. An enjoyable route (VD).
The left overhanging wall climbed up the centre (VS 5a). Easier variations are possible.

Middle Buttress

Middle Buttress is reached by following the path up past the left-hand side of the *Lower Buttress* for about five minutes. Its main feature is a prominent overhang on its left side. This overhang is formed by a huge detached block which appears precariously balanced, though, as it hasn't fallen down yet, it might be mechanically sound – tread carefully.

The routes are described from **right** to **left**.

1 **The Whisperer**	12m	E3		2003

Climbs the overhang and buttress right of *Whistle Away*. There has been a recent rockfall on the right side of this overhang – treat the holds with care.

(6a). Step off the block and move up to the overhang - good thread on *Whistle Away*. Make a long reach right from undercuts then swing out and up to good holds and easier ground.

2 **Whistle Away**	12m	HVS		

(5a). Climb the overhung small cave on the right side of the crag and finish up the crack above.

3 **The Whistler**	24m	MVS	★★	1966

A delightful little route which follows the blunt rib just right of the main overhang. Start at the lowest point of the crag.

(4b). Climb the blunt rib, move right to overcome the overlap (crux) and then trend back left to follow the arête.

4 **The Whinger**	15m	E3		2003

The overhang between *Valicide* and the *Whistler* is more challenging for the vertically challenged. Start 4 metres left of *The Whistler* at a flat ledge.

(5b). Climb up right to the small tree. Climb boldly over the overhang directly above to reach good holds then up to join the last few moves of *The Whistler*.

Gowbarrow Middle Buttress

1	The Whisperer	E3
2	Whistle Away	HVS
3	The Whistler	MVS **
4	The Whinger	E3
5	Valicide	E3
6	Please Release Me	HVS
7	Shamrock Crack	VD

5 **Valicide**	15m	E3		1982

Unprotected. Start just left of *The Whinger* at a groove leading to the left end of the large overhang.

(5c). Climb the groove to the large overhang. Gird your loins and climb boldly over it.

6 **Please Release Me**	20m	HVS-		1998

Start just left of *Valicide* at a short groove. A very unbalanced route with a short bold section.

(4c). Climb the groove to reach the ledge at the foot of *Shamrock Crack*. From here move boldly right across the steep wall on good handholds then up and right to a good ledge. Climb the slab above and finish by an overlap via a short groove on the left.

7 **Shamrock Crack**	24m	VD		

Bridge up a short corner to the right of a detached block and climb the cracks above finishing either left or right.

Dave's Slab	15m	VD		

Climb the right-hand side of the obvious slab on the left of the crag.

Upper Buttress

The *Upper Buttress* is the largest of the three buttresses. The buttress is not popular so some climbs have reverted to their natural state and are not recognisable as rock climbs. In addition, the lower parts of this buttress are heavily overgrown, dirty and off-putting but there is reasonable rock above – honest!

From the right side of *Middle Buttress*, follow a faint track up rightwards to an obvious large yew tree. A stepped path ascends to the left immediately under the crag though it has fallen into disuse following recent rockfalls.

Descent is by the path on the left of the crag.

The routes are described from **left** to **right**.

The first six routes start from the large bay high up on the left-hand side of the crag. They can be reached by following the steps up left under the crag until a short scramble rightwards leads to a grassy bay.

Left: Catherine Kenyon on the blocky holds of **The Whistler** (MVS), Yew Crag, Gowbarrow.
Photo: Ron Kenyon

Some of these routes originally had introductory pitches up the jungle below the grassy bay.

Gruesome Twosome	18m	HVS		1991

Start 2 metres left of the crack of *Mike's Dilemma* below a thin 2 metre long crack. A pointless unprotected pitch.

(5b). Climb a direct line through the crack and bulge above avoiding temptations rightwards.

8 **"It's a good job the Vulture's got Long Wings!"**	20m	HVS		1991

Start one metre left of the crack of *Mike's Dilemma* in the left wall of the bay.

(5a). Climb upwards passing a bush on the right. Take the broken arête above.

9 **Mike's Dilemma**	17m	MVS		1973

(4b). Climb the prominent crack in the left wall of the bay, finishing with an awkward layback.

10 **Gowbarrow Corner**	17m	S		

The grassy corner at the back of the bay.

Snapshot	17m	HVS		1991

(5a). Climb a direct line up the filthy lichen covered wall one metre right of *Gowbarrow Corner*.

Gowbarrow Bastion	20m	HVS		1974

Dirty, unprotected and one to avoid. Start at the large oak at the right end of the grassy bay.

(5a). Climb to a ledge on the left above the oak. Move up right and climb a shallow groove with difficulty.

The next routes can be located from the large yew tree at the foot of the crag.

11 **Gowbarrow Buttress**	40m	VS		

This route was recleaned in 2009, restoring it to its former glory. However it is still rather dirty and there is a very dubious spike guarding entry to the final chimney. It starts behind the large yew at the foot of the steps.

1 22m. Climb the wall just right of a tree to gain a shallow groove which is followed easily to a ledge on the left.

Right: Michael Kenyon on the classic layback section of **Susan** (HVS), Yew Crag, Gowbarrow.
Photo: Ron Kenyon

2 18m (4b). Move up and right, then traverse along a ledge to a wide crack. The crack is hard to start but can be protected by large cams or hexes. Climb more easily past a worrying jammed (hopefully well-jammed) spike to a narrow chimney. This is climbed with interest (or difficulty – according to taste). If the final chimney does not appeal, an escape can be made along the crack system rightwards.

The Thin Blue Line	18m	E1		1984

A rather pointless route with easy climbing leading to a difficult but avoidable finish. Start from the wide crack on pitch 2 of *Gowbarrow Buttress*.

(5b). Climb the crack for 4 metres, step right to a small ledge and up a flake crack to a bulge. Climb this then move left over the top of a chimney onto a steep headwall. Move diagonally left to finish up a groove.

12 **Susan**	24m	HVS	★★	1960

An excellent route providing elegant crack climbing – well worth seeking out. From the yew at the foot of the steps a prominent crooked crack can be seen up on the right. From the yew, go right and scramble up vegetated steps past a silver birch to the foot of the crack.

(5a). Climb the initial bulges to reach and follow the crack. Move left slightly and follow a groove to the top.

Two poor routes **Gravy Booby** (1971) and **Birkett's View** (1960) have disappeared into the undergrowth.

13 **Birkett's Direct**	18m	E2		1978

Start from the shattered ledge at the right side of the crag. The difficulties are short but unprotected. Serious.

(5b). Climb straight up the steep yellow rib.

Girdle Traverse	77m	HVS		1966

A varied and interesting route which climbs mainly above the vegetated lower rock. Above and right of the lowest point of the right-hand side of the buttress is a corner hidden by trees.

1 23m (4b). Climb the corner and twisted crack above to reach a large ledge and oak tree.

2 17m (5a). Traverse left below the rib to the crack of *Susan*. Climb this to below a block then traverse left to the foot of the chimney of *Gowbarrow Buttress*.

3 12m (5a). Move left round the rib and down across the slab to a corner. Climb this moving left at the top.

4 25m (4b). Make an ascending traverse into the corner (*Gowbarrow Corner*), cross it and the wall beyond to finish up the arête on the left.

Bypass 20m HVS 1975

A variation to the *Girdle Traverse*, starting from the top of pitch 1.

2 (5a). Traverse left to ***Susan***, step left and continue traversing the mossy slab to a crack. Climb the crack for 3 metres, move left around a rib and traverse left to an oak, from which you can easily scramble off.

Diagonal Route (1972), a poor right to left girdle, has been mercifully reclaimed by nature.

Arthur's Pike

Grid Reference: **NY 463 217**
Altitude: **350m**
Faces: **North-West**
Approach: **10 mins**

Arthur's Pike (marked on the map as *Long Crag*) stands above the road from Pooley Bridge to Howtown.

Approach:

Leave the road at Thwaite Hill Farm 3 kilometres from Pooley Bridge. The rocks, in three tiers ascending from right to left, are on the hillside behind the farm.

The best climbing is on a tiny slab with a crack on each side which lies on the *Lower Tier*. The climbs are **Left-Hand Crack** (MS), **The Slab** (VS 4b) and **Right-Hand Crack** (HS).

The *Middle Tier* is the home of two historical curiosities which only an archaeologist might want to unearth.

Above: Arthur's Pike, centre, on the east side of Ullswater. **Photo:** Eric Shaw

Thrang Crags

Grid Reference: **NY 431 177** Altitude: **300m**
Faces: **East** Approach: **10 mins to the Lower Crag**

This sadly neglected crag has a lovely setting and gives good steep climbing when clean. The upper crag is currently very dirty and covered in a deep coat of lichen with large mossy areas. The lower crag still has some very worthwhile routes which are clean enough to be enjoyable.

Approach:
The crags are approached from Pooley Bridge at the head of Ullswater by following the road through Howtown to Martindale. The *Upper* and *Lower Crags* are seen on the west side of the valley. Park at the old Martindale Church in the valley bottom and walk south along the road for 200 metres. An obvious small track slants diagonally up to the *Lower Crag*.

Both crags are usually affected by a bird restriction in the nesting season.

Lower Thrang Crag (correctly known as Raven Crag)

This crag gives good climbing only a couple of hundred metres from the road. Unfortunately, the initial pitches are currently cloaked in a dense layer of lichen. It may be best to use the first pitch of *The Lurcher* to gain access to the better climbing above.

Descent is to the left.

The routes are described from **left** to **right**.

1 **Locusts** (HVS, 1977) is truly filthy and best avoided like the plague.

2 **Return of the Natives**	32m	E3		1981

Start at the lowest point at the centre of the crag.
1 16m (5a). Climb the obvious thin crack to the terrace (or better, the first pitch of *The Lurcher*).
2 16m (6a). Climb the short groove and then the overhanging wall right of *The Lurcher*, first leftwards to a pocket, then rightwards to the top.

3 **The Lurcher**	43m	HVS	★	1966

A direct line up the crag which is both steep and well-protected. Very enjoyable. Start at the centre of the crag, 3 metres right of the lowest point.
1 16m (4c). Climb the open groove to a grassy stance and chockstone

Lower Thrang Crag

1	Locusts	HVS
2	Return of the Natives	E3
3	The Lurcher	HVS *
4	Jude the Obscure	E1 *
5	The Dynasts	E2
6	Far from the Madding Crowd	E2 **

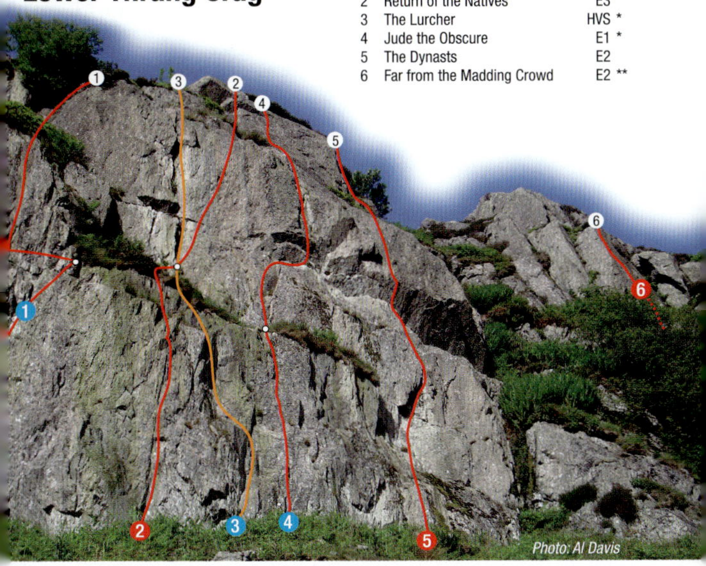

Photo: Al Davis

belay on the left.

2 27m (5a). Climb the steep crack direct and then scramble to the top of the crag.

4 **Jude the Obscure**	40m	E1	★	1977

The main pitch takes the wall to the right of *The Lurcher*.

1 15m (5a). Climb the rib just right of *The Lurcher* (or the first pitch of *The Lurcher*) to a grass terrace.

2 25m (5b). Climb the wall behind the belay and then move right to below the overhang. Pull over this with difficulty and continue up the dirty crack to another grass ledge. Climb the thin crack above, step left and finish over the overhang.

5 **The Dynasts**	40m	E2		1981

A serious and committing lead with sparse protection which climbs the right edge of the buttress. Start at the right-hand end of the crag below a white groove.

(5b). Climb the groove to a ledge below the overhang. Pull straight over the overhang, step up rightwards, then climb the slab and overlap to below the crack in the right-hand edge of the final wall. Climb the crack/groove to the top.

6 Far from the Madding Crowd	37m	E2-	★★	1981

This superb little climb lies on a wall about 15 metres above and to the right of *Lower Thrang Crag*. It is fairly clean and well worth seeking out. The crack is hard to start and sustained thereafter. Start at the foot of a slab.

1 25m (5c). Climb the slab to below a prominent thin crack in the middle of the wall. Follow the crack to a ledge.

2 12m (4c). Pull up the left-hand side of the rib and continue more easily to the top.

Never, and Again	25m	E3		1989

A serious lead with no protection.

(5c). Climb the wall to the right of the crack moving right near the top to a worrying finish.

Upper Thrang Crag (correctly known as Allen Crag)

This is the largest of the crags but unfortunately it has been neglected over the years despite the quality of the climbing. Many of the routes have reverted to their natural state of verdant, vegetated hillside. However, the routes described are still recognisable as rock climbs, though perhaps not clean enough for modern tastes.

Approach:

Follow the track under the *Lower Crag* to where an open gully leads to the *Upper Crag*.

The best **descent** is on the right.

The routes are described from **left** to **right**.

Southern Slab (1969), **Thrang Slab** (1966) and **Thrangstone** (1966) burrow pointlessly up the left-hand side of the crag.

1 Desperate Remedies	40m	E4		1981

This once excellent route takes an obvious slim groove in the steep filthy wall in the centre of the crag. Telescopic arms are an asset.

(6a). Climb directly to a large hanging flake at 6 metres. Climb up the right-hand side of the flake and over the bulge to sloping ledges. Climb the slim groove above to its end at an undercut flake. Pull up to a ledge then follow the obvious hand-traverse line rightwards into a shallow groove. Step right and pull up onto a slab. Easy climbing leads to belays.

Upper Thrang Crag

1	Desperate Remedies	E4
2	Simple Solution	E3
3	Microcosm	E1
4	Vaccination	HVS
5	Stern Test	E5
6	Responsibility	E1
7	Gouttes d'Eau	E3

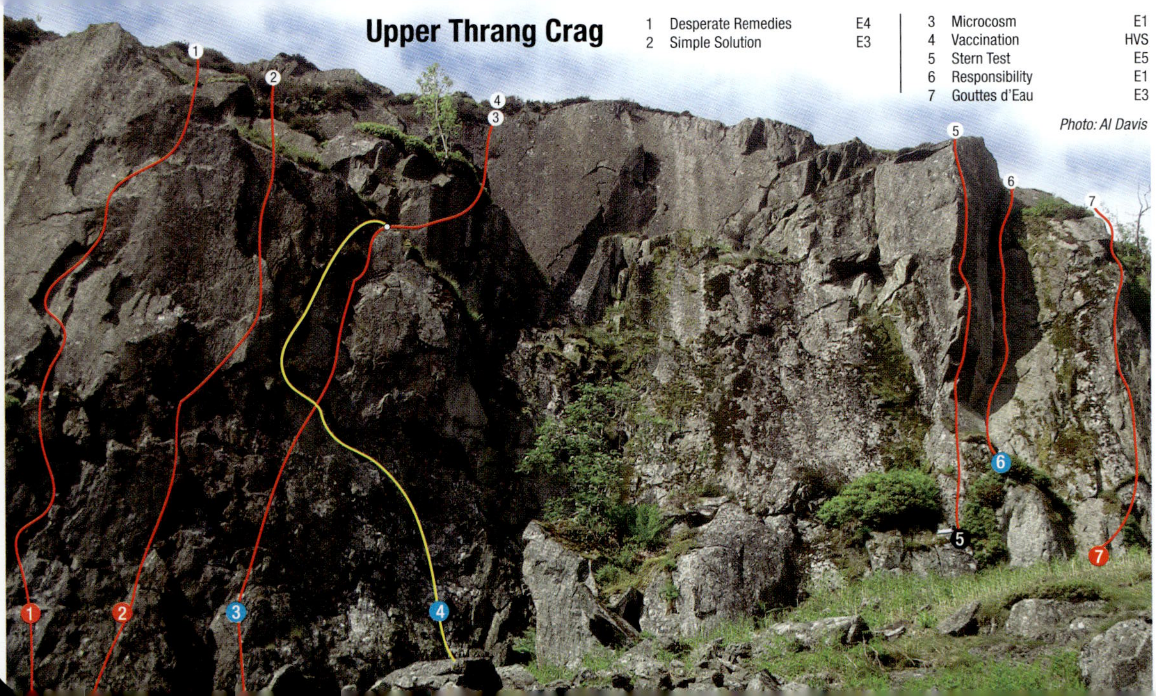

Photo: Al Davis

2 **Simple Solution**	40m	E3		1985

Start at the small stacked pinnacle 2 metres right of *Desperate Remedies*.

(5c). From the top of the pinnacle, climb the wall until forced right then move up and back left to ledges. Climb the short groove to gain a standing position on the shoulder on the left. Follow the diagonal crack to gain the groove above at the large spike. Continue up the groove to the top.

3 **Microcosm**	42m	E1		1966

The first pitch climbs the shallow recess in the impending wall. The first half of the pitch has no protection but the harder climbing above is well-protected. Currently it is very mossy. Start just left of the recess 3 metres right of the stacked pinnacle.

1 27m (5a). Climb the wall to the recess and then the recess itself.

2 15m (4a). Traverse right into a corner and follow it to the top of the crag.

4 **Vaccination**	44m	HVS+		1978

Dirty climbing leads to a bold finish. Start 6 metres right of *Microcosm* behind a large pinnacle.

1 29m (5a). Climb the wall trending left to the bottom of the recess on *Microcosm*. Move up and left into a mossy groove in the wall. Climb this to a rounded finish.

2 15m (4a). As for *Microcosm*.

Tinker, Tailor, Soldier, Spy (1980), **The Mole** (1968), **Big Dick Lustrum** (1981), **Bomber Wall** (1969) and **The Wilderness** (1977) all tackle the *Hanging Gardens* in the centre of the crag. They are best left to the vibrant eco-systems which are more naturally suited to this area of hillside.

5 **Stern Test**	25m	E5		1985

A tremendous route up the impressive prow left of the deep groove of *Responsibility*. The climb is currently filthy and the pegs will now be in a very dubious condition.

(6b). Scramble up to a ledge and large flake beneath the prow. Starting on the left side of the prow, climb up to a peg runner on its right side. A long reach or awkward moves enable the horizontal break and a second peg runner to be reached. Move up to a large foothold just on the left of the arête. A couple of thin moves lead to an overlap then easy climbing to a ledge.

6 **Responsibility**	25m	E1		1973

A fine line up the deep groove at the right end of the crag. Unfortunately it gets very dirty and usually contains a large nest which should not be removed.

(5a). Climb the groove direct.

Night of The Long Knives (E1, 1981) climbs the moss immediately right of *Responsibility*.

7 **Gouttes d'Eau**	25m	E3		1985

This climb takes the arête right of *Night of The Long Knives*.

(5c). Climb the arête on its right-hand side.

Odile (HVS, 1995) climbs the filthy wall right of *Gouttes d'Eau*.

Farm Buttress lies directly behind the farm and about 100 metres beyond the main crags. Access is currently denied by the farmer.

Rampsgill Head

Grid Reference: **NY 443 129** Altitude: **750m**
Faces: **North-West** Approach: **1 hr 30 mins**

A remote buttress in a wild setting tucked just below the summit of Rampsgill Head and overlooking the length of Ramps Gill to Martindale. In autumn, rutting stags in the valley add to the atmosphere.

Rampsgill Head
Broatch's Buttress

1	Alfie	E1 **
2	Ask Jim	VS
3	Validation	VS
4	Conundrum	E1
5	Go Mamasike	MVS

Photo: Steve Broatch

Approach:

From Hartsop follow the path to Hayeswater then take the path towards The Knott. From here the Rampsgill Head crags can be viewed; a prominent buttress can be seen at the far (east) end of the crags – this is *Broatch's Buttress*.

To the east of the buttress is a broad gully which allows **descent** to the base of the crag.

The routes are described from **left** to **right**.

Broatch's Buttress

1 **Alfie**	35m	E1	★★	2008

Start at the lowest point of the buttress beneath a square-cut roof.

(5b). Enter an open groove below the left of the roof and ascend into the open groove on the left. Climb up this to a flake-crack on the left at the top of the groove. Follow the flake-crack up and rightwards to exit on the right whence easier ground leads to the top of the buttress. Alternatively exit the flake-crack direct.

2 **Ask Jim**	35m	VS		2008

Start as for *Alfie*.

(4c). Trend right to below the right end of the square-cut roof. Move up the groove on the right for 2 metres and step right with difficulty onto the higher slab and continue up the left edge of the slab.

3 **Validation**	30m	VS		2008

Start 3 metres right of *Alfie* below a short grass rake left of a small rock pinnacle.

(4c). Climb up to and follow a left-curving open groove above the square cut roof to finish up Alfie.

4 **Conundrum**	30m	E1		2008

Start at the grass rake level with a rowan tree.

(5b). Climb a faint steep rib right of the scoop of *Validation* until the slab is reached. Cross the slab to a large overhanging corner, climb it, and continue up easier ground to the top.

5 **Go Mamasike**	30m	MVS		2008

Scramble 2 metres up the grass rake directly below the large overhanging corner of *Conundrum*.

(4b). Pull up onto the steep slab using hidden holds and ascend to the right-hand end of the lower of two roofs. Continue up the blunt arête to join the top of *Conundrum*.

Widdowson's Buttress

The next buttress to the west has a prominent steep arête. This is best approached by descending the adjoining gully.

Rudd	25m	VS		2008

(4c). Climb the arête.

Place Fell has two optimistically developed crags. **Roscombe Rigg (NY 408 193)** is the incredible shrinking crag on Place Fell, which looks great from a distance in the evening sun but is sadly disappointing on closer acquaintance. The routes do not justify the effort required to reach them. **Durple Crag (NY 399 163)**, a small slate quarry hidden low on the side of Place Fell, is best left hidden.

Dubhow Crag

Grid Reference: **NY 408 147** Altitude: **400m**
Faces: **South-West** Approach: **30 mins**

This crag is situated on the south-west flank of Stony Rigg (itself a north-west outlier of Angletarn Pikes) and overlooks Bridgend. The rocks in the main are broken and juniper infested, but high on the left is a worthwhile buttress identified by a 3 metre high pinnacle at its base with a right-angled corner above and to the right.

Approach:

Follow the Boredale Hause track for 300 metres before striking directly up the fell and contouring rightwards above the broken area. The buttress offers very pleasant climbing in a superb situation with a classic Lakeland panorama. The rock is steeper than it looks but is adorned with incuts and solid spikes and though the crag sprouts heathery ledges these barely affect the climbing.

1 **Goldrill Thrill**	11m	MVS		2007

Start 2 metres left of the pinnacle below a small recess in the wall.
(4b). Climb the steep wall just left of the recess to a ledge. The climbing now deteriorates but continue anyway, up a shallow crack-line to the top.

2 **Trill Groove**	12m	MVS+		2009

Start one metre right of *Goldrill Thrill* below and left of a steep faint groove.
(4b). Step right into the groove and follow it to a ledge. Continue slightly rightwards up the slab to finish right of the small circular scoop.

Dubhow Crag

1	Goldrill Thrill	MVS
2	Trill Groove	MVS
3	Ker-ching	HS
4	Beckstones Buttress	MVS
5	Hobblit	HS
6	Goldrill Grooves	HS
7	Flossy	VS

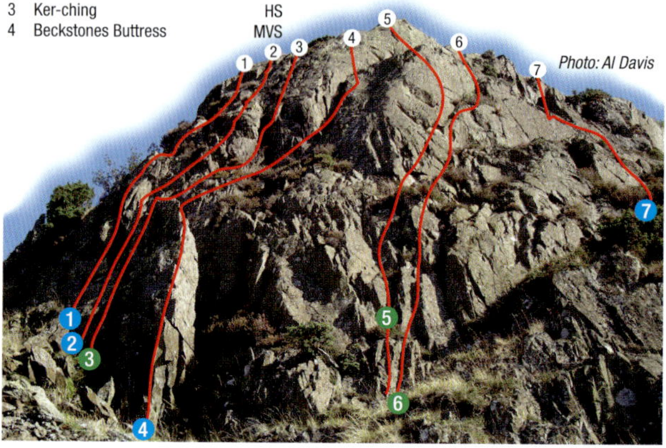

3 **Ker-ching**	13m	HS		2007

Takes the obvious V-groove just left of ***Beckstones Buttress***. Start one metre right of ***Goldrill Thrill*** at the left side of the pinnacle.

Move up the wall utilising the pinnacle. Step right and climb the V-groove then continue up the slab slightly leftwards, to finish above and left of the small circular recess.

4 **Beckstones Buttress**	14m	MVS		2007

Good climbing with a bold finish. Despite its brevity, it feels bizarrely like mountaineering rather than rock climbing. Start at the pinnacle.

(4b). Climb the right arête of the pinnacle to its top. Step across and move up to reach the right-angled corner which is followed to a ledge. Swing left and finish up the wall.

5 **Hobblit**	15m	HS-		2009

Start 3 metres right of the pinnacle below a series of grooves, as for ***Goldrill Grooves***.

Step left and follow a smooth groove to below a steep arête. Step right and gain the tiny holly in the groove from the left. Swing left and climb the upper portion of the arête to reach a ledge. Finish up cracks just right of the nose.

6 **Goldrill Grooves**	14m	HS		2007

Start 3 metres right of the pinnacle, below a series of grooves.

Climb the grooves to a ledge below a steep wall. Gain the groove above containing a tiny holly from the right. Move up the groove and finish up a scooped wall above and slightly right.

7 **Flossy**	12m	VS		2007

One for the connoisseur of the esoteric. A climb with unsuspected difficulty and an exciting finish. Start 7 metres right of *Goldrill Grooves* on a grass terrace at a stance with a juniper belay below an easy-angled mossy scoop.

(4b). Move up the scoop for one metre then step left and climb the slab to a ledge. Move right and climb up to the base of an impending corner defining the right end of the headwall. Bridge up to reach good holds on the clean overhanging wall on the left.

Thirty metres to the right along a goat track is a rib rising through the greenery.

Old Bones Rib	20m	S-		2007

Start 3 metres up and left of the toe of the rib.

Move rightwards onto the rib by utilizing the hollow flakes and continue to large spikes below the rib proper. Climb the rib keeping slightly to the left to reach a ledge. Step right and climb the upper rib via scoops.

Caterpillar Ridge	30m	S		2010

Follows a short ridge some distance below and to the right of the rest of the routes. It's the obvious pillar of continuous rock visible on the walk in. Approach by a traverse from the left, following a sheep track starting by a large tree. Start at the first unbroken rocks, just left of the foot of the ridge.

A tricky start is followed by easier climbing above. The angle eases after about 30m and the ridge becomes more broken - either walk off over loose ground to the right, or scramble to the top.

Directly below *Dubhow Crag* and just above the track lies a tiny brown-coloured **Coffee Slab**. The dark colouring is due to the scummy layer of grease fed by the water course affecting its five pointless routes.

Fall Crag

Grid Reference: **NY 409 142** Altitude: **330m**
Faces: **West** Approach: **20 mins**

A small crag found on the left of the beck which drains Angle Tarn. It is a pleasant place to while away a summer's evening.

Approach:

Park at Cow Bridge (NY 403133) and walk towards Hartsop. Immediately after the turn off for Hartsop, a tarmac road leads north. Walk to the end of the track (300m), through a gate and on to the fell. Cross Angle Tarn Beck and *Fall Crag* is visible as the most prominent outcrop of rock 300 metres up the hillside. The routes start from a terrace above a small crag.

1 **Lost Left Sock**	17m	S		1994

Start at the green corner on the left of the prominent slab.

Climb the corner direct, step left at the top and climb direct above to easier ground.

2 **Broken Jinx**	17m	VS		1994

Start 2m right of *Lost Left Sock*.

(4c). Climb the right-hand edge of the slab. Step left at the top of the slab and climb the steep central groove directly above to easier ground and a belay.

3 **Dobby's Sock**	15m	E2		2003

Takes the obvious groove on the right of the crag.

(5b). Climb the groove to the large overhang. Step right and move up the wall.

Fall Crag

1 Lost Left Sock S
2 Broken Jinx VS
3 Dobby's Sock E2

Photo: Al Davis

Raven Crag, Threshthwaite Cove

Grid Reference: **NY 419 112** Altitude: **450m**
Faces: **South-East** Approach: **45 mins**

This excellent crag, situated in the lower part of Threshthwaite Cove, is one of the best crags in the Lake District for the climber operating at E3 and above. It has more stars than a night at the Oscars; but these have not been scattered too liberally, all the routes really are that good!

The rock on the main area of the crag is solid and compact lending itself to tremendous climbing on edges and thin cracks. Where protection exists it is generally bomb-proof!

The upper section of the crag is dominated by the huge ***Shield*** which offers exposed and technical climbing on perfect rock. The lower section gives some tremendous wall and crack climbing with its upper tier bounded by prominent grooves which are deceptively steep. Most of the belays are spikes set well back from the crag.

Approach:

The best approach is from the Patterdale to Kirkstone road turning off at the small hamlet of Hartsop. Continue through Hartsop to a large parking area at the end of the road. An easy and pleasant three-quarter of an hour's walk follows Pasture Beck up the valley. As you leave the parking area, turn right. Follow the track over the bridge and through the gate. The track bears left and initially follows the wall, eventually bending to the right into the valley proper. From here, the crag can be seen on the right, slanting diagonally up the hillside.

The best **descent** is on the right or more sensibly use the abseil point in the centre of the crag directly above the excellent clean corner of *Boy Racer*.

The climbs are described from **left** to **right**.

There is likely to be a bird restriction on these crags between 1st May and 31st June. Please consult the FRCC website for details.

Two routes to the left of the main crag have been omitted from the guide on account of large rock falls in this area in the past.

1
2
3
4
5
6
7
8
9
10
11
12

Raven Crag

Threshthwaite Cove

1	Baby Driver	E3 *
2	Grand Prix	E3 ***
3	Road Rage	E7 ***
4	Internal Combustion	E6 ***
5	Top Gear	E4 ***
6	Overdrive	E4 *
7	Cabriolet	E5 *
8	Redex	E2 **
9	G.T.X.	E3 ***
10	Running On Empty	E4 ***
11	Lady Driver	E5 **
12	Dipstick	E4 *
13	Boy Racer	E4 ***
14	Liquid Engineering	E6 ***
15	Liquid Wall	E8 **
16	High Performance	E5 ***
17	Silverstone	E4
18	Chicane	E3

Photo: Steve Crowe

1 **Baby Driver**	38m	E3	★	1985

A bold climb at the far left-hand side of the crag. Not one of the best but worthwhile.

(5c). Six metres left of *Grand Prix* is an obvious grassy groove. Climb this to a sloping ledge below the horizontal break beneath the right end of a blocky overhang. Climb to the right of the overhang past a peg on the left beneath the pink wall. Move up and right across the wall using faint flakes to join *Grand Prix*. Tricky climbing up and left leads eventually to an undercling and then on to the top. Belay 9 metres up on the left.

2 **Grand Prix**	40m	E3	★★★	1980

A great climb up the left side of the *Shield*. Start up the left hand of two grooves directly below the left side of the *Shield*.

(5c). Climb the corner to a ledge below the overhang at the break. Move right slightly and climb the overhang (good protection here) to the leftward-slanting ramp which is followed to a short groove. Race up this, and finish up the obvious crack system.

3 **Road Rage**	40m	E7	★★★	1995

Try to stay calm! An exciting route up the left of the *Shield* with some bold thin climbing. Start as for *Grand Prix*.

(6b). Climb *Grand Prix* as far as the leftward-slanting ramp: arrange good gear here. Step right onto the *Shield* underneath a small overlap. Move right to a good flake then make hard committing moves up the wall on poor holds to a flat hand ledge. Peg on left - first gear since *Grand Prix*! Continue directly up until the headwall is reached left of the finish of *Top Gear*. Step up and right onto a ledge (peg) before finishing directly up the crack.

4 **Internal Combustion**	40m	E6	★★★	1986

An excellent climb up the middle of the *Shield*. Bold to start then technically very demanding and finger testing. High octane fuel recommended.

1 8m (5a). Climb the groove a few metres right of *Grand Prix* to the break.
2 32m (6b). Make committing moves over the first overlap to reach a peg on the right. Surmount the next overlap by pulling leftwards towards the crack before stepping back right above the peg. Climb the wall to a short diagonal crack and follow this to cross *Top Gear*. Climb the wall and cracks above to a small overhang (peg up and right). Step left to clip another peg on the left, then climb straight up – hard but well-protected. Finish up the slab and corner above.

Right: Ged Desforges getting into **Top Gear** (E4) as he moves across the Shield, a major feature of Raven Crag, Thresthwaite Cove. **Photo:** Rob Fielding

5 **Top Gear**	40m	E4	★★★	1981

Top Route! A superb bold climb taking a diagonal line across the *Shield*. Start below the middle of the *Shield* between the groove of *Grand Prix* and the crack of *Redex*.

(6a). Climb the wall, crack and groove to reach ledges below the right edge of the *Shield*. Move right and climb a short flake-crack until a pull up left can be made into a steep groove. Swing left to gain a large sloping foothold on the bottom right-hand edge of the *Shield*. Move up on good holds to reach the obvious line of holds which trend leftwards across the *Shield* until a vague groove is reached. Follow this then step right and mantelshelf onto the large sloping ramp. Step right and climb the short corner to the top.

6 **Overdrive**	35m	E4	★	1981

A great committing climb taking the prominent groove on the right-hand side of the *Shield* and left of *G.T.X.*

1 13m (4c). Follow *Top Gear* to the ledge at the right-hand side of the Shield.

2 22m (6a). Follow *Top Gear* up the flake-crack into the groove. Continue up rightwards to the roof and make a hard pull over using a large sloping hold on the lip. Continue up the groove above to the top.

7 **Cabriolet**	40m	E5	★	1985

A challenging climb which follows the rightward-slanting crack just above and parallel to the crack of *Redex* and which terminates at the large obvious roof between the upper grooves of *G.T.X.* and *Redex*.

1 25m (5b). Follow the crack rightwards, crossing the horizontal fault, until a step right can be made at the tree. Belay on the right.

2 15m (6b). Climb up to gain a good handhold on the large flake beneath the roof. Use the large undercling right of the flake to initiate difficult and puzzling moves across left and round the lip of the roof to gain the ledges above. Climb straight up the rib above and move left at the top to a crack. Nut belays and two spikes up and right.

8 **Redex**	30m	E2	★★	1976

This classic line, taking the prominent diagonal crack sweeping from left to right across the centre of the crag, gives fine sustained climbing.

1 13m (5b). Climb the diagonal crack to the horizontal fault.

2 17m (5c). Follow the crack to the small tree. Step right into the steep groove and follow this to the top.

Right: Wes Hunter on **G.T.X.** (E3), Raven Crag, Threshthwaite Cove. **Photo:** Nick Wharton

9 **G.T.X.**	40m	E3	★★★	1980

An impressive and sustained route taking a direct line through *Redex*. Start 5 metres right of *Redex* at a shallow groove.

(5c). Climb the groove rightwards to the scoop, step left and climb steeply to the horizontal fault. Follow *Redex* to the small tree and then climb left and up to the overhang. Pull over this into the groove and up to a second overhang. Climb this on the right and up to finish.

10 **Running on Empty**	35m	E4	★★★	1981

You may well be by the time you reach the top! Excellent climbing taking the stepped groove right of *G.T.X.* and the wall and groove right of the final groove of *Redex*. Start at the left end of the easy grassy ramp below a large overhang at half-height. Small wires will be found useful.

(6a). Climb the groove (quite bold) heading for the right end of the large overhang where a large spike will be found. Use this to swing right with a committing move onto the wall above, which is climbed delicately to a large groove right of *Redex*. Follow the groove to the top with an awkward finish.

11 **Lady Driver**	35m	E5	★★	2009

A dangerous and unpredictable route clumsily parked between *Running on Empty* and *Boy Racer*. Start at the foot of the grassy ramp.

1 5m. Climb onto the grassy ramp and belay at a peg halfway along.

2 30m (6a). Climb up to the roof and go straight over just right of the elder tree into the moon-shaped groove. Try not to get flustered as technical climbing leads to a good hold at the top, reach up and right to another good hold then straight up to the break. Rattle up the twisting groove above totally oblivious to what is going on behind you! Could be done in one pitch, if you don't get lost that is.

12 **Dipstick**	40m	E4	★	1986

The main substance of this route is provided by the rightward-facing corner/groove at the upper left-hand end of the gangway. Start at the foot of the arch near the base of the crag on its left-hand side at a grass rake.

1 21m (5b). Follow the grass rake rightwards to its end. Climb back up and left along a short steep left-slanting ramp/groove to the first quartzy crack. Follow this out right to the large gangway beneath the upper groove.

2 19m (6a). Climb the corner/groove to a good flake. Move up and left to a small foothold on the arête whence a long reach off a sloping handhold enables two knobbles to be gained in the vague upper

Left: Mark Johnston **Running on Empty** (E4), Raven Crag, Threshthwaite Cove.
Photo: Nick Wharton

groove. The large jug above is followed by easier climbing to a short sloping ledge which is hand traversed to its right-hand end. Continue straight up to finish.

13 **Boy Racer**	37m	E4	★★★	1981

A great climb starting at the right-hand side of the arch down and right of the easy ramp.

(6a). Hoon up the right-hand side of the arch and make a tough move into a slim groove on the right. Follow this boldly to a good ledge and up the ramp to the break, down and right of a raven's nest (possible belay but better to continue). Climb the short left-slanting ramp/groove past the first quartzy crack of ***Dipstick*** then make a thin move to reach the next crack and so into the groove. Climb the groove and rib on the left up to the break. Excellent climbing into and up the groove above leads to the top.

14 **Liquid Engineering**	38m	E6	★★★	1984

A magnificent climb requiring a well-oiled performance. Sustained, steep and sparsely protected with a most deceptive and serious top pitch. Start at the vague white scoop a few metres down from the arch.

Above: Rob Fielding pulling smoothly through the crux of **Liquid Engineering** (E6), Raven Crag, Threshwaite Cove. **Photo:** Ged Desforges

1 24m (6b). Climb into the scoop and head up and leftwards until above a peg (wires). Step down left to clip the peg. Alternatively, from the scoop, move across left and up on layaways to the peg. Climb back up until above the peg and tentatively move left across the blank slab to a good sidehold. Climb the wall above to a diagonal crack then more easily to a ledge. Step right to a scoop and follow the slab to belay at the large block.

2 14m (6b). Move up the ramp for 2 metres to below a large bottomless groove. Pull into the groove (tape runner) to some good footholds. Climb up the groove making some very technical moves (may be easier for the tall) and then continue with a little more ease to the top. Spike belays well back.

15 **Liquid Wall**	25m	E8	★★	2004

The bulging wall between *Liquid Engineering* and *High Performance* requires a fluid ascent if success is to be achieved.

(6c). Start up *Liquid Engineering* and climb to the good holds (and a Rock 2 and 1) up and right of the peg. From the jugs, undercut upwards to an obvious edge and snatch back left on small crimps and slopers to the left of the obvious bulge. Continue more easily past a Friend 00.

16 **High Performance**	40m	E5	★★★	1981

A tremendous climb aptly named and giving very varied climbing. Start as for *Liquid Engineering* below the vague white scoop in the lower wall.

1 25m (6b). Climb into the scoop and then up to a thin diagonal crack. Follow this until it is possible to move up to the large slot which forms the start of the thin crack and which is followed up the wall above. Continue with ease to a horizontal break and large block belay.

2 15m (6a). Climb into the large groove above the belay. Move across right to a good jug on the arête and then step back left into the groove which is followed to the ledge above the capping roof. Finish up the wall above. Belay well back to the left on spikes.

17 **Silverstone**	40m	E4		1985

A fair climb with a poor bottom pitch but a very good and technical top pitch just right of the top groove of *High Performance*.

1 22m (5b). Climb the faint groove just right of *High Performance* on good holds to the spike at its top. Move right and then up the short diagonal groove to the horizontal fault. The largest scoop in the slab above leads to the belay below a white groove: good thread up and right.

2 18m (6b). Make an awkward move onto the sloping ledge and so gain the white groove right of *High Performance*, which is climbed to a good ledge at two thirds height. Continue up the groove with a hard move right at the top to finish. Belay well back on spikes.

18 **Chicane**	40m	E3		1985

A good route taking the most right-hand fault on the crag. Start at the white groove immediately left of the descent path at the right-hand side of the crag.

1 25m (5c). Climb the groove which curves left at the top to a ledge. Follow the cracks diagonally rightwards to a sloping grass ledge. Continue straight up the slab via the faint groove directly above and belay beneath the groove immediately left of the right arête.

2 15m (6a). Move up to a thread left of the groove. Traverse right on the obvious fault and move up to a large flat hold in the groove. A desperate move off this leads to a niche. Climb the crack on the left to a large ledge. From the higher ledge on the right one move leads to a pleasant slab and the top.

A Lap of Honour	90m	E4	★★	1981

A high level girdle from right to left following a natural traverse line. It gives some excellent and sustained climbing crossing some very exposed areas of rock. Start on a ledge at the right-hand end of the crag level with the top break.

1 23m. A pleasant stroll along the ledges.

2 23m (6a). Follow the break, crossing *Boy Racer*, to reach *Running on Empty*. Climb down this a couple of metres then cross the slab on the left to belay at the tree on *Redex*.

3 30m (6a). Climb up left to beneath the roof of *G.T.X.* Continue leftwards into *Overdrive* beneath its roof and, using poor holds, swing onto the *Shield*. Descend to a junction with *Top Gear* and follow it across the wall, continuing into *Grand Prix*. Nut belays and poor stance.

4 14m (5c). Climb up and traverse the wall on the left to finish.

Echo (VS, 1964), which takes the lower of the horizontal fault lines, is of historical interest only.

Right: Mike Norbury getting revved up on **Boy Racer** (E4), Raven Crag, Thresthwaite Cove.
Photo: Nick Wharton

Grisedale

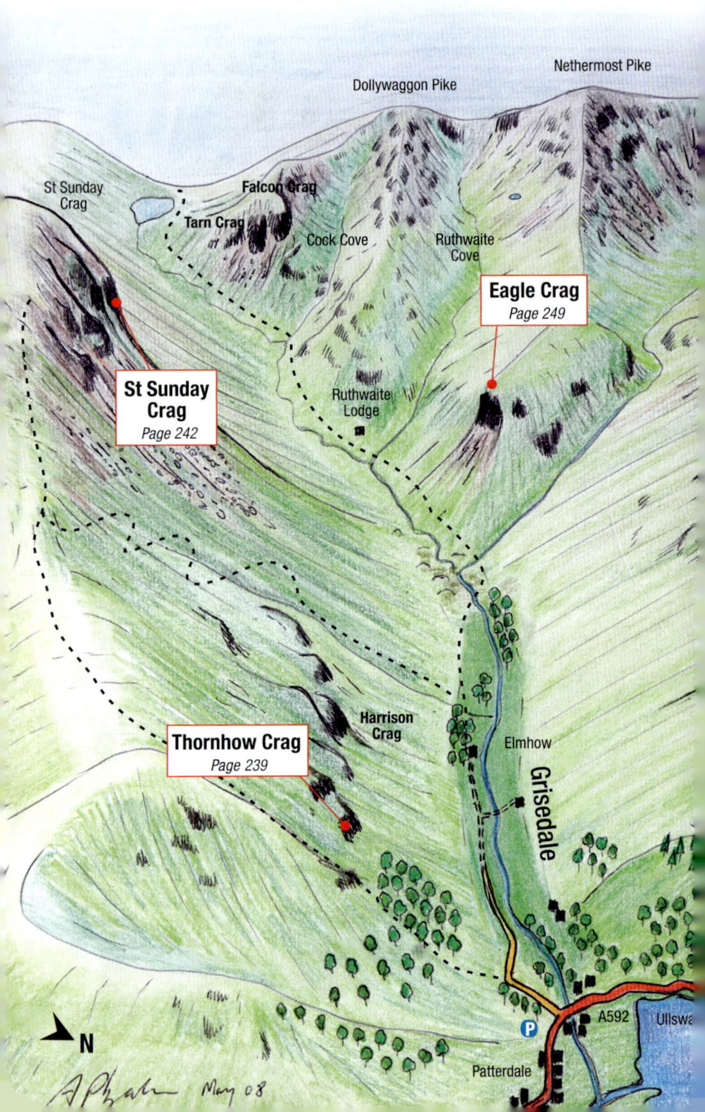

Nethermost Pike
Dollywaggon Pike
St Sunday Crag
Falcon Crag
Tarn Crag
Cock Cove
Ruthwaite Cove
Eagle Crag
Page 249
St Sunday Crag
Page 242
Ruthwaite Lodge
Harrison Crag
Thornhow Crag
Page 239
Elmhow
Grisedale
A592
Ullswa
P
Patterdale
N
May 08

Grisedale

Grisedale descends north-east from Grisedale Tarn to the Ullswater valley at Patterdale. It is about 6 kilometres long and contains one major climbing ground, *Eagle Crag*. The crags are listed clockwise around the valley.

Thornhow Crag

Grid Reference: **NY 382 154** Altitude: **260m**
Faces: **North-West** Approach: **30 mins**

This small crag lies low on the hillside directly above the point where the road to Braesteads Farm meets the main valley road. The routes described give pleasant climbing. As the crag is popular with groups, the routes are rather polished, though this doesn't spoil the climbing. The top of the crag has been equipped with seven bolt belays.

Approach:
It is best approached past Thornhow Barn (the first building after passing through the gate at the start of the level part of the valley). Follow a track to a gate in the intake wall and then follow the wall to below the crag.
There is no parking in the valley and cars should be left in Patterdale. A mountain bike can be used until directly below the crag which makes the approach much shorter and is highly recommended.

Descend to the right.

The routes are described from **left** to **right**, with reference to the large ash tree at the foot of the crag.

Two poorly protected routes (**Thornhow Wall**, MVS, 1986 and **The Groove**, S, 1986) have been climbed on a short filthy slab facing east on the left side of the buttress.

1 **Keep Left of the Crack!**	24m	VS		1991

A contrived pitch which offers pleasant climbing. A few metres left of the ash tree is a prominent crack. Start just left of this.
(4c). Climb the rock to the left of the crack.

Thornhow Crag

1 Keep Left of the Crack! VS
2 Kneewrecker Wall S *
3 Kneewrecker Direct S *
4 Gossamer VS

Photos: Al Davis

2 **Kneewrecker Wall**	27m	S	★	1965

Climb up behind the ash and move left above a large recess to reach a crack. The crack is followed to a small ledge. Traverse left and up to the large ledge (serious - poorly protected). Bolt belays.

3 **Kneewrecker Direct**	24m	S	★	1966

From the ash, climb directly to a small niche and then up the arête to a ledge. Move right and up a crack to the large ledge and bolt belays.

4 **Gossamer**	24m	VS		1966

Start on small ledges 3 metres right of the ash.

(4c). Delicately climb the faint cracks in the slab just right of *Kneewrecker Direct* to a ledge. Continue straight up to a large ledge.

Sundown Slab	20m	D		1961

Start 6 metres right of the ash.

Follow the obvious crack in the slab. Harder variations are possible.

Above: Al Davis in golden sunlight on **Kneewrecker Direct** (S), Thornhow Crag.
Photo: Ron Kenyon

A number of well-polished lines are obvious to the right for those who need more.

Above and to the left lies a rather broken buttress. **Grisedale Slabs** (43m, D, 1964) makes the best of the slabs on the right side of the crag. **Gambol Rib** (47m, S, 1964) starts at a flake at the lowest point of the crag and tries to find rock up the ridge above.

Harrison Crag (NY 381 151) is the line of outcrops lying some way above Thornhow Crag. **Elm How Crag** (NY 377 149) is the last outcrop on the right of the small crags not quite overlooking Elmhow Farm. Routes were dug out in the dark ages. Thankfully, we climb in more enlightened times.

Bouldering in Grisedale in 1896

"After lunch we walked down Grisedale together and when passing a rock we used to call Elephant Rock, near Elm How, Haskett Smith showed us what he could do with a running start and maintained his momentum to the top."

Horace Westmorland recalls, when aged 10, seeing the founding father of British rock climbing pre-empt Johnny Dawes by a century, ***The Ullswater Fells Round the Turn of the Century***, FRCC Journal 1945

St Sunday Crag

Grid Reference: **NY 368 137** Altitude: **650m**
Faces: **North-West** Approach: **1hr 45 mins**

High on the north-west slopes of St Sunday Crag a long line of broken crags face towards Helvellyn. The layout of the crags is complex but the gullies (which are only worth climbing in winter) give useful landmarks. Using the usual approach, ***East Chockstone Gully*** is the first reached. It is easily identified because a massive boulder lies in the scree well below it. To the right of this gully are some conspicuously striped light rocks called the ***Tiger-Banded Rocks***. ***Pillar Gully*** lies about 150 metres to the right of ***East Chockstone Gully***. It is separated from the obvious ***Y Gully*** to its right by the ***Pillar*** which is an almost detached buttress. Just to the right of this and set further back up the hillside is the ***Great Nose*** which is defined by the two branches of ***Y Gully***. The limit of the crag on the right is marked by ***West Chockstone Gully*** which lies 75 metres right of ***Y Gully***.

The crags appear insignificant from the valley floor but there is a lot of climbing here in the lower grades on generally sound and surprisingly clean rock.

Approach:

The best overall view of the crags is gained by an approach from directly below but this involves a steep grind up scree-covered slopes. The easiest and more usual approach is to turn left at the end of the plantation beyond Elmhow and take the path which zig-zags up the hillside to a grassy shelf. From here a path traverses right to below the crags. It is also feasible to approach the crag from Dunmail Raise via Grisedale Tarn.

The best **descent** for the routes on the *Pillar* is to traverse left into *Pillar Gully*. For the *Nose Direct* and all the routes to the right the best **descent** is down the right branch of *Y Gully*.

The routes are described from **left** to **right**.

St Sunday Crag Overview

1 **Blade Buttress**	14m	HS		2006

A small pear-shaped buttress riven by cracks lies 25 metres left of the start of *Pinnacle Ridge*. Start at the toe of the buttress.

(4b). Climb the awkward crack over a small bulge to reach a block. Step left and follow the *Blade* boldly to gain the top of the buttress. Scramble up for 20 metres then descend the gully on the right.

2 **Pinnacle Ridge**	185m	M	★★	1955

This is the serrated ridge about 150 metres left of *East Chockstone Gully*. *The Pinnacle* is not easily seen from below but the ridge is a well worn scramble and the route is obvious. Many variations are possible.

The following routes are located just left of *East Chockstone Gully*. A reference point is the slab with two prominent cracks 30 metres left of the gully. This is where *Slab Route* is located and this area provides some very enjoyable climbing on excellent rock

3 **Sine Nomine**	14m	VS		2006

The prominent rib 30 metres left of *Slab Route* identified by a perched flake at half-height and a short impending striated wall at its base. Start below the striated wall.

(4b). Climb the wall to a ledge. Continue up the arête past the perched flake and a shallow groove to finally pull over the slight nose to finish.

4 **Santiago**	35m	S		2006

Start 3 metres left of *Slab Route* at the left-hand crack in the slab.

Gain the crack delicately from the right and follow it to a ledge. Trend leftwards up slabby walls to finish up a blunt rib.

Descend down grassy ledges to the right (looking-out) eventually reaching a small gully which is descended.

5 **Sensor Slab**	7m	HVS		2006

The slab immediately left of *Slab Route* gives a delicate though pointless pitch. Start one metre left of *Slab Route*.

(5b). Climb the slab just right of the faint vein on tiny chickenheads and reach the first break. Move up to finish by utilising undercut flakes.

6 **Slab Route**	32m	VD	★	1954

A pleasant route with good protection and on good rock. Start 20 metres left of *East Chockstone Gully* at a slab with two prominent cracks.

Climb the right-hand crack and continue up a wall and groove.

St Sunday Crag

1	Blade Buttress	HS	
2	Pinnacle Ridge	M	**
3	Sine Nomine	VS	
4	Santiago	S	
5	Sensor Slab	HVS	
6	Slab Route	VD	*
7	Slab Route Continuation	VD	
8	La Haye Sante	VS	
9	Sable Wall	VD	
10	Ocelot	MVS	
11	Dimanche	VD	
12	Pillar Front	VS	
13	The Nose Direct	S	*
14	Three Tier Climb	VD	

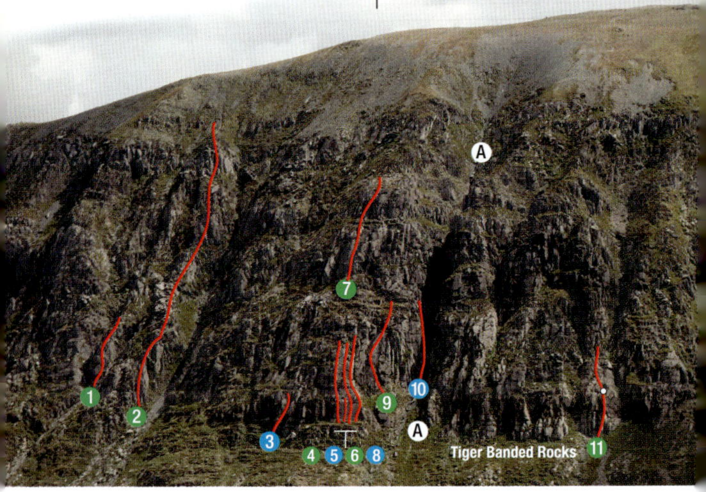

7 **Slab Route Continuation**	43m	VD		1956

Start well above the finish of *Slab Route* at the next steep rocks.

Ascend the wall then a short crack over a bulge. Climb the groove above then move up the face on the left. Scramble up rightwards to the next buttress and climb this.

8 **La Haye Sainte**	35m	VS		2006

Good climbing up the slab, rib and buttress just right of *Slab Route*. Start 2 metres right of that route at a block.

(4c). Step off the block and climb the slab somewhat gingerly. Continue up the rib to a ledge below the final impressive buttress. Ascend a series of flakes on the right side of the buttress to the top.

9 **Sable Wall**	47m	VD		1958

This climb takes the mossy slabs to the left of *East Chockstone Gully* and is a poor, very vegetated route. Start at the bottom right of the slabs (but don't say you weren't warned).

A East Chockstone Gully
B Pillar Gully
C Y Gully
D West Chockstone Gully
E Far West Gully
P The Pinnacle

Photo: Eric Shaw

1 20m. Ascend diagonally left across the slabs towards a corner-crack. Climb an indefinite crack 2 metres right of the corner and belay at its top.

2 27m. Move back right and climb the face crack until it lies back into a grassy corner beneath an overhang. Turn the overhang on the right and continue up a break to a grassy terrace.

10 **Ocelot**	42m	MVS		1982

The left arête of *East Chockstone Gully*. Fine positions, sparse protection and a little dubious rock make for an interesting climb.

(4b). Follow the arête throughout with deviations left onto the slabs for small wires.

Chockstone Gully Rib	74m	VD		1956

A continuation to *Sable Wall* or *Ocelot* taking the buttress left of the upper part of *East Chockstone Gully*. Start at the foot of a 7 metre groove immediately above the right side of a deep cave in the left wall of the gully.

From the top of *Sable Wall* make a rightward traverse leading into the gully over the roof of the cave. Superb positions on the first pitch.

1 **27m.** Climb the groove to small ledges. Step right across the exposed nose and climb up to a grassy terrace.

2 **30m.** Ascend broken rocks to the left of an overhang. Climb the crack and continue to a wide grass terrace.

3 **17m.** Climb the slabby face of the buttress just left of a small overhang to a perched block.

11 **Dimanche**	44m	VD		1956

This route lies between *East Chockstone Gully* and *Pillar Gully* at the right end of the *Tiger-Banded Rocks*. A miniature gully just to the right leads up to a gap in the ridge. The start is at the foot of a broken rib.

1 **20m.** Climb up to a bollard beneath a wall.

2 **24m.** Surmount the bulge by the slanting weakness on the left and ascend the triangular slab.

Two poor routes have been made in *Pillar Gully* which runs up to the left of the *Pillar*. **Sontag** (30m, D, 1956) takes the easiest line up the second rock step on the left of the gully. **Tumbledown Grooves** (35m, VD, 1958) climbs the right wall of the gully starting 7 metres below the first waterslide. It starts at a corner and then takes the grassy right-hand groove.

12 **Pillar Front**	52m	VS		1954

This climb takes the right-hand ridge of the *Pillar* as seen from directly beneath. Pleasant scrambling leads to a steep finish. Originally graded Mild Severe, despite, or perhaps because of, being climbed in tricounis and the rain. Rather loose and dirty in places.

1 **35m.** Climb the ridge immediately left of *Y Gully* to a ledge beneath a steep little tower.

2 **17m.** (4c). Climb the face 3 metres left of the corner surmounting some small overhangs. Continue more easily up the arête.

Pillar Direct	32m	S	★	1956

A steep route. Start in *Y Gully* at a corner 12 metres below the chockstones barring the left branch.

Climb the rib on the left taking care with some dubious rock and then surmount the inverted V-overhang in the headwall.

Domingo	30m	S		1956

This climb starts 3 metres left of the chockstones barring the left branch of *Y Gully*.

Climb a bulge and a scoop then move right to a grass-filled groove. Finish direct up a steep tower.

13 **The Nose Direct**	58m	S	★	1958

A good route up the arête overlooking the left branch of *Y Gully*. It has an exposed and committing crux. Start at the foot of the *Great Nose* defined by the two branches of *Y Gully*.

1 **20m.** Follow the line of least resistance to a grass ledge and pedestal on the arête.

2 **18m.** Pull onto the exposed arête and follow it, moving leftwards slightly, to a ledge. Ascend a crack with jammed blocks.

3 **20m.** Climb easier rocks trending rightwards.

Boneyard Wall	42m	MS	★	1958

A good climb. From the start of *Arpeggio* follow the grassy ledge down left for 10 metres. Belay where the ledge ends beneath an exposed wall.

1 **20m.** Climb diagonally left across the wall to reach a flat ledge at the base of a clean-cut corner. Climb the slab on the right and belay at the top of the corner.

2 **22m.** Move back right and climb the overhang. Turn a second overhang on the left and move up over a nose to easier rocks.

Arpeggio	38m	D		1955

A worthwhile route which starts about 35 metres up the right branch of *Y Gully* at a big right-angled corner above a triangle of ribs and grass.

Climb the grassy crack then the crack on the left. Move left to the arête and finish over the nose.

Two poor routes have been made up the rocks to the right of *Y Gully*. **Renaissance Route** (30m, D, 1955) starts 10 metres right of *Y Gully* at a V-chimney in a grassy recess. It climbs the chimney and grassy groove above. **Subsidiary Rib** (50m, S, 1957) starts at a slab 20 metres right of *Y Gully* and below the previous route. Scramble up for about 40 metres to a steep slab and make one hard nasty move up its left edge to enter a small recess.

14 **Three Tier Climb**	65m	VD		1955

This climb takes the three step ridge on the left of *West Chockstone Gully*. The climbing is pleasant but spoiled by the large terraces between the rock steps. The line is obvious. The best descent is down Y Gully.

A number of small routes have been climbed beyond *West Chockstone Gully* but do not reward the effort made in reaching them.

Tarn Crag (NY 352 125) and **Falcon Crag (NY 351 127)** lie on the flank of Dollywaggon Pike and face east across the head of Grisedale. They stand about half a kilometre north of the tarn. *Tarn Crag* is the broken series of outcrops on the gully-seamed hillside on the left. There is some impressive rock scenery and the routes include two of the earliest climbs in the Eastern Crags, but the rock is not good, though this has not stopped people climbing there, and on surrounding craglets. *Falcon Crag* is a steep compact buttress of jointed walls and overhangs, almost separated from the fellside by two deeply-cut gullies.
The extensive vegetation is home to rare alpine plants, mainly in the gullies but also at the bases of routes and on the buttresses, and the area is much better visited in a hard winter.

On *Tarn Crag*, **High Noon** (D, 1965) takes a line up the extreme left-hand arête and **Dollywaggon Gully** (D, 1896) is the right-hand of the four gullies whilst **Chock Gully** (VD, 1910) lies about 200 metres right of *Dollywaggon Gully* and somewhat higher. It is the deeply cut gully to the left of *Falcon Crag* and gives a good traditional route though it has a lot of dangerous scree. **Fiasco** (MVS, 1961) climbs a steep groove on the left of *Chock Gully*.

On *Falcon Crag*, **Sideline** (VS, 1958) takes a crack in the right wall of *Chock Gully*, **Limbo** (VS, 1958) takes the easiest line up the front of the buttress and **Bottleneck** (HVS, 1957) takes the overhanging groove in the nose of the buttress. **Dollywaggon Great Chimney** (VD, 1957) is the loose and vegetated cleft on the right-hand side of the crag, **Falcon Front** (HVS, 1959) takes the steep but loose buttress left of *Dollywaggon Great Chimney* and **Merlin** (VS, 1963) is a steep loose route which starts 10 metres right of *Dollywaggon Great Chimney*.

Other inconsequential climbs have been consigned to www.frcc.co.uk.

Spout Crag (NY 354 134) is a small crag behind Ruthwaite Lodge whose route names say all you need to know: **Moss Wall** (MVS, 1957) and **Moss Groove** (VS, 1958).

High Crag (NY 344 137) is the large broken buttress which divides the upper part of Ruthwaite Cove. The rock is fissile and there is a lot of grass. Two routes have been climbed - but why?

Eagle Crag

Grid Reference: **NY 357 143**
Faces: **East**
Altitude: **396m**
Approach: **1hr 30 mins**
(greatly reduced by mountain bike)

Eagle Crag stands at the base of the east ridge of Nethermost Pike, about 4 kilometres from Patterdale. There are some old mine workings just below the crag. From the valley approach two sections may be seen: *The North Crag* which is damp, vegetated and justly neglected lies to the right. *The South Crag* on the left is clean and quick-drying.

Approach:

A good track runs all the way up the valley starting as a metalled road, from the Grisedale Bridge at Patterdale. There is no parking in the valley and cars should be left in Patterdale. A mountain bike can be used until almost below the crag which makes the approach much shorter and is highly recommended.

The South Crag

The most popular routes are on the left-hand side of the *South Crag* which receives most sunshine. The rock is generally sound though of a rather flaky nature on some routes. A good spread of grades is available.

Descent from all routes is to the left. In addition, at half height the crag

Eagle Crag Overview

Eagle Crag Left Side

1	Grisedale Corner	VD *
2	Cold Frontier	VS *
3	Taliban	VS

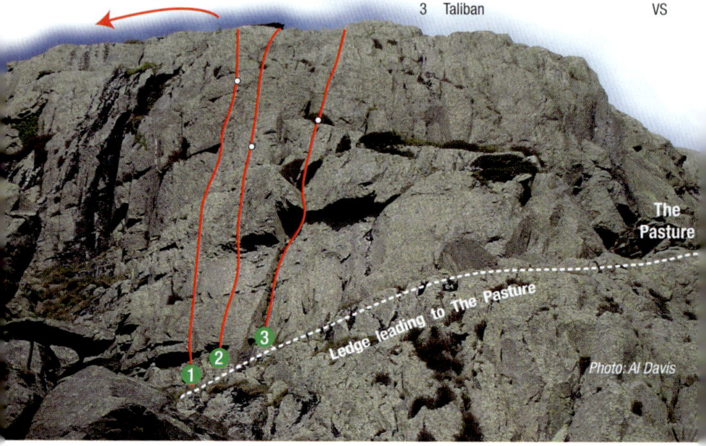

is crossed by a broad terrace, the *Pasture*, which can be accessed along a ledge from the left side of the crag. This provides an easy descent from many of the routes and gives access to pitches higher up the crag.

The routes are described from **left** to **right**.

Left Side

The following routes start 30 metres up the open gully on the left of the crag at a rib by two tall blocks. The ledge which leads rightwards onto the *Pasture* begins at the same point.

1 **Grisedale Corner**	37m	VD	★	1954

1 18m. Climb the rib and then the crack between the two blocks. Surmount the wall above to reach a bilberry ledge.

2 19m. Climb easily up the slabs and walls above.

2 **Cold Frontier**	37m	VS+	★	2004

A good route. Begin as for *Grisedale Corner* below a smooth wall capped by an overlap. This is at the left end of the ledge which leads to the *Pasture*.

1 12m (5a). Climb up via an awkward mantel onto a ledge to gain the smooth wall. Climb straight up the wall and over the left side of the overlap to a small ledge and flake belay.

2 25m (4c). Climb the front face of a slender pillar, then up to a ledge below the wall. Climb this, left of the finish of *Taliban*.

3 **Taliban**	37m	VS+		2001

A pleasant little climb with a worthwhile first pitch. Start just right of *Cold Frontier* at the left end of the ledge leading to the *Pasture*, below a prominent overhang.

1 12m (5a). Climb a shallow corner to beneath a small overhang. Move right and up to enter a short V-groove. Climb the wall on its right to a ledge and spike belay.

2 25m. Climb directly over two short steps to the final headwall and ascend it directly on fingery holds.

Central Area

4 **Full Circle**	15m	VS		2008

Start (as for *Original Route*) at a flat ledge at the left corner of the crag as it starts to bend up left into an open gully. An enjoyable pitch with some worthwhile climbing.

(4c). Move up leftwards to a grassy ledge below a shallow groove. Climb the groove delicately to join *Original Route* on the *Pasture* descent path by the stone wall.

5 **Original Route**	54m	D		1954

Start at a flat ledge at the left corner of the crag as it starts to bend up left into an open gully. This is below a well-worn crack.

1 24m. Climb the crack, move left to the nose and ascend to the *Pasture* at the stone wall. Belay on the juniper ledge above.

2 30m. Continue up easy rocks to the top.

6 **90 Years Young**	26m	E1		2002

Poorly protected climbing with flaky rock. Start below the left end of the broad ledge.

(5a). Climb to the ledge and then up to a short groove. Gain a small ledge on *Raptor* below a rock nose. Move left under the rock nose and climb the wall above and another short wall to the *Pasture*.

7 **Raptor**	25m	HVS+		1999

Delicate climbing with doubtful protection.
Start below the left end of a broad ledge to the right of *Original Route*, below the left end of a large chamfered bulge at about 4 metres.

(5a). Climb straight up the left side of the bulge into a shallow groove. Cross the wall leftwards past a rock scar to a higher resting place. Trend right and follow the shallow corner direct. Cross a ramp and continue up to the *Pasture*.

Eagle Crag Central Area

4	Full Circle	VS
5	Original Route	D
6	90 Years Young	E1
7	Raptor	HVS
8	Hawkeye	VS **
9	Kestrel Wall	S **
10	Pericles	HVS *
11	Warbird	VS
12	Horse Power	E2 **
13	Thoroughbred	E2 *
14	Grand Day Out	HVS **
15	Sobrenada	VS **
16	Solioquy	E2 **

Routes 9, 10, 11, 12, 15 16 show Pitch 1 only.

Photo: Al Davis

14
13
13
14
16
13
14
15
16

8 **Hawkeye**	25m	VS	★★	2008

An excellent pitch with good positions. Start as for *Raptor*.

(4b). Follow *Raptor* to the shallow groove at 4 metres. Continue up the groove rightwards onto the rib. Climb straight up keeping to the left of the large perched block and finish straight up to the *Pasture*.

9 **Kestrel Wall**	45m	S	★★	1954

A superb climb starting up and left of the 15 metre slab which lies at the foot of the buttress. There is a prominent flake crack above.

1 27m. Climb to the rock ledge and ascend the crack moving left at the top to a stance behind a perched block. Continue directly to the *Pasture*.

2 18m. Climb the steep slab, 8 metres right of the stone wall, to the upper ledge. Climb into the scoop above the right end of the ledge, move right to the rib and up to the top.

10 **Pericles**	45m	HVS	★	1960

A good route with a definite crux. Three metres right of the flake crack of *Kestrel Wall* a line of flakes forms a shallow groove leading to an overhang. Start directly below this, just right of *Kestrel Wall*.

1 27m (4c). Climb to the groove and move up this until it is possible to step right below a big spike. Climb up to this and continue to the *Pasture*.

2 18m (5a). Directly above the highest blocks on the ledge is an overhanging V-chimney containing an obvious quartz jug. Surmount the overlap and move left on the slab below the chimney. Climb this to the final slab of *Sobrenada* and the top. An intimidating pitch.

11 **Warbird**	45m	VS		2008

Good enjoyable well-protected climbing. Start just right of *Pericles* at a V-corner.

1 27m (4c). Climb the corner, step left at the top and gain a ledge. Follow the groove of *Pericles* for 2 metres, then step left and climb the wall just left of the arête to a small corner. Trend left to a corner/crack (above and right of *Kestrel Wall*). Climb up the wall just right of the crack to belay on the *Pasture*.

2 18m (4a). Climb the slab 2 metres right of the stone wall to the upper ledge. Finish up the final wall 2 metres left of *Kestrel Wall*.

12 **Horse Power**	65m	E2	★★	1989

Three metres right of the groove of *Pericles* is a large overhang with a groove on its right. Start up slabs below this groove.

1 35m (5c). Climb up the slab to just right of the V-groove. Use the crack to gain a layaway flake on the right of the groove. Climb up

Left: Guidebook writer Al Davis enjoying his research on **Hawkeye** (VS), Eagle Crag, Grisedale. **Photo:** Steve Prior

Eagle Crag Upper Tier

10	Pericles	HVS *
12	Horse Power	E2 **
17	Swoop	E2 **
18	Nexus	E1 **
15	Sobrenada	VS **
16	Soliloquy	E2 **

Photo: Ron Kenyon

with interest to gain better holds then follow a crack-line up leftwards to join *Pericles* at the big spike. With a runner on this, step back right and climb the steep delicate slab boldly to the *Pasture*.

2 30m (5c). Climb straight up the black-streaked slab between *Pericles* and *Sobrenada* to gain the foot of a short hanging groove. Pull steeply out right and up with difficulty to gain the top of *Sobrenada's* chimney. Follow the steep corner above finishing out left.

13 **Thoroughbred**	40m	E2	★	1999

Excellent climbing with generally good protection except for a short bold section. Start as for *Horse Power*.

(5b). Climb the slab to the right of the obvious V-groove as for *Horse Power*. Using the horizontal crack-line, gain a layaway flake which is followed boldly to a good resting place. Follow the diagonal fault to its right-hand end and then pull up to a small platform (junction with *Grand Day Out*). Climb the awkward tapering groove on the right to pull out leftwards at the top and follow easier rock to the *Pasture*.

Right: Eric Parker following the slim groove of **Pericles** (HVS), Eagle Crag, Grisedale.
Photo: Ron Kenyon

14 **Grand Day Out**	37m	HVS+	★★	1999

Although this climb lies close to ***Sobrenada*** it gives superb well-protected climbing with good positions. Start at the left of the obvious slabs.

(5a). Climb easily rightwards and gain a higher grass ledge. Step right and climb a steep rib/groove (to the left of the cave of ***Sobrenada***) to pull leftwards onto the slab. Trend slightly left beneath a small shelf and gain this direct or slightly to its left. Pull out left and follow a steep shallow groove direct to the *Pasture*.

15 **Sobrenada**	59m	VS	★★	1957

An excellent climb starting at the foot of the 15 metre slab beneath the buttress.

1 36m (4b). Climb the slab. Move up into the cave, pull out to the left and ascend the corner. Move right to the nose, climb the short wall and follow the sharp rib to the *Pasture*.

2 23m (4c). Starting to the right of the piled blocks, traverse 5 metres right to below a flat-topped spike. Climb up to this and traverse back left until it is possible to gain the large shallow chimney. Ascend the chimney with interest and pull out left to a slab. Climb the slab and ribs to the top.

16 **Soliloquy**	76m	E2	★★	1975

The second pitch is superb though poorly protected. Start as for ***Sobrenada***.

1 36m (4b). Climb to the cave as for ***Sobrenada***. Mantelshelf out onto the right-hand rib. Pull out of the groove and, keeping to the edge of the rib, ascend to the *Pasture*.

2 40m (5a). Follow the ascending traverse of ***Sobrenada*** to its end below the prominent rib. Climb up to an obvious flat hold and, using the groove on the left, ascend to a ledge leading back to the rib. Continue up the rib and then slabs to the top.

Upper Tier

The following routes start from the *Pasture*. This can be reached easily along a ledge from the left or by climbing one of the routes up the rocks below.

17 **Swoop**	25m	E2-	★★	2009

A good climb on excellent rock. It starts on the ***Pasture*** 3 metres right of pitch 3 of *Kestrel Wall*.

(5b). Ascend the slab to the obvious groove in the overhang. Climb the groove (crux, poorly protected) to a small pinnacle (junction with *High Girdle*). Step off the top of the pinnacle and finish straight up the wall.

18 **Nexus**	25m	E1	★★	1999

Excellent climbing throughout, well-protected and with fine positions. It climbs very close to the second pitch of *Horse Power*. Start from the *Pasture* just to the right of the piled blocks (same point as *Sobrenada* pitch 2).

(5b). Climb directly up the black-streaked slab and into the triangular niche. Step right, then climb shallow cracks with interest to join *Sobrenada*. Step right again (above the chimney of *Sobrenada*) and climb the corner directly to the top (as for *Horse Power* pitch 2).

19 **The Worm**	37m	E2		1978

Start at the corner at the left end of the green wall, 2 metres left of *Earlybirds*.

(5c). Climb the groove, using holds on the right wall, to the ledge below the continuation groove. Move up into this groove and exit immediately left. Climb the arête and then move right into the groove near its top.

20 **Earlybirds**	40m	E2	★★	1976

A bold move is the highlight of this pitch. Start at the thin crack in the green wall below and right of the top pitch of *Sobrenada*.

(5b). Climb the crack to the overhang, move left and break over the overhang, moving right to the base of a groove. Climb this to the *High Girdle* ledge and move leftwards into a slabby groove. Climb this and slabs to the top.

21 **Chalk Walk**	40m	E3	★	1979

Good climbing over the roof to the right of *Earlybirds*.

(5c). Follow *Earlybirds* to the overhang. Traverse right to the end of the overhangs and pull over into a slim groove, immediately swinging left into the left-hand groove. Continue up to the quartz band and traverse left to the peg runner on the *High Girdle*. Step right and pull over the bulge and head for the obvious rock scar. An arête and slabs lead to the top.

22 **Dandelion Groove**	38m	VS		1959

A good line but with some loose rock. Start at a groove at the right-hand end of the green wall of *Earlybirds*.

1 12m (4b). Climb onto a pinnacle and then up the steep groove to an awkward landing on the right. Poor belays.

2 26m (4b). Step left into the subsidiary groove and climb it to a flat ledge. Go up past an insecure tree and move round the rib into the main groove. Follow this to the top.

Eagle Crag Right Side

19	The Worm	E2	
20	Earlybirds	E2	**
21	Chalk Walk	E3	*
22	Dandelion Groove	VS	
23	Dandelion Wall	HVS	
24	Summit Crisis	E3	
25	Poisoned Arrow	E1	
26	Morning Slab	E1	**
27	Burdock	VS	*
28	Curtain Call	HVS	
29	Ghoul	VS	
30	The Sting	E2	
31	Good Friday	VS	
32	Doctor's Grooves	HS	*

Photo: Al Davis

28
27
26
25
27
28
29
30
31
32

23 **Dandelion Wall**	45m	HVS		1961

Start from the grass ledge level with the first stance of *Dandelion Groove*. This can be reached either by scrambling or by pitch 1 of *Dandelion Groove*. Belay in the corner.

1 24m (5a). Move right to a block below a steep wall. Gain the block from its left then climb the wall above until it is possible to get into the V-groove on the left. Climb this and then traverse right round a corner into an easier groove. Ascend this to a grass ledge and move down rightwards to a tree belay.

2 21m (4c). Climb the steep groove behind the tree direct to the top.

24 **Summit Crisis**	24m	E3		1982

The striking arête right of the last pitch of *Doctor's Grooves*. Start below the big groove at the top right-hand side of the *Pasture*.

(5c). Move right and climb a subsidiary groove then straight up to a small overhanging flake. Pull straight over the overhang on layaways then move right to a rest and runner. Continue up the wall slightly left of the arête with difficulty to gain a glacis below the final sharp arête which is climbed strenuously and precariously to the top. Belay well back.

Right Side

The following routes start from the foot of the crag. About 18 metres right of *Sobrenada* there is a large flake at the foot of the crag and an easy gangway leading up to the right.

25 **Poisoned Arrow**	37m	E1		1982

Start at the large flake 18 metres right of *Sobrenada*.

(5a). Climb a crack and slab left of *Morning Slab* to a ledge. Finish up the short slab above.

26 **Morning Slab**	37m	E1	★★	1976

A fine but poorly protected climb taking the faint groove-line in the slab left of *Burdock*. Start at a large flake as for *Poisoned Arrow*.

(5a). Traverse easily for 5 metres along the gangway to the undercut slab. Pull up left onto the slab and continue more delicately up the groove to a ledge. Climb the continuation groove above to join *Burdock* at its final crack. Follow this to the ash tree.

27 **Burdock**	39m	VS	★	1961

A pleasant route. Start at the large flake as for *Poisoned Arrow* where the easy gangway leads up to the right.

1 10m. Traverse easily right across a gangway to a stance below the overhanging chimney.

2 14m (4c). Climb or struggle up the chimney. Ascend the slabs above trending right with difficulty to a ledge. Continue up leftwards to a large flake and belay on its right end.

3 15m (4a). Traverse left along the flake to a crack in the slabs above. Climb this to an ash tree.

28 **Curtain Call**	37m	HVS		1979

A poor route which takes the area of moss between *Burdock* and *Ghoul*. Start at grooves 6 metres right of *Burdock*.

1 12m (4a). Climb the grooves to the easy gangway. Belay in the chimney of *Burdock*. This may be reached more pleasantly by following pitch 1 of *Burdock*.

2 25m (5b). Start up the groove just right of the chimney and climb to a grass ledge. Climb the crack on the right into a niche with detached blocks. Finish up cracks.

Above: Eric Parker runs out **Morning Slab** (E1), Eagle Crag. **Photo:** Ron Kenyon

29 **Ghoul**	34m	VS		1964

Undistinguished climbing except for the lower part of pitch 2. Start a few metres to the right of ***Burdock*** at an open mossy corner.

1 **14m.** Climb the corner and move up to the right to a grass ledge and belay.
2 **20m (4c).** Climb up into the overhanging groove above. Move to the right into a subsidiary groove and climb this, exiting on the left. Mossy slabs on the right lead to easier ground and a junction with *Doctor's Grooves*.

30 **The Sting**	42m	E2		1975

An overgrown and filthy climb. Start, if you must, below a crack 3 metres left of the start of *Good Friday*.

1 **18m (5c).** Climb the crack exiting right to the good ledge.
2 **24m (5b).** Ascend directly to the block. Climb the difficult slab and follow the groove system to join pitch 3 of *Doctor's Grooves*.

31 **Good Friday**	78m	VS		1965

A series of variations to *Doctor's Grooves* which is varied and interesting. Start at the two thin cracks left of *Doctor's Grooves* leading to the corner.

1 **18m (5a).** Climb the cracks to the slab and ascend to the tree belay of the parent route.
2 **15m (4c).** Move left from the stance and climb the steep groove moving left at the top to a flake on the arête. Continue above to ledges.
3 **27m (4b).** Step round the rib to the right and ascend the groove to the *Pasture*. Scramble up for 18 metres to the foot of a steep wall just left of *Doctor's Grooves* pitch 4. Block belay.
4 **18m (4c).** Step off a sharp flake to the left of the block and climb the steep wall with an awkward landing on the slab above. Climb the slab and step left to belay below the final chimney. Climb the chimney as for *Doctor's Grooves*.

32 **Doctor's Grooves**	87m	HS	★	1956

An interesting route. Start at the very right-hand end of the lower wall.

1 **14m.** Pull up left to a slab, move left into a corner and climb up to an obvious tree belay.
2 **15m.** Climb the steep groove up to the arête.
3 **32m.** Move up and left into the corner. Hand-traverse the slab on the right and ascend to the ***Pasture***. Scramble up for 18 metres and belay below the big groove at the top right-hand side of the ***Pasture***. Block belay.
4 **26m.** Move right and climb a subsidiary groove. Traverse across the big groove to its left arête. Climb this and traverse left again and up to belay below the final chimney. Climb the chimney to the top.

High Girdle	121m	HVS		1964

The route traverses the rock above the ***Pasture*** from left to right, just above the overhangs, and then continues across difficult corners and grooves in the upper right part of the crag. The good climbing stops at the ledge of ***Dandelion Groove***. Start on the ***Pasture*** below pitch 3 of ***Kestrel Wall***, a little left of the last pitch of ***Pericles***.

1 21m (4c). Ascend easily for 5 metres to a large ledge on the left. Climb the wall on the right for 3 metres then move to the right, round the corner and make an exposed step down to a small pinnacle. Traverse the mossy wall to a stance and belay on ***Pericles***.

2 15m (5a). Traverse to the right above the crux of ***Sobrenada*** then follow an obvious slightly descending traverse line to the nose. Climb up a little then move to the right to an exposed stance and peg belay.

3 21m (5a). Move round the arête and mantelshelf on to the flat ledge on pitch 2 of ***Dandelion Groove***. Descend this to the grass ledge.

4 20m (5a). As for ***Dandelion Wall***. Traverse right, mount an overhanging block and climb the steep wall above until a groove on the left can be gained. Ascend this with difficulty then traverse to the right to an easy groove which leads up to a ledge. Descend to the right to a stance and tree below a groove.

5 15m (4c). Climb up the groove until a traverse can be made to the impending arête on the right. Turn this to land on a mossy slab. Move up to the stance below the last pitch of ***Doctor's Grooves***.

6 20m (4c). Descend to the right (reversing ***Doctor's Grooves***) down two 3 metre steps. Make a delicate step across a groove to a ledge on the right and follow this until it peters out. Move up to the bulging arête and turn this by an awkward step to reach a large grass ledge. Belay to the right of an obvious corner/groove.

7 9m. Climb the corner to the top of the crag.

The rock below the ***Pasture*** has been girdled, **Lower Traverse** (S, 1957), from embedded boulders 6 metres above ***Original Route*** to ***Sobrenada***.

The North Crag

The *North Crag*, which lies 400 metres right of the *South Crag*, is both dirty, overgrown and damp. One would be bad enough. It and its routes are best left to themselves.

Deepdale

Deepdale lies to the south-east of Grisedale, joining the Ullswater valley at Bridgend (limited parking) about 1½ kilometres south of Patterdale. It is a long valley flanked by the ridge of St. Sunday Crag to the north and the Hartsop above How ridge to the south with Fairfield standing at the head. The spur of Greenhow End splits the upper valley into two parts: Sleet Cove, the more northerly, lies below Fairfield, and Link Cove below *Hart Crag*.

The main crags are high and the rock quickly becomes greasy in poor conditions. The major crags are *Scrubby Crag* high up in Link Cove and *Hutaple Crag* in Sleet Cove. *Mart Crag*, just above the valley floor, may be climbable when these are shrouded in mist. The valley approach to these crags involves a delightful level walk followed by steep ascents at the end. From Bridgend, a track leads to Wallend and then a path is followed along the northern side of the beck as far as the drumlins beneath *Greenhow End*. To reach Link Cove, Deepdale Beck is crossed before Greenhow End and a line taken roughly following the line of the stream which flows from the cove. The continuation of the path leads into Sleet Cove where *Hutaple Crag* lies high up to the left. The crags are listed clockwise around the valley.

Erne Nest Crag

Grid Reference: **NY 374 119** Altitude: **450m**
Faces: **North** Approach: **1 hr**

This collection of buttresses lies just left of Link Cove.

The Main Crag (NY 374 119)

This is a small crag of once clean, sound, rough pocketed rock and was home to some good climbs. Sadly it has reverted to its natural state of being filthy and unclimbable due to years of neglect.

The Slabs (NY 378 121)

Two hundred metres left of the *Main Crag*, and at a higher level, is a grassy promontory below a broken slabby buttress. One hundred metres

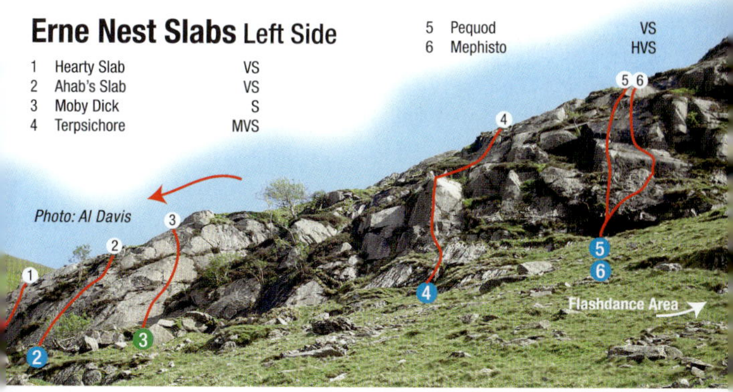

further left is a line of slabs interspersed with more broken walls. The slabs provide pleasant climbing.

The best **descent** is to the left.

The routes are described from **left** to **right**.

1 **Hearty Slab**	11m	VS		2007

This climb takes a series of shallow grooves up the left-hand side of the first slab on the left of the crag. Start immediately right of the left edge of the slab at a thin crack.

(4c). Climb the crack and meander up shallow grooves to the top.

2 **Ahab's Slab**	23m	VS		2006

Pleasant climbing up the slab between two rowan trees. Start 8 metres right of *Hearty Slab* and below a twin-stemmed tree.

(4c). Climb the slab (easing in difficulty as height is gained) keeping to the right of the twin-stemmed tree and trend right to finish as for *Moby Dick*.

3 **Moby Dick**	23m	S		2006

Pleasant padding up the slabby whaleback buttress 6 metres right of *Ahab's Slab*. Poorly protected but delightful.

Start just left of a slabby corner and follow a broad rib, thin crack and a final arête to the top.

4 **Terpsichore**	25m	MVS		2007

Twelve metres left of the series of black water-washed slabs left of centre of the crag, and 20 metres right of *Moby Dick*, an attractive arête rises above the lower rocks. This route makes best use of the available rock. Poorly protected.

(4b). Gain the arête and follow it direct on positive but hidden holds. From the ledge at its end, step right and follow the pleasant slabby rib to the top.

Thirty metres right of *Moby Dick* is an area of black water-streaked slabs just left of the centre of the crag. Low-angled clean rough rock compensates for the almost complete lack of protection though this wet area of rock requires drought conditions.

5 **Pequod**	35m	VS		2007

Start at a projecting block with a small holly below a black bulge. Very bold for the grade.

(4b). Climb over the bulge as for *Mephisto* but continue direct up the fine bubbly wall to reach the ledge below the left side of the black wall. Pull directly onto the slab and follow its left side to another black wall. Pull up the black wall, a metre left of *Mephisto*, and continue direct to gain a ledge up and left and a small spike runner. Finish up the blunt rib on the left.

6 **Mephisto**	35m	HVS		2007

Bold. Start as for *Pequod* at a projecting block with a small holly below a black bulge.

(4c). Climb the bulge then trend right up the bubbly wall to gain a ledge below the right side of a black wall guarding access to the main slab. Move up and step left onto the dark slab. Follow this trending slightly leftwards. Overcome another black wall and reach a large hidden pocket. Continue direct up the steeper slab to a ledge and finish up a rib and a short corner-crack.

Erne Nest Slabs Right Side

7	Eachan Trillvite	HVS *
8	Flashdance	VS
9	Slaberitif	MVS

The following three climbs are located on the right side of the crag.

7 **Eachan Trillvite**	27m	HVS	★	2007

A fine climb up the rib, crack and slab just to the right of the thin slanting crack set in the overhanging wall up and left of *Flashdance*. Start 7 metres left of *Flashdance* at a clean wall.

(5a). Climb the wall to a ledge, then the rib on the right to below twin cracks. Move up the left-hand crack with difficulty for 3 metres, then step left. Pull over the slight bulge using a pocket and tiptoe up the slab to a ledge. Continue up a steeper slabby wall whence easier slabs lead to the top.

8 **Flashdance**	16m	VS		2006

The razor-slashed thin crack in the right flank of the buttress at the right-hand end of the crag. Start below and just right of a small rowan tree at a free-standing finger of rock.

(5a). From the finger of rock, climb the slab and rib to a ledge below the headwall. Step left and follow the excellent thin crack, with initial use of the crack on the right, and finish up the arête.

9 **Slaberitif**	19m	MVS		2007

Two pleasant pitches at the right end of the crag only marred by a large grass terrace. Start 8 metres right of *Flashdance* at a stand-alone rib.

1 9m (4a). Climb the rib, mainly on its right side, and cross the terrace to a slab.

2 10m (4c). Climb the slab via the slanting crack and left rib to reach a spike. Finish up the blunt arête.

To the right of *Erne Nest Crag* and left of *Greenhow End* lies the hanging valley of Link Cove.

Hart Crag

Grid Reference: **NY 372 114** Altitude: **650m**
Faces: **North** Approach: **1 hr 15 mins**

The Deepdale flank of Hart Crag is a maze of outcrops and rocky ridges. The crag is on the extreme left of the fellside close to the point where the Hartsop above How ridge begins to rise steeply to the summit of Hart Crag. The crag is steep and compact with rough rock which is surprisingly clean. The crag is worth a visit and can easily be linked with *Gill Crag* in Dovedale to give a fine mountain day.

 Photo: Eric Shaw

The routes start from a terrace, broad on the left and narrowing to a quartz gangway on the right.

The easiest **descent** is on the left.

The climbs are described from **left** to **right**.

1 **Wildebeest**	17m	MVS		2007

Twenty metres down and left of the cairn at the foot of *Zip*, a 2 metre high pinnacle stands below slabs with a prominent stepped arête above.

(4b). Step off the pinnacle and climb the slabs to a ledge below the arête (not the undercut arête to the right). Continue up the right-hand side of the stepped arête. Step left on to a cracked block (loose) before finishing up the rib above.

2 **Zip**	36m	VD		1957

Pleasant climbing. Start at the left end of the terrace at a cairn below prominent vertical ribs and corners high on the crag.

1 15m. Climb the slabs to a ledge below the corners.

2 21m. Ascend diagonally right below the wall and then move back left across the slabs to finish directly above the start.

3 **The Greybeards**	30m	VS		1990

Start 12 metres right of the left end of the terrace and 3 metres left of a shallow cave.

(4c). Climb the obvious steep filthy left-hand corner.

4 **Dividend**	38m	S		1956

Start about 20 metres right of the left end of the terrace at a pointed rock spike leaning against the wall. There is a small roof at 2 metres. A poorly protected pitch.

Hart Crag

1	Wildebeest	MVS
2	Zip	VD
3	Greybeards	VS
4	Dividend	S
5	Slape	S
6	Spiral	HS**
7	Sickle	S
8	Gazelle	VS

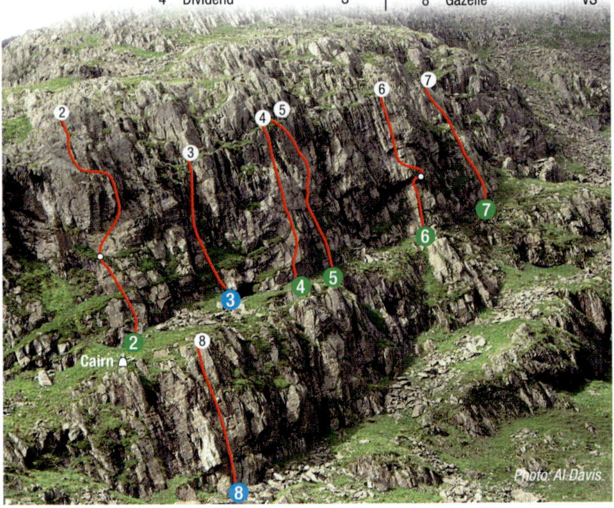

Climb the bulge to the right of the spike and follow the slab rightwards to some broken rock. Move out left, then up again and rightwards via a little scoop to a ledge (possible poor belay but best to carry on). Climb the wall on the left and then up a little chimney.

5 **Slape**	35m	S		1956

Start 6 metres right of ***Dividend*** below a leftward-slanting chimney/groove. There is a grassy slab 3 metres to the right of the start. It is very vegetated and slape - best avoided.

Climb up to the chimney/groove. Continue up this using the slab on the left. Continue up the groove above the chimney to a nose. Step left up a scoop and climb up to a ledge. Traverse the slab delicately to the right and climb the rib or groove. Climb the undercut crack, or the wall, to the top.

6 **Spiral**	32m	HS+	★★	1956

Start 22 metres right of ***Slape*** at the obvious quartz gangway. A rib runs up to the right end of an overhang. A little gem but it is very bold for the grade.

1 **12m.** Climb the groove on the right of the rib to a stance and belay.
2 **20m.** Continue to the right and traverse left above the first overhangs. Climb a groove on the left to reach a small ledge above the second overhang. Continue up the arête to finish on the left. A bold pitch.

7 **Sickle**	32m	S		1956

Start at a large perched block 7 metres right and up from the start of ***Spiral***. Climb up rightwards to ledges and then up by the right side of the arête to the top.

Blip	24m	VD		1956

Start 9 metres right of ***Sickle*** at two grooved arêtes.

1 **12m.** Climb either arête to a ledge on the left.
2 **12m.** Start up the slab on the left for 5 metres. Move right and up the centre of the face to an awkward finish.

A lower tier of rock is shorter but cleaner.

8 **Gazelle**	15m	VS		2007

Halfway along the lower tier an easy-looking groove snakes up a rounded buttress.

(4c). Gain the groove from the left, step up right to a sloping ledge and then back left into the groove. Follow its left rib and make a few awkward moves up the headwall to the top.

Impala (VS, 2007) climbs a gendarme and slabby pinnacle below the start of ***Spiral*** but could not be located with any certainty.

One hundred metres north of ***Hart Crag*** a stand-alone rocky knoll presents a fine-looking buttress to Link Cove.

Norwester	17m	S		2007

Start 10 metres up and right of the lowest rocks on a grassy ramp at a tiny slab. Pleasant climbing on rough rock.

(4a). Climb the right-trending shallow groove and knobbly wall above to a ledge. Finish up a series of grooves in the arête.

The right wall of this buttress is **Grate Wall** (8m, VD, 2007).

Scrubby Crag

Grid Reference: **NY 367 115** Altitude: **710m**
Faces: **South-East** Approach: **1 hr 30 mins**

Scrubby Crag stands at the top of Link Cove, its southern end almost reaching Link Hause, the shallow col between Hart Crag and Fairfield. It is about 60 metres high, a steep wall cut by vertical corners and grooves, and stands above steep grassy slabs. An easy traverse from the left leads to the cliff above these lower rocks. Near the point where this traverse begins, a big right-angled corner (*Juniper Crack*) runs up the cliff. About 60 metres right of this, a deep V-chimney (*Grendel*) rises from the easy traverse as far as *Long Ledge*, a grass balcony which crosses the central part of the cliff. Immediately right again is the big open groove of *Hrothgar*.

The crag is steep and there is considerable exposure outside the groove-lines. The rock is generally sound and the holds tend to be good. The crag is very vegetated in places but the recommended routes give excellent climbing in an atmospheric mountain setting.

Approach:

The crag may be approached via Deepdale and Link Cove or, much more pleasantly, via the Hartsop above How ridge, each taking about 1½ hours. It is perhaps slightly shorter (1¼ hours) from the top of Dunmail Raise via Grisedale Tarn and the summit of Fairfield.

Descent is on the left, towards Link Hause.

The climbs are described from **left** to **right**.

The first 3 routes lie on the short clean wall at the left end of the crag. The climbs start on a grassy ledge below the wall above the main descent path.

1 **Interlude**	25m	HVS		1982

(5a). Climb the left to right diagonal line starting up a ramp at the left side of the buttress.

2 **Bar Sinister**	35m	VS		1960

Start at a thin crack in the centre of the wall.

Move up then left to a gangway before finishing up the left arête.

3 **Premier**	25m	E1		1982

(5b). Climb the thin crack in the centre of the wall direct.

4 **Wall Climb**	49m	S		1952

A steep route up the buttress left of ***Juniper Crack***. The wall is defined by a diagonal fault on the left and the big corner of ***Juniper Crack*** on the right. Start from the initial ledge of ***Juniper Crack***.

1 **9m.** Climb up the vegetated grooves on the left to a ledge below a steep wall.

2 **31m.** Climb the wall to a juniper ledge and follow the crack on the left. Climb the wall above over a wedged block then traverse left to a steep rake and move up to a stance.

3 **9m.** Finish easily up the rake.

Variations

1 **9m.** It is possible to reach the stance from the left.

2 **31m.** From the top of the crack it is possible to traverse right and up to a ledge. Move left and up a corner and then trend left to the arête to rejoin the main line at the stance.

3 **9m (4b).** The attractive corner-crack, or the rib on its right.

5 **Juniper Crack**	51m	HS	★	1952

The route starts up the mossy corner but then crosses its left wall onto the edge of the buttress. Start from the ledge at the foot of the corner which is reached by scrambling up from the right.

1 **23m.** Climb the corner to a stance on the slabs below the steep upper wall.

2 **11m.** Move up the corner until it becomes difficult and then step onto the left wall. Traverse left over some wedged blocks and behind a small pinnacle on the arête to a ledge.

3 **17m.** Climb the crack near the corner and move round the rib to a ledge on the right. Finish by the corner-crack or by the arête.

6 **Juniper Crack Direct**	47m	HVS		1977

This takes the upper corner.

1 **23m.** As for ***Juniper Crack***.

2 **24m (5a).** Climb the corner to the top.

Long Ledge Entry and Exit	113m	VD		1956

This takes the easiest line to ***Long Ledge*** and traverses off from its right-hand end. Start as for ***Juniper Crack***.

1 **18m.** Climb the corner and belay at the foot of the slabs (most of pitch 1 of ***Juniper Crack***).

2 **20m.** Traverse up to the right across the slabs, move down and cross a short wall. Ascend and traverse a rock ledge to a corner. Move right to a belay.

3 **21m.** Walk along the ledge to the right and traverse round the corner to ***Long Ledge***. Belay by a cave.

Scrubby Crag

1	Interlude	HVS
2	Bar Sinister	VS
3	Premier	E1

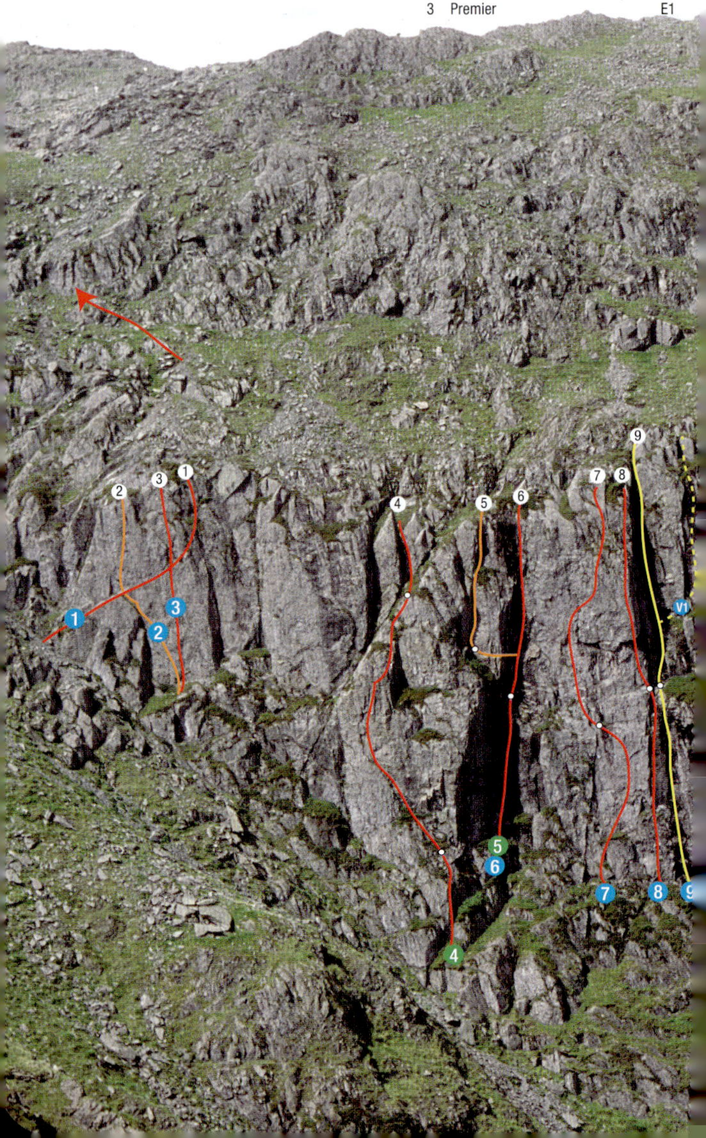

4	Wall Climb	S	8	Darth Vader	HVS
5	Juniper Crack	HS *	9	Heorot	HVS
6	Juniper Crack Direct	HVS	v1	Variation Finish	
7	Beowulf	VS ***	10	Grendel	MVS ***
			11	Hrothgar	HVS **

Photo: Eric Shaw

4 45m. Walk along the exposed *Long Ledge* to its right end passing a 3 metre chimney-crack at 18 metres. Belays can be taken as required.
5 9m. Step down and move round the corner. Traverse for 2 metres and move rightwards over ledges to belay. Reach the top of the cliff via a corner above on the left and then go up grassy rakes diagonally left for 30 metres.

7 **Beowulf**	54m	VS+	★★★	1959

This excellent route climbs the wall to the right of *Juniper Crack*. Pitch 1 is poorly protected.
1 27m (4c). A bold pitch. Climb a short wall to a grassy ledge. Climb the wall above on small holds, first trending rightwards to surmount a slight bulge then making an ascending traverse to the left into and across a shallow groove. Climb to a stance with a flake belay 5 metres up on the right.
2 27m (4b). Ascend past the belay to a prominent overhang which is reached at its left end. Climb the overhang on superb flake holds and continue up the curved crack to a flake. Traverse to the right for about 5 metres and ascend to the top of the crag.

Ringway (1956) found an inferior line up the same area of rock as the following two routes.

8 **Darth Vader**	50m	HVS		1978

Start as for *Heorot* at a black mossy streak.
1 24m (4c). Climb into the slim groove on the left of the *Heorot* groove. Follow this to a belay below the corner.
2 26m (5a). Climb the left edge of the left wall of the corner to reach a wide crack. Follow this and easier rocks to the top.

9 **Heorot**	50m	HVS		1974

A black mossy streak leads up twin grooves to the main corner climbed by this route. Start at a ledge which cuts across the mossy streak at the same level as the start of *Beowulf* and 6 metres right of that route. The black moss of pitch 1 barely affects the climbing. The green moss of pitch 2 is made of sterner stuff.
1 26m (4c). Climb up from the left end of a ledge to a flake. Move into the groove and follow it to where a step left leads to the rib. Continue up the easy section of the corner to a grass ledge and belays on the right.
2 24m (5a). Climb the corner. When clean, this pitch is superb, though currently it is lushly green.

Right: Al Davis on the superb rough rock of **Beowulf** (VS), Scrubby Crag. **Photo:** Ron Kenyon

v1 ***Variation Finish*** 20m

An easier and inferior finish which proves useful when the main corner becomes mossy.

2 (4c). Climb the groove directly above the belay, moving diagonally right after 10 metres.

The overgrown wall right of *Heorot* has been climbed by two routes, **Midnight Special** (VS, 1957) and **Sennapod** (VS, 1958).

10 **Grendel**	67m	MVS	★★★	1956

An excellent route which takes the deep V-groove in the centre of the crag. It is slow to dry but climbable when damp. Scramble across to the start, below and slightly left of the main groove.

1 39m (4b). Climb up rightwards to gain the groove. Climb onto the flake, traverse left across the groove and move up to a ledge on the left. Re-enter the groove and climb to *Long Ledge* using the right wall as necessary. Near the top, exit the groove finishing up the rib on the right.

2 28m (4a). Climb the corner passing a pedestal and continue straight up towards poised blocks and on to the top.

Anabasis (HVS, 1975) and **The Pillar** (E1, 1975) lie on the steep and impressive pillar between *Grendel* and *Hrothgar*. Unfortunately, they are so overgrown they are barely climbable in their present condition and cannot be recommended.

11 **Hrothgar**	84m	HVS	★★	1960

An impressive and excellent climb which takes the steep open groove to the right of *Grendel*. Below the groove there is a vegetated amphitheatre. The first ramp on the left simply leads back to the start of *Grendel*. Scramble up into a damp bay below and slightly right of a second ramp.

1 17m. Step left and go up the grass ramp to the foot of a rock corner. Climb this, exit left and then traverse right to a good stance and belay below the groove. In damp conditions it is much more pleasant to traverse right from pitch 1 of *Grendel* to reach the same stance (4a).

2 37m (5a). Move easily rightwards then go back left up an awkward gangway to the foot of the groove. Climb the groove to where it steepens, move onto the left wall and make an exposed mantelshelf and continue up to *Long Ledge*. Walk 11 metres right to a flake belay.

3 30m (4c). Climb up above the belay to a bilberry ledge. Work right and surmount a bulge on flaky holds. Continue up with decreasing difficulty and scramble to a good belay. A serious pitch.

Firedragon (HVS, 1957) is a poor route which climbs the wall 25m right of *Grendel*.

The Girdle Traverse (HVS,1961) traverses the crag from right to left. The central section is poor and the rest is not much better.

A few other routes have been climbed even further to the right: **The Outsider** (VS, 1957), **Green Buttress** (S, 1955), **Halcyon** (VD, 1956) and **Pendulum Gully** (D, 1956). This vegetated area of hillside is best left undisturbed so that its diverse ecosystems can continue to flourish.

Right of Link Cove, the terminal cliffs of **Greenhow End (NY 369 121)** on the Sleet Cove flank are steep but heavily vegetated. Climbs have been made here but the place is best left until winter conditions prevail.

Mart Crag

Grid Reference: **NY 372 123** Altitude: **360m**
Faces: **East** Approach: **1 hr**

This pleasant crag is situated at the head of Deepdale and close to the valley floor. The crag comprises a large triangular-shaped slab with steep walls above and right. The rock is superbly sound and rough but, due to its compact nature, protection is scarce on some routes and a bold approach helps - a good selection of cams of all sizes is useful booster of boldness. Unfortunately the crag is currently sprouting moss and vegetation in the cracks so that some once fine lines are virtually unclimbable. However, the areas between the cracks are relatively clean. When clean, the climbing is excellent and the crag is well worth a visit.

Approach:

Park at Bridgend and follow the track up Deepdale - a delightful walk up the valley.

There is an easy **descent** down either side.

The routes are described from **left** to **right**.

Chameleon	35m	E3	★	1997

Starts on the far left side of the crag at an easy-angled slab.

(6a). Climb easy right-slanting cracks to a ledge and possible belay. A short shallow corner leads to a hidden jug on the blank wall above. Climb this to a precarious exit onto the slab above and finish up slabs to the top.

Mart Crag

1	Gremlin Groove	E2
2	Badger Wall	E3 *
3	Polecat	VS
4	The Widowmaker	VS *
5	Ghetto Blaster	HVS
6	Ride the Wild Turf	E2
7	Parched Parakeet	E2 **
8	Chocolate Frog	E1
9	Rabbit Run	E1
10	Slab and Groove	E2 *
11	Diamond Wall	E4 *
12	Route Twelve	E4 *
v1	Variation Direct Finish	E4
13	Route Thirteen	E5 *
14	Route Fourteen	E3 *
15	Jumblat	E2 *
16	Jungle Genocide	E2 **
17	Route Seventeen	E3 *
18	Minuteman	E3 *

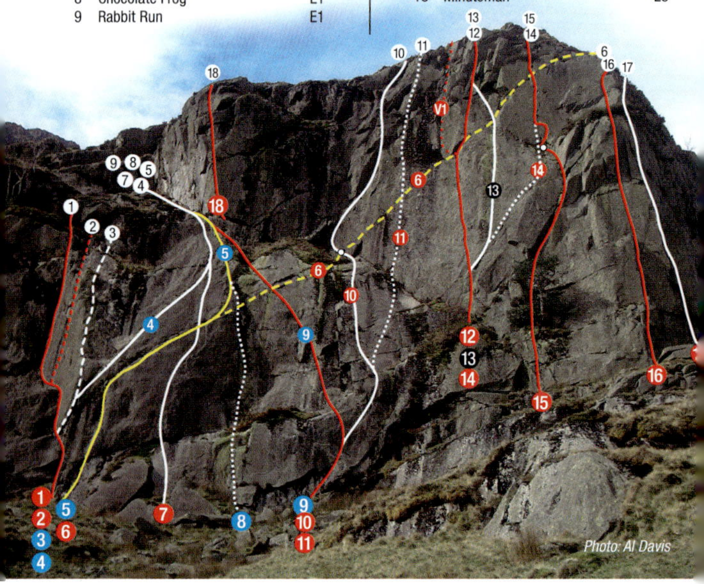

Bat Crack	35m	E2	★	1997

(5c). Follow *Chameleon* to the ledge and a possible belay. The overhanging crack/chimney on the right gives a well-protected jamming exercise. Finish up slabs above.

Grotto Crack	25m	E1	★	1997

Midway between the easy slab of *Chameleon* and the main slab, a vague rib leads to an obvious cave feature.

(5b). The vague grassy rib leads to a jamming crack and the left-hand side of a hanging slab forming the base of a cave. Gain the slab and cross it precariously to gain jamming cracks leading to the top.

1 **Gremlin Groove**	20m	E2		1997

(5b). The filthy corner; if you really want to know.

2 **Badger Wall**	20m	E3	★	1997

(5c). Start up *Gremlin Groove* but move right onto the wall after 2 metres. Climb the centre of the wall over a small roof and rock scar, then move right on easier ground and climb through the bulge via a diagonal crack.

3 **Polecat**	30m	VS		1997

(4b). The left arête of the main slab provides a fairly clean climb.

4 **The Widowmaker**	30m	VS	★	1984

Fairly clean! Start in the left-bounding groove of the large slab.

(4b). Climb the easy groove to a large sloping rock ledge. Cross the wall on the right to the arête and move round to a smaller ledge with a large unsound block. Climb straight up for a metre then diagonally right to gain the shallow scoop in the slab. Go up this to a grass ledge on the left. Move up and right to finish over a bulge to a nut belay on the large ledge.

5 **Ghetto Blaster**	35m	HVS		1984

The lower of the two obvious slanting cracks in the slabs; currently choked with vegetation. Start up a thin crack just right of *The Widowmaker*.

(5a). Climb up the thin crack (crux) and follow the slanting vegetated crack rightwards to a large grass ledge. Traverse left to finish over the bulge, as for *The Widowmaker*, to a nut belay.

6 **Ride the Wild Turf**	80m	E2		1997

Starts as for *Ghetto Blaster* and follows its initial highly vegetated crack.

1 40m (5b). Gain the obvious diagonal crack-line across the crag (as for *Ghetto Blaster*). Follow the crack to climb over or pass under the turf just before the belay.

2 40m (5b). Follow the continuation diagonal crack.

7 **Parched Parakeet**	35m	E2	★★	1984

A good but poorly protected climb up the slim curving groove on the big slab just left of the central bay. Serious but low in the grade.

(5a). Climb up to the sloping ledge and follow the line of big holds to below the slim curving groove just right of the hairline crack. Climb the groove delicately (crux and unprotected) to gain the first diagonal crack and then continue directly up the faint weakness above to the second crack. Follow the slab to its apex and over a bulge to a nut belay on a large ledge on the left.

8 **Chocolate Frog**	30m	E1		1984

The big bay above the grass ledge and just right of ***Parched Parakeet*** is currently liberally coated in lurid green moss. If that hasn't put you off, start at the short groove 3 metres right of ***Parched Parakeet***.

(5a). Climb the short groove to the large grass ledge then up the thin crack in the back of the bay on small holds. Move out left (crux) to a slanting crack and follow this rightwards to a large grass ledge. Traverse left to the bulge of ***Parched Parakeet*** and over this to a nut belay on the ledge.

9 **Rabbit Run**	30m	E1		1997

(5b). The diagonal crack-line was an excellent three star climb when clean. Unfortunately it is currently very grassy, though possibly more appealing to rabbits.

10 **Slab and Groove**	50m	E2	★	1997

1 30m (5b). Climb a ramp-line rightwards for 8 metres then trend left to an obvious blocky spike. Stand on this and make a committing move rightwards before running it out to the grass ledge up on the left.

2 20m (5b). Climb over a blocky ramp (more stable than it looks) and up narrow grooves left of the larger blank one. Near the top, mantelshelf left and then trend rightwards.

11 **Diamond Wall**	45m	E4	★	1997

(6a). Climb ***Slab and Groove*** for 10 metres, then climb a short thin crack to the base of the steep upper wall. Move left up the main ramp for a few metres, then climb onto a narrow ramp leading back right. Move left into a shallow scoop and climb it boldly to a good hold (hidden RP 4 or 5). Make a long reach to the traverse line of ***Ride the Wild Turf***, then move left and climb another shallow scoop to easier ground and a finish at the same point as ***Slab and Groove***.

The next three routes share the same start.

12 **Route Twelve**	40m	E4	★	1995

The obvious shallow groove-line. Serious. Start between the two trees at a short corner.

(5c). Climb up and leftwards on grass and occasional rock to below the groove. Climb up a couple of metres to a Friend 3 placement and then continue delicately up the groove. At the top of the groove, a move right is followed by easier climbing through the bulges passing to the left of some hanging blocks.

v1 ***Direct Finish*** 1997

(5b). The direct continuation of the groove. Still dirty but a lot easier than the climbing below.

13 **Route Thirteen**	40m	E5	★	1995

Very serious. Start as for ***Route Twelve***.

(6a). Follow ***Route Fourteen*** up the diagonal crack for a few metres before following the vague crack-line a couple of metres right of ***Route Twelve***. Finish easily up this route. Could be unlucky 13 if you miss the RP and small spike runner placements en route.

14 **Route Fourteen**	40m	E3	★	1997

Start as for ***Route Twelve***. Rather artificial and hard to start for the short.

(6a). Climb to the Friend 3 placement then follow the diagonal crack rightwards to climb the slab a few metres left of the groove of ***Jumblat***. Finish by climbing directly up the top crack of ***Jumblat***.

15 **Jumblat**	30m	E2	★	1984

Start below the holly tree at the foot of the grass rake, right of the big slab.

1 20m (5b). Climb past the holly into the V-groove. Climb this, over the bulge, and up a corner to a large ledge.

2 10m (5b). The thin crack directly above the corner is gained awkwardly from the right. Peg belay.

16 **Jungle Genocide**	30m	E2	★★	1984

A good route which takes the obvious groove, wall and narrow chimney up the blunt right rib of the crag.

(5b). Move up to beneath the groove and climb it boldly via its left edge to a sloping ledge at its top. Thin moves up the wall (peg runner) lead to the chimney which is followed to a large ledge. The wall above is climbed on its right side. Peg belay.

17 **Route Seventeen**	30m	E3	★	1997

(6a). The arête 2 metres right of ***Jungle Genocide***.

The final route starts on the large ledge at the top of ***Parched Parakeet***, ***Rabbit Run*** etc, at the left side of the arête.

18 **Minuteman**	20m	E3	★	1998

(6a). Climb the flared crack to the arête and good handholds around the corner. Continue steeply up the right-hand side of the arête. Two Friend 2s are useful after the initial crack.

> *"Grisedale is very pleasant; which, ultimately, may mean no more than there is usually evidence of man, people to be shouted to in case of need: whilst in Deepdale one has no such recourse"*
> Harold Drasdo, ***Extremes and Excesses***, FRCC Journal 1960

Hutaple Crag

Grid Reference: **NY 367 120** Altitude: **640m**
Faces: **North-West** Approach: **1 hr 15 mins**

Hutaple Crag stands in Sleet Cove, about 500 metres beyond Greenhow End, with a maze of broken rock and little gullies separating the two. It is a large rather grassy crag about 150 metres high and the main mass is defined on either side by two deep gullies, *East* and *West Hutaple Gullies*. Just left of the centre of the crag, a steep open corner, the *Amphitheatre*, stands above a triangle of grassy slabs. Further right, the long curving open chimney splitting the crag from top to bottom is *Curving Gully*. The crag is cut by two major grassy terraces (*Lower* and *Upper Terraces*) which provide the best, though seriously exposed, means of descent (see below). The rock is generally sound but care is needed with debris on the ledges. Belays and protection can be difficult to arrange and the crag quickly becomes a serious place in poor conditions. The crag has a mountaineering atmosphere and variation of line is often possible on the upper pitches.

Approach:

Park at Bridgend follow the track up Deepdale. The track climbs steeply past *Mart Crag* and, as it levels off, head directly for the crag. It may also be approached from Dunmail Raise, via Grisedale Tarn and Deepdale Hause.

Great care is needed finding a safe descent. The best is to the right. Scramble up from the top of the climbs until it is possible to traverse right along the *Upper Terrace* into and across the grassy funnel above *West Hutaple Gully* and then descend beyond the shoulder above *Far West Rib*. It is also possible to descend at half height, above the interest of the harder climbs, by following the *Lower Terrace* to *West Hutaple Gully* (a scramble is involved at the crossing of *Curving Gully*). Do not descend *West Hutaple Gully* but, either precariously descend vertical vegetation on the right side (facing out) or preferably cross the gully and traverse easy rock rightwards to link up with the usual descent.

The routes are described from **left** to **right**.

The first two routes start from a large terrace, the *Lowest Terrace*, a third of the way up the left side of the crag. This is reached by the first pitch of *East Wall* or by scrambling up from the left.

1 **Scallywag**	40m	E1	★	1991

A good route on rough clean rock taking the steep buttress just right of *East Hutaple Gully*. Start on the left of the *Lowest Terrace* at a short groove.

(5a). Climb the groove and then a short corner above, exiting right and go up to an obvious wide crack. Climb this and the slab above to a narrow ledge then move right slightly and continue to the top.

2 **Exhaustion**	53m	VS		1962

A very disjointed route with a good final pitch. The top pitch climbs the corner-crack at the left end of the crag, overlooking *East Hutaple Gully*. Start at the right end of the *Lowest Terrace* above a scarred area of rock (there is a leftward-slanting chimney high above).

1 35m (4a). Climb up the filthy leftward-slanting groove below the chimney to a ledge. From its left end climb up to a traverse line leading leftwards to a stance overlooking *East Hutaple Gully* and below a prominent corner-crack.

2 18m (4b). Climb the corner-crack or its left wall.

3 **East Wall**	90m	HS	★	1950

A good mountaineering route up generally clean rock. Start at the steep water-worn slab near the left end of the crag.

1 40m. Climb the slabs boldly to the *Lowest Terrace* (or an easier variation up the more broken rock up the left side of the slabs). Walk 18 metres right to a belay.

2 35m. Step down and around a rib to the right and then work steadily upwards to grassy ledges. Climb up to pleasant steep slabs which are tackled directly to a recess and large bollards.

3 15m. Climb the little corner and continue up scoops and slabs to the *Upper Terrace* and a huge block belay. Scrambling leads up to the traverse line for descent.

An inferior variant, **Migraine** (MS, 1950), covered similar ground to *East Wall* but is very dirty.

4 **Sleet Wall**	108m	VS+	★★	1952

A good route up the middle of the steep buttress on the left of *The Amphitheatre*. One of the best climbs in the cove. Start at the foot of a slim left-slanting groove above 9 metres of steep grass and mossy rocks about 10 metres left of the *Amphitheatre*.

1 20m (4b). Follow the left-slanting groove for 6 metres until it is possible to traverse 5 metres left on good holds to a small ledge. Climb the wall above to belay on an overhung ledge.

2 18m (4a). Traverse right and then climb the leftward-slanting weakness to a big grass ledge. Bold.

Hutaple Crag

1	Scallywag	E1	*
2	Exhaustion	VS	
3	East Wall	HS	*
4	Sleet Wall	VS	**
5	Summer Diversion	E2	
6	Heat Wave	E2	
7	The Amphitheatre	HVS	**
8	Amphitheatre Rib	MVS	
9	North-West Grooves	VS	*
10	Cyrano	HS	
11	Curving Gully	MS	**
12	Terrace Wall	VD	*
13	Terrace Wall Variant	VD	
14	Gully Wall	S	
15	Waiting for Laura	HVS	
16	Late Back for Laura	E1	

17	Brown Study	HVS
18	Interrupted Grooves	MVS
19	Broken Ridge	MS
20	Far West Rib	D
21	Western Avenue	D

3 50m (5a). Traverse right and make a very thin move round the right arête to a small ledge. Another tricky move up gains easier rock which is followed to *Lower Terrace* below the steep wall above. Move up leftwards to belay at a block on a ledge on the rib on the left.

4 20m. Climb the rib and then grass on the left to a broad terrace. The terrace above this is the start of the *Upper Terrace* traverse descent.

5 **Summer Diversion**	45m	E2		1978

Start at the leftmost groove in the centre of the wall between *Sleet Wall* and *The Amphitheatre*. The main pitch is very dirty due to years of neglect.

1 20m (4c). Climb the groove and continue up the slabs above to a belay.

2 25m (5b). Move up right into a prominent groove and climb it to the overhang. Swing out left round the arête into an overhung groove. Exit from this on good holds and climb the easier groove above.

Descend via the *Lower Terrace* (see above), or finish up *Sleet Wall* or *The Amphitheatre*.

6 **Heat Wave**	45m	E2		1978

Start up the wall just left of *The Amphitheatre*. Another route which is wearing its neglect like a green mantle.

1 20m (4c). Start up the wall, move right to the arête and follow this to a large ledge. Move left to belay.

2 25m (5b). Move up right into a prominent groove and climb this to the overhang. Surmount the overhang and climb the overhanging groove above with difficulty to a ledge. Continue up a final groove to a grass stance.

Descend via the *Lower Terrace* (see above), or finish up *Sleet Wall* or *The Amphitheatre*.

7 **The Amphitheatre**	138m	HVS	★★	1955

An impressive route up the big corner. The main pitch is delicate, exposed and poorly protected. Start at the left of the triangle of slabs below the corner.

1 26m (4a). Climb the slab until it steepens. Move right to a shallow groove and climb this to a big ledge. Walk right to the foot of a wide broken groove.

2 27m (4c). Climb up on the right of the groove, cross it for a few moves and then step right to pull up onto the steep slab above. Climb delicately up and across the slab to the right (rather bold) to the obvious exit line through the overhangs leading to a good ledge.

3 20m (4c). Move awkwardly into and up the groove on the left. Continue up the groove to the *Lower Terrace* (it is possible to make

a descending traverse left at the start of this pitch and climb the rocks on the left of the groove before moving back right above the awkward section). Scramble up to the right side of a prominent buttress, bounded on the right by a chimney groove.

4 **25m (4a).** Climb up into a recess and cross its left wall onto the front of the buttress. Continue up to a grassy ledge.

5 **40m.** Climb the buttress on the right.

8 **Amphitheatre Rib**	109m	MVS		1955

A poor indirect route. It starts as for *The Amphitheatre*.

1 **26m (4a).** Climb pitch 1 of *The Amphitheatre*.

2 **27m (4a).** Move down to the right and climb a 3 metre corner. Make a long traverse right (about 20 metres) to a small exposed foothold and then surmount the bulge above.

3 **18m (4a).** Climb the groove and continue up to the *Lower Terrace*. Cross the terrace to a prominent buttress on the left with a chimney/groove on its right. (A descent is possible from here by following the *Lower Terrace* to the right).

4 **18m.** Climb the chimney/groove and pull out right. Climb to the ledge above and belay in the chimney.

5 **20m.** Traverse right across the slab for 5 metres and then climb the rib trending rightwards to broken rocks. Scramble up to the *Upper Terrace* traverse descent.

The next feature to the right is a huge corner.

9 **North-West Grooves**	115m	VS+	★	1952

A good mountaineering route with interesting climbing on clean rock. Start on a ledge a short way up the huge corner, gained by scrambling up mossy grassy rock.

1 **24m (4b).** Climb the right wall of the corner (or the corner itself) to a ledge. Move up right to a large grass ledge and belay at its left end.

2 **48m (5a).** Climb easy-angled rock directly above to the left end of a recessed grass ledge. Move 2.5 metres right and mantelshelf up into a groove (crux), which is followed with further interest to the *Lower Terrace*. Trend slightly leftwards up the terrace to a huge block belay below a wall capped by overhangs.

3 **18m (4c).** Turn the first few metres of the wall on the left then climb a steep crack up the left side of the wall to a ledge. Ascend the short wall at its right end and walk right to a large flake.

4 **25m (4b).** Move right for 4 metres and climb over huge perched blocks. Move onto the delightfully exposed nose and climb this and the ridge above direct on good holds to the *Upper Terrace*. An optional continuation up the easier ridge above can be made (22m).

Above: Looking up Deepdale with Link Cove and Scrubby Crag on the left and Sleet Cove on the right. The large crag just left of centre is Greenhow End and Hutaple Crag lies hidden around its right edge. Mart Crag is the small crag peeping over the bracken just right of centre. **Photo:** Eric Shaw

10 **Cyrano**	106m	HS		1954

Takes a line between *North-West Grooves* and *Curving Gully*. Start at a sentry-box at the foot of a large recess midway between *North-West Grooves* and *Curving Gully*.

1 20m. Climb the recess and exit on the left. Step right and climb the rib on the right of a slight groove to the overhang. Move right and climb a steep shallow groove.

2 20m. Climb to the foot of an obvious V-chimney. Avoid the chimney on the left and move back right.

3 16m. Traverse right for 6 metres and climb an awkward scoop to reach the *Lower Terrace*. (It is easier to continue the traverse to the right and climb up just before reaching *Curving Gully*).

4 15m. Cross a series of three walls and grassy ledges.

5 12m. Move to the right and climb a groove containing a pedestal to a grassy platform on the left. Pull across the wall, above the groove, to a ledge.

6 23m. Climb the wall on the right and ascend the groove on the left of a large nose. Move diagonally up to the nose and climb it to the *Upper Terrace*. An optional continuation up the easier ridge above can be made, as for *North-West Grooves* (22m).

11 **Curving Gully**	142m	MS	★★	1952

The most obvious line on the crag. A classic climb with more climbing than scrambling.

The climbing starts with a chimney 20 metres up the gully bed. The line thereafter is obvious with stances and belays at frequent intervals.

To the right of *Curving Gully* there is a slabby area of rock beneath the *Lower Terrace*. Two routes climb these slabs. **Descent** from these two routes is rightwards along the terrace to *West Hutaple Gully* – this is not straightforward (see above). It may be preferable to continue up *Broken Ridge*.

12 **Terrace Wall**	64m	VD	★	1952

A pleasant route on sound rock. Belays can be taken at will. Start 12 metres right of *Curving Gully*.

Climb a series of short walls to a stance below steep slabs. Take the centre of the slabs, just left of a doubtful flake, up to a grassy ledge. Climb the wall above directly and continue more easily to the *Lower Terrace*.

13 **Terrace Wall Variant**	60m	VD		1952

A totally independent route, despite its name. Belays can be taken at will. Start 18 metres right of *Terrace Wall* at the bottom right-hand corner of the crag.

Climb rock steps to a ledge below a steep wall. Climb the groove in the centre of the wall, move right to a ledge and continue up the slabs to the *Lower Terrace*.

Several climbs start from the *Lower Terrace*, above the last two climbs, where a steep wall rises to the right of *Curving Gully*.

14 **Gully Wall**	60m	S		1954

A series of harder variations to the upper part of *Curving Gully*. It climbs the rock just right of the gully and may sometimes offer a drier route. The route starts at a little corner-crack just right of the gully.

15 **Waiting for Laura**	55m	HVS		1990

A good but unfortunately neglected route up the slabby wall just right of *Curving Gully*. It is currently very dirty. It starts on the *Lower Terrace* just right of the gully.

1 40m (5b). Climb the crack on the left-hand side of the slab to a pinnacle on a ledge (as for *Gully Wall*). Step right off the top of the pinnacle and climb the mossy slab to a resting place below a corner/groove. Ascend the corner to a loose spike. Move left to a bulge and pull over this to a good ledge. Climb stepped corners to a large grass ledge.

2 15m (4c). Climb the thin left-slanting cracks above.

16 **Late Back for Laura**	40m	E1		1990

This route starts from the *Lower Terrace*, up the narrow rightward-slanting slab 10 metres right of the *Curving Gully*.

1 16m (5a). Move rightwards onto the slab and climb it to ledge system. Scramble up to belay in the obvious corner.

2 24m (5c). Bridge up the corner with difficulty to a higher rock ledge. Move very slightly rightwards into a steep shallow groove. Make some hard moves up the groove to reach good jugs and pull steeply up to a narrow grass ledge. Follow the obvious crack above more easily to belay on the left of a huge square block.

17 **Brown Study**	46m	HVS		1958

A steep and quite awkward climb, poorly protected but worthwhile. Start on the *Lower Terrace*, 15 metres right of *Curving Gully*. A slab with three big footholds is set in the overhanging wall.

1 26m (5a). Step onto the left-hand side of the slab and traverse rightwards. Move awkwardly up into the sentry-box. Pull out and up to the left into a small recess. Gain a large foothold on the right and climb up to a terrace.

2 20m (4a). Climb the obvious corner-groove. Scrambling for 45 metres leads to the top.

18 **Interrupted Grooves**	53m	MVS		1958

A steep climb on sound rock taking the centre of the upper wall. Start 12 metres right of *Brown Study* up the right-hand of two grooves at the lowest point of the wall.

1 14m. Climb the wall using the grooves alternately.

2 18m. Climb the continuation groove, step right to a grass ledge and move up to a terrace.

3 9m. Move up to the left to the foot of a big groove containing a small square overhang.

4 12m. Climb the groove, passing the overhang with difficulty, to a big grassy ledge with a huge square block 5 metres to the left. Scrambling leads to the *Upper Terrace*.

19 **Broken Ridge**	60m	MS		1952

A scrappy start up the broken rocks to the left of *West Hutaple Gully*. Start from a boulder about 9 metres right of *Interrupted Grooves*. The final pitch is quite hard.

1 24m. Climb the broken ridge to a grass ledge.

2 24m. Climb the wall moving slightly right to a recess under an overhang. Step left to a grass ledge and climb a 3 metre corner-crack and the short wall above to a wide grassy terrace.

3 **12m.** Climb the steep wall near its left-hand side and move up to broad grassy ledges. Scramble to the top or traverse right to join the normal descent.

West Hutaple Gully (75m, D, 1954), which defines the right side of the crag, is dangerously loose.

Two climbs have been made to the right of *West Hutaple Gully*. Both routes are on solid clean rock but they lack continuity.

20 **Far West Rib** (50m, D, 1954) climbs the rib to the right of the gully. It starts 9 metres right of and slightly up from the foot of the gully and thereafter the line is obvious.

21 **Western Avenue** (55m, D, 1954) is a natural continuation to *Far West Rib*. It starts about 60 metres above and slightly right of the finish of that climb and ascends a little buttress and the rib above.

Black Buttress

Grid Reference: **NY 365 118** Altitude: **640m**
Faces: **North** Approach: **1 hr 30 mins**

Black Buttress is a prominent pillar to the right of *Hutaple Crag* and separated from it by the big scree shoot called the *Black Tippet*. The buttress stands out from the hillside and offers a good classic route which is very worthwhile. It could easily be combined with a route on *Cofa Pike Slabs* to give an excellent mountain day in a wild setting.

Portcullis Ridge	58m	VD	★★	1952

Start just right of the toe of the buttress at a small chimney.

1 **18m.** Climb the rib on the left of the chimney, move 2 metres left and then up to a ledge. Move right and climb up pocketed rock to a platform on the top of the buttress.

2 **3m.** Climb the short wall on the right, move up a little groove and traverse diagonally left to a small stance on the edge of the slabs. Climb the groove to a large ledge. Belay well back.

3 **17m.** Continue to the next ledge on the left side of the arête. Climb the wall just right of the corner to a hard but well-protected finish.

Scramble on upwards until it is possible to traverse left to **descend** the *Black Tippet*. An excellent alternative is to climb with rucksacs and continue upwards to reach the summit plateau of Fairfield.

Black Buttress

Two other climbs have been made. **The Tippet** (MVS, 1964) starts 18 metres left and above *Portcullis Ridge* and climbs the face with increasing difficulty. **Cofa Wall** (S, 1954) finds a way up the uninviting and vegetated rocks to the right of *Portcullis Ridge*.

Cofa Pike Slabs

Grid Reference: **NY 359 121** Altitude: **750m**
Faces: **South-East** Approach: **2 hr**

On Cofa Pike's east flank overlooking the upper reaches of Sleet Cove is a small sweep of fairly continuous slabs. Despite the presence of tussocky ledges, the rock in between is rough and clean giving good but bold climbing. The crag would suit a team which fancied a long walk and not much climbing, though climbing here could follow a route on *Black Buttress* to give an excellent mountain day.

Cofa Pike

1 Sofa on Cofa VS *

Approach:
Follow the track up Deepdale and, as it levels off past *Mart Crag*, head directly for the crag high on Cofa Pike. Alternatively, approach from Dunmail Raise via Grisedale Tarn and Deepdale Hause.

Descend to the right.

The climbs are described from **left** to **right**.

1 **Sofa on Cofa**	34m	VS	★	2007

Start at the left-hand side of the slabs below a small roofed recess at 3 metres: cairn. A delightful route giving fine sustained slab climbing.

1 19m (4c). Gain the recess and pull over its left side before trending right to a ledge. Move up slightly leftwards to reach and climb the faint seam up the slab above and so reach a comfortable bilberry ledge with spike belays (the *Sofa*), a delightful place, especially in August.

2 15m (4b). Pull out to the left and climb the pleasant slab to a ledge then follow a left-trending ramp. The cracked slab above is optional.

Yonder Slab	30m	MVS		2007

Follows the right-hand side of the slabs. Start 3 metres right of *Sofa on Cofa*.

1 18m (4b). Climb the blunt rib keeping just left of the grassy fault to reach the *Sofa*.

2 12m (4b). Step right up a short gangway and climb the slabby wall towards the prominent bulbous headwall. Avoid this on the left and reach the top.

It's Easily Done	25m	MVS		2007

Very contrived but pleasant enough. Just down and left of *Sofa on Cofa* is an undercut buttress marking the lowest point of the rocks. 40 metres left and up from here a grassy terrace (cairn) leads right to blocks below a slabby arête. A razor-slashed crack cleaving an overhanging wall high up is clearly visible and forms pitch 2. Start at the blocks.

1 15m (4a). Climb the right-hand side of the slabby arête pleasantly and its continuation to a ledge and belay. Scramble 10 metres right and up to gain a comfortable grassy ledge below the razor-slashed crack.

2 10m (4b). Climb the steep wall to gain the crack. Follow the crack using a specially-designed set of footholds on the left until a final move gains the finishing slab. **Descend** to the right.

Other micro routes have been recorded on outcrops in this area and more forgettable routes have been recorded on **Grey Crag (NY 363 126)** on the south-east flank of St Sunday Crag.

Dovedale

Dovedale lies to the south of Deepdale. It is about 3 kilometres long and runs north-east to join the main valley to the south of Brothers Water. The Patterdale to Kirkstone road crosses Goldrill Beck just north of the lake at Cow Bridge and a track leads into Dovedale from this point. Alternatively, from the Brothers Water Hotel, walk through the campsite to Hartsop Hall. Just beyond the Hall, follow the right-hand path ascending the hillside. The crags are listed anticlockwise around the valley.

Gill Crag

Grid Reference: **NY 387 119**
Faces: **South**
Altitude: **490m**
Approach: **1 hr**

Gill Crag (sometimes called *Dovedale Slabs*) lies close to the summit of Hartsop above How. A 15 metre wall is separated from the main slabs by a grassy terrace called *Bird Cage Walk*. The rock is excellent and the climbs are great fun. Variation is possible almost anywhere but the routes listed take the best lines.

Approach:

The crag can be approached directly from the track up Dovedale. Follow the track from Hartsop Hall for 1 km. As the trees finish the wall ends. Go through the final gate and ascend steeply near the stream on the right. The crag can be seen on the skyline to the left of the stream. 1 hour from Cow Bridge/50 minutes from the campsite.

Alternatively and much more pleasantly, starting from Bridgend in Deepdale, follow the wall along the Hartsop above How ridge. As the wall bears left away from the ridge, follow it until it begins to drop steeply into Dovedale. The crag is across the gully on the right.

The easiest **descent** is on the right.

The climbs are described from **left** to **right**.

Gill Crag

1	Younger Days	S
2	Left Ridge	VD
3	Gill Crag Grooves	VD
4	Flake Buttress	D *
5	Main Slab Route to the Perch	VD **
6	Table de Roc	MVS
7	Right Ridge	HS *

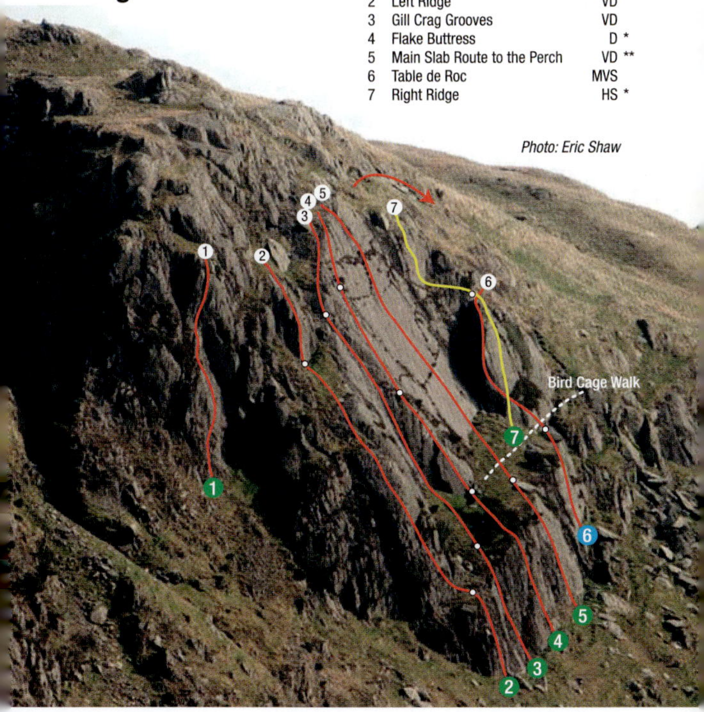

Photo: Eric Shaw

1 **Younger Days**	38m	S		1979

High on the left of the crag, above a rowan, is an overhung cave/corner with a left-leaning corner-crack to its left. The slab forming the left side of the corner is climbed. Start at an embedded flake at the base of the slab down to the left. Bold and poorly protected.

Climb straight up for 5 metres before trending rightwards almost into the corner and then straight up. At the top of the corner, move right onto a grooved arête directly above the corner to finish in an exposed position.

2 **Left Ridge**	53m	VD		1938

The climb starts by a boulder on the left of the lowest part of the crag.

1 9m. Climb the rib behind the boulder to *Bird Cage Walk*.

2 36m. Climb the ridge on the left finishing up easy slabs and grass to

the foot of a steep nose. Large flake belay.

3 **8m.** Climb the left edge of the nose directly or, more easily, gain it from the right.

3	**Gill Crag Grooves**	50m	VD		1983

Start 4 metres right of ***Left Ridge*** at clean rock just left of a heathery/grassy groove.

1 **15m.** Climb clean rock to ***Bird Cage Walk***.

2 **20m.** Ascend to the flake of ***Flake Buttress*** and climb a groove to its left.

3 **15m.** Easily to the top.

4	**Flake Buttress**	53m	D	★	1937

The climb starts 12 metres right of ***Left Ridge*** at the centre of the lower wall.

1 **15m.** Climb the clean rib to ***Bird Cage Walk***.

2 **15m.** Climb the flake at the back of the ***Bird Cage Walk*** by its face, or by a through route, or as a chimney, and continue to the foot of the next pitch.

3 **18m.** Climb the slab to a stance on the left edge and scramble up into a grassy recess.

4 **5m.** Climb the steep corner or the nose on its right.

5	**Main Slab Route to the Perch**	47m	VD	★★	1937

Delightful climbing on the main pitch but with no protection. Start 12 metres right of ***Flake Buttress*** at a boulder by the right end of the crag.

1 **14m.** Climb the wall to ***Bird Cage Walk***.

2 **33m.** Climb the main slab directly to the top. Superb. Scrambling leads to the ***Perch***.

6	**Table de Roc**	24m	MVS		2002

Start 10 metres right of ***Main Slab Route*** on top of the perched rock table.

1 **12m.** Climb the wall to ***Bird Cage Walk***.

2 **12m.** Gain the juniper ledge on pitch 1 of ***Right Ridge*** from the left. Step left immediately onto the rib and climb it, then follow the horizontal section above leading to easier ground.

7	**Right Ridge**	28m	HS	★	

Start at the right-hand end of ***Bird Cage Walk*** at a steep rib leaning towards the main slab. Two pleasant little pitches but with no protection.

1 **15m.** Ascend 2 metres to a juniper ledge. Continue up the south-east facing slab to the arête above the rib which is followed until it joins the main face.

2 **13m.** Traverse 5 metres left across the little gully and climb the steep wall.

Corner and Wall 18m 1937

The original way but much less enjoyable.

1 **15m.** Climb the corner on the left of the rib, or the chimney next to it. Continue up and right to join the arête.

Black Crag

Grid Reference: **NY 378 116** Altitude: **520m**

Faces: **South-East** Approach: **1 hr**

Black Crag, sometimes called *Dovedale Buttress*, faces across the head of the valley. It is about 60 metres high and, though its generally vegetated appearance is extremely off-putting, the left-hand section is actually relatively clean and dries quickly.

The approach from the track up Dovedale is obvious.

The best **descent** is on the left.

The climbs are described from **left** to **right**.

Black Crag Dovedale

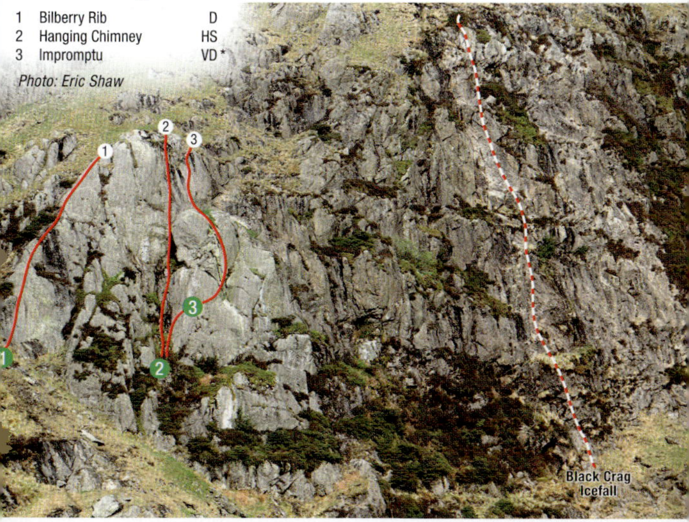

1	Bilberry Rib	D
2	Hanging Chimney	HS
3	Impromptu	VD *

Photo: Eric Shaw

At the left end of the crag, about 20 metres above and left of the lowest point, a grassy bay 10 metres above the base of the crag is guarded by juniper bushes. This bay is a marker for the three described routes.

1 **Bilberry Rib**	40m	D		1947

This route climbs some ribs on the left flank of the crag. At the left end, at the foot of the crag, there is a juniper by the start of ***Impromptu***. This climb starts at the foot of a rib 9 metres up to the left from this tree.

1 20m. Climb the rib. Move right to the arête and continue to a ledge.

2 20m. Follow the arête and finish up the slab on the right. A very pleasant pitch.

2 **Hanging Chimney**	26m	HS		1947

A poor, loose and vegetated route. Start in the grassy bay above the juniper.

Climb the obvious narrow chimney on the right side (crux) and continue to the top.

3 **Impromptu**	38m	VD	★	1947

Start by the juniper below the grassy bay at the left-hand end of the crag. Scramble up into the bay. A pleasant climb on clean rough rock.

1 28m. Climb the arête on the right to a small ledge and traverse right to a corner-crack. Follow the crack for a few moves, then climb the slab to a grass ledge.

2 10m. Climb the wall near its left edge.

Further routes have been recorded on the central slabby area of the crag but they are wet, very vegetated and are best left undisturbed in their splendid verdant obscurity. In fact they are unrecognisable as rock climbs, which indeed they really aren't. In winter though it is a different matter – this is the area that forms *Black Crag Icefall*.

Dove Crag

Grid Reference: **NY 376 109** Altitude: **580m**
Faces: **North-East** Approach: **1 hr 15 mins**

This magnificent crag is one of the most impressive pieces of rock in the district, its central and right-hand sections being sheer or overhanging for most of their height. The main face consists of two buttresses separated by a triangle of slabs leading up to steep corners and overhangs. *North Buttress*, on the right, is about 60 metres high and is a sustained overhang with excellent rock; the *Main Crag*, about 90 metres at the highest point, is almost vertical. From the southern end of this face a sharp ridge, *Westmorland's Route*, descends forming the lower part of the wall of *South Gully*, the left-hand limit of the crag. The gully wall forms another face to the crag, looking to the south-east. The main feature of this face is a hanging gully, *Inaccessible Gully*.

Approach:
The crag is a very obvious presence to the left of the main track up Dovedale.

Descent is to the right.

The climbs are described from **right** to **left**.

High on the right side of the crag is the well-known *Priest's Hole*, a cave which is a popular bivvy site. The following route starts here.

Xoanan	25m	E4		1991

(6b). Climb up the left side of the cave. Reach out right to a good spike and up to a peg. Pull over a bulge and up to a second peg. Pull over a roof and climb up past a peg to pull over another roof. Move slightly right then up to a horizontal break. Move up to a second break then up to a finishing crux.

Above: Sunrise from the **Priest Hole**, Dove Crag. **Photo:** Ron Kenyon

16
17
10
11
9
6
V3
17
18
6
11
13
10
V3
V4
17
18
9
8
11
8
12
14
15
7
8
9
12
13
14
15
17
16

Dove Crag North Buttress

1	Explosion	E4 *
v1	FFF Link	E5 *
2	Outside Edge	E5 **
3	Yorkshire Pudding	E3 *
4	Fetish For Fear	E7 *
5	Fast and Furious	E5 ***
v2	Flying Fissure Finish	E5 **
6	Bucket City	E6 ***
7	Fear and Fascination	E5 ***
8	Vlad the Impaler	E7 ***
9	Beyond the Pail	E7 **
v3	Original Finish	
10	Fear of Failure	E8 ***
11	Pail Face	E6 ***
v4	Original Finish	
12	Bucket Dynasty	E7 ***
13	Dusk Till Dawn	E7 ***
14	The Darkest Hour	E7 ***
15	The Brasov Incident	E6 ***
16	Hangover	HVS *
17	Asolo	E3 *
18	Problem Child	E4

Photo: Steve Crowe

North Buttress

All the climbs on this tremendous leaning wall offer good climbing on rock which is (mostly) covered with good flat or incut holds. The protection is generally adequate, though a selection of small flexible Friends up to size 2 will be found useful. The routes on the *North Buttress* have seen a lot of attention over recent years and as a result are generally clean and well equipped with in situ gear (where mentioned).

Where French grades have been assigned in brackets, these do not suggest a clip-up! However they are meant to give some idea of the equivalent difficulty of climbing you can expect to find – but without the bolts.

1 **Explosion**	30m	E4	★	1976

A deceptive pitch which is very strenuous and poorly protected. Not a soft touch. Start at the very right of the buttress where an obvious easy gangway leads up and left.

(5c). Climb the steepening gangway up leftwards and then climb more directly upwards to the obvious corner which provides a rest and an easier finish.

v1 ***FFF Link*** 30m E5 {F7a+} ★ 2003

(6b). Start up ***Explosion*** and follow it until it steepens. Step left and reach down to clip the thread on ***Fetish for Fear***. Continue as for ***Fetish for Fear***, finishing up the ***Flying Fissure Finish***.

2 **Outside Edge**	33m	E5 {F7a+}	★★	1990

Really a variation finish to ***Explosion*** but providing it with a sensational and photogenic finish.

(6b). Follow ***Explosion*** to the foot of the final easy corner then traverse left to the arête. Arrange protection, then wild moves up the arête past a thread lead to the top.

3 **Yorkshire Pudding**	20m	E3	★	1988

The thin crack that cuts through the traverse of ***Explosion*** is harder than it looks. Start about 3 metres left of ***Explosion*** below the obvious thin crack.

(5c). Climb the crack to the top.

The next five climbs all have a common start at an obvious flake about 10 metres left of the right end of the buttress and 3 metres to the right of the rock step at the base of the crag.

Right: Duncan Booth exhibits a **Fetish for Fear** (E7), Dove Crag. **Photo:** Al Wilson/Chris Hope

4 **Fetish For Fear**	30m	E7 {F7b}	★	2003

(6b). Follow the initial flake of *Fast and Furious* to its top. Move up and right, passing a loose block, to the base of a slim left-leaning groove. Climb this (cams) to an overlap. Reach over this to good holds and make committing moves leftwards (serious) to an obvious large flat hold and in situ thread on the left. Move up and right on large spaced holds to join the *Flying Fissure Finish* at its peg. Continue up this to the top.

5 **Fast and Furious**	45m	E5 {F7a}	★★★	1982

A bold and sustained climb of great quality which takes the shallow groove and headwall directly above the starting flake. The name suggests the required approach! Several longish narrow tapes are useful for the small spikes encountered on the wall.

(6a). Layback to the top of the flake then climb the short bold rib to the base of a smooth wall guarding entry to the groove. Neatly avoid this obstacle with a step up to the right before hand-traversing back left to a peg (new) at the base of the groove. Layback boldly up the groove to better holds and runners then trend rightwards passing a tiny spike to a long reach (crux) to gain a superb hidden jug on top of a short rib. The wall above is climbed boldly, first right, then left, then straight up, aiming for the obvious finishing chimney. Belay above this or continue to better nuts further up to the left.

v2 ***Flying Fissure Finish*** E5 {F7a+} ★★ 1990

A very steep right-hand finish to *Fast and Furious* following the hanging groove left of *Outside Edge* and right of the chimney of *Fast and Furious.*

(6b). Follow *Fast and Furious* to the superb jug after the crux. Move right to a peg runner (new) then race up the wall past an in situ thread runner to gain a line of buckets which lead up the sensational groove to the top.

The Inside Out Link 30m E5/6 {F7b} ★★ 2003

(6b). Start up *Fast and Furious* following the rightwards traverse (past the peg on *Flying Fissure Finish*) to finish up *Outside Edge*. Mega pump! (Shown on the diagram as the finish of *The Brasov Incident*).

6 **Bucket City**	45m	E6 {F7b}	★★★	1988

Another tremendous pitch, this time taking the obvious diagonal crack to the left of *Fast and Furious* and an intricate line up the superb headwall.

(6b). Layback the starting flake of *Fast and Furious* but step left into

Left: Al Wilson prepares for a mega pump on **The Inside Out Link** (E6), Dove Crag.
Photo: Steve Crowe

a shallow cave. Pull over the bulge and climb up to the break. Step left round the rib to the base of a thin diagonal crack sporting several old pegs. Fight the stubborn crack to a rest in the niche (*Fear and Fascination* gains this point from the left) then climb up and rightwards as for *Fear and Fascination*, passing an obvious spike to gain the right end of the obvious ledge system and a good rest. Make a couple of moves up the groove above before breaking out left via a line of holds on the lip of an overlap. These lead to an obvious slot from which a line of reasonable holds, breaks and ledges lead directly up the wall passing a peg runner just below the top.

North Buttress	59m	E6		1969

The original aid climb is now free after a series of attempts over many years. Although difficult the climb is somewhat disjointed.

1 37m (6b/c). Follow *Bucket City* to the niche at the top of the diagonal crack. Climb the short technical wall above, past a line of decaying pegs and bolts, to the ledge system. Traverse left for 10 metres to an uncomfortable niche with a peg and bolt belay and assorted nuts.

2 22m (5c). Climb up the back of the niche to an old peg runner then move left and climb the ramp to more rusting horrors. Move up and right and climb the wall, traversing rightwards past a groove to a gangway leading leftwards to a tree and belays just above.

Fast City	37m	E5 {F7a}	★★★	2003

(6a). A direct line up *North Buttress* linking the start of *Fast and Furious* with the top of *Bucket City*. It follows *Fast and Furious* to the top of the groove and moves left to gain the prominent spike (junction with *Fear and Fascination/Bucket City*). Climb up to the ledge system then make a couple of moves up the groove above before breaking out left via a line of holds above the lip of an overlap. These lead to a slot (small cams) from which a line of reasonable holds, breaks and ledges lead directly up the wall, slightly right, passing a peg runner just below the top.

The next feature is a two metre rock-step at the foot of the crag behind a large block. The following four climbs all start at the foot of this feature where an obvious flake crack leads up and left to a rock shelf at 6 metres.

7 **Fear and Fascination**	48m	E5+ {F7a+}	★★★	1980

A classic climb; bold, strenuous, intimidating and maintaining interest right to the top. Brilliant.

(6a). Climb the flake crack to the rock shelf and pull up the wall at the

Right: Karin Magog on the big lead of **Vlad the Impailer** (E7), Dove Crag. **Photo:** Steve Crowe

right end of the shelf to an old peg runner. Continue up the wall to a good flake and then less easily to a short crozzly crack. Hand-traverse right and pull into the niche on *Bucket City* (old pegs). Step right and up, as for *Bucket City*, passing an obvious spike to gain the right end of the ledge system and a good rest. Climb the fine groove-line above, making a sneaky step out right when all the holds seem to run out, and finishing via the obvious deep groove. A belay may be taken on the shelf at 6 metres to reduce the runout, though this is not normally necessary.

8 **Vlad the Impailer**	35m	E7 {F7c}	★★★	1990

This is the obvious fault-line leading out leftwards from *Fear and Fascination* to the bay of *Asolo*. Stupendous, bold and very strenuous climbing make this an unforgettable route. The pegs and in situ tat were replaced not long before this guide was published. Long slings are essential to prevent rope drag higher up the pitch. Start at the foot of the rock step.

(6b). Follow *Fear and Fascination* to the good flake. Swing left to a jug and then another (0 Friend above), then traverse left to an in situ Rock 1 and vital Friend 2.5 just above it. Undercut left to a downward pointing spike and good footholds, then pull up left to a Rock 1 and crucial Friend 0.5 or Wallnut 6 above. Swing down across left (Friend 3) then climb up past a peg runner to a jug (Friend 1 or 1.5 on right). Gain the block and niche up and left (crux, peg runner) and continue up the fault-line (peg runner and thread on rock chock) to gain the belay of *Asolo*. Either finish up *Asolo*, or alternatively the leader can reverse to the in situ gear, the

Above: Vlad Stones and remnants of Dove Crag's in situ finds cleaned from the crag.
Photo: Steve Crowe

second climb up to the rock shelf and, from here, lower the leader to the ground. Karabiners are in situ to facilitate this more convenient option.

9 **Beyond the Pail**	50m	E7 {F7b+}	★★	1989

A difficult climb which has now been extended to the top of the crag giving one magnificent pitch. Start at the foot of the rock step.

(6b). Follow *Fear and Fascination* to the crozzly crack. Climb directly above this aiming for a peg just below the ledges. Traverse right easily to join *Bucket City* and follow this to the top.

v3 ***Beyond the Pail – Original Start and Finish*** 53m 1989

The route was first climbed in two contrasting pitches. The second is very bold and dirty and has probably not seen a second ascent.

1 27m (6b). Follow *Fear and Fascination* to the crozzly crack. Climb directly above this aiming for a peg just below the ledges. Traverse left along the ledge system to belay in the niche of *North Buttress* on a poor bolt, thread and good peg up and right.

2 26m (6a). Climb up past the good peg and continue up passing a pathetic blade peg runner on its right until better holds eventually arrive. Climb up to finish at the obvious tree.

10 **Fear of Failure**	50m	E8 {F7c+}	★★★	2002

A very big route, freeing the old aided first pitch of *Broken Arrow* before taking a sweeping run-out across the top wall.

(6c). Climb the wall as for *Vlad the Impailer* but pull up with difficulty to good side-pulls (peg from old aid section). Make a hard move via sloping pinch and continue with exciting moves to reach the ledge. Step up left to clip the first peg on the second pitch of *Beyond the Pail* then make a harrowing traverse up rightwards to buckets on *Bucket City* and finish up this, or the groove on the left. Exciting!

11 **Pail Face**	50m	E6 {F7b+}	★★★	1990

A magnificent route which has now been extended to the top of the crag. Start at the foot of the rock step. Long slings essential.

(6b). Follow *Vlad the Impailer* to the 2.5 Friend. Make hard moves directly up the wall above then slightly rightwards to a good ledge with a spike runner and rest. Climb into the niche above then traverse right for 2 metres to join *Bucket City* which is followed to the top of the crag.

Original Finish

The route originally climbed into the niche at the end of pitch 1 of *North Buttress*. From here there are three alternatives, each less palatable than the last. The first is to lower off! The second is to climb pitch 2 of *Beyond the Pail*. The third and now mostly of historic interest is:

Broken Arrow	50m	E5		1980

2 25m (5c). Follow pitch 2 of *North Buttress* but where it moves right continue up the easy ramp to the edge of the buttress. Traverse the ledge leftwards and cross the steep groove of *Asolo* to belay below the last pitch of *Hangover*.

3 25m (4c). The last pitch of *Hangover*.

The first pitch of *Broken Arrow* followed a line 3 metres right of *Pail Face* by using both an aid nut (missing and impossible to place from below) and a poor aid peg to gain better holds and the ledge system. Nowadays there seems little point in such antics.

The next climb starts about 15 metres left of the previous climbs below the right end of an obvious grassy terrace (top of pitch 1 of *Hangover*).

12 **Bucket Dynasty**	25m	E7 {F7c}	★★★	1991

Another steep exciting climb on good rock. Start at the obvious layback crack below the right end of the grassy terrace of *Hangover*.

(6b). Climb the crack to its top and follow the wall above until a move left leads to huge holds (2.5 Friend). Climb the intimidating wall above to a good layaway (1 and 00 Friends). Pull up again to gain *Vlad the Impailer* at the Friend 3. Finish up *Vlad the Impailer*.

13 **Dusk till Dawn**	30m	E7 {F7c}	★★★	2003

This route climbs the huge leaning pillar on the *North Buttress*. An awesome route, one of the steepest lines in the Lakes. A double set of small cams is recommended. Start as for *Bucket Dynasty* at the obvious layback crack below the right end of the grassy terrace.

(6b). Follow *Bucket Dynasty* to the junction with *Vlad the Impailer* at the Friend 3 – i.e. all of it! Reverse *Vlad the Impailer* for a couple of metres to good holds (Friend 0.5 or Wallnut 6). Make moves up and rightwards to gain the right side of the pillar. A series of big moves on good holds following a leftwards-leaning ramp leads to a huge shake out below a ramp sporting a peg at its top. Make hard moves up to and past the peg (leftwards) to superb jugs on the left side of the pillar. More huge moves upwards lead to a small ledge. The tricky groove above is climbed to another ledge. Abseil descent (in situ).

Right-Hand Start E7 {F7c} 2003

Marginally less serious than the original start, but not much.

(6b). Follow *Vlad the Impailer* to the junction with *Dusk till Dawn* and finish up *Dusk till Dawn*.

Right: Chris Hope finds a bucket on **Bucket Dynasty** (E7), Dove Crag. **Photo:** Steve Crowe

Above: A slab it ain't! Steve Crowe on very steep ground on **The Brasov Incident** (E6), Dove Crag. **Photo:** Steve Crowe Collection

14 **The Darkest Hour**	30m	E7+ {F7c+}	★★★	2005

A direct start to *Dusk till Dawn*.

(6c). Follow the initial layback flake of *Bucket Dynasty* then step right onto the first ledge. Starting below the weakness in the roof above, climb directly up to the point where *Dusk till Dawn* leaves *Vlad the Impailer*. Follow *Dusk till Dawn* to the top.

15 **The Brasov Incident**	30m	E6 {F7b+}	★★★	2003

A big sweeping left to right girdle which starts up *Bucket Dynasty* at the layback flake.

(6b). Climb *Bucket Dynasty* to the bulge. Traverse right beneath the roof, passing two pegs, to join *Fear and Fascination* at the spike below its crux. Move up and across, as for *Fear and Fascination*, to a junction with *Bucket City* and continue up until it is possible to step right at a good spike on *Fast and Furious* below its crux. Move up to the good jug, then continue rightwards beneath the *Flying Fissure Finish* to finish up *Outside Edge*. It is possible to lower-off the in situ slings with a 60 metre rope.

Left: Al Wilson on his own creation, **Dusk Till Dawn** (E7), Dove Crag. **Photo:** Steve Crowe

Dove Crag

Not all routes marked.

1	Explosion	E4	*
2	Outside Edge	E5	**
3	Yorkshire Pudding	E3	*
5	Fast and Furious	E5	***
6	Bucket City	E6	***
7	Fear and Fascination	E5	***
8	Vlad the Impaler	E7	***

11	Pail Face	E6 ***
12	Bucket Dynasty	E7 ***
16	Hangover	HVS *

18	Problem Child	E4
19	Extol	E2 **
20	Aurora	E3 *
21	Mordor	E3
22	Phobos	E2 **
23	Hiraeth	E2 *
v5	Variation	
24	Dovedale Groove	E1 **
25	Ommadawn	E5
26	Westmorland's Route	MS **

Photo: Al Phizacklea

Main Crag

Sadly, some of the routes on the rest of the crag have not seen so many ascents recently and are subsequently rather dirty – take care!

16 **Hangover**	72m	HVS	★	1939

A fine route once, though now quite dirty, weaving the easiest way up the centre of this daunting crag. The upper part is exposed and some of the rock needs care. Start at the right side of the triangle of slabs just left of a big boulder.

1 18m. Climb the grassy groove and then traverse right to a belay below the corner (or continue up the next pitch).

2 29m (5a). Climb the corner for 12 metres then traverse left with difficulty for 3 metres. Step up and re-enter the corner over a bulge. Move up and climb a small chimney then step round the rib to a good stance.

3 25m (4c). Traverse right with care along the shattered ledge and climb a pinnacle. Move up to a groove, step right across a rib into a corner and climb the V-chimney to the top.

> *"I had heard that Jim Birkett had found and was developing a new crag and thought this was Dove Crag so I went there and climbed Hangover. I later found that the crag in question was Castle Rock and Birkett had just climbed Overhanging Bastion and Zig Zag so I did the second ascents."* Jim Haggas in old age, being quite matter of fact about his days of glory.

17 **Asolo**	81m	E3	★	1981

Follows the groove on the left of *North Buttress*. The final pitch is bold and serious. Start left of *Hangover* at the short slab with a faint crack running diagonally across it.

1 34m (5c). Climb the thin crack in the mossy slab to a dirty stance. Continue up the wall and climb the groove to a junction with *Hangover*. This pitch is very dirty.

2 10m (6a). Move up *Hangover* and traverse right at an old peg passing a large spike to the base of the large groove. Poor belays.

3 37m (5c). Climb the groove to a glacis on the right. Traverse right then climb directly up to the break. Pull out left at the lip. Finish on the right over a pointed block.

18 **Problem Child**	86m	E4		1976

Start at the tree belay just right of the chimney of *Extol*. A serious route.

1 33m (5c). Climb across to the right then via a glacis back left and up to an overhung niche. Pull over the roof using a doubtful block. Climb up and slightly right until below a short groove. Climb this on the right and continue direct to the belay on *Hangover*.

2 33m (6a). Step left into the steep groove and climb it until moves

right can be made onto some large blocks below an overhanging rib. Pull onto this and continue up until a traverse right can be made to a belay in a groove.

3 20m (6a). Climb the groove and the crack above to the overhang. Step left, layback round this on poor holds and follow a short crack to the top.

19 **Extol**	75m	E2+	★★	1960

A classic of the Sixties finding its way up the centre of the crag with some exposed positions in its upper reaches. Although most of the route is rather broken and dirty, the section of worthwhile climbing at the top is clean and still remains a good challenge. Start at the left end of the triangular slab. Scramble up broken rocks to some trees below a chimney.

1 30m (5a). Climb the unpleasant and unprotected chimney to join *Hangover* at the top of pitch 2. A more enjoyable alternative is to follow *Hangover* to the good stance at the top of pitch 2 – but what would Whillans say?!

"Extol is rather like Whillans; direct, uncompromising and hard."
Chris Bonington, Hard Rock, 1973.

2 45m (5b). The grassy leftward-slanting line 6 metres left of the stance is the initial objective. Cross the main groove and then swing left on a series of good jugs to reach the ramp. Climb this with a brief excursion on the right wall at its top to reach a position below the steep wall beneath the overhang. Climb the short steep wall to the big overhang. Step right and pull into a bottomless groove which splits the overhang. Follow the groove until forced to move right to finish up the rib.

Above: Cherrie Whiteley on the finishing holds of **Extol** (E2), Dove Crag. **Photo:** Tim Whiteley

20 **Aurora**	78m	E3	★	1977

A good climb taking the steep upper wall between *Mordor* and *Hiraeth*. Start a few metres left of the triangular slab.

1 30m (5b). Climb easily up leftwards over ledges to a break in the overhangs. Climb up the corner and traverse left above the overhangs to reach a vague groove-line. Follow this, passing a steep scoop, and take the slabs above to a peg belay at the top of pitch 1 of *Mordor*.

2 27m (5c). Step up a groove behind the belay and traverse left above the large overhang for 6 metres. Climb straight up over large hanging flakes to a ledge. Step right and climb a wall and short groove to a good spike. Move right and climb the wall just right of the prominent groove to a resting place. Step left and climb up on undercuts, move left to a groove beneath the overhang and surmount this to a belay on *Hiraeth*.

3 21m (5a). Step up from the belay and traverse right across slabs to the arête. Climb this to join *Hiraeth* and follow it to the top.

21 **Mordor**	75m	E3		1965

A serious climb with a loose second pitch. Start 6 metres left of the triangular slab below a grassy groove with a smooth left wall above.

1 30m (5a). Climb a grassy rib on the right of the groove to steeper rock. Pull into a small niche above, step right and climb up left to a resting place. Trend rightwards up an overhanging wall and pull onto the large slab above. Climb the slab rightwards to a small stance and peg belay in the centre of the slab.

2 12m (5c). Climb the overhangs at their weakest point some 3 metres right of the stance and make a hard move left. Continue up and right to a ledge and peg belay.

3 33m (5b). Climb the bulge above into a groove. After a metre or so, move round the arête and cross onto *Extol*. Finish up this.

22 **Phobos**	69m	E2	★★	1972

A steep wall climb taking the challenges that *Hiraeth* avoids. Many slings are recommended for runners – not less than six should suffice. To the left of *Mordor* the path at the foot of the crag steepens to a scramble leading up to the obvious crack of *Dovedale Groove*. Start at the foot of the scramble.

1 30m (5c). Climb vegetated rock to reach a clean crack on the left of an overhang. Follow this crack to the middle of the traverse of *Hiraeth* and move up right to the highest of the flat rock ledges. Climb leftwards for 6 metres up the steep wall then move right to a shallow niche. Step back left and climb the groove, stepping left below the bulge, to the overhang above. Turn this on the right and take a stance at the foot of the terrace.

2 15m (4b). Step right and climb leftwards to a gangway parallel to the terrace. Ascend the gangway and the chimney above rightwards to a stance on *Hiraeth*.

3 24m (5a). Climb the short corner of *Hiraeth* and move right past a large spike to below a large corner. Ascend the corner and hand-traverse right along a thin crack below a roof, then move up to gain easier ground and the top.

23 **Hiraeth**	75m	E2	★	1962

A climb of contrasts; the bold poorly protected first pitch leading to a well-protected crux. Scramble up to a belay some 6 metres below the crack of *Dovedale Groove*. Unfortunately rather grubby.

1 27m (5a). Climb a thin crack to the top of the slab then follow the obvious line rightwards to a small ledge then up to grass on the left and continue up the steep wall above to a small stance.

2 15m (5b). Move up to a sloping ledge on the left. The green groove above is climbed direct and constitutes the crux of the climb.

3 15m (5a). Move left and ascend a short overhung corner. Traverse right for 10 metres to a rib and drop down a groove to a stance (or continue).

4 18m (5a). Climb back up the groove and ascend a steeper groove to the right of the rib. Move right, then leftwards up overlapping mossy slabs to the top.

v5 ***Variation*** 27m 1973

3 (5b/c). To the right of the stance is a short groove with a jammed spike. Climb to it, cross the wall on the right to gain a ledge of detached blocks and climb up to re-join the original route below the steep groove.

Above: Hiraeth (E2), Dove Crag. **Photo:** Nick Wharton

24 **Dovedale Groove**	54m	E1+	★★	1953

A classic product of the 'Rock and Ice' years which takes the impending crack-line to the left of *Hiraeth*. Start at the foot of the obvious crack behind a large boulder.

1 15m (5b). From the top of the slab make an awkward move into the groove and continue by bridging and jamming to a stance below a conspicuous overhanging crack.

2 18m (5b). Climb the crack to a chockstone then pull awkwardly out left onto a slab. Continue more easily up a groove and slab to a large grass ledge.

3 8m. Move up to a grass ledge below some overhangs.

4 13m (5a). Above a short slab is a gap in the overhangs. Climb through this and step left into the left-hand groove. Follow the groove to the top.

Dove Crag Far Left

26	Westmorland's Route	MS **
27	Up Hellya	E8 **

25 **Ommadawn**	88m	E5		1978

Sustained and strenuous climbing with poor protection. It starts at the foot of *Dovedale Groove* and climbs the wall to its left.

1 17m (5b). Climb the first 6 metres of *Dovedale Groove* until it is possible to step onto a sloping ledge on the left. Climb the wall above slightly leftwards to a ledge below a steep wall. Traverse left for 4 metres to a good spike belay.

2 36m (6a). Traverse back right to the ledge. Climb straight up the wall to a peg runner below the overhang. Pull strenuously onto the wall above and continue in the same line to a good ledge. Climb the wall above to a large grassy ramp and block belay.

3 35m (5c). Move 5 metres down the ramp to a slim mossy groove which is climbed to small ledges beneath *Dovedale Groove's* finish. Climb across right towards two indefinite grooves. Climb the left-hand groove until it is necessary to pull onto the rib on the right. Pull up the rib and into a groove that slants up rightwards and leads to the top.

26 **Westmorland's Route**	110m	MS	★★	1910

An interesting mountaineering route which takes the ridge bounding *South Gully* to its right and abuts against the left end of the main face. It becomes much harder in anything less than perfect conditions and should not be underestimated. Start at the foot of the ridge just below a huge boulder in *South Gully*.

1 21m. Easy rock steps lead rightwards to the grassy ridge which is followed easily to a large ledge below the obvious rock ridge.

2 21m. Ascend the ridge on its slabby right side to a sloping stance on the ridge by a pinnacle belay.

3 15m. Follow the ridge directly to a grassy ledge below a wall.

4 20m. Traverse right on spiky brackets for 5 metres above a gully and ascend the mossy leftward-slanting slab to a grassy ledge on the ridge.

5 21m. Climb the little wall and traverse up to the left to the end of the gangway. Move up to a large bilberry covered ledge and traverse this rightwards to the belay.

6 12m. Climb the final wall.

South Gully is loose and usually wet and not recommended either for ascent or descent except when frozen.

A poor route, **The Tarsus** (HS, 1937), climbs the wall of *South Gully* to reach pitch 5 of *Westmorland's Route*. It is loose and not recommended.

Overleaf: Dave Birkett breaks new ground on the first ascent of the spectacular **Up Hellya** (E8), Dove Crag. **Photo:** Another great shot by Alastair Lee

Inaccessible Gully	57m	VS		1937

This is the hanging gully which falls into ***South Gully*** and splits the south-east aspect of the crag. It gives a fine winter climb but not such a good summer one. Start directly below the gully.

1 27m (4c). Climb up to the right over some blocks and pull on to a sloping platform. Climb the wall either directly or by backing and footing up the right-hand corner. Move up to the left into the crack and climb it, or the crack on the right above the wall. Belay 6 metres up the slabs on the right.

2 15m. Ascend the gully to a belay beneath a chockstone.

3 9m (4b). Climb the left wall and move to the right to a stance beneath a second chockstone.

4 6m. Pull out onto the right wall. Scramble up for 24 metres.

Entity	63m	VS		1963

This route takes the face left of ***Inaccessible Gully*** as far as the very steep upper wall then moves round the arête and climbs the left wall of the gully. Start as for ***Inaccessible Gully***.

1 24m (4b). Vegetated rocks lead up leftwards to a grass ledge then climb a groove system to a rowan tree.

2 18m (4a). Take the gangway to the right then follow another gangway slanting back left to a sloping ledge. Traverse right and slightly downwards and swing round the arête into the gully.

3 21m (4b). Climb the chimney/groove on the left wall until it is possible to traverse left to the arête. Traverse left across a slab to reach easier ground.

27 Up Hellya	35m	E8?	☆☆	2009

Climbs the biggest overhanging wall and capping roof left of ***Inaccessible Gully***. Follow ***South Gully*** past the base of ***Inaccessible Gully*** to where the scramble becomes damp and difficult. Belay in the gully above this, directly below the obvious groove/corner-line in the centre of the wall.

(6c). Climb easy ledges to a peg runner. Hard moves lead past the peg and wires to the base of the corner. Climb the corner with difficulty to gain ledges beneath the roof. Taking great care with what you pull on, move slightly rightwards through the roof to the obvious easy groove above.

Eilethgia	51m	MVS		1968

A poor route. Half way up ***South Gully*** is an area of overhangs, on the left of which there is a V-shaped groove. Start 12 metres left of this groove.

1 33m. Traverse right along a ledge and climb a large block to gain the groove which is followed to a belay above some large chockstones.

2 18m. Traverse left until a groove is reached and then up this to the top.

Girdle Traverse	167m	E3	☆	1971

Probably unrepeated in its entirety. Start at the foot of *Inaccessible Gully*.

1 36m (4b). Climb up for a short distance then traverse right. At the end of the traverse climb up diagonally left to gain a gangway. Follow this to join *Westmorland's Route* at the top of pitch 5.

2 28m (5a). Descend the gangway on the right for 5 metres then pull up the steep wall and traverse right round some perched blocks to gain a small ledge. Climb the wall until it is possible to move right into a V-groove. Traverse right to gain another small ledge (peg runner). Descend for 3 metres and continue to a junction with *Dovedale Groove* above pitch 2.

3 12m (5a). Stride across the crack and pull up to a grass ledge. Descend the grass ramp to a peg belay on *Phobos*.

4 15m (5a). Move right to the stance of *Hiraeth* (peg runner). Descend pitch 2 of *Hiraeth* to the traverse of *Aurora*.

5 30m (5a). Descend for 3 metres then traverse right to join pitch 2 of *Mordor*. Follow this to a stance and continue traversing until forced to descend. Move into the chimney of *Extol* and follow it to belay on *Hangover*.

6 24m (6a). Traverse the wall at the level of an old peg to the ledges. Up the groove to the glacis (*Asolo*). Cross the glacis and descend the groove on the far side for 3 metres to a ledge (hanging stance, or better, move down on the right to an old bolt and peg belay on *North Buttress*).

7 22m (5c). As for *North Buttress* pitch 2.

Lower Dove Crag

Grid Reference: **NY 377 110** Altitude: **500m**
Faces: **North-East** Approach: **1 hr 15 mins**

This small rib lies just below and right of *Dove Crag*. It is just left of the main track up Dovedale, about 100 metres above and left of an old quarry hut. The rough bubbly rock is pleasant if inconsequential.

Rusty Fish	25m	VS		1987

Start below the rib on the lower part of the little crag.

(5a). Move into a scoop below the diagonal overhang. Move up to the rib which is followed direct to the top.

Polish Pork	20m	S		1987

Climb the slab 10 metres right of *Rusty Fish* direct, finishing up right.

Heirloom Crag

Grid Reference: **NY 377 107**
Altitude: **750m**
Faces: **North-East**
Approach: **1 hr 30 mins**

This small crag is located about half a kilometre to the left of *Dove Crag* at a slightly higher level.

The rock at the base of the crag is fissile and unpleasant. The routes start from a terrace above this loose lower tier and are on steep compact rock. This terrace is reached from the right-hand side of the crag by a downwards traverse. It should not be approached by the central gully as this too is loose and dangerous.

The main feature of the crag is an obvious central groove taken by *Heirloom*. The best routes lie on the steep rock just to the left.

The routes are described from **right** to **left**

Heirloom Crag

1	Josse F. Boyas	E2
2	Reunion	E1
3	Heirloom	HVS *
4	Relative Ease	HVS
5	Like Father, Like Son	E4
6	Family Affair	E4 **
7	Bloodline	E3 *
8	Genetic Edge	E4

Photo: Al Davis

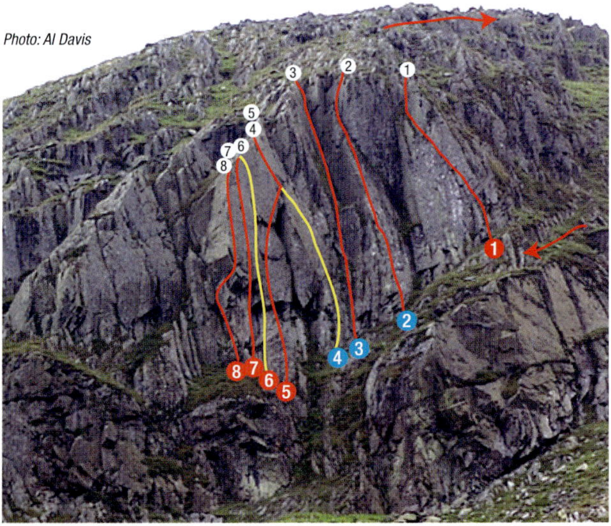

1 **Josse F. Boyas**	10m	E2		1991

A short climb starting at the right end of the terrace.

(5c). Climb leftwards on undercut flakes and cracks.

2 **Reunion**	28m	E1		1991

A direct line up the edge above and to the right of *Heirloom*.

(5b). Start from the foot of the edge, which is followed straight up, passing a delicate slab, and finish via the tricky top right-hand scoop.

3 **Heirloom**	36m	HVS	★	1991

The obvious central groove. Well protected.

(5a). Climb the groove.

4 **Relative Ease**	33m	HVS		1991

Start at the foot of the central groove.

(5a). Follow the dog-leg crack on the left to a crevasse and finish up cracks on the left.

The next three routes start from a stance above the short 3 metre chimney just left of the obvious off-width crack.

5 **Like Father, Like Son**	30m	E4?		1991

The brutally obvious off-width crack gives a similar (but slightly more strenuous!) problem to the *Post Mortem* crack in Borrowdale. A true collector's item.

(6a). Move right into the crack and try to climb it. Belay in the crevasse to avoid rope drag.

6 **Family Affair**	30m	E4	★★	1991

Excellent climbing up the very steep groove and crack about 3 metres left of the off-width crack.

(6a). Make awkward moves over the overhang to enter the groove. Climb this then pull out left to a finger-crack which leads to the top.

7 **Bloodline**	30m	E3	★	1991

Intricate and sustained climbing about 5 metres left of the off-width crack.

(6a). Move out left onto the rib, then go straight up and pull through the overhang via a narrow groove. Above the overhangs, follow the thin finger-crack to the top.

8 **Genetic Edge**	30m	E4		1991

A very exciting line up the left edge of the crag. Start from the large sloping bilberry ledge directly below the arête.

(6a). Climb the rib to a peg, move left up a scoop, then through the overhang's edge by the small groove. A few difficult moves lead to a rest just to the left of the edge. Climb directly to the top.

The rock to the left is far less impressive. The three obvious cracks have all been climbed nevertheless. About 6 metres left of the arête of *Genetic Edge* an open inverted scoop gives a couple of strenuous moves into an easy crack, **Her Indoors** (MS, 15m, 1991). The obvious crack just to the left is **Tying the Knot** (VS, 17m, 1991). Around the corner on the left the obvious right-slanting crack gives **Under the Thumb** (VS, 10m, 1991).

Stang Crag (NY 382 110) is the crag on the east side of the ridge overlooking Hogget Gill. It has one route which has achieved well-deserved obscurity.

Above: Early morning at Brothers Water. **Photo:** Eric Shaw

Mardale (Haweswater)

The delightful head of Haweswater has more to offer the walker than the climber. A number of small crags have been explored but only *Birks Crag* is worthwhile. Although recent exploration of *Whelter Crag* has produced a number of excellent routes, these are not described due to ongoing access problems at this sensitive site. See map on page 336.

Wallow Crag (NY 496 151), a gabbro crag above the road along Haweswater, about 1 kilometre beyond the dam, has a few poor routes.

Harter Fell Gully (M, 1926) on the **North-Eastern Face of Harter Fell (NY467 098)** gives 30 metres of dangerously loose climbing which is much better left for winter.

Birks Crag

Grid Reference: **NY 468 128** Altitude: **400m**
Faces: **East** Approach: **40 mins**

This small crag is pleasantly situated on the west side of Haweswater on the lower slopes of High Raise. It is easily visible from the road and can be reached by an easy walk from the car park at the head of the lake. In periods of severe drought, the approach via the submerged village of Mardale is much shorter but this cannot be recommended in normal summers.

The crag is composed of steep flaky rock. In the nose of the crag is a prominent central groove capped by an overhang - an obvious reference point.

1 **The Ramp**	39m	HS		1966

This climb takes the prominent leftward-slanting ramp up to the left of *Quail*. A poor first pitch leads to good climbing above.

1 15m. At the foot of the groove of ***Quail*** a short thin groove trends left. Follow this groove to a good ledge. Pull over a steep little wall to gain the ledge of *Quail*.

Birks Crag

1	The Ramp	HS
2	Quail	E1
3	Groove Central	E6 **
4	The Wasp	HVS

2 24m. Climb the wall on the left to the foot of the ramp. Follow the ramp up to the right to its end where a short wall leads on to a comfortable ledge. Easier rocks on the right lead up to the top.

2 **Quail**	48m	E1		1966

This uneven route has one short hard section. It climbs the groove immediately left of the main groove. Start up a subsidiary ridge from the lowest point of the crag.

1 23m (4c). Follow the ridge then traverse left into the leftward-slanting V-groove and climb it on good jams to exit left to a good ledge and belay.

25m (5b). Climb the rib on the right. Bold! Step right into the continuation of the groove and follow it to a junction with *The Ramp*. Climb a short wall on the left and the wall above.

3 **Groove Central**	38m	E6 {F7b+}?	☆☆	1999

This route accepts the obvious "challenge for the future" mentioned in the last guidebook.

(6c). Climb the obvious central groove.

4 **The Wasp**	38m	HVS		1966

Scramble up to the foot of the right wall of the central groove.

1 20m (5a). Climb steeply up the wall until it is possible to move rightwards to a crack in the rib. Climb this to a tree.

2 18m (4a). Move left under the overhang and climb a slab. Easier climbing leads to the top.

A poor route, **Chicken** (S, 1971) climbs a rib on the upper right buttress, just left of a prominent corner and overhang.

Whelter Crags (NY 462 137) are situated on the east facing hillside overlooking Whelter Bottom on the west side of Haweswater. A number of excellent routes have been climbed on the slabby buttress in the centre of the craggy hillside. However the RSPB has raised concern about the use of the hillside as an occasional roost by the golden eagle from the reserve in Riggindale. As the situation is delicate, it has been decided not to publicise the routes and the descriptions have been archived until the access difficulties are resolved.

Above: Birks Crag on the west side of Haweswater Reservoir. **Photo:** Al Davis

Swindale

This lovely secluded valley lies between Haweswater and the A6 Kendal–Penrith road over Shap Fell. The valley descends to the north-east, the lower part being about 3 kilometres west of Shap. The approach is by Askham and Bampton from Penrith; by Rosgill from Shap.

Gouther Crag

Grid Reference: **NY 515 127**
Altitude: **350m**
Faces: **North-West**
Approach: **30 mins**

The cliffs stand on the eastern side of the valley opposite Truss Gap Farm. The crag consists of four main buttresses: *North-East Buttress, Truss Buttress, Fang Buttress* and *Nymph Buttress*.

The crags may be dry when the central Lakes areas are wet. The rock is clean and sound and provides excellent climbing in a variety of grades.

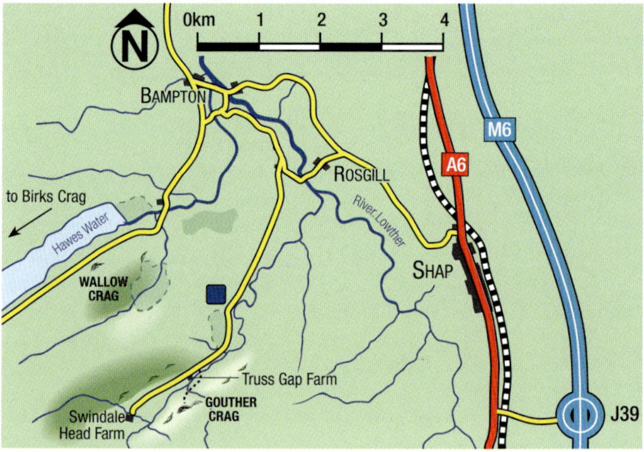

Approach:

The official parking approved by Cumbria County Council is signed 1.2 kilometres before Truss Gap Farm. The walk to the crags from just prior to the farm, via a bridge over the river, takes about 10 to 15 minutes from the bridge (30 mins in total).

The buttresses are described from **left** to **right**.

North-East Buttress

This is the large evil-looking left-hand buttress almost opposite Truss Gap Farm. Numerous routes have been recorded on this buttress over the years, some of dubious worth. They have been totally neglected and are now very mossy and unrecognisable as rock climbs. **The buttress sometimes has a bird restriction which gives you a good excuse to keep away.**

Gouther Crag

Castration Crack Area

1	The Gelding	E3 *
2	A Snip in Time	E3 *
3	Surgical Cut	E3 *
4	Vasectomy	E3 *
5	Incision	E4 *
6	Castration Crak	E3 **
7	First Cut	E3 *

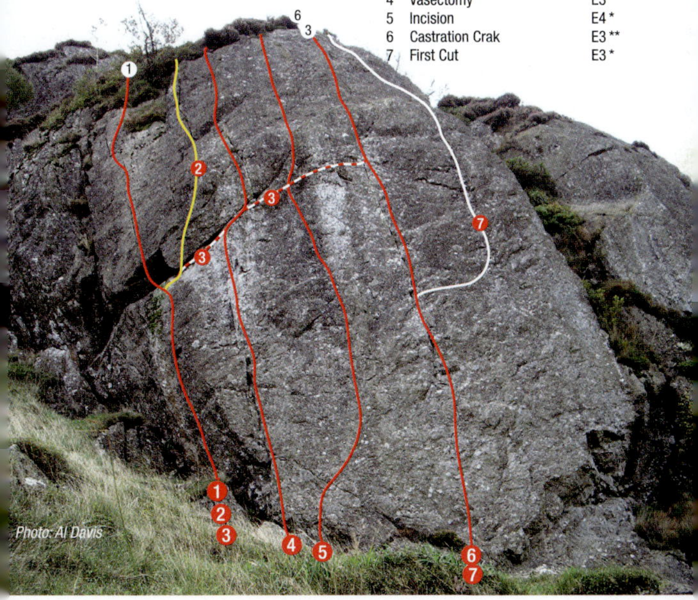

Gouther Crag Overview

Truss Buttress

This excellent buttress lies just to the right of *North-East Buttress*. It is easily identified by its main feature, the stepped ridge of the original route.

Descend to the right.

The routes are described from **left** to **right**.

Thirty metres up to the left of the toe of the buttress is a steep clean face of immaculate rock containing the following routes.

1 **The Gelding**	20m	E3	★	1993

Start 4 metres left of *Vasectomy* in a grassy corner.

(6a). Climb the overhanging wall to flat holds and move up left on sharp incuts to reach a small spike. Pull right into a niche below an overhang (peg). Move slightly left and pull around a bulge on small holds to reach a good layaway. Step left to a flake and climb back right to a crack-line. Follow this up and left with excellent protection but dirty rock. Step right to a grass ledge and exit easily rightwards.

2 **A Snip In Time**	20m	E3	★	1993

Very close to its parent route.

(6a). Climb *The Gelding* to beneath the overhang (peg). Exit rightwards from the niche to reach a thin crack with difficulty. Pull up to reach a jug and follow the crack above more easily.

3 **Surgical Cut**	30m	E3	★	1999

A good route which takes the obvious diagonal crack across the left-hand side of *Truss Buttress*. Almost a girdle of this fine wall. Start as for *The Gelding*, 4 metres left of *Vasectomy* in a grassy corner.

(6a). Pull into the niche (peg runner on *The Gelding*) and follow the crack rightwards across *Vasectomy*. Make a hard move into the top of *Castration Crack* and follow this to the top.

4 **Vasectomy**	24m	E3	★	1980

Start at a cracked rib 5 metres left of the thin crack-line up the centre of the face and follow a parallel line.

(5c). Climb easily for 3 metres then make awkward moves to reach a good hold in a rightward-slanting crack. Climb the bulge above via a thin crack and follow slabs to the top.

5 **Incision**	27m	E4	★	1999

A good route that requires a bold approach tackling the wall between *Vasectomy* and *Castration Crack*.

(6a). Climb the tricky wall (unprotected) to gain a scoop. Move up this to a good ledge and runner. Climb the steepening wall leftwards (runner in *Vasectomy*). Pull back right and climb the narrowing diagonal crack to a good jug over the bulge. Climb the easy rib on the right to the top.

6 **Castration Crack**	27m	E3	★★	1980

A very good route up the thin crack-line in the centre of the face.

(6a). Climb the wall to gain the crack and follow it with increasing difficulty to a ledge. Continue in the same line to the top.

7 **First Cut**	24m	E3	★	1983

(6a). Start as for *Castration Crack* but move right from the bottom of the crack and climb the groove and a vague crack-line to the top.

8 **The Snip**	36m	VS		1982

Start 15 metres up left from the toe of the buttress.

1 21m (4b). Climb to a tiny overlap just to the right of a grass ledge. Go straight up the mossy slab to a small grass ledge with a sapling and embedded flake. All very dirty.

2 15m (4b). Climb straight up behind the belay for 3 metres to a small tree. Step left and follow a slab and groove to the top.

9 **Zhivago Sassenach**	22m	S		1974

Start 7 metres up left from the toe of the buttress. A poor dirty route.

Climb more or less direct passing a slight bulge on the left. Trend up leftwards crossing a ledge with saplings and climb the crack above. Scramble up to finish.

10 **The Bone**	22m	S		1974

Start 5 metres up left from the toe of the buttress.

Climb up leftwards, struggling to avoid the routes on either side, and follow the right side of the *Zhivago Sassenach* slab and the groove above.

11 **Slab Start**	20m	S	★	1974

Start 5 metres up to the left of the toe of the buttress as for *The Bone*. Protection is sparse – get it where you can.

Climb the slab and rightwards-facing groove above to join *Truss Buttress* and continue up this.

12 **Truss Buttress**	38m	VD	★★	1933

A fine route on clean sound rock taking the prominent ridge. Start just left of the foot of the ridge.

1 20m. Climb the arête using thin cracks in the middle section to a point where the angle eases.

2 18m. Continue up a little slab to the left and ascend the rib above.

13 **One Hang Low**	8m	E1		1978

Just round to the right of the toe of the buttress is a short wall. Two metres right of the wall is this attractive but sadly short problem crack.

(5c). Climb the overhanging crack to a difficult pull out on to *Truss Buttress*. Follow the buttress to finish or reverse it to the bottom.

14 **Razorback**	35m	VS		1978

Twenty metres up right from the toe of the buttress there is a right-facing corner. This poor line starts here.

(4c). Climb the groove, step left over the bulge and on to an easy-angled slab above. Finish up a groove above.

v1 ***Alternative Start*** 1999

(4b). The obvious groove left of the start provides a better introduction but is unprotected.

15 **Mist Arête**	25m	E1		1999

Takes the arête just left of the corner of *Sam*. Take some microwires and start below the mottled wall 5 metres left of the start of *Sam*.

(5b). Climb the wall to gain the easy slab. Continue up to the left of the arête. Runners are available above the large block (of doubtful stability). Move up the wall to gain the arête and follow the arête more easily to the top.

16 **Sam**	20m	S	★	1976

Thirty metres right of the toe of the buttress is an easy slab leading leftwards. An enjoyable pitch.

Follow the slab and the obvious V-corner above.

17 **Strider**	33m	E1		1976

A poor route. After a difficult first pitch, the climb follows the left-hand arête of the steep rounded buttress. Start as for *Sam*.

1 15m (5b). Climb the easy slab to the foot of the corner then step right and ascend the blunt rib to a ledge and tree belay. Serious.

2 18m (4c). Steep cracks on the right of the arête above lead to the top of a flake. A shallow groove then leads to easier ground.

Gouther Crag
Truss Buttress

6	Castration Crack	E3**
8	The Snip	VS
9	Zhivago Sassenach	S
10	The Bone	S
11	Slab Start	S*
12	Truss Buttress	VD**
13	One Hang Low	E1
14	Razorback	VS
v1	Variation	
15	Mist Arête	E1
16	Sam	S*
17	Strider	E1
18	Times of Stress	E3**
19	Appliance of Science	MVS*
20	Hernia	E1**
21	Scabby Horse Direct	E3
22	Scabby Horse	VS

Not all routes shown

Photo: Al Phizacklea

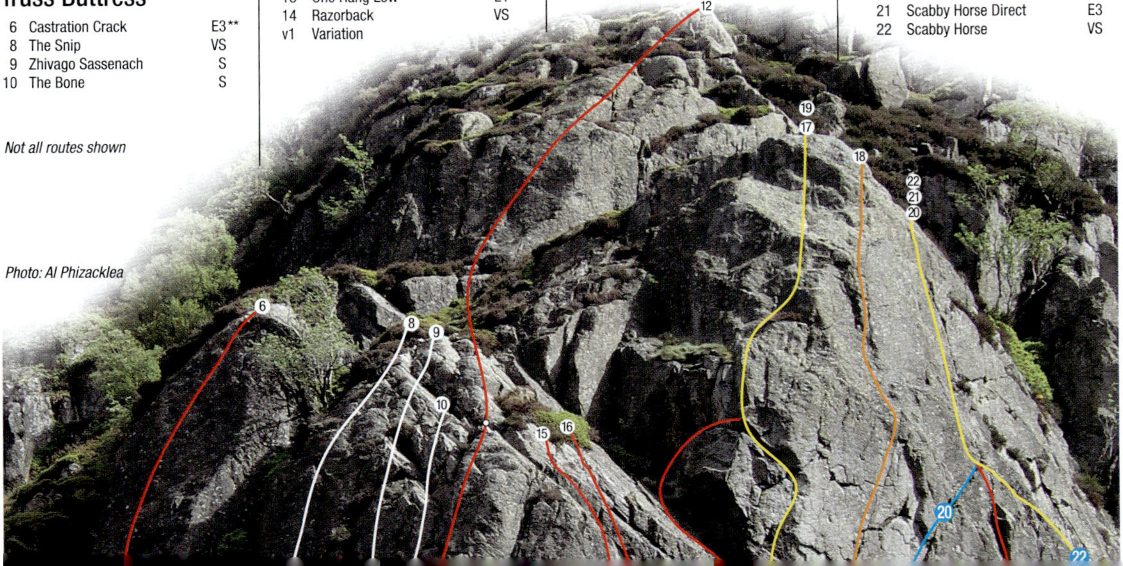

6
8
9
10
11
12
13
14
v1
15
16
17
17
18
19
20
21
See Castration
Crack diagram
for missing routes
Page 337

Gouther Crag Truss Buttress Right Flank

14	Razorback	VS
15	Mist Arête	E1
16	Sam	S *
17	Strider	E1
18	Times of Stress	E3 **
19	Appliance of Science	MVS *
20	Hernia	E1 **
21	Scabby Horse Direct	E3
22	Scabby Horse	VS
23	Misplaced Trussed	VD
24	Slab in the Face	MS

Photo: Al Davis

18 **Times of Stress**	30m	E3	★★	1980

The thin overhanging crack in the centre of the buttress. Start just right of *Sam* at a small tree. Good well-protected climbing.

(6a). Climb a short steep crack onto a slab. Pull up past a break to reach a thin crack which is followed to a good spike. Move right then up left to regain the crack which leads to a good ledge. The scoop left of the thin crack leads to a ledge and easier ground.

19 **Appliance of Science**	40m	MVS	★	2004

An intricate and exciting route. Rope drag can be a problem - take lots of slings to use as extenders. Start as for *Hernia*.

1 20m (4a). Climb the easy ramp as for ***Hernia*** but from its left end descend a corner and traverse left to behind a tree.

2 20m (4b). Climb the slab behind the tree, pull over a bulge onto an upper slab and climb boldly up this. Then traverse right into a corner where there is a huge flake (Friend 3.5 or 4). Hand-traverse the flake rightwards to below a slim groove cutting through the bulge above. Climb the groove to a ledge (possible belay in the corner on the left)

Above: Toby Denny on **Scabby Horse Direct** (E3), Gouther Crag. **Photo:** Tim Whiteley

From the right end of the ledge, climb boldly up rightwards to gain a slab which leads back leftwards to the top.

20 **Hernia**	22m	E1-	★★	1976

A strenuous and well-protected route with some entertaining moves. The grade is contentious - some say HVS. Start at a huge flake which leans against the foot of the rounded buttress to the right.

(5b). Climb the flake by an easy slab on its right and from its pointed top climb steeply rightwards and round a bulge to join *Scabby Horse*. Finish up this.

21 **Scabby Horse Direct**	18m	E3		1981

The steep wall directly below the upper groove. Hard and very serious unprotected climbing.

(5c). Climb straight up the steep wall to the ramp and finish up the groove.

22 **Scabby Horse**	20m	VS		1973

At the right-hand side of the buttress is a leftward-slanting ramp with a tree at its foot. This gives a pleasant route with one hard move.

(5a). Climb to the top of the ramp and finish up a steep shallow groove.

23 **Misplaced Trussed**	15m	VD		2004

Start 3 metres right of the tree of *Scabby Horse* at a small heather-filled groove.
From the groove, climb on the right up the clean slab directly to the top.

24 **Slab in the Face**	15m	MS		1997

Sparsely protected but delightful climbing.
Start 4 metres right of *Scabby Horse* and climb the slab direct.

Practice Wall

The small outcrop below the left-hand side of *Fang Buttress* provides the following poor dirty routes.

Practice Wall	18m	S		1975

Start below the centre of the crag.
Climb the mossy rib of rock then rightwards up a gangway to finish on the right.

The Beat Goes On HVS 1999
(5b). A direct finish - carry on up when the parent route moves right.

Late Night Groove	17m	VS		1999

(4c). About 5 metres to the right of *Practice Wall* is a groove. Climb this, moving right to a ledge near the top. Some of the rock is friable.

Fang Buttress

This is the steep clean buttress some 200m horizontally to the right of *Truss Buttress*. Just below the foot of *Truss Buttress*, a faint track leads rightwards over a shoulder through trees to a large buttress with a shallow cave at its foot.

Descent is down the grassy ridge on the right (much better and safer than the grotty gully).

The routes are described from **left** to **right**.

1 **The Stopper**	40m	HVS		2004

Rather scrappy low down but improves with height. Start 3 metres left of *The Filling* on the very left-hand side of the pillar on the left of the buttress.
1 20m (4c). Step off a block on the left and follow a series of jugs up the left side of the short wall to gain an easy-angled grassy ramp. Follow this to a spike at the foot of the upper wall. Climb a short groove on the

left of the spike to gain a large horizontal flake. Traverse this rightwards until you can stand on it and then sidle rightwards round the arête to a belay in the groove below the huge poised flake on *Tamarist*.

2 20m (5a). Step back along the flake and move to a short impending groove. Make a long reach up rightwards for a spike (thin sling) and pull out leftwards onto the buttress above. Keep moving up leftwards and then scramble to the top.

2 **The Filling**	30m	HVS		1985

Start 5 metres left of the cave at an upstanding flake in a groove.

1 10m (4c). Climb up from the flake then move right into a short groove before exiting left onto a block belay on the arête.

2 20m (5a). Traverse right and go up to a rowan on *Tamarist*. Step right and climb the steep crack up to the right of the flake (*Tamarist* takes the left crack).

3 **Tautalist**	27m	E4		1994

Climbs the steep line out of the cave to the left of *Tamarist*.

(6a). Bridge out of the back of the cave moving left to good undercuts. Powerful moves lead up to a good fingerlock and large Rock. Climb strenuously to a ledge. From the ledge, follow the thin crack to the top via a niche and small roof which is overcome on the left.

v1 ***Boddycount Start*** 1997

A left-hand start is possible stepping off the pinnacle to the left of the cave and climbing up to a peg before following the parent route.

4 **Tamarist**	27m	HVS		1975

Start at the cave.

1 15m (5a). Ascend the back of the cave and the short crack above until moves left can be made to reach small ledges and a rowan.

2 12m (4a). Climb the cracked groove above stepping left at the final flake.

5 **Sforzando**	25m	VS		1959

Start 5 metres to the right of the cave at the black mossy groove.

(4c). Climb the groove which may be split into two pitches or, more sensibly, avoided altogether.

6 **Loaded Dice**	25m	E3		1995

Varied climbing with a technical start and a bold finish. Start just left of *Sostenuto* below a short groove capped by a small roof with a diagonal groove above.

(5c). Move up the groove to below the roof then move left along a

Gouther Crag Fang Buttress

1	The Stopper	HVS	
2	The Filling	HVS	
3	Tautalist	E4	
v1	Boddycount		
4	Tamarist	HVS	
5	Sforzando	VS	
6	Loaded Dice	E3	
7	Sostenuto	HVS	**
8	Relentless Rage	E7	**
9	The Fells! The Fells!	E1	
10	Fang Direct	E1	**
11	The Fang	MVS	***
v2	Variation	VS	
12	Cerberus	E2	
13	The Doghouse	MVS	**
14	Left Edge	S	*
17	Kennel Wall	MS	**
20	Bloodhound	E2	***
21	Hindleg Crack	S	**
22	The Dalesman	E4	*
23	One Step Beyond	E4	***
24	Dogleg Crack	HVS	*
25	One Step Right	E2	

Not all routes shown.

Photo: Al Phizacklea

11
17
20
21
23
22
24
25
23
22
23
24
25
14
13
12
21
17
20
13
14
11
12
10
See closeup diagram on Page 353

horizontal crack. Use undercuts above the left of the crack to ascend a slight groove to gain a good hold. Move up right and ascend slanting ledges to the ledge on the *Girdle Traverse* (peg runner). Gain the flake crack above and move up (Friend 3.5) to flat holds on a slanting broken crack. Worryingly move up, then move back right in an exposed position to gain the last few moves of *Sostenuto* at its finishing crack.

7 **Sostenuto**	36m	HVS	★★	1958

A good exposed climb up the front of the buttress. Start from a rock gangway midway between *Sforzando* and the right edge of the face.

1 28m (5a). Climb the flake crack just left of a thin leftwards-slanting crack and then the steep wall to ledges below an impressive smooth groove. Move left along a slanting crack to an easy rib which leads to a stance.

2 8m. The easy crack on the right is followed to the top.

Variation Start E1

1 (5b). Climb the thin slanting crack on the right to join the ordinary start at 4 metres.

8 **Relentless Rage**	30m	E7	★★	2003

A superb and very bold route.

(6a). Follow *Sostenuto* to ledges below an impressive steep groove. Fill the ragged horizontal crack with runners (last before the top), step right and climb the groove directly to a small overhang. Pull straight through this onto a large ledge to belay.

9 **The Fells! The Fells!**	30m	E1		1988

The hanging arête to the right of the pink groove of *Relentless Rage* provides the meat of this climb. The grade assumes that high side runners are placed in *The Fang*; without these it could be E3. Start as for *Sostenuto*.

(5c). Climb the thin slanting crack (as for the variation start to *Sostenuto*). Traverse right under a small overhang. Move back left and up a short crack to a ledge. Move right to the bottom of the corner on *The Fang*. Step up left and climb the hanging arête (with high side runners in *The Fang*) to the top.

10 **Fang Direct**	30m	E1	★★	1974

A very good but rather bold route. Start at the blunt arête to the left of *The Fang*.

Right: Debbie Wilkinson gets her teeth into **The Fang** (MVS), Gouther Crag, Swindale.
Photo: Roger Wilkinson

(5a). Climb the crack past the overlap to the traverse of *The Fang*. Continue in the same line to gain the shallow scoop to the right of the layback on *The Fang* then exit rightwards. Finish easily up the blunt rib.

11 **The Fang**	40m	MVS	★★★	1946

A fine steep climb. It is exposed with adequate protection. Start directly below a holly under an overhang at the right edge of the buttress.

1 20m (4a). Climb up to the holly and make a bold ascending traverse left to ledges on the front of the buttress. Ascend a steep thin crack to a ledge on the right on the edge of the face.

2 20m. Ascend the steep arête at the right end of the ledge to a platform and climb the blunt rib above.

v2 ***Variation*** VS 1988

2 (4c). From the ledge at the top of pitch 1, it is possible to traverse leftwards to the arête of *The Fells! The Fells!* and finish up this.

12 **Cerberus**	30m	E2		1979

A climb that will only appeal to the connoisseur of bold routes with loose holds and poor protection. Extend your neck and start as for *The Fang*.

(5b). Climb up to the holly as for *The Fang* then move right using a hidden hold. Continue steeply to the overhang. Climb over this into a shallow niche and onto good holds on the left. Continue up the slightly protruding buttress to belay on the big ledge on *The Fang*.

The buttress now bends round to form the slabby left wall of a gully.

Above: Tim Whiteley, right on **The Fang** (MVS) and Amy Heys on **Sostenuto** (HVS), Gouther Crag.
Photo: Phil Rigby

Gouther Crag Kennel Wall

13	The Doghouse	MVS **
14	Left Edge	S *
15	Dog on the Edge	E2
16	Foreleg Wall	D
17	Kennel Wall	MS **
18	Bloodletting	E2 **
19	Bloodpoisoning	E3 **
20	Bloodhound	E2 ***
21	Hindleg Crack	S **

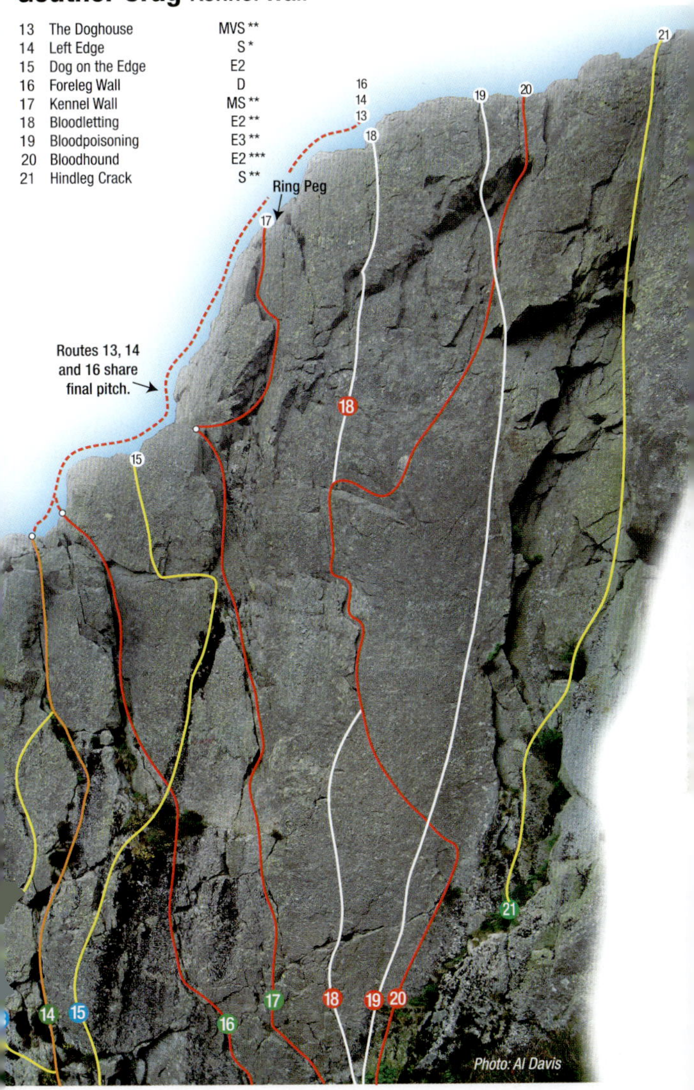

13 **The Doghouse**	39m	MVS	★★	2003

A straightening out and improvement of ***Left Edge*** avoiding all the moss and heather-ridden cracks at mid-height. Start as for ***Left Edge***, at the left-hand edge of the gully wall below a short right-facing V-groove.

1 **24m (4b).** Climb the groove and walk along the ledge to a niche. Climb the steep crack to a narrow ledge. Step off the triangular block and climb the wall slightly leftwards on a series of good ledges. Move back slightly right and climb boldly to the foot of the right-facing V-groove of ***Left Edge*** which is followed to the belay ledge.

2 **15m.** Ascend the wall to a ledge (ring peg). Continue up the groove above.

14 **Left Edge**	39m	S	★	1966

A steep but well-protected route. It is very worthwhile and the heather does not detract from the climbing. Start at the left-hand edge of the gully wall below a short right-facing V-groove.

1 **24m.** Climb the groove and move out left to a patch of vegetation. Surmount the small overhang and climb a crack and wall to finish up the V-corner 3 metres left of the similar corner of ***Foreleg Wall***.

2 **15m.** Ascend the wall to a ledge (ring peg). Continue up the groove above.

15 **Dog On The Edge**	22m	E2-		2008

A surprisingly independent route starting at the rib of rock midway between ***Left Edge*** and ***Foreleg Wall***. A series of three sections with the final wall providing the crux, which is protected by a small sling on a small spike (as long as it lasts).

(5b). Either climb the short corner on the right of the rib or the wall and overhang on its left. Continue up the wall above, to the left of an edge, to gain the ledge of ***Foreleg Wall***. Move rightwards up a gangway to join ***Kennel Wall***. Move left below the top wall (sling placement on spike in centre) and use edges and dinky footwork to get your left foot onto a foothold, then creep up the wall to gain a good edge at the top. An easy pitch remains.

16 **Foreleg Wall**	37m	D		1946

Start 5 metres right of the V-groove of ***Left Edge*** at a large block at the top of the scree.

1 **22m.** Climb a crack to the left edge of a narrow ledge and then the vegetated groove above.

2 **15m.** Ascend the wall to a ledge (ring peg). Continue up the groove above.

17 **Kennel Wall**	37m	MS	★★	1946

This very good climb takes the middle of the slabs. Start as for *Foreleg Wall* at a large block at the top of the scree.

1 26m. Climb the indefinite crack to the right end of a narrow ledge. Ascend the crack and groove above.

2 11m. Moving right, ascend a crack to a large ledge with a ring peg and follow easier rocks above.

An artificial route on the left of the *Bloodhound* slab (**Keep out of the Kennel**, E1, 1999) has been climbed using *Kennel Wall* for protection but not for holds.

18 **Bloodletting**	37m	E2	★★	1988

A superb line up the *Bloodhound* slab starting directly below the flake on *Bloodhound*. The moves up to the flake are thin and bold.

(5c). Climb directly to the flake on *Bloodhound* then follow the original route to a sloping ledge. From the left end of this pull into a short corner. Climb the corner and then the right-hand of two cracks.

19 **Blood Poisoning**	37m	E3+	★★	1989

Thin climbing directly up the right-hand side of the *Bloodhound* slab but unfortunately it is extremely contrived. The grade assumes that the crack on the right is ignored. Start below the centre of the slab.

(6b). Climb up easily to a diagonal crack and climb directly to the traverse of *Bloodhound* (skyhook and nut in the crack on the right). Climb up (avoiding the crack on the right) to a blunt spike and continue up to a good hold at the base of a shallow groove. Go up to the roof, swing left into the final groove of *Bloodhound* and climb the roof above directly using a small right-facing flake.

20 **Bloodhound**	37m	E2	★★★	1978

An excellent sustained but very bold route up the slabs between *Kennel Wall* and *Hindleg Crack*. Start in the centre of the slabs.

(5b). Climb easily up right then left with difficulty to gain an obvious flake in the middle of the slab. Continue directly upwards, then move right to the base of an obvious groove in the right-hand side of the top overhang. Climb the groove and the wall above.

21 **Hindleg Crack**	22m	S	★★	1946

The steep chimney on the right of the slab provides an interesting experience.

Overleaf: Precise footwork from Nick Wharton on **The Dalesman** (E4), Gouther Crag.
Photo: Tim Whiteley

Hindleg Crack Direct VS+ ★★

(4c). Instead of entering the bowels of the chimney, continue directly up the groove to rejoin the main route where it moves left from the chimney.

The right wall of *Hindleg Crack* is formed by an undercut buttress split by an offwidth crack.

22 **The Dalesman**	20m	E4+	★	1998

Takes the wall of *One Step Beyond* direct.

(6b). Start as for *Dogleg Crack* but where the crack turns horizontally right, go left, direct through the roof, via a hard move to good holds and a peg then finish straight up the slab (as for ***One Small Step***).

23 **One Step Beyond**	24m	E4-	★★★	1980

This superb climb crosses the hanging slab between ***Hindleg Crack*** and *Dogleg Crack*. Start up *Dogleg Crack*.

(6a). Follow the crack to above the roof then traverse down across the lip of the roof to a good hold and low peg runner. Up to another peg runner and then move down slightly to make a delicate series of moves to reach a resting foothold just right of the arête. Bold climbing on small holds just right of the arête leads to the top.

One Small Step E2 1985

From the high peg, cop out by climbing straight up to the top – then go back and do it properly!

24 **Dogleg Crack**	13m	HVS	★	1977

(5a). The short offwidth crack through the roof to the right of the hanging slab provides good climbing.

25 **One Step Right**	12m	E2		1992

The clean slab right of ***Dogleg Crack*** has one very short difficult section but is serious as the hard moves are unprotected.

(5b). Start at the right-hand end of the overhang and move onto the slab and left to its centre. A long reach allows a good hold to be gained. Easier climbing leads to the top.

Girdle Traverse of Fang Buttress	72m	E1		1962

An interesting and exposed climb. The first three pitches are awful. However, if ***Sostenuto*** is used as a start it gives a very worthwhile climb. Start at an upstanding flake in a groove 5 metres to the left of the cave.

Left: Ben Smith teeters on the edge of **One Step Beyond** (E4), Gouther Crag.
Photo: Ron Kenyon

Gouther Crag Nymph Buttress

1	Above the Timberline	HVS
2	The Nymph	HVS
3	Golden Shot	HVS
4	Showtime	HVS
5	Crack of the Under-Table World	HVS
6	Time Stops for No-One	E2

Photo: Al Phizacklea

1 9m (4c). Mount the flake, step left, and climb steeply to block belays on the left arête of the crag.
2 8m (4a). Make an ascending traverse to the right to a grass ledge and rowan belay on *Tamarist*.
3 13m (4a). Climb the crack behind the tree to a huge detached flake and traverse right. Continue on bilberry ledges, descending slightly to a stance and peg belay.
4 21m (5b). Climb the wall on the right (*Sostenuto*) then move up small ledges to join *The Fang*. Step down and move to the right to the arête. Move round the arête (crux) and up to a small ledge on the slab beyond. Climb up to a good line of holds which lead easily rightwards to a stance on the narrow ledge on *Kennel Wall*.
5 21m (4c). Move up until it is possible to traverse into *Hindleg Crack*. Finish up this.

Nymph Buttress

A steep buttress which is reached by traversing rightwards for 100 metres from the foot of *Fang Buttress*, crossing two small ridges.

The routes are described from **left** to **right**.

1 **Above the Timberline**	30m	HVS		1978

Start as for *The Nymph* below a steep groove at the toe of the buttress.
1 18m (5a). Climb the groove.
2 12m. The slabby groove in the back wall.

2 **The Nymph**	36m	HVS		1966

A steep and fingery climb which makes the most of the available rock on this buttress. It is now rather neglected and dirty. Start on a grass ledge 6 metres above the toe of the buttress below an overhanging groove.
1 14m (4c). Climb up to a ledge below the groove. Step right and pull round the steep rib to gain a line of holds which lead to the right to a ledge with flake and rowan belays. Poor belays - it may be prudent to run both pitches together but beware of rope drag.
2 22m (5a). Climb up steeply to another diagonal line. Follow this easily at first but with increasing difficulty to a niche. Continue steeply to a resting place below a crack then move to the right to a short slab and the top.

An historical curiosity, **Finale** (D, 1946), climbs the broken rock below and left of the holly in the centre of the crag.

The following routes lie on a short outcrop just left of a dry stone wall some 50 metres to the right of the start of *The Nymph*.

3 Golden Shot	16m	HVS		1992

(5b). The prominent crack just left of *Showtime* gives a short struggle.

4 Showtime	16m	HVS		1992

In the centre of the wall, just left of the crack of *Crack of the Under-Table World*, is an obvious nose of rock with a crack-line on its left.

(5a). Attain the crack and follow it to a ledge. Move left to finish.

5 Crack of the Under-Table World	16m	HVS		1992

(5a). Start 7 metres left of the stone wall and climb the crack in the left wall of a slanting vegetated corner.

6 Time Stops for No-One	16m	E2		1992

Start 5 metres left of the stone wall at a large block near the base of the buttress.

(5b). Step up left off the block and climb to a sloping ledge and corner and up to a precarious block. Continue up and right to a good hold. A short corner leads to the top.

A few intrepid explorers have ventured into **Shap Pink Quarry (NY 557 084)**, the obvious huge but tottering and chossy presence on the left of the road when traveling north from Kendal to Shap via the A6. None of them have ever been heard of since.

Above: The long and winding road – Longsleddale. **Photo:** Al Phizacklea

Longsleddale

by James and Kerrie Bumby

Longsleddale runs in a south-easterly direction and is reached from the A6 seven kilometres north of Kendal near Garnett Bridge. There is limited parking at Garnett Bridge for *Nether Crag*. The road further up the valley is metalled as far as Sadgill where parking is available for *Buckbarrow*. Please park here with consideration and don't block access to the gates or track.

Longsleddale is a beautiful quiet valley and a place to get away from the crowds. It is also the setting for the Postman Pat stories! The crags are listed clockwise around the valley.

Nether Crag

Grid Reference: **NY 512 003**
Faces: **South-East**
Altitude: **180m**
Approach: **30 mins**

Nether Crag catches the morning sun. The main buttress is approximately 18 metres high with a second smaller buttress above; both are quick to dry. There is also a north-facing buttress that is rather vegetated and as yet has no routes. Trees shade the main crag so it is best visited in the early spring. These make it hard to produce a useful photodiagram, and in fact the lines are obvious. There is some evidence of quarrying but the rock on the crag appears to be natural.

Approach:

From Garnett Bridge, Longsleddale, follow the public bridleway on the west side of the river to Nether House Farm. Take the footpath from the farm up the hill to a gate. Follow the wall on the right until a small stone stile gives access to the wood. Follow a broken crag/quarry around until the obvious *Main Buttress* is reached. The *Upper Tier* is just above the main buttress and can be accessed by not crossing the stile and following the wall around until above the *Main Buttress*.

Descents can be made to either side of the crag. The drystone walls should not be climbed.

The climbs are described from **left** to **right**.

Main Buttress

Nether Pillar	18m	E1	★	2007

(5b). To the right of a gully is an obvious pillar split by horizontal cracks - climb the pillar as directly as possible.

Never say Nether	18m	E2		2007

(5c). Gain the hanging gangway on the right-hand side of the pillar and climb up the crack above to a blank groove. Make a hard pull onto the sloping ledge and then finish easily to the left of the tree.

Netherlands	18m	VS		2007

(4c). Climb the obvious wide crack in the centre of the buttress by traditional thrutching. Pass the tree to its right and move out onto the wall for an airy finish.

Better Late than Nether	18m	HVS		2007

(5a). To the right of *Netherlands* is a series of discontinuous cracks and flakes - climb these to a good jamming crack finish.

Nether Never	18m	HVS	★	2007

(5a). On the right-hand side of the main wall is a continuous crack that reaches almost to the top. Follow this and finish up the wall above.

Upper Tier

Last Knight	10m	HVS		2007

(5a). Follow the deep V-crack on the left-hand side of the crag.

Good Knight	10m	VS		2007

(4a). Follow the left rib of the large block with no protection.

Second Knight	10m	S		2007

Climb the right side of the large block and follow the crack.

First Knight	10m	HVS		2007

(5a). Follow the crack right of the block to a bulge. The move over the bulge is harder than it looks.

Pacemaker Special	10m	HS		2007

The obvious right-trending crack on the right-hand side of the buttress.

Goat Scar (NY 478069) faces east and lies opposite *Buckbarrow Crag* a little further down the valley. It is a rambling grassy area of rock standing above long slopes of small scree and its few poor, loose and vegetated routes are best left for the enjoyment of the goats.

Buckbarrow Crag

Grid Reference: **NY 483 073**
Altitude: **350m**
Faces: **South-West**
Approach: **30 mins**

Buckbarrow Crag lies towards the top of the valley. It dries quickly and can be a good evening crag, particularly if a mountain bike is used to speed up access along the track. It is worthy of more attention. There is great swimming in the gorge below the crag.

The obvious main buttress is about 90 metres high and is called the *Dandle*. It is bounded on its right by *Camera Gully*. Some broad faults slant up to the left from the foot of this buttress. Below these faults and to the left is *Low Crag*.

Above the faults lies *High Crag* which is separated from the *Dandle* by a deep and loose gully, *Cleft Ghyll*. This is not obvious from the usual approach. To the right of the *Dandle* there are some shallow heathery gullies. Well to the right a stream runs down the hillside with a group of small buttresses beyond it.

A seasonal nesting restriction (raven or peregrine) may be in place during the spring.

Approach:

From Sadgill follow the main track up the valley for 2 kilometres until below the main crag. A gate gives access to the steep final approach. It is worth identifying the topography of the crag from here.

Descents:

For *Low Crag* the easiest descent is down to the left. For *High Crag* the easiest descent is also to the left. For the *Dandle* it is best to traverse the hillside to the right. This involves a climb down into and across the top of a grassy gully. It is graded Difficult for a move and can be awkward if wet. The slope and scree can be descended beyond this. *Cleft Ghyll* and *Camera Gully* are dangerous descents.

The climbs are described from **left** to **right**.

Buckbarrow Crag Overview

1	The Crystal Maze	HVS
2	Linjeston's Climb	VS *
3	The Blunder	HVS *
6	Express Crack	E1 ***
9	The Clangers	E1 **
11	The Hog's Back	HVS **
14	Slab and Rib	VD *
15	Low Crag Chimney	D
16	Geronimo	VS
17	Crazy Horse	E2 *
18	Domination	MVS *
19	Waterfall Buttress	S *
20	The Fondue Party	HVS *
22	The Minotaur	HVS **
23	Dandle Buttress	S *
24	Sleep Walk	VS
26	Sadgill Wall	S **

Not all routes shown.

Low Crag

When viewed from the track, *Low Crag* appears as a line of shorter buttresses to the left of the main buttress and nearest the track. The routes in the vicinity of the right-angled corner of *Express Crack* provide good climbing on sound rock.

1 **The Crystal Maze**	17m	HVS		1995

Above and behind *Linjeston's Climb* is the descent gully. This route is found on its left wall and starts at its lowest point.

(5a). Climb the wall past a quartz vein crack to reach the right end of an overhang. Use a flake crack to move past this and finish up the groove above.

2 **Linjeston's Climb**	24m	VS-	★	1927

Start 9 metres left of the corner of *Express Crack* at a large pinnacle.

(4b). Climb the front of the pinnacle. Traverse left for 6 metres and climb a short steep corner exiting to the right.

Buckbarrow Crag Express Crack Area

1	The Crystal Maze	HVS	
2	Linjeston's Climb	VS	*
3	The Blunder	HVS	*
4	Shed Shifters of the World Unite	E3	
5	The Soup Dragon	E5	*
6	Express Crack	E1	***
7	Hot Wheels of Steele	E2	
8	The Shackle	E2	
9	The Clangers	E1	**
10	Shed Shifting for Beginners	E4	
11	The Hog's Back	HVS	**
12	The Iron Chicken	E3	*
13	A Century on the Crags	E2	

3 **The Blunder**	25m	HVS	★	1982

The steep chimney-crack just right of the large pinnacle.

(5a). Climb the right rib awkwardly until the crack can be gained. Follow this to the top. A slightly easier and more obvious alternative is to climb the crack throughout.

4 **Shed Shifters of the World Unite**	22m	E3		1998

Sustained climbing up the crozzly wall right of *The Blunder*.

(5c). Climb up to a small overhang with a black streak below it. Pull left into a small groove then climb direct to the excellent halfway break. Pull into a vague groove above and climb up and out left onto the foot of the top slab (*The Blunder* is just to the left). Step up and right across the slab to finish.

5 **The Soup Dragon**	33m	E5	★	1986

A good route up the grooves left of the corner.

(6a). Climb the shattered groove to a good ledge. Climb the groove above using sloping layaways to another good ledge (runners down and right in a short crack). Make a long reach to gain the short overhanging crack; a big pull leads to the slabs above which are followed to below a short wall. Climb this via an obvious weakness on the right.

6 **Express Crack**	33m	E1	★★★	1969

(5b). The right-angled corner gives an excellent pitch. It is strenuous but well-protected by large cams.

7 **Hot Wheels of Steele**	30m	E2+		2003

A contrived eliminate which nonetheless contains some worthwhile climbing. It uses *Express Crack* for protection but avoids using its holds.

(5c). Climb the bubbly wall just right of *Express Crack* to a shallow curved feature at five metres. Follow this on the right to the base of a shallow V-groove which is climbed with difficulty until the tree on *Express Crack* can be grabbed. *Express Crack* is only a metre away at this point but should not be used! Step right and follow the bubbly arête to the top.

8 **The Shackle**	33m	E2	★	1963

A bold route with a short but poorly protected crux. It starts 2 metres right of the corner.

(5b). Climb the steepening wall to a small ledge. Move up and slightly right, then up a short wall to a large ledge. Climb the groove above.

9 **The Clangers**	33m	E1-	★★	1986

A very good climb which feels quite bold and reachy in its lower half. Start beneath the overhang 3 metres right of the corner.

(5b). Climb up to the obvious line of flakes and follow them to the large ledge. Continue up the slab above just left of the arête.

10 **Shed Shifting For Beginners**	35m	E4		1998

Thin technical climbing that takes a line leftwards through *The Clangers*. Start as for *The Hog's Back*.

(6a). Follow *The Hog's Back* to the roof. Step left into *The Clangers* and follow it for 3 metres until moves left again lead to a spike in the centre of the wall. Make a hard move up to a halfway ledge and follow the thin pocketed crack (hard) to quartz pockets. Reach right for a rib and pull up to a ledge below the top arête. Climb the left-hand side of the arête to the top.

11 **The Hog's Back**	34m	HVS	★★	1956

A fine route up the grooved arête 5 metres right of the corner.

(5a). Climb up to enter a slim groove with difficulty by pulling over a small roof. Follow this to a yew. Move onto the rib on the right and climb up to a bulge. Turn this on the right and move back left to the arête which is followed to a ledge. Easier rocks lead to the top.

Above: James Bumby on **The Hog's Back** (HVS), Buckbarrow. **Photo:** Kerrie Bumby

12 **The Iron Chicken**	34m	E3	★	1986

A good route up the narrow black overhanging wall right of *The Hog's Back*.

(5c). Climb the centre of the wall to below the bulge, swing up and right to a good downward-pointing spike and then back left to the arête which is followed to a ledge. Scrambling leads to the top.

13 **A Century on the Crags**	40m	E2		2007

A good strenuous line, well-protected but with a couple of suspect holds. Start at the foot of *The Iron Chicken*.

(5b). Follow the crack-line in the right side of the steep wall that curves rightwards through the bulge to reach a good spike. Climb the blunt arête directly above to finish.

14 **Slab and Rib**	32m	VD	★	1956

A worthwhile climb which starts up the slab to the right of *The Hog's Back* and then moves left to finish as for that route.

Climb the slab, then work left to the rib and ascend this steeply leftwards on good holds. Climb the right-hand side of the rib, turning the bulge at the top on the right.

15 **Low Crag Chimney**	18m	D		1929

The miniature gully in the centre of the crags. A poor climb and more awkward than it first appears.

16 **Geronimo**	60m	VS		1961

Start a little to the right of *Low Crag Chimney* at the foot of an undercut slab. Good climbing but with poor protection and sadly becoming overgrown.

1 30m (4b). Turn the overhang on the right (or climb it direct if you can!) Step left to a crack above the overhang and climb this to a ledge (possible belay on the right). Climb the slab above by a shallow groove with an awkward dirty finish. Serious.

2 30m (4b). A final pitch (which may be avoided) has been made up suspect rock on the buttress above and to the left. Climb up diagonally left, traverse left beneath the prow and finish up a steep and dirty chimney.

Two poor variations have been climbed to the last pitch of *Geronimo*. They start just to the left of its last pitch, beneath the obvious prow.

Jude Said Yes 30m HVS 1989

(5a). Climb the large leaning flake to step left and up. Hand-traverse right below an overlap to the top of the slim corner. Climb up to join *Geronimo* beneath the main prow. Traverse left and finish up the dirty chimney.

The Challenge Side Stepped 30m E1 2004

(5b). Pull up into the slim left-facing corner just right of the large leaning flake. Climb the corner to join *Geronimo* beneath the main prow. Traverse left and finish up the dirty chimney.

17 **Crazy Horse**	20m	E2	★	1995

Start in a small grassy bay right of *Geronimo* below a smooth wall seamed by three parallel slanting cracks.

(5c). Climb the awkward groove to reach the middle crack. Follow this out right to the arête and finish more easily up this.

18 **Domination**	40m	MVS	★	1961

An interesting route. Start 9 metres right of *Low Crag Chimney* at a notched arête.

1 20m (4a). Climb up to the left of the arête and move right below the overhang to the notch (much easier than it looks). Step right and climb a crack which leads back to the arête. Follow this to a belay below a prominent prow.

2 20m (4b). Traverse right below the prow and pull into the chimney on large flakes. Climb the chimney and then the easy arête on the right.

Two poor routes have been made right of *Domination*. An obvious right-slanting line is Very Difficult and a chimney with a rotten tree is Severe.

19 **Waterfall Buttress**	32m	S	★	1953

This pleasant climb takes the ridge at the right end of *Low Crag*. Start from a sloping rock ledge on the right flank of the ridge.

Climb up from the right end of the sloping ledge and traverse left to the arête. Ascend to a ledge and climb the ridge above to the top.

20 **The Fondue Party**	16m	HVS	★	1994

This route lies on the steep buttress above and to the right of *Waterfall Buttress*. An alcove with a crack in its back marks the start.

(5a). Climb the slab steeply until a pull at half height leads left onto a steep slab to finish. Belay on blocks well back.

High Crag

This steep buttress lies to the left of the upper part of *Cleft Ghyll*. Its most obvious feature is a steep arête flanked on the left by a wide grassy gully. An 8 metre block stands at the foot of the arête. Access to the buttress is best gained by scrambling up steep grass diagonally leftwards from the bottom of *Cleft Ghyll*.

21 **The Eagle's Nest**	34m	S		1927

A disjointed climb with one very hard move. It takes a corner to the left side of the main arête running into the gully at half height. Start at the left-hand side of the 8 metre block.

1 25m. Climb up to the left of the block and move up left to a corner. Climb this with difficulty moving leftwards from a flake on the right wall by a wide bridging move.

2 9m. Scramble up the grassy gully until it is possible to climb its right wall. Ascend rightwards to a stance on the nose of the buttress.

Buckbarrow Crag High Crag

21 The Eagle's Nest S
22 The Minotaur HVS **

Photo: Al Phizacklea

22 **The Minotaur**	42m	HVS	★★	1964

A sensational climb up the main nose of the crag. It is sustained, exposed and not too well-protected but the holds are good. Start directly below the arête just left of the 8 metre block.

1 12m (4a). Climb a little arête just left of a chimney and traverse right to the platform on top of the block.

2 30m (4c). Climb a slanting crack to gain the arête at a flake. Climb the bulging arête to a prominent overhang. Turn this on the left (it can be climbed directly), regain the arête and follow it to the top. It is also possible to step down and right at the overhang and then to move up the impending wall.

The Dandle

The Dandle is the largest buttress on the crag. It is largely detached from the hillside behind by *Cleft Ghyll* (NB This is not the Cleft Ghyll marked on the 1:25000 Ordnance Survey map) but a short and narrow ridge connects its top to the hillside. It is bounded on its right by *Camera Gully*. The rock is good but the less popular routes are grassy and have some loose rock on the ledges. The climbs have a mountaineering air to them.

Some routes have been climbed on the steep face of *The Dandle* above the chockstone in *Cleft Ghyll*. They are unattractive and on suspect rock. **Dandle Direct** (VS, 1964) climbs the chimney/groove at the left end of the wall, 12 metres above the chockstone. The crack and chimney line 3 metres right of *Dandle Direct* gives a steep and rather loose route, **Cleft Ghyll Chimney** (VS). **Nimbus** (MVS, 1963) is an ascending traverse to the right, starting 6 metres above the chockstone. The left-hand rib of *Cleft Ghyll*, above the chockstone, gives a poor climb, **Falcon Ridge** (S, 1961).

23 **Dandle Buttress**	46m	S	★	1926

A good climb up the left-hand ridge of the *Dandle*. The first pitch is considerably harder than the rest of the route. Start on the right wall of *Cleft Ghyll*, 6 metres below the large chockstone.

1 14m. Climb polished slabs to a corner and then climb steeply up twin cracks to a stance on the edge of the buttress.

2 15m. Follow the broad ridge to a ledge and climb a chimney on the left to *Spike Minor*.

3 17m. Continue, passing *Spike Major*, to the top. The descent route now lies straight ahead. However, it is also possible to continue up the rock above and onto the fell.

Buckbarrow Crag The Dandle

22	The Minotaur	HVS **
23	Dandle Buttress	S *
24	Sleep Walk	VS
25	Dandle Chimney	VD
26	Sadgill Wall	S **
27	Sadgit Wall	HVS

Photo: Nick Wharton

24 **Sleep Walk**	70m	VS		1962

An unbalanced route with a hard start leading to easier meanderings above. Start 12 metres left of the bottom left-hand corner of the crag at an open groove.

1 23m (4c). Climb the groove then swing left to a small ledge. Climb diagonally right over a bulge then go up a rib to a grass ledge. Hard to protect.

2 12m. Climb the groove above past an overhang. Traverse right to belay by some large flakes. (The overhanging groove to the right has also been climbed using a peg and sling for aid.)

3 35m. Move left to a slab. Climb it, over a bulge, and traverse left to join *Dandle Buttress* at *Spike Minor*. Finish as for that route.

Dandle Face Direct (HS, 1931) has been described as grassy and insecure in the past. It is even grassier and more insecure now.

25 **Dandle Chimney**	105m	VD		1986

A natural line. The chimney is in fact a basalt dyke which winds its way up the crag. The climb starts 8 metres right of the bottom left corner of the crag.

1 18m. Climb the chimney to a ledge and belay.

2 23m. Climb the chimney in two stages to ledges and belays.

3 27m. Climb the chimney to a small rocky bay and exit up right to a bilberry terrace. Belay up in a small bay.

4 37m. Climb leftwards behind pinnacles and go up the first break in the wall starting it on the left. Belays are possible at 24 metres. The rough wall on the left then leads to the top and a belay well back.

Dandle Slabs (S, 1926) was recorded in the 1992 guide as being mainly of botanical interest. The intervening 18 years have not changed it for the better, except perhaps for botanists.

26 **Sadgill Wall**	100m	S-	★★	1949

A very good climb which unfortunately deteriorates for the final pitch. Start at the foot of a slabby rib between *Dandle Chimney* and *Camera Gully* about 6 metres right of a rowan.

1 20m. Climb the slab until it steepens. Step right and ascend to a grassy ledge. Continue up to the left to belay at the foot of a steep wall.

2 20m. Climb the rightward-slanting flake crack to a thread runner then climb the slab on the left to a stance by *Dandle Chimney*.

3 30m. Traverse sensationally right across the steep slab to its right edge. Ascend directly and continue up ledges to a rowan. Scramble up into the grassy bay above.

Right: Al Phizacklea on **Dandle Buttress** (S), Buckbarrow. **Photo:** John Holden

4 **30m.** Cross the right wall of the bay and climb the broken ridge to a ledge by a 3 metre crack. Climb the corner and the easier rocks above.

Alternative Finish

4 **25m.** Trend left to a flaky spike, then climb the steep cracked wall above to finish up a vague short chimney. Better and more exposed than the normal finish.

27 **Sadgit Wall**	105m	HVS+		2003

Start below a stepped rib some 8 metres right of *Sadgill Wall*. The steep crack on the first pitch is visible from the foot of the crag. This is the only redeeming feature of this route.

1 **35m (5b).** Climb the rib to a poor spike at 15 metres just below the heather. Traverse the mossy slab leftwards to reach a ledge below the crack. Follow the superb short crack to belay on the big flake of *Sadgill Wall* above just below the prominent overhang.

2 **30m (5a).** Follow the ramp leftwards (as for *Sadgill Wall*) to the left end of the overlap then pull onto the steep slab above. Step right and climb the centre of the slab to a heathery finish. Belay next to the small rowan above.

3 **40m.** Scramble into the grassy bay above then take a blocky ramp out left where a shallow groove-line leads to the top of the buttress.

Camera Gully (VD, 1926) lies right of *Sadgill Wall*. It is not worth climbing except in a very good winter.

The **Southern Buttresses** are the small buttresses just right of the stream and a long way to the right of the *Dandle*. Climbs have been recorded here but they are scrappy and overgrown.

Left: Joyce Evans crossing the pinnacles at the top of **The Dandle**, Buckbarrow.
Photo: James Bumby

Kentmere

Kentmere, or Kentdale, lies north of Staveley which is on the main Windermere–Kendal road. The valley lies on a north-south axis running from Kentmere Reservoir in the north down to the village. There is a metalled road up the valley but cars should be parked at Kentmere Church as there is no parking beyond this. Alternatively a field is sometimes available as a car park at the foot of the hill before the church (payments are donated to charities).

The valley contains numerous small outcrops in a delightful setting. They are described clockwise around the valley.

Iving Crag

Grid Reference: **NY 453 049** Altitude: **250m**
Faces: **East** Approach: **15 mins**

This ferocious little crag is situated one kilometre north of Kentmere church providing easy access from the south. The rock on the whole is good and dries quickly though some parts of the crag are currently a bit dirty and overgrown. The climbing is very steep and, although the majority of routes are protected by in situ pegs, a bold approach is still needed. Moreover, some of the in situ gear is showing its age and should be treated with great caution.

Approach:

There is no parking whatsoever beyond the church/village hall, as detailed above. Follow the road beyond the village hall for half a kilometre, passing through a gate on the right as it bends to the left. The crag can be seen slanting up the left-hand side of the narrow side valley. Follow the road until approximately 100 metres short of the cattle grid then follow the wall on the left to below the crag.

A very easy **descent** is on the right.

The routes are described from **left** to **right**.

Right: Steve Merry on **Day of the Squid** (E5), Iving Scar. **Photo:** Al Phizacklea

Iving Crag Lower
1 Never Ending Story E2
2 Pagan Life E2 *
v1 Easy Way HVS
3 Smooth Operator E3 **
4 Day of the Squid E5 *
5 Blind Vision E4
6 Diamond Life E3
7 Left-Hand Slab S *
8 Right-Hand Slab S
Photo: Nick Wharton

1 **Never Ending Story**	10m	E2		1986

The climb has a very bold start and is not inspiring. Start 9 metres right of the stone wall at a shallow groove just left of a black streak.

(6a). Move up on layaways for 3 metres to a horizontal break then move right to good pockets. Continue directly then left to the top.

2 **Pagan Life**	14m	E2	★	1986

A good route with an airy upper section. Start at the left side of the overhangs at the corner.

(5b). Climb directly up the wall then trend right to a good ledge below the thin leftward-slanting groove. Follow this to the top.

v1 ***Easy Way*** 14m HVS

An escape can be made leftwards into the obvious groove before the trend rightwards.

3 **Smooth Operator**	14m	E3	★★	1986

A great climb with a hard awkward start. Start below a smooth horizontal crack beneath the left end of the overhangs.

(5c). Make awkward moves over the initial overlaps to a small incut ledge. Climb up and right past the next small overhang, using the groove on the right, past a peg. Continue up to a thread and a ledge on the left (junction with *Pagan Life*). Move up and right then climb the wall above following the faint fault on the right.

4 **Day of the Squid**	17m	E5	★	1986

An excellent and technical route with some committing moves under the overhangs. Start on the right of the overhangs below a large sloping ledge. Beware of the old protection.

(6b). Climb up to the large sloping ledge. Move across left under the overhang on layaways to a large hold (peg runner). Swing across left to another good hold then continue up the wall to another peg runner. Move up slightly left then directly up the wall above.

5 **Blind Vision**	15m	E4		1986

A good climb taking the start of *Day of the Squid* and finishing up the large groove on the right.

(6b). Climb *Day of the Squid* to the large hold (peg runner). Pull directly up and enter the groove above which is followed to the top.

6 **Diamond Life**	18m	E3		1986

Start on the large sloping shelf up and right of *Day of the Squid*.

(6a). Climb up and left to a niche. Gain good holds above the niche, then move right on good holds to join *Left-Hand Slab*. Continue up and right to an overlap then move right to finish just left of a crack.

7 **Left-Hand Slab**	20m	S	★	1986

Very good climbing making the best of the slab. Start on a grassy ledge below the cracked wall right of *Diamond Life*.

Climb the wall then step left onto the ledge. Climb leftwards up the slab to its left edge. Move right along the crack-line then go straight up to the top.

8 **Right-Hand Slab**	15m	S		1986

A poor route, very overgrown. Botanists may find it interesting!

Climb the little corner beneath the slab to a grass ledge then continue directly up on good holds to the top.

9 **Grubby Mitts**	17m	HVS		1986

Rather overgrown at the moment which is a shame as this is a good route.

(4c). Climb *Right-Hand Slab* a little way, then the corner on the right, passing a small tree at 3 metres.

10 **Under Pressure**	18m	E4	★	1986

Takes the right side of the blunt rib left of *The Old Aid Route* and then the impending wall just left of the overhang. Start just below a projecting block under the rib.

(6a). Climb up to the block then the short wall above, trending slightly right to the bottom of the obvious groove. Follow the groove to the left side of the overhang, then the impending wall to a tree belay.

11 **The Old Aid Route**	18m	E5	★★	1986

A superb route taking the large overhang just right of the centre of the crag. The climbing is technical, strenuous and adequately protected, though some of the in situ gear is now rather ancient. Start at the perched blocks.

(6b). Climb the pocketed wall to the right of the rib past an old bent peg runner. Move left onto the slab below the short steep shallow corner. Go up this and then the slab to beneath the overhang. Using poor undercuts in the back of the roof, pull up and across right to a good hold on the right of the roof – hard! Pull over and climb the wall above with more ease.

12 **Langdale Lads**	18m	E6	★	1998

Another tough route up the leaning wall.

(6b). Start up *The Old Aid Route* to the old bent peg. Move up and right, climbing the steep wall between the arête of *The Old Aid Route* and the upper ramp of *Shaken Not Stirred* past a peg.

Iving Crag Upper

8	Right-Hand Slab	S	
9	Grubby Mitts	HVS	
10	Under Pressure	E4	*
11	The Old Aid Route	E5	**
12	Langdale Lads	E6	*
13	Shaken Not Stirred	E6	**
14	Mindscape	E7	**
15	Physical Test	E4	**
16	Ted's Route	E1	
17	Dream Chaser	E1	
18	Slanting Corner	E1	*
19	Pig Balls	HVS	

13 **Shaken Not Stirred**	17m	E6	★★	1986

A ferocious route with technical and sustained climbing throughout. Start just right of ***The Old Aid Route***, below the downward-pointing flake with the protruding peg!

(6b). Climb the steep wall with hard moves past pegs until it is possible to step left and make a very exposed move to gain the diagonal ramp. Hand-traverse this leftwards to a good hold whereupon easier climbing leads to the top.

14 **Mindscape**	16m	E7	★★	1989

The improbable leaning wall right of ***Shaken Not Stirred*** gives steep fingery technical climbing.

(6c). Climb directly to the first peg runner. Pass this on the left on sharp painful quartz holds to gain the second peg runner. Continue to a small pod in the thin crack (crux). An awkward pull over a bulge leads into a groove which is followed to the top.

15 **Physical Test**	15m	E4	★★	1986

A tremendous steep route with widely spaced holds on the first 9 metres which is very strenuous but well-protected. Start just left of the large flake.

(6b). Climb the steep wall direct passing three peg runners to a good finger-lock just above the top peg. Step left to large slots and continue up to a short groove which is followed to the top.

16 **Ted's Route**	15m	E1		1986

(5b). Climb the chimney behind the large flake. Step off the flake into the groove which is followed to the top.

17 **Dream Chaser**	14m	E1		1986

Takes the front of the large flake before stepping onto the crag proper. Start just right of the left edge of the large flake.

(5c). Climb precariously for 3 metres to good holds. From the top of the flake gain the wall awkwardly and move up left then up right to finish in a short groove.

18 **Slanting Corner**	13m	E1	★	1986

A good climb taking the obvious slanting corner at the right side of the crag.

(5b). Climb the left wall of the corner to the short groove of ***Dream Chaser*** which is followed to the top.

19 **Pig Balls**	12m	HVS		1986

Start just right of the arête right of *Slanting Corner*.

(5a). Climb up the wall past a small overhang then trend left to the arête which leads to the top. An easier variation is possible by trending right through the bulge instead of left to the arête.

Raven Crag (NY 455 050) overlooks the cattle grid just north of *Iving Crag*. Its two poor routes are deservedly left to the ravens.

Calf Howe Crag

Grid Reference: **NY 458 052** Altitude: **200m**
Faces: **North and East** Approach: **20 mins**

This pleasantly situated crag offers a variety of easier grade climbs which complement the harder routes on *Iving Crag*. Once quite popular, a lack of use over recent years has allowed vegetation to flourish and led to a general veneer of moss and grime and all the routes would benefit from a spring clean. With more traffic, several of the routes would justify stars.

Approach:

The crag lies 400 metres north-east of *Iving Crag*. It is close to the road on the left, just before Scales Farm.

The crag is divided into three main sections rising rightwards up the hillside.

The routes are described from **left** to **right**.

A bird restriction may affect the crag in Spring.

Lower Buttress

This collection of steep buttresses can be identified by the right-facing ramp-like corner/groove rising from its centre. To the right lies a prominent 5 metre cracked pinnacle, whilst the left half of the buttress is split into two distinct tiers. The lower tier is a long low wall, the steep right-hand end of which is home to the following short entertaining routes.

Descent is by the same break that gives access to the upper tier.

The wall beneath the bulging prow defining the right-hand end of this lower wall is split by two thin diagonal cracks running up leftwards.

Calf Howe Crag Lower Buttress

1	Splashdown	VS
2	Eddie the Eagle	E2
3	Glaslost	E3
4	The Bulger	E1
5	No Picnic on Mt Kenya	E1
6	Nanga Parbat Pilgrimage	E3
7	Route 1	HS *
8	Ken's Wall	VS *
9	Kenny the Lad	VS
10	Taurus	HVS *
11	Route 3	VS

Photo: Nick Wharton

1 Splashdown	12m	VS		1988

The juggy wall just left of the overhanging prow. Start below the middle of the left-hand slanting crack-line.

(5a). Strenuous climbing up the steep wall, passing a small ledge, leads to a finish up a short wide crack behind the left side of the prow.

The shallow groove immediately to the left and sharing the same halfway ledge has also been climbed at a similar grade (VS 5a).

2 Eddie the Eagle	12m	E2		1988

Start just right of the overhanging prow and in between the base of the two thin diagonal crack-lines slanting up left.

(5b). Using a prominent spike, climb impending rock diagonally leftwards, then make a thin move up and reach left for a jug (in situ thread) beneath the prow. Swing up right and finish more easily.

The upper tier lies immediately above and the starts to its routes are gained leftwards along the lower of two breaks.

3 Glaslost	13m	E3		1991

The overhanging wall immediately left of *The Bulger* is split by three thin crack-lines. Start 3 metres left of *The Bulger*, below the middle and longest of these cracks.

(5c). The overhanging crack is climbed past pegs; very fingery and strenuous.

4 **The Bulger**	21m	E1		1988

Takes the prominent groove-line in the bulbous arête. It free climbs an old aid route with a short hard well-protected crux.

(5c). Climb into and up the curving groove to the overhang. Move out left beneath this to the second of the three peg runners and, using a small hold over the bulge, pull awkwardly up left. Step immediately back right and follow the rib to the top.

The following two climbs start on the grassy ledge higher up to the right. The steep wall left of the upper half of *Route 1* is split by a prominent short crack. Immediately left of this is a slanting overhung break.

5 **No Picnic on Mt Kenya**	10m	E1		1996

Start below the middle of the slanting break and 3 metres left of the prominent crack.

(5b). From the leftward-slanting break, pull rightwards across the overlap on small flakes to gain the wall, whence steep moves lead to easier ground. Poor protection from small wires.

6 **Nanga Parbat Pilgrimage**	10m	E3		1996

Takes the challenge of the prominent crack.

(5c). Climb the slanting crack in the centre of the wall using laybacks and bridging. Pull over to a small ledge and continue more easily to the top. Belay well back on boulders. Well-protected but strenuous to place.

Returning to the centre point of the *Lower Buttress* at the obvious slanting ramp-like corner/groove that gives:

7 **Route 1**	23m	HS	★	pre 1969

Start below the right-facing ramp-like groove.

(4b). Climb the corner/groove to a grass ledge. Continue in the same line up the corner-crack above, utilising the slab on the left.

8 **Ken's Wall**	24m	VS	★	pre 1969

A very good pitch up the steep wall between *Route 1* and the cracked pinnacle. Start 5 metres right of *Route 1*.

(4c). Climb a steep line of left-trending flake cracks to the right end of a ledge. Pull up to the right and climb the short corner directly above.

9 **Kenny the Lad**	27m	VS		pre 1969

Start at the cracked pinnacle.

(4c). Climb the crack in the pinnacle. Step across and left into the broken corner, which is climbed to the top via a final steep crack.

10 **Taurus**	27m	HVS	★	pre 1969

A good line up the highest part of the buttress. Start 3 metres right of the cracked pinnacle below a vague thin groove in the steep slab.

(5a). Climb the vague groove in the slab to a grass ledge. From its left end, pull up awkwardly to gain a ramp which is followed left for 5 metres to gain a shallow scoop which leads directly to the top.

11 **Route 3**	27m	VS		pre 1969

Four metres right of ***Taurus***, the slab is bounded on its right by a deeper groove with a mossy left wall.

(4c). The groove is presently dirty and unprotected and leads to the right end of a grass ledge. Move right for a metre and climb up to gain a steep slab which leads to the top. It is also possible to continue directly above the groove by difficult moves up steep rock leading into a vegetated crack (HVS).

Right of ***Route 3***, the buttress bends round to form an easy-angled slab of diminishing height. The left-hand edge of this gives a pleasant 25-metre scramble (**Birkett's Arête**, M, pre 1969), whilst the descent for ***Lower Buttress*** takes the right-hand edge. To the right of this lies:

Central Slabs

12 **Route 4**	30m	S		pre 1969

Climb the short corner to the grass ledge. Step right and then follow the narrow continuation gangway leftwards to the top.

The grassy gangway has been climbed, followed by the break running up the slab to finish up a final gangway (**Route 5**, 37m, MS, pre 1969).

13 **Calf Howe Slab**	37m	VD		pre 1969

Start at the toe of the slab.

Climb up to a grass ledge then follow a ramp-line diagonally left to the top.

14 **Kentmere Slab**	33m	VD	★	pre 1969

By far the best route when clean. Start at a faint break, halfway between the toe of the slab and the right-hand corner.

Weave your way up the cleanest rock on small holds, crossing two diagonal fault-lines, until below the left-hand of two final clean slabs. The best finish lies up this. Alternatively, finish leftwards along the fault-line, or escape off rightwards.

Left: Tim Whiteley looking for holds on **Kenny the Lad** (VS), Calf Howe Crag. **Photo:** Nick Wharton

Calf Howe Crag Upper Buttress

12	Route 4	S	
13	Calf Howe Slab	VD	
14	Kentmere Slab	VD	*
15	Ancients' Crack	VS	
16	Resurrection	E4	
17	Calf Chimney	D	*
18	Victory V	E1	
19	Twilight Slab	MVS	

Photo: Nick Wharton

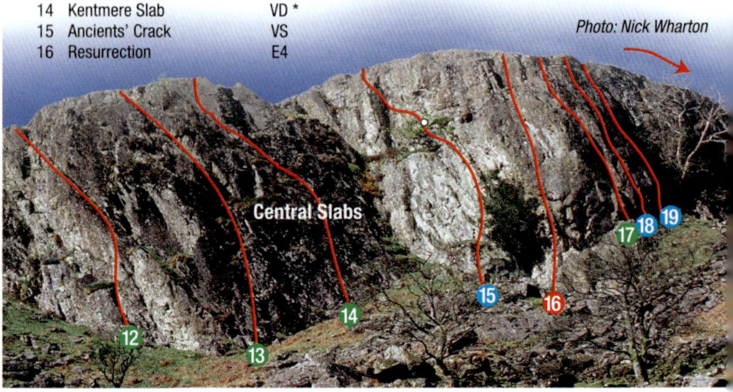

Upper Buttress

This is the steep buttress lying initially at right-angles to the *Central Slabs*. There is an obvious holly on its left-hand side.

15 **Ancients' Crack**	28m	VS		pre 1969

1 16m (4c). Scramble up to a ledge left of the holly and climb the steep off-width crack behind it using the left wall to gain a small tree. Move up right to a thread belay.

2 12m (5a). Traverse left for 4 metres and climb the short steep corner using the left arête to finish.

16 **Resurrection**	25m	E4		1988

Start just right of the holly.

(6a). Climb the groove in the impending prow (peg runner) to a jug on the left (sideways Rock 7 under your fingers!) Bridge right and climb strenuously through bulging rock to gain and climb the centre of the slabby wall above (as for ***Route 8***) to a belay ledge. An easy 3 metres leads to the top.

Route 8	25m	MVS		pre 1969

Follow *Calf Chimney* for 5 metres then traverse leftwards around onto the front of the buttress to finish up what is now the upper half of *Resurrection* in an impressive position.

17 **Calf Chimney**	23m	D	★	1921

A good route starting 10 metres right of the holly tree.

Climb the prominent chimney-crack and short wall above.

The final two routes climb the undercut steep slim slab right of *Calf Chimney*.

18 **Victory V**	20m	E1		1988

Start just right of *Calf Chimney*.

(5c). Climb the undercut V-groove direct (awkward to start), then follow the thin crack-line up the left side of the slab.

19 **Twilight Slab**	17m	MVS		pre 1969

Start at the right-hand side of the undercut slab.

Pull over the overlap and climb the right side of the slab to a small ledge at 10 metres. Either move back left and finish up the centre of the slab, or continue up its right side.

Rainsborrow Crag (NY 444 067) is the big broken crag on the western side of Kentmere about 1 kilometre below the reservoir. It was briefly popular in the late sixties but new route fever blinded the explorers to its obvious shortcomings. Owing to loose rock and vegetation none of the routes are recommended.

Tongue Scar (NY 453 071) is a steep but broken crag lying above Tongue House and half hidden by a belt of trees. The state of its routes might make you wish it were fully hidden.

Above: Boulderers on the secluded single track road that runs up the Kentmere valley.
Photo: Nick Wharton

Kentmere Bouldering

There is a wealth of bouldering in the Kentmere valley. Two boulders are described in detail but further fun can be found at the optimistically named Little Font area in the wooded hillside above Badger Rock and in the grandly titled Valley of the Kings area which is located on the hillside right of Garburn Pass. Further details can be found at www.lakesbloc.co.uk or in the Rockfax guidebook *Lakes Bouldering 2006*.

Right: Looking down into Kentmere past the Garburn Pass Boulder. **Photo:** Nick Wharton

Garburn Pass Boulder

A superb boulder which complements the more traditional fare on offer at *Badger Rock*. The problems are more demanding but excellent rock and landings make the pleasant walk up to it very worthwhile.

Approach:

Follow the Garburn Pass track for about three quarters of a kilometre until a large boulder is clearly seen to the left of the track. Stay on the track until level with the boulder, then head left across the hillside.

Photos: Al Davis

1	Easy Slab	V0
2	The Arête Recusant †	V1
3	Traverse wall †	V2
4	Paradigm †	V9
5	Over the Lip †	V5

† Sitting start

Photos: Nick Wharton

Overleaf: Girl power: Mari Cole is spotted by Flora Wharton on **Badger Rock**, Kentmere. **Photo:** Iain Cole

NY 442 045

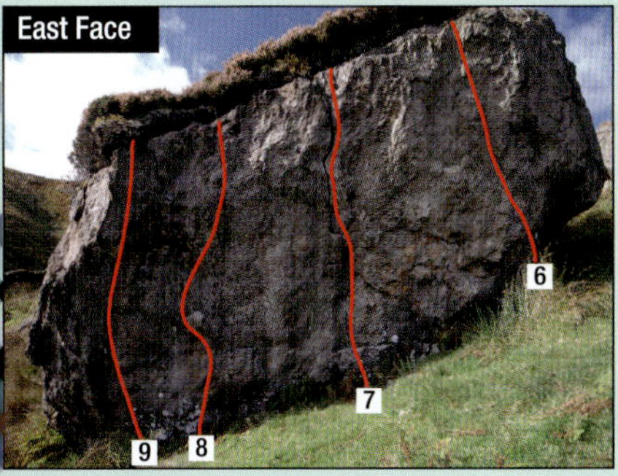

6	Thin Crack	V3
7	Release the Pressure	V3
8	Phantasmagorica †	V7
9	The Symbiant †	V4

† Sitting start

10	Quixotic Arête	V1
11	Wall left of scoop	V1
12	Right Side of Arête	V2

Photos: Nick Wharton

Badger Rock

Sometimes referred to as the *Brockstone*, Badger Rock is an isolated boulder (of similar size to the Bowderstone) pleasantly situated in a field near Kentmere Hall.

Approach:

Follow the metalled road from the church for some 500 metres until it ends as a track between buildings (The Nook). Turn right here (signposted Garburn Pass) and follow that track for a further 200 metres to where the boulder will be seen in a field on the left. It is on private farmland but access has been negotiated by the BMC on condition that **no dogs are taken into the field**.

Badger Rock provides good clean rock and gives some fingery problems with the bonus of a well-tested flat landing! Some are of sufficient length (10 metres) to feel rather highball so that the timid (or sensible) may feel a top rope is justified. Most people prefer to enjoy the obvious traverse lines. The traverse left of the crack (facing Garburn) is traditionally referred to as **Oliversons' Traverse**.

> *"There is a very interesting boulder about half a mile from the Church, just off the Garburn Pass track. It is very well scratched, and has about ten climbs up and two traverses. The Chimney on the West Face is very good, and another route just to the left of it up an overhang goes very well, and is difficult. On the Eastern Face is a big sloping slab, with many small holds, and also a narrow crack which is rather devoid of anything to hang on to. The rock is called Brockstone Crag…"*
> Gilbert Wilson, 'Some Climbs Round Kentmere', FRCC Journal 1922

Above: Flora Wharton, right and Mari Cole on **Badger Rock**, Kentmere.
Photo: Nick Wharton

NY 450 042

Photos: Nick Wharton

1	Low traverse to groove	V5
2	The Arête	V1
3	The Scoop	V1
4	Hard start	V1
5	The Groove	V0
6	Traverse under overlap	V3
7	The Slab	V6
8	Quartzy Groove	V2
9	Quartzy slab	V0

10	Traverse	V3
11	Wall	V0
12	The Arête	V0
13	Wall right of arête	V1
14	Steep wall	V1

10	Traverse	V3
14	Steep wall	V1
15	The Nose	V0
16	Quartz wall	V0
17	Wall	V0
18	Chimney	V0

Ambleside, Rydal and Grasmere

These areas comprise the major valley that is marked by the course of the A591 from Ambleside northwards to Dunmail Raise. There are no important crags in this area and it is rarely visited by climbers unless in search of food, beer or yet more equipment.

Raven Crag, Troutbeck (NY 416 046) is only about 2 minutes from the A592 about one kilometre north of Troutbeck village and Town Head. However that is all it has to recommend it, being green and loose. It enjoyed its 15 minutes of fame when a foot and mouth epidemic forced rock starved climbers to see if it was worth developing – it wasn't.

Rothay Bridge Crag

Grid Reference: **NY 368 039** Altitude: **100m**
Faces: **East** Approach: **10 mins**

This steep and vegetated crag is located in delightful woodland above the Rothay Bridge, on the outskirts of Ambleside. There is only one route here, but it is a real gem.

Approach:

Leave Ambleside on foot, following the Coniston road, and turn right just after crossing the narrow Rothay Bridge. After a short way, a small road leads up to the left, through a gate. Go through the gate and strike up the steep grassy field to where the angle eases and a wall can be seen below the woodland. Cross the wall with care and head leftwards up through the wood to reach the crag.

Crack in the Woods	20m	E4	★	1981

The climb takes the striking thin crack-line which splits the centre of the smoothest face. Start beneath the crack.

(6a). Scramble up leftwards for a couple of metres and step across onto a good foothold on the slab on the right. A delicate move up leads to the small overhang and a further move right leads to a jug at the base of the crack. The crack is well-protected but gets progressively harder towards the top, where the final pull over onto the slab, via a poor jam and a pinch, proves to be a difficult and frustrating crux.

The groove to the right has been top-roped but it is loose, unpleasant and not worth the effort.

Erne Crag and *Black Crag* are situated in the Rydal Valley which runs due south from Fairfield. The valley is about 5 kilometres long and is formed by the Great Rigg – Heron Pike ridge of Fairfield and the Hart Crag – High Pike ridge. Rydal village, at the foot of the valley, is 2 kilometres north of Ambleside on the Keswick road. There are good swimming pools in Rydal Beck.

Erne Crag

Grid Reference: **NY 359 087** Altitude: **450m**
Faces: **East** Approach: **45 mins**

Erne Crag is the long steep crag on the east flank of Heron Pike above the Rydal Valley. The cliff is extensive but the best section is the zone of white rock to the left of the obvious tree-filled gully in the centre of the crag. This *White Zone* has two conspicuous deep corners. The rock is slatey and friable and with some poor protection. The climbing is a little dirty and would benefit from more traffic.

Approach:
The crag is reached by following the track up the Rydal Valley from the church which is opposite the Rydal Hall entrance (NY 364 064). From the track in the valley floor the easiest approach is by slanting up the fell as the crag appears. Make for a dry stone wall that comes down from the left end of the crag. From its top, traverse right to the *White Zone*.

Ravens nest on this crag and it should be avoided in the Spring.

Descent can be made down a system of rakes at the left end of the crag but abseiling off is recommended. The best anchor for this is the pinnacle of *The Vorpal Blade* itself.

The climbs are described from **left** to **right**.

Erne Crag

1	Silhouette Arête	VS
2	The Grater	E2
3	The Vorpal Blade	VS **
4	The Cutter	E1 *
5	The Slicer	E2 *
6	The Cleaver	HVS
7	The Slasher	E1
8	The Keenest	E2

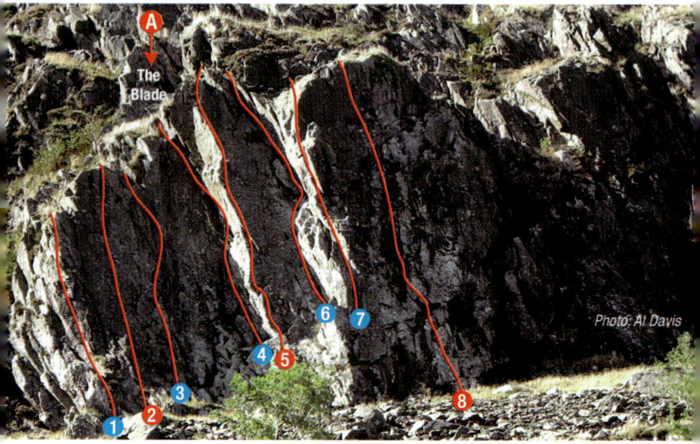

1	Silhouette Arête	33m	VS		1986

The left-flanking arête of the *White Zone*. A bold first pitch which is serious for the grade.

1 24m (4c). Climb the system of cracks up the leaning edge to a ledge and belay below a deep corner.

2 9m (4a). Ascend the steep corner to a small pinnacle as for *The Vorpal Blade*.

2	The Grater	33m	E2		1987

The wall between *Silhouette Arête* and *The Vorpal Blade*. The crux is poorly protected and committing.

1 24m (5b). Start up *Silhouette Arête* and then continue straight up the wall to a ledge and belay below a deep corner.

2 9m (4a). Ascend the steep corner to a small pinnacle as for *The Vorpal Blade*.

3	The Vorpal Blade	33m	VS	★★	1986

A good climb taking the twisting crack up the centre of the wall right of *Silhouette Arête*.

1 24m (4c). Climb the thin bow-shaped crack up a shallow curving scoop. As the crack widens continue up steeply to an awkward move left at the top. Belay in a deep cleaned corner.

2 9m (4a). Ascend the steep corner to a small pinnacle (the *Blade*).

4 **The Cutter**	33m	E1	★	1986

A well-protected and classic struggle up the obvious left-leaning groove right of *The Vorpal Blade*.

(5b). Easy ground leads up to a tiny tree. Jam and bridge the corner, exiting right over a bulge into a subsidiary hanging groove.

5 **The Slicer**	33m	E2	★	1986

A fine route up the striking slender arête in the centre of the *White Zone*.

(5c). Climb the leaning crack in the corner to the right of the arête. From a runner, climb down to good footholds at the base of the arête which is climbed with difficulty to a small square hold. Continue up the arête which provides exposed and excellent climbing.

6 **The Cleaver**	33m	HVS		1986

(5a). The right-hand corner. Serious to start but then has good protection and continuous interest.

7 **The Slasher**	33m	E1		1987

The steep arête between *The Cleaver* and *The Keenest*.

(5b). Climb two slim grooves in the crest, finishing up the arête.

8 **The Keenest**	33m	E2		1986

Start right of centre of the long wall to the right of *The Cleaver*. Bold.

(5c). Move up and left to gain the middle of the wall. Continue straight up then step right onto a ramp and move up to the thin crack in the headwall. Climb this using a movable dog-tooth flake and then up to the top (crux).

Black Crag

Grid Reference: **NY 361 108** Altitude: **530m**
Faces: **South-East** Approach: **1 hr 15 mins**

Black Crag is situated at the head of Rydal Valley. It is steep and consists of three distinct pillars, the middle one being broken and short. The routes are unfrequented and you are likely to have the valley to yourselves – not really surprising considering the length of the walk in.

Approach:

The crag is reached by following the track up the Rydal Valley from the church which is opposite the Rydal Hall entrance (NY 364 064).

Black Crag Rydal

1	Fish Fryers Convention	E2
2	Piglet's Wall	VS
3	Two Pockets	E4
4	Dizzy	E1

Descent is at either end.

The climbs are described from **left** to **right**.

1 **Fish Fryers Convention**	30m	E2		1986

Takes two walls to the left of the left pillar.

(5b). Follow a leftward-trending faint groove to a wilting little tree and ledge. Continue straight up the wall above (crux).

2 **Piglet's Wall**	33m	VS		1986

Start in the groove to the left of the edge of the pillar.

(4c). Climb the groove to a ledge. Move left onto a large pinnacle flake and continue up to a ramp which is followed rightwards, then up to the top.

3 **Two Pockets**	33m	E4		1986

Takes the edge of the left-hand pillar. Start just right of the arête.

(5c). Using two pockets, pull into a niche. Step right and climb a crack to a ledge. Go straight up the wall above on small friable holds, move left to a flake hold and then back right up the centre of the wall.

4 **Dizzy**	33m	E1		1986

Takes the right-hand pillar. Start from a large flake.

(5a). Climb a green groove to an obvious sloping gangway leading right to the arête. Gain the arête then move right into a diagonal crack which is followed up the wall.

Moving north into the Grasmere Valley, some poor loose climbs have been made up the vegetated rock of **Nab Scar (NY 355 067)** and further routes have been climbed up the loose slatey rock of **White Moss Car Park Crag (NY 348 066)** - fortunately most of them have fallen down. In the same area, but on the south side of Rydal Water lies the huge quarried **Rydal Cave (NY 355 058)**. Some good hard routes were made across the headwall of the cave but have been neglected and the slabby rock they cross has accumulated a luxuriant carpet of moss.

The remaining crags lie north of Grasmere, near Dunmail Raise.

Low Raven Crag

Grid Reference: **NY 330 093** Altitude: **200m**
Faces: **East** Approach: **20 mins**

This is the steep little outcrop low down on the east side of Helm Crag. It is very clearly seen across the valley from the Traveller's Rest. The crag has a reddish look to it and has an obvious barrel shape in the upper two thirds of the front face. This results in a very steep section which is breached by the crag's star attraction – *Meltdown.*

On the whole, the rock is sound and the climbing good though, as with many crags, it would benefit from more traffic and some cleaning.

Approach:

Parking for the crag is easily reached from the Grasmere side of the A591, Dunmail Raise road. Heading north, turn left just after the left-hand bend north of the Traveller's Rest. Follow this narrow road over a bridge and past a junction on the left. Continue straight on for another 400 metres to a farm on the left and a junction on the right where the road crosses another bridge. Limited parking is available on the left. Alternatively park on the main road and walk the short distance. The easiest access to the crag is to the right of the farm. The initial part of the route to reach the open fell crosses private land so permission should be sought at the farm.

Descent is down a grass ramp on the right.

The routes are described from **right** to **left**.

Low Raven Crag Grasmere

1	Punter's Rib	HS	
2	While the Cat's Away	HS	
3	Bantam	HVS	
4	Rampart Road	HVS	*
5	A Crow Flies North	E3	
6	Meltdown	E7	**
7	The Necker	E5	*
8	Climbs of Quality	E1	

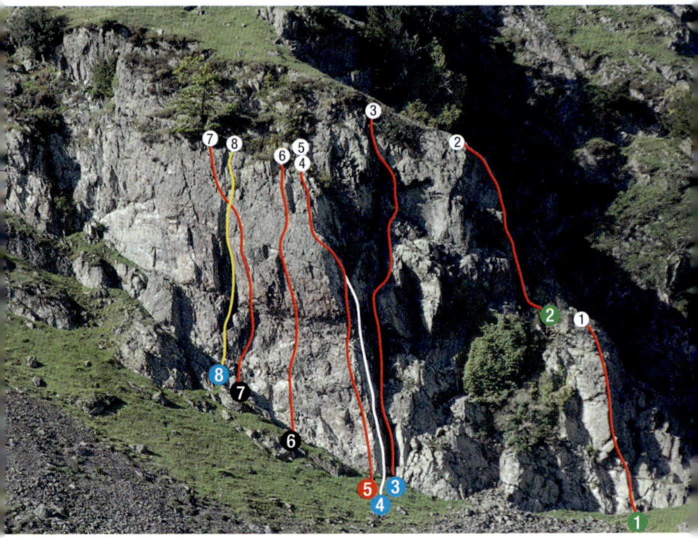

1 **Punter's Rib**	14m	HS		1997

Climb the broken rib on the right edge of the crag.

2 **While the Cat's Away**	15m	HS		1990

Climb the upper arête, left of the grassy ramp, to the top. Care is needed with some of the rock.

3 **Bantam**	30m	HVS		1963

(5a). Follow the stepped groove right of the main wall. Some good climbing.

4 **Rampart Road**	30m	HVS	★	2007

An excellent slab climb up the green left-slanting ramp near the centre of the crag, just right of the main wall. Start at the obvious, deep V-groove as for *Bantam*.

(5a). Climb the groove then move left onto the slab. Continue up the slab in exciting positions to a large ledge. Climb the wall to reach the narrow gangway heading left to the arête. Climb this on poorer rock to the top – as for *A Crow Flies North*.

5 **A Crow Flies North**	30m	E3		1993

Starts 2 metres left of the left-hand arête of the central ramp.

(5c). Step up and go right to swing round the arête and gain a ledge below an obvious flake on the arête. Boldly climb the hollow flake to a large ledge then climb the wall to reach the narrow gangway heading left to the arête. Climb this on poorer rock to the top.

6 **Meltdown**	25m	E7 {F7b}	★★	1997

A slightly different proposition to the other routes on offer, this fine climb accepts the challenge of the bulging red wall in the middle of the crag. The main difficulties centre around a superb sequence of gymnastic moves at half height. Start under the wall below the line of the overhang.

(6b). Climb up to a flaky diagonal crack at about 3 metres. Follow the crack up and left to a ledge. Continue up the short bulging wall to a good ledge beneath the main roof – arrange protection. Stretch around the roof to a flat hold. Clip four poor pegs, all close together, then take a deep breath and sprint up the wall to where the angle eases – breathe again! The remainder of the wall is much easier but without protection until almost at the top.

7 **The Necker**	25m	E5	★	2007

The thin crack on the left edge of the central overhanging red wall. Good climbing protected by small wires. Start at a short corner below the crack.

(6a). Climb the corner to pull out left onto a ledge at 6 metres. Fire your way up the bulging crack, using holds on both sides, to reach a resting place on the slab above. Continue up and left, crossing ***Climbs of Quality***, to finish at a tree belay.

8 **Climbs of Quality**	20m	E1		1985

(5b). Climb the steep pod/crack at the left end of the main wall.

Cotra Breast (NY 324 107), which stands just north of the entrance to the delightful valley of Greenburn Bottom, has been thoroughly examined by one indefatigable explorer. His few short climbs are left for others of a similar ilk to rediscover. **Gavel Crag (NY 347 113)** lies on the south-east slope of Seat Sandal. There is one short climb which doesn't justify carrying climbing gear – better to go for the walk.

Crag Guide

Crag Name	Seasonal Restrictions (R)	Aspect	Alt (m)	Approach Time (mins)
Thirlmere				
Shundraw Quarry		E	180	3
Church Crag		E	240	5
Bramcrag Quarry		W	200	5
Sandbed Ghyll Crags		N – W	390	15
Castle Rock		W – S	275	10
Lower Piketoe Knott		W	300	5
Swirl Crags		W	400	10
Nab Crag		S – E	400	30
Harrop Tarn Crag		E	400	25
Standing Crag		N – W	560	60
Thackmell Crag	R	N – E	360	10
Raven Crag	R	E	350	15
Smaithwaite Banks		E	370	15
Sippling Crag		W	350	30
Iron Crag		E	350	40
Goat Crag		E	400	40
Yew Crag		W	200	10
Northern Fells				
Black Crag		E	330	15
Snail Shell Crag		E	330	15
Slape Crag		E	300	15
The Trough Area		E	450	15
Patterdale & Ullswater				
Kirkstone Crag		E	400	3
Raven Crag Keldas		E	200	3
Edmund's Castle		N	400	10 / 45

al ns	Total Routes 761	M D VD	MS S HS	MVS VS	HVS E1	E2 E3	E4+
		To 5+	F6a/a+	F6b/b+	F6c/c+	F7a/a+	>F7a+
	6				4		2
	9	7		2			
	36	1		7	18	9	1
	25		2	4	7	7	5
0	59	3	5	9	18	18	6
	8	1	2	4	1		
	29	2	6	4	5	7	5
	11	3		1	5	1	1
	4		1		1	1	1
	10		1	3	1	4	1
	11			4	4	3	
	25		1	4	1	6	12
	2					2	
	3			1	1	1	
	20			1	4	3	12
	17		2		8	6	1
	19		1	3	7	8	
	1						1
	6	7	2	1			
	4	1		1		2	
	4	3		1			
	14	2	3	1	6	1	1
	3				2	1	
	5	2	2	1			

Crag Guide

Crag Name	Seasonal Restrictions (R)	Aspect	Alt (m)	Approach Time (mins)
Brunt Crag		E	300	2
Gowbarrow		SE	245	10
Thrang Crag	R	E	300	10
Rampsgill Head		NW	750	90
Dubhow Crag		SW	400	30
Fall Crag		W	330	20
Raven Crag Threshwaite	R	SE	450	45
Grisedale				
Thornhow Crag		NW	260	30
St Sunday Crag		NW	650	105
Eagle Crag		E	396	90
Deepdale				
Erne Nest Crag		N	450	60
Hart Crag		N	650	75
Scrubby Crag		SE	710	90
Mart Crag		E	360	60
Hutaple Crag		NW	640	75
Black Buttress		N	640	90
Cofa Pike Slabs		SE	750	120
Dovedale				
Gill Crag		SE	490	60
Black Crag		SE	520	60
Dove Crag		NE	580	75
Lower Dove Crag		NE	500	75
Heirloom Crag		NE	750	90
Haweswater				
Birks Crag		E	400	40

al e ns	Total Routes 761	M D VD To 5+	MS S HS F6a/a+	MVS VS F6b/b+	HVS E1 F6c/c+	E2 E3 F7a/a+	E4+ >F7a+
	4	3			1		
	19	2	1	3	9	4	
	13				5	6	2
	6			4	2		
	9		5	4			
	3		1	1		1	
	19					5	14
	5	1	2	2			
5	19	8	6	4	1		
	33	2	2	10	10	9	
	9		1	6	2		
	10	2	5	3			
3	12	1	2	3	6		
	21			2	4	12	3
3	19	2	5	5	5	2	
	1	1					
	3			3			
	7	4	2	1			
	3	2	1				
	35		1	3	2	8	21
	2		1	1			
	8				3	2	3
	4		1		2		1

Crag Guide

Crag Name	Seasonal Restrictions (R)	Aspect	Alt (m)	Approach Time (mins)	D
Swindale					
Gouther Crag	R	NW	350	30	
Longsleddale					
Nether Crag		SE	180	30	
Buckbarrow Crag	R	SW	350	30	
Kentmere					
Iving Crag		E	250	15	
Calf Howe Crag		E	200	20	
Ambleside, Rydal & Grasmere					
Rothay Bridge Crag		E	100	10	
Erne Crag	R	E	450	45	
Black Crag		SE	530	75	
Low Raven Crag		E	200	20	

Crags Suitable for Group

Church Crag (NY 305 227)

Described in the text on page 47. However group use is currently restricted to the Calvert Trust.

Snail Shell Crag (NY 355 327)

Described in the text on page 181.

Edmund's Castle (NY 365 172)

Described in the text on page 201.

al e ns	Total Routes 761	M D VD	MS S HS	MVS VS	HVS E1	E2 E3	E4+
		To 5+	F6a/a+	F6b/b+	F6c/c+	F7a/a+	>F7a+
)	58	3	9	8	18	16	5
	10		2	2	5	1	
5	27	3	4	4	8	6	2
	19		2		5	4	8
	20	3	2	7	4	3	1
	1						1
	8			2	3	3	
	4			1	1	1	1
	8		2		3	1	2

Brunt Crag (NY 397 210)

Described in the text on page 202.

Gowbarrow – Lower Buttress (NY 414 205)

Described in the text on page 205. Please see page 206 for booking system and code of practice.

Thornhow Crag (NY 382 154)

Described in the text on page 239.

Climbing Walls

There is a good range of climbing walls available to those living in or visiting the Lake District. They are described here for use on those occasional rainy days and dank evenings:

Ambleside: Ambleside Climbing Wall

10.5 metre lead wall with 45+ routes of all grades from 3 to hard. Dedicated bouldering room. Open 09:00 to 22:00 every day.

Access check – tel: 015394 33794, www.adventurepeaks.com

Ambleside: University of Cumbria (ex-Charlotte Mason's College)

Low cost revamped wall at the college, with good bouldering but no leading. Now only available to students at the college.

Access check – tel: 015394 30210, www.cumbria.ac.uk

Barrow in Furness: Park Leisure Centre

Good access and low cost, but very limited lead climbing and a cramped bouldering area. Excellent other facilities. Open all day until 21:45 weekdays, 10:00 to 18:00 weekends.

Access check – tel: 01229 871146, www.barrowbc.gov.uk

Carlisle: The Sands Centre

Reasonable low cost climbing facility in a large sports centre. Good bouldering and leading. Very good access and excellent general facilities. Open 09:30 to 22:30 seven days a week.

Access check – tel: 01228 625222, www.thesandscentre.co.uk

Carlisle: Richard Rose Central Academy

Previously called St Aidan's School. Good freeform featured leading wall open to the public. Bouldering may be possible but you might need your own mat. Open 17:00 to 21:00 Monday to Friday (last admission 20:00), 10:00 to 17:00 Saturday and Sunday (last admission 16:00).

Access check – tel: 01228 822060, www.richardroseacademies.org

Cockermouth: Leisure Centre

Varied bouldering with natural stonework and Bendcrete. Low cost and good access. Other sports facilities available. Open 08:00 to 22:00 Monday to Friday, 09:00 to 17:00 weekends.

Access check – tel: 01900 823596, www.allerdale.gov.uk

Egremont: Wyndham Sports Centre

A good facility located in the centre of Egremont on the west coast, only half an hour from Wasdale Head. There are practice areas, bouldering, leading walls and a huge roof. Unfortunately no longer open to the public except on a club booking basis.

Access check – tel: 01946 820356

Ingleton: Inglesport Climbing Barn

Best of the small walls. Very good use of space with leading and bouldering. Regular innovations. Relaxed friendly atmosphere. Cafe and shop nearby. Open 09:00 to 22:00 Monday to Thursday, 09:00 to 17:30 Friday, 08:30 to 18:00 weekends.

Access check – tel: 015242 41146, www.inglesport.co.uk/wall.html

Kendal: The Lakeland Climbing Centre

A magnificent indoor climbing facility with excellent bouldering and leading. Includes a very impressive 18 metre main wall and a huge roof. Located on the Lake District Business Park, across the A6 from Morrison's supermarket. Changing and shower facilities. Open: Winter (September to April) 16:00 to 22:00 Monday, 10:00 to 22:00 Tuesday to Friday, 10:00 to 19:00 weekends and Bank Holidays. Summer (May to August): 10:00 to 22:00 Tuesday to Friday, 10:00 to 17:00 weekends and Bank Holidays.

Access check – tel: 01539 721766, www.kendalwall.co.uk

Keswick: Keswick Climbing Wall and Activity Centre

Located to the east of Keswick at Goosewell Farm. From the A66, approach from "the old road", near Naddle Bridge, following a road towards Castlerigg Stone Circle - the farm is on the right just before this. Bright, airy climbing wall and bouldering wall with a stunning view of Helvellyn out of the main barn doors, you feel you are climbing outdoors no matter what the weather - the Outdoors "Indoors". Open 9:00 - 17:00 Friday to Monday, 9:00 to 21:00 Tuesday to Thursday.

Access check – tel: 017687 72000, www.keswickclimbingwall.co.uk

Penrith: Penrith Leisure Centre – Eden Climbing Wall

An excellent leading wall adjoining the town's swimming pool. Open 9:30 to 21:30 weekdays, 9:30 to 21:00 weekends.

Access check – tel: 01768 863450, www.leisure-centre.com

Penrith: University of Cumbria (Newton Rigg)

Leading and bouldering wall open as part of the campus but also available for public use.

Access check – tel: 01768 863450, www.cumbria.ac.uk

Useful Contacts

Climbing

British Mountaineering Council
0870 0104878 www.thebmc.co.uk
Fell & Rock Climbing Club www.frcc.co.uk

Lake District Weather

Weather Forecast
0844 846 2444 www.lake-district.gov.uk/weatherline/home/index.php

Lake District National Park Authority www.lake-district.gov.uk

Bird Restrictions
017687 79633 www.frcc.co.uk/conservation_birdrestrictions.asp
Brockhole National Park Centre
015394 46601
Head Office
01539 724555

Above: Mirror image of Thirlmere looking towards Dunmail Raise. **Photo:** Al Phizacklea

Tourist Information

Cumbria Tourism
01539 8222 222 www.golakes.co.uk

Ambleside	015394 32582
Ambleside (Waterhead)	015394 32729
Appleby	017683 51177
Bowness-on-Windermere	015394 42895
Brampton	016977 3433
Carlisle	01228 625600
Glenridding	017684 82414
Grange-over-Sands	015395 34026
Grasmere	015394 35245
Kendal	01539 725758
Keswick	017687 72645
Killington Lake (M6 Services)	015396 20138
Kirkby Stephen	017683 71199
Penrith	01768 867466
Pooley Bridge	017684 86530
Rheged (Junction 40)	01768 860034
Sedburgh	015396 20125
Southwaite (M6 Services)	016974 73445
Windermere	015394 46499

Journey Planners

Cumbria County Council www.cumbria.gov.uk

Public Transport Information – Traveline
0871 200 2233 www.traveline.org.uk

Where to Stay

This list of Youth Hostels, Campsites and Camping Barns on the eastern side of the Lake District is fairly comprehensive, but there are no doubt more, and fuller details will be available from Tourist Information Offices. This information is current in 2011 but will almost certainly alter and it is probably best to make telephone contact before going to a particular hostel, site or barn.

Youth Hostels	Grid Ref	Telephone
www.yha.org.uk		
Ambleside, Waterhead	NY 377 031	0870 770 5672
Gilsland, Birdoswald	NY 616 664	0870 770 6124
Carlisle, Old Brewery Residences	NY 393 561	0870 770 5752
Borrowdale – Longthwaite	NY 254 142	0870 770 5706
Derwentwater – Barrow House	NY 268 200	0870 770 5792
Dufton	NY 688 251	0870 770 5800
Grasmere		
Butharlyp Howe	NY 337 079	0870 770 5836
Thorney How	NY 332 084	0870 770 5836
Broadrayne Farm (not YHA)	NY 337 094	05394 35055
Glenridding, Helvellyn	NY 366 173	0870 770 6110
Kendal	NY 514 923	0870 770 5892
Keswick	NY 267 235	0870 770 5894
Patterdale	NY 398 157	0870 770 5986
Skiddaw House	NY 287 291	07747 174293
Windermere, Troutbeck	NY 405 013	0870 770 6094

Bunkhouses	Grid Ref	Telephone
Hartsop, Syke Farm	NY 401 120	017684 82239
Glenridding, Gillside	NY 382 168	017684 82346

Camping Barns	Grid Ref	Telephone
www.lakelandcampingbarns.co.uk		01946 758198
Caldbeck, Hudscales	NY 331 375	017687 72645
St Johns in the Vale, Low Bridge End	NY 316 205	01946 758198
www.campingbarn.com		
Thirlmere, Causeway Foot	NY 294 218	017687 72290
Newlands, Catbells	NY 245 208	01946 758 198

Rosthwaite, Dinas Hoggas Barn	NY 259 150	01946 758 198
Ullswater, Swirral	NY 365 174	01946 758 198
Kendal, Wythmoor Farm	SD 588 954	01946 758 198
Kirkby Stephen, Bents Farm	NY 708 065	01946 758 198

Campsites	Grid Ref	Telephone
Braithwaite, Scotgate	NY 235 236	017687 78343
Keswick		
Castlerigg Hall	NY 280 225	017687 74499
Castlerigg	NY 283 223	017687 72479
Derwentwater	NY 260 232	017687 72392
Threlkeld		
Burns Farm	NY 305 242	017687 79225
Setmabanning	NY 322 247	017687 79229
Thirlmere		
Dale Bottom	NY 295 220	017687 72176
Thirlspot	NY 317 177	017687 72551
Bridge End Farm	NY 315 192	017687 72166
Troutbeck		
Gill Head	NY 378 268	017687 79652
Hutton Moor End	NY 364 270	017687 79615
Gillhead	NY 364 270	017687 79652
Hartsop, Syke Farm	NY 401 120	017684 82239
Patterdale, Side Farm	NY 397 167	017684 82337
Glenridding, Gillside	NY 382 168	017684 82346
Watermillock		
Cove Park	NY 432 234	017684 86549
The Quiet Site	NY 428 235	017684 86337
Ullswater	NY 435 229	017684 86666
Pooley Bridge		
Park Foot	NY 470 235	017684 86309
Waterside	NY 463 231	017684 86332
Roehead (Hillcroft Park)	NY 475 242	017684 86363
Penrith, Lowther	NY 526 263	01768 863631
Penruddock, Beckces	NY 417 277	017684 83224
Berrier, Hopkinson Park	NY 405 288	017684 83456
Greystoke, Thanet Well	NY 398 350	017684 84262

Caldbeck, Throstle Hall	NY 332 398	016974 68618
Ainstable, Faugh Head	NY 522 458	016974 72229
Kirkoswald, The Mains	NY 562 398	01768 898342
Dufton, Edenstone	NY 688 252	017683 51573
Morland, Newby End	NY 599 213	01931 714338
Ambleside, Low Wray	NY 015 372	015394 32810
Windermere		
Limefitt Park	NY 414 032	015394 32300
Park Cliffe	SD 388 909	015395 31344
Staveley, Ashes Lane	SD 478 965	01539 821119
Crook		
Rather Heath	SD 479 958	01539 821154
Pound Farm	SD 472 953	01539 821220
Kendal, Millcrest	SD 526 948	01539 741363

Above: Patterdale Mountain Rescue team in action. **Photo:** www.mountainrescue.org.uk

Mountain Accidents

by Dr John Ellerton (LDSAMRA)

Procedure for climbers in the Lake District

Mountain rescue in the Lake District is well served by 13 voluntary teams backed up by special search and cave/mine rescue units. They are equipped to a high standard and work closely with the RAF helicopters and Air Ambulance services. Consequently, only minor casualties should come within the scope of treatment and evacuation by the climber's companions. The rule for all other cases is; to make the casualty safe, to start first aid, and to send for a Mountain Rescue Team.

Sending for Help

A reliable member of the party, with full information about the nature of the injuries and the position of the incident (including, if possible, the map reference) should be sent to find the nearest telephone. He should dial 999, and ask for the Police, who will notify the appropriate team/agency. The sender of the message should stay by the telephone until he receives instructions from the Team Leader. Mobile phones can save a considerable amount of time - please use them to call the Police. Have the mobile phone number handy and keep within reception range (reception is often better on the tops or ridges of the mountains). Do not switch the phone off - the team leader will call back.

Lack of help

You have a difficult decision to make when the casualty is severely injured, possibly unconscious, and you are alone. You should try to summon help from nearby climbers or walkers by shouting, giving the distress call on a whistle (6 blasts repeated regularly), flashing a torch (6 flashes repeated regularly), or sending up a red flare. If there is no response then assess the relative dangers of leaving the casualty, or of failing to get help, and then act decisively in the interest of the casualty.

Emergency precautions and first aid

While waiting for the rescue team, you should check for further danger, and then carry out basic first-aid treatment.

Safety first

Are you and the casualty safe from further danger?

If not try and make yourselves safe: either by moving, or anchoring yourselves, or both. Is the casualty responsive?

Is the casualty's Airway open?

If necessary, open it by a simple jaw thrust or lift. If possible, avoid moving the neck after trauma. An open airway is essential if the casualty is unconscious or semi-conscious as reduced consciousness can cause death from asphyxia as the tongue falls back blocking the airway. The position of the casualty, in particular his head and tongue, should be adjusted to open the airway and continually reassessed.

Is the casualty Breathing?

Look, feel and listen for breathing. Basic Life Support should be started, if you are trained, when the casualty is unconscious and shows no signs of breathing, and it can be continued until help arrives and where there is a chance of recovery (lightning, drowning, heart attack). It is usually futile in casualties with internal injuries and is probably best to defer in cases of severe exposure/hypothermia until expert help is available An unconscious and breathing casualty should be put in the Recovery Position if possible. Check the airway is still open.

Is the casualty's Circulation adequate?

Stop any bleeding from wounds by elevation and direct pressure with dressings or clothing. The pressure needs to be applied continuously for at least 10 minutes. Raising the legs and/or lowering the head may be appropriate. Internal haemorrhage should be suspected if the casualty has sustained blows to the chest or abdomen or broken the femur (thigh bone). The condition often deteriorates and all steps should be taken to facilitate the rapid arrival of the Mountain Rescue Team and, if possible, a helicopter. A record of the pulse rate and consciousness level is very helpful.

Is the casualty Disabled due to damage to head or spine?

Record the casualty's consciousness level – alert, responsive to voice, responsive to pain or unresponsive? Has the spine been damaged? If so, do not move the casualty unless essential for safety reasons. Maintain the head in the normal straight position using your hands.

Check the limbs for fractures

If present, immobilise the limb by the simplest method available. In the case of the arm, pad it and bandage it to the chest, and in the case of the leg, pad it and bandage it to the other leg.

Prevent hypothermia (exposure)

Shelter the casualty from wind and rain. Wrap them in as many layers of clothing as possible and encase them in a 'poly bag' or other impermeable barrier. Do not forget to insulate the head and underneath the casualty.

A **helicopter** may arrive before the mountain rescue team. Extinguish all flames and secure all equipment. The downdraught can knock you over, so get in a safe position. Do not approach the helicopter until clearly signalled to do so by the pilot.

Further points to consider

Large **organised groups** should bear in mind that Mountain Rescue Teams are a finite resource and it is wrong to assume their availability.

The majority of climbers killed in the Lake District as a result of a climbing accident die from a head injury. A **helmet**, whilst not being 100% effective, can make the difference between living and dying.

Whilst **mobile phones** can be very useful in emergencies, any temptation to use them in the hills to call the emergency services in non-emergency circumstances should be resisted. If you are not sure whether it is an emergency or not, please investigate a little yourself first before reaching for your phone.

GPS systems, whilst also useful, are no substitute for carrying a **map** and **compass** and knowing how to use them.

The routine carrying of a suitable **head-torch** would save many needless call-outs.

Lake District Mountain Rescue Teams are made up of unpaid volunteers and rely on charitable contributions. Your consideration and a "Thank you" go a long way to ensure the service continues.

The **Lake District Search and Mountain Rescue Association** (LDSAMRA) acts as an umbrella body for the Lakeland Mountain Rescue Teams. It has a website, which gives contact details for the individual teams, at: http://homepages enterprise net/ldsamra

First Ascents

Alternate and varied leads are indicated by (**alt**) and (**var**)

1890 **Sandbed Ghyll** – GD Abraham, AP Abraham

1896 Jun **Iron Crag Chimney** – GD Abraham, A Abraham, JW Robinson, FW Jackson

"I shall never forget how white the face of one member of the party was when it appeared over the top of the [second] pitch, how he yelled to us to "haul in the taut," how he 'quoth, "nevermore,"'and how impolitely he spoke to the leader for having climbed it at all."

"The upper rocks … were of the worst description imaginable. Great pieces as large as one's head came away at once and every step had to be most carefully tested before we could proceed… Several big pieces had to be removed and some came whizzing past in much too close proximity to be pleasant."

GD Abraham recounts episodes from the first and second ascents, in an appendix to ***Rock Climbing in the English Lake District*** by OG Jones, 3rd Edition, 1900.

1896 Jul 22 **Dollywaggon Gully** – Wilberforce, N Tribe, JW Robinson

"Dollywaggon Gully, climbed by Col Westmorland when he was a little lad and probably never repeated until our ascent generations later. That was our impression at the time anyway. This gully is now rather safer than it was before, large portions of its retaining walls having peeled off during our ascent."
Harry Griffin, 'Innocents in the East', ***FRCC Journal 1955.***

1910 Sep 23 **Chock Gully** – H Westmorland, J Mounsey, WA North

"The names of Mr Hudson, who so unfortunately came to grief inTwll Dhu, of Mr Haskett Smith, and of Mr John Mounsey, my companion in September, had been connected with earlier ascents, but a complete direct ascent still remained to be made." Horace Westmorland, 'Climbs Old and New', ***FRCC Journal 1910.***

1910 Oct 3 **Westmorland's Route** – H Westmorland, J Mounsey, WA North

A local newspaper reported that a doctor and ambulance were on stand-by during Westmorland's ascent!

It has long been recorded in FRCC guidebooks that *"The first four pitches were added by a party consisting of CR Wilson, Mabel M Barker,*

Top Right: Rusty Westmorland, creator of the eponymous **Westmorland's Route**. **Photo:** Unknown. From *"Adventures in Climbing"* by Rusty Westmorland (Pelham, 1964)
Bottom Left: Rusty Westmorland. **Photo:** R Cook. From *"Adventures in Climbing"* by Rusty Westmorland (Pelham, 1964)

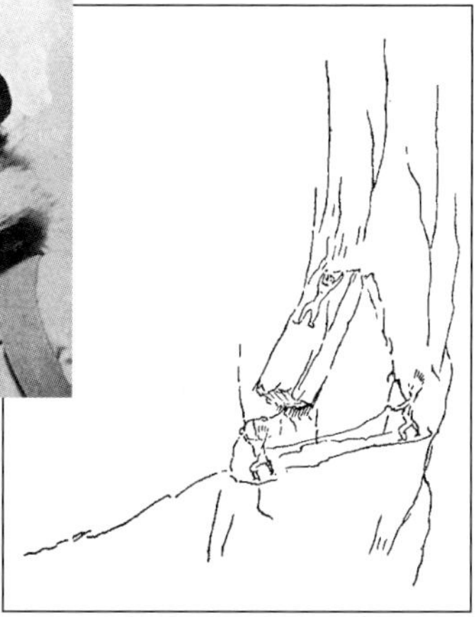

Bottom right: First Ascent of Westmorland's Route: *"John Mounsey and WA North were on a narrow ledge and I was leading up a slab which formed one side of a gable-shaped rock abutting against the over-hanging wall of the cliff; as I climbed carefully up this slab, the portion I was on, about the size of two large tombstones end to end, slid outwards, and as Dove Crag overhangs twenty feet in three hundred or so, the prospect was at least exciting. However after moving outwards about four inches, the slab for some reason came to a stop and I was able to go on without dislodging it, and finish the climb."* H Westmorland (sketch by WA North) (FRCC Journal 1939)

D Tweddle, J Bell, and NH Hamilton, 30th May 1937 and that they called the climb Wing Ridge, unaware that the upper part had been ascended earlier." However in a letter in the ***FRCC Journal 1940***, MABEL BARKER states, *"So far as I can tell from the route marked on the photograph, it* [Westmorland's Route] *is indeed to all intents and purposes the same route as the one we made up 'Wing Ridge'."*

1921 **Calf Chimney** – G WILSON and his two brothers
Both the Oak Tree Traverse and the Direct Finish were climbed. *"A big detached flake (the Pinnacle) has a crack behind it which forms a very jolly climb. There is a chockstone in it, which seems somewhat loose, so each time I have led the crack I have tried to avoid putting weight on it. The upper stone, which is a very big wedge, can be climbed on both sides."* GILBERT WILSON, 'Some Climbs around Kentmere', ***FRCC Journal 1922***.

1924 Three short climbs recorded on **The Benn** – RW HALL, AR THOMSON, DEBONER

1926 May 27 **Camera Gully** – JD BEST, B SEDDEN, H JOHNSON

1926 Jun 5 **Dandle Buttress** – JD BEST, M LINNELL, H JOHNSON

1926 Jun 17 **Dandle Slabs** – JD BEST, M LINNELL H JOHNSON

1926 Jun 30 **Harter Fell Gully** – WT ELMSLIE

1927 Aug 4 **The Eagle's Nest** – H JOHNSON, M LINNELL, JD BEST

1927 Aug 4 **Linjeston's Climb** – JD BEST, M LINNELL, H JOHNSON

1927 **The Trough** – MABEL M BARKER, F POWER

1927 **Eighty Foot Slab** – MABEL M BARKER, AVS LOCHEAD, AF AIREY and others.

1928 Mar 31 **Yew Tree Climb** – GG MACPHEE, MABEL M BARKER
The first route on Castle Rock. MACPHEE'S attempts on the North Crag were thwarted by a combination of *'meteorology, geology and forestry.'*

1928 May 19 **Gangway Climb** – GG MACPHEE, JW BAXTER
Gangway Direct was added by F WILKINSON, M BEBBINGTON, I KNIGHT, 10th October 2007, though M TURNER had previously climbed most it on 9th April 1995 as the upper part of Commemoration.

1928 Jul 3 **Slab Climb** – MABEL M BARKER, GG MACPHEE
Finished direct by AT HARGREAVES, GG MACPHEE, 29th September 1929.

1928 Jul 3 **Scoop and Crack** – GG MACPHEE, MABEL M BARKER
The climb originally finished up the full length of the crack of Via Media.

1929 **Low Crag Chimney** – JD BEST and Party

1930 May 10 **Direct Route** – AT HARGREAVES, GG MACPHEE

1931 Sep 27 **Dandle Face Direct** – A WALMSLEY, L HAMILTON, MEW NORTH, J BRADY

1931 **Three Tier Climb** – MABEL M BARKER, JA MUSGRAVE, NANCY EG RIDYARD

1932 Jul 9 **Juniper Crack** – JA Musgrave, Nancy EG Ridyard, Mabel M Barker

1932 or before **Eighty Foot Slab Left-Hand** – Mabel M Barker and party

1933 Apr **Slape Crag Arête** – AVS Lochead, Mabel M Barker

1933 Aug 7 **Truss Buttress** – RH Fidler, CE Arnison

1934 Aug 5 **Rose Tree Route, North Climb** – Mabel M Barker

1935 Aug 21 **Slape Crags Direct** – A Horne, Mabel M Barker (var). The ***Original Start*** up Lower Slape Crag was climbed by A Horne on the same day.

1936 Feb **Weeping Wall** – CR Wilson, E Thomson, D Tweddle

1937 Jun 20 **Corner and Wall** – BGS Ward, Mabel M Barker

1937 Jun 20 **Main Slab Route to the Perch** – BGS Ward, CR Wilson, Mabel M Barker, Nancy EG Ridyard (alt)

1937 Jun 20 **Flake Buttress** – Mabel M Barker, BGS Ward, CR Wilson, Nancy EG Ridyard (alt)

1937 Jul 25 **Tarsus** – RJ Birkett, Mabel M Barker, Nancy EG Ridyard
Jim Birkett's first new route - he went on to better things.

1937 Aug 21 **Inaccessible Gully** – CR Wilson, BGS Ward (var)
"Conditions did not look so cheerful as water was spraying over the lip of the 'hanging gully' on to the platform, and more than half of the unclimbed wall and the first two pitches were wet:

Above: Eric Arnison, first ascentionist of **Truss Buttress** in 1933.
Photo: FRCC Archive

Above: Mabel Barker climbing on Gill Crag around the time she was involved in several first ascents there.
Photo: The Barker Collection

Above: Ernest Wood Johnson and Mabel Barker attempting **Inaccessible Gully** on Dove Crag some time before the successful first ascent by BGS Ward and CR Wilson in 1937.
Photo: The Barker Collection

but we decided to have a look at it. I led the first two pitches and tied on to very doubtful spike embedded in the platform, enjoying all the discomforts of a cold shower until Gilpin Ward arrived. He stood on my feet, carefully dried his rubbers, then moved to the sloping right-end of the platform which was comparatively dry. Bracing myself, I got into the 'combined antics' position, impressing on GW the negative value of the belay and the distance to the gully floor. It was hardly necessary as he had already looked and no hasty moves were likely to be made by him. He then stood on my right leg, and so to my shoulders, the bulge in the wall and the wet platform making 'combined antics' in rubbers very precarious. Three times he moved up on small damp holds, and on the fourth glided up the wall to grasp the 'jug handle' at the very top."
CR Wilson, 'Dove Crag', *FRCC Journal 1939.*

Above: Jim Birkett on the first ascent of **Overhanging Bastion** in 1939.
Photo: Charlie Wilson

Above: Jim Haggas, left and Robert Clough c1947 who put up **Hangover** (HVS), Dove Crag with JK Booth in 1939. **Photo:** Jim Haggas Collection

1938 Feb 6 **Left Ridge** – CR Wilson, Mabel M Barker

1939 Apr 1 **Overhanging Bastion** – RJ Birkett, CR Wilson, L Muscroft

The first successful attack on the main face of Castle Rock and hailed by the press with their usual accuracy as *"Lakeland Everest Conquered."*

"On the early part of the climb Birkett experimented with a new idea for protection. He took some pebbles along in his pocket and when he saw a convenient crack he would wedge a pebble in it and then thread a length of line behind the pebble to afford a running belay. It cannot have been very reassuring. The line was not very strong. Birkett once said: 'I wouldn't trust my mother's washing on it.' But he advanced steadily and had no trouble with what is now regarded as the crux – the committing step from the pinnacle to the foot of the gangway. He judged the whole route 'easy for a Very Severe'." Alan Hankinson, *A Century on the Crags* 1988.

The first pitch described was climbed as part of an eliminate called **One World, One Family** by RJ Kenyon, C King, G Baum, J Grinbergs, August 1990.

1939 Apr 22 **Zig Zag** – RJ Birkett, CR Wilson, L Muscroft

1939 May 20 **Hangover** – JW Haggas, JK Booth, R Clough

"The only possible line of ascent and must rank as one of the purest lines in the country… There was the usual choice of handholds – loose rock or grass I chose the grass. It would, at least, give way with less abruptness." AR Dolphin, 'Recent Developments in Lakeland', *FRCC Journal 1948.*

"All I can say about the climb is that the crux seemed to be both strenuous and delicate at one and the same moment, and that nylon rope is extremely reliable " Harry Griffin is press ganged into route checking for the guidebook, 'Innocents in the East', *FRCC Journal 1955.*

	The block on pitch 1 came off attached to the landlord of the Golden Rule, John Lockley, October 1985.
1944 Apr 22	**Southern Traverse, Companion Way** – E Banner-Mendus, W Peascod The latter climb is basically pitch 1 of Southern Traverse. It was named and recorded in 2008.
1945 May 10	**Via Media** – GF Parkinson, W Rae Originally started to the right of the initial rib. The left-hand start as described was added by E Lomas and P Wittwell, 7th September 1952, as part of a climb called **Turret Wall**, which then traversed left and avoided the main issue. The upper crack, and arguably the major part of the route, had first been climbed by GG MacPhee and Mabel M Barker as the original finish to **Scoop and Crack**, 3rd July 1928.
1946 Oct 20	**Kennel Wall, Hindleg Crack** – JS Williams, CR Wilson, T Nicholson, RA Ewin, GH Tyson
1946 Oct 27	**The Fang** – JS Williams, CR Wilson, T Nicholson, RA Ewin ***Variation to pitch 2*** added by SJH Reid, I Conway, 15th August 1988.
1946 Oct 27	**Foreleg Wall** – T Nicholson, GH Tyson, F Holmes
1946 Nov 3	**Finale** – GT Hetterick, D Hetterick
1947 May 1	**May Day Cracks** – RJ Birkett, L Muscroft
1947 May 25	**The Gossard** – RJ Birkett, L Muscroft, T Hill
1947 May 25	**Castle Wall** – L Muscroft, T Hill, RJ Birkett
1947 Oct 8	**Impromptu** – A Gregory, L Roberts, JW Tucker, J Ward
1947 Oct 18	**Bilberry Rib** – A Gregory, L Roberts
1947 Oct 18	**Hanging Chimney** – JW Tucker, A Gregory (var), J Ward
1947 Oct 26	**Flying Buttress, Chapel Cracks** – RJ Birkett, L Muscroft
1949 Jun 26	**Harlot Face** – RJ Birkett, L Muscroft Much the hardest route in the area at this time. Pitch 3 added by N and D Craig, 29th June 1984. ***Walsh's Blind Variant*** was added by Patsy Walsh, one of the best climbers in the Creagh Dhu, ca 1960, reputedly due to the fact that he was so short sighted that he missed the correct line.
1949	**Sadgill Wall** – AH Griffin, CE Arnison, T Philipson A similar line was climbed in 1948 by KSL Hunt, PE Brown and FG Jones.
1950 Jun 11	**East Wall** – A Gregory, CH Peckett
1950 Jul 9	**Migraine** – A Gregory, J Woods
1951 Jun 3	**The Barbican** – H Drasdo, D Hopkin (var)
1951 Jul 15	**Ferrous Buttress** – AR Dolphin, E Hodgson
1952 Easter	**Wall Climb** – JC Duckworth, G Batty (alt) Variation to pitch 3 (***Howard's Finish***), JE Howard, RB Jones, 19th June 1956. Variations to pitches 1 and 2 (***Right-Hand Variant***), H Drasdo, GD Roberts, 21nd August 1957.

1952 Easter **Portcullis Ridge** – G Batty, JC Duckworth, K Miller

1952 Easter **Broken Ridge, Terrace Wall** – JC Duckworth, G Batty (alt)

1952 May 20 **Curving Gully** – JC Duckworth, G Batty (alt)

1952 May 22 **North-West Grooves** – JC Duckworth, G Batty (alt)

1952 May 22 **Juniper Crack** – JC Duckworth, G Batty (alt)
Via the original finish. The current finish was climbed free by GN Higginson in 1977.

1952 May **Sleet Wall** – JC Duckworth, G Batty (alt)

1952 May **Terrace Wall Variant** – JC Duckworth, G Batty

Above: Harold Draso of **North Crag Eliminate** fame. **Photo:** Bob Allen

1952 Sep 7 **North Crag Eliminate** – H Drasdo, D Gray
"Volumes might be written about the botany of the crag; but not by me… The cautious climber may even go off the route to attain arboreal excrescences…"
G Graham Macphee prophesies the shape of holds to come in 'The Castle Rock of Triermain', ***FRCC Journal 1929***.
"Here, at least ten cigarettes were required before the crux was overcome." Paul Ross, Castle Rock of Triermain, ***FRCC Journal 1961***.
"Gangway? It was more like the road to Hades!…I turned the corner and the rest seemed easy. We laughed at the top as we coiled the ropes and we went to the pub and we were very happy and a few weeks later Rob was dead and I went on to climb sometimes harder and sometimes easier things. "What for? To experience the very things I felt as I turned that corner: to escape the potted, computerized, cellophane existence which is ours in the twentieth century; to play at life's brinksmanship, find freedom and the right to escape a challenge, test oneself to the limit, plumb the extremes of emotion and exhilaration, brain, heart, eye, strength and balance united in a single purpose - to live like a searchlight of survival searing through the total darkness of failure; to taste the stinging wine of danger, but to sweeten it with the total joy of existence, "That's what life is all about, That's what dreams are made of.'"
Neil Allinson, Hard Rock ***(Ken Wilson, 1974)***

1952 Sep 28 **Genesis** – H Drasdo, PJ Greenwood

1952 Oct 4 **Exodus** – A Beanland, M Dawson, E Leach

1953 Mar 15 **Triermain Eliminate** – DD Whillans, J Brown, D Cowan

"This climb is like Whillans himself, hard and very fierce." ALLAN AUSTIN, Lakeland Report, ***CC Journal 1961.***

1953 May 4 **Dovedale Groove** – DD WHILLANS, J BROWN, D COWAN

One point of aid was used on the first pitch, now free. Defied many attempts to repeat it over the following decade.

"It is not for want of trying that only one new route has appeared on Dove Crag in the last twenty years; and this route – Dovedale Groove, by Whillans and Brown – indicates at what level the next ones will be carried out. I have not seen a more impressive piece of igneous rock, of similar size, anywhere. All we can say is that we have failed; others can try." HAROLD DRASDO, 'Extremes and Excesses, ***FRCC Journal 1960.***

Above: Joe Brown partnered Don Whillans on **Dovedale Groove** in 1953. **Photo:** Ken Wilson

"The thing was a lot steeper than I remembered. It seemed to be overhanging quite a lot, in fact. At last, after about 60 feet I came to a small chock. A hand-jam, a very wide bridging move and out with my threader. After a few minutes during which I lost a sling, straightened the hook out on my threader, got cramp in one hand and attempted to bridge even wider, I was reluctantly forced to the conclusion that I would have been better off somewhere else. Not that but I wanted to get this thread on or I would be going rather quicker than I wanted. There was a steady light-hearted chatter coming up from below. This soon stopped when I announced that it looked as if I was going to fall off. 'That's shown them,' I thought, before I began feeling sorry for myself again and wishing I was somewhere else. I bent the hook back into the threader with my teeth, dropped another sling and started threading operations again. At last, as my fingers were tightening up, I got the thing on and clipped in. The position was terrific. On either side rose smooth impending walls. Above, huge bulges ended in a vicious overhanging crack and below, from a group of white faces, rose the thin white line of the rope, nailed by slings into the groove, before it came freely up the last stretch to me. 'It's not bad', I announced. 'Just a bit awkward to fix the runner'. The effect was somewhat spoiled when Jack relaxed the rope a little and my voice rose sharply on the last word." ALLAN AUSTIN recalls making an early repeat with JACK SOPER, 'Dovedale Groove', ***FRCC Journal 1964.***

Above: Arthur Dolphin, one of the most important of Lake District activists, exploring on Raven Crag, Thirlmere. His route here, Communist Convert (1953) was remarkable for the exposed terrain it crossed. Tragically it was his last new route – he was to die in the Alps two months later after slipping on the descent from the Dent du Géant. He was only 28. **Inset:** Arthur Dolphin. **Photos:** Marie Blake Collection

Pitch 4 was added by JA Austin and NJ Soper, 2nd June 1963.

1953 May 5 **Waterfall Buttress** – E Lomas, J Townsend (alt) P Whitwell

1953 May 9 **Necropolis** – PJ Greenwood, JW Bradley

1953 May 10 **Communist Convert** – AR Dolphin, D Hopkin, M Dwyer, J Ramsden (var)
So named because *"it started on the left and finished on the right." The Gritstone Club Diary 1953.*
Direct Finish added by E Metcalf, JA Austin, June 1961.

1953 Jun 6 **Anarchist** – PJ Greenwood, R Miller
The original lower pitches are overgrown. The first two pitches described were climbed as **Genesis** by H Drasdo and PJ Greenwood, 28th September 1952.

1954 Apr 11 **West Hutaple Gully** – AH Griffin, GB Spenceley

1954 May 9 **Far West Rib** – GB Spenceley, AH Griffin, CE Arnison

1954 May 11 **Gully Wall** – G Batty, AD Marsden (alt)

1954 May 12 **Cyrano** – G Batty, AD Marsden (alt)

1954 May 30 **Cofa Wall** – AH Griffin, GB Spenceley (alt)

1954 Jun 7 **Original Route** – F Fitzgerald, D Bond
A route was made in this area in the thirties by W Heaton Cooper.
"Far more time was spent working [on Ruthwaite Lodge] than climbing and the weather was not always good. And the SUMC's strong climbers apart from Don Wooller never went to the place and he only worked, so climbing partners were initially in short supply. Amazingly, the general feeling of that generation of SUMC climbers was that there was little to do in the area. That view was put right later when Soper and others discovered the delights available. I did Original Route on Eagle Crag in the rain with D Bond, a schoolboy aged about ten or twelve years, one of a party of Sheffield schoolkids on a trip to the Lakes who stayed at the hut. I've never seen or heard of him since but he was quite unflappable! He followed with real style." Frank Fitzgerald reminisces on goings on of half a century ago.

1954 Jul 4 **Grisedale Corner** – AH Griffin, GB Spenceley (alt)
"...after watching a nimble sheep accomplishing the last few feet of what looked a pleasant climb – we thought that if a sheep could get up there must be holds on it and we might even be able to get up ourselves." Harry Griffin, 'Innocents in the East', *FRCC Journal 1955.*

1954 Jul 19 **Kestrel Wall** – RJ Birkett, AH Griffin

1954 Dec 13 **Pillar Front** – F Fitzgerald, GA Leaver, Miss SA Evans, E J Clegg
"Although all the negotiating work had been done by others I signed the final legal documents for the lease of Ruthawaite Lodge at Mr Barr-Smith's solicitor's office in Kendal in March 1953. Jim Hutchinson took me up to Patterdale on his motorbike and we slept in the hut which had a great hole in the roof and a thick layer of sheep droppings on the floor. It poured with rain! On the way to Kendal Jim lost control of the motor-bike in the field below Elm Howe and we arrived at the signing smelling a bit of sheep and with our right sides plastered

with mud and grass. I judged they must have been really keen to lease the place! I would have done more climbing had I not spent a lot of time rebuilding the hut. The doors and windows were made in Sheffield and transported up, we used naturally occuring sand from a source just below the bridge and cement came in bags and was dropped at the barn above Elm Howe. We used to have 'cement races' up to the hut, half a hundredweight (half a bag) on an Everest carrier. Later, corrugated-iron races (for the roof) took over. I first saw The Pillar Ridge from the front door of the hut whilst working on a misty day when the mist went behind it. I kept seeing it whilst we were rebuilding and it exerted a sort of fascination for me. It was two years after the signing of the lease before I put a foot on it." FRANK FITZGERALD reminisces further.

1954 Dec 13 **Slab Route** – F FITZGERALD, GA LEAVER, MISS SA EVANS, E J CLEGG

1955 Jan 1 **Pinnacle Ridge** – GA LEAVER, MISS SA EVANS, BW LOWTHIAN, ME TWENTYMAN

1955 Mar **Green Buttress** – R PEART, G BATTY

1955 Apr 14 **Arpeggio** – G SUDDABY, F FITZGERALD, JM BEELEY

1955 Apr 14 **Renaissance Route** – F FITZGERALD, JM BEELEY

1955 May 30 **Amphitheatre Rib** – R PEART, G BATTY (alt)

1955 Jun 26 **Thirlmere Eliminate** – P ROSS, P J GREENWOOD (var)

A peg was used for aid - now free. The original route traversed left to the arête after the overhang. The direct ascent of the top pitch was added in 1956 by J BROWN and DD WHILLANS. *"Above us was a frightening-looking bulge, and above that extremely steep rock. Peter climbed a few feet up the right wall and, after almost exhausting himself, planted a peg half-way up the bulge. I offered to have a go and, unfortunately he agreed. With the aid of the piton and after much struggling, I managed to pull over this obstacle. Going quickly a few feet to the left, I made one upward move and, not to my surprise, found the crux of the climb. The next two or three moves were of the 'up or off' variety, mainly due to my rubbers on the rounded and very lichenous holds. With great relief I reached a belay."* PAUL ROSS, 'Castle Rock of Triermain', *FRCC Journal 1961*.

Above: Don Whillans: first ascents of **Triermain Eliminate** and **Dovedale Groove** (1953), **Delphinus** (1956) and **Extol** (1960). **Photo:** Ken Wilson

	Wet Day Wander was added by J Handley, T Page
1955 Jul 30	**Three Tier Climb** – GA Leaver, Miss SA Evans
1955 Aug 15	**The Amphitheatre** – AD Marsden, G Batty (alt)
1955 Sep 6	**Angel's Highway** – PJ Greenwood, P Whitwell *"Greenwood was responsible for Angel's Highway. An excellent name this, even if it is hard to see where Greenwood fits in."* Allan Austin, Lakeland Report, *CC Journal 1961.*
1956 Jan 4	**Pillar Direct** – JE Howard, RB Jones, GA Leaver
1956 Jan	**Pendulum Gully** – W Kelsey, C Chattaway
1956 Feb 26	**Delphinus** – DD Whillans, J Smith Climbed free but a later rockfall made pegs necessary on the third pitch. *"The route, which had been attempted first by Arthur Dolphin and later by Harold Drasdo, took a fine line up the cliff and included one or two exciting, exposed traverses. When Morty and I did it, the whole crag was plastered with snow although it was not frozen over. It was a magnificent climb which gave me great pleasure."* Don Whillans quoted by Alan Hankinson, A Century on the Crags, 1988.
1956 Apr 1	**Long Ledge Entry and Exit** – C Chattaway, G Batty
1956 May 12	**The Raven Traverse** – PJ Greenwood, DD Whillans (alt)
1956 May 12	**Doctor's Grooves** – F Fitzgerald, GA Leaver
1956 May 20	**Dividend** – GA Leaver, K Twyford
1956 May 21	**Chockstone Gully Rib** – GA Leaver, K Twyford
1956 May 24	**Slab Route Continuation** – K Twyford, GA Leaver
1956 May 25	**Slape** – K Twyford, GA Leaver
1956 May 26	**Spiral, Sickle, Blip** – K Twyford, GA Leaver
1956 May	**Ringway** – G Batty, H Drasdo
1956 Jun 3	**Grendel** – H Drasdo, G Batty
1956 Jun 20	**Halcyon** – MA James, RB Jones
1956 Jun 24	**Dimanche, Domingo, Sontag** – MA James, Miss J Mattocks
1956 Sep 15	**Slab and Rib** – D Atherton, JD Llewellyn
1956 Sep 16	**The Hog's Back** – JD Llewellyn, A Sutton
1957 Apr 15	**Miranda** – D Johnson and party
1957 Apr 22	**Dollywaggon Great Chimney** – F Fitzgerald, JM Beeley
1957 Jun 11	**Sobrenada** – MA James, GA Leaver, KA Brookes
1957 Jun 11	**Subsidiary Rib** – MA James, GA Leaver
1957 Jun 12	**Zip** – GA Leaver, MA James, KA Brookes
1957 Jun 13	**Lower Traverse** – MA James, NA Busby
1957 Jul 2	**The Outsider** – H Drasdo, C Buckley
1957 Jul 4	**Firedragon** – H Drasdo, C Buckley
1957 Aug 21	**Midnight Special** – H Drasdo, GD Roberts (var) The last pitch was added in September 1959 by NJ Soper.

Right: Eagle (VS), Eagle Crag Grisedale. Probably a first ascent picture. The climb was later incorporated into the **High Girdle**. **Photo:** Mike James

1957 Aug 30 **Irony** – H Drasdo, L Clark (var)
1957 Sep 27 **Moss Wall** – NJ Soper, NA Busby
1957 Oct 10 **Bottleneck** – H Drasdo, GD Roberts (alt)
1958 Apr 13 **Interrupted Grooves** – H Drasdo, G Batty, N Drasdo
1958 Apr 29 **Brown Study** – H Drasdo, AJ Maxwell
A peg was used - now free.
1958 May 29 **Western Avenue** – KA Brookes, GA Leaver
1958 Jun 15 **Nose Direct** – N Crowther, Miss E Cannon
1958 Jun 16 **Moss Groove** – NJ Soper, N Crowther, Miss E Cannon
1958 Jun 17 **Sennapod** – N Crowther, NJ Soper
1958 Jun 18 **Limbo** – N Crowther, NJ Soper
1958 Jul 12 **Sideline** – H Drasdo, NJ Soper
1958 Jul 21 **Boneyard Wall, Tumbledown Grooves** – MA James, Miss E Cannon
1958 Jul 24 **Sable Wall** – MA James, Miss E Cannon
1958 Aug 23 **Sostenuto** – H Drasdo, RB Evans, NJ Soper, RP Harris (var)
1958 Aug 28 **Valedictory** – H Drasdo, T Parker
1958 Sep 14 **Crypt and Fingers Climb, Sisters Ridge** – DN Greenup, JP Greenup
However: *"Nab Crag offers innumerable short routes, though rather indefinite, on splendid rock."* GD Abraham, 'Round and About Thirlmere – Old and New', *FRCC Journal 1915*.
1959 Feb 8 **Prenotion** – R McHaffie, J Douglas
1959 Apr 18 **Rigor Mortis** – P Ross, B Aughton
So named because the first ascentionists thought it "a rather stiff problem". Five points of aid were used.
"Once again I started to chip; this time I had to be extremely careful as only in one place, towards the middle of the wall did there appear to be anything that could be made into a hold for a sling. When I had finished there were three minute projections, within the space of an inch, the largest being about half the size of a thumb nail. A very delicate operation was necessary to move into this sling and, once there, I realised, after both the smaller projections had broken with loud twangs, that this was not a very healthy situation." Paul Ross admits to crimes past in 'Castle Rock of Triermain', *FRCC Journal 1961*.
First free ascent by M Boysen who mistook it for Thirlmere Eliminate!
1959 May 24 **Agony** – G Oliver, N Brown
The climb originally had more flakes and thus more holds and protection slings. Most of these have now fallen off.
Direct Finish, C Dale, A Wilkey, 1984.
1959 Jun 13 **Falcon Front** – NJ Soper, JM Rogers
Three points of aid used.

Right: Jack Soper and Dave Gregory on the first ascent of **Beowulf** (VS), 1959, Scrubby Crag. Note the runout! **Photo:** Rosemary Soper

1959 Jun 17 **Sennapod** – N Crowther, NJ Soper (alt)

1959 Aug **Sforzando** – H Drasdo, N Drasdo

1959 Sep 19 **Dandelion Groove** – NJ Soper, Rosemary Collier

1959 Sep 29 **Beowulf** – NJ Soper, PE Brown

1960 Apr 17 **Extol** – DD Whillans, C Mortlock

One point of aid was used Now free

"Easter 1960. A crowded camp site at Dale Bottom Farm near Keswick. The 'Rock and Ice were there in force, with numerous hangers on like myself. The 'Boys' were doing a few routes of top quality and a large number of pubs of low quality… We shot round to Dove Crag on Don's bike. It was a perfect day, even if ruddy cold at that hour on a bike. An hour's walk, and the little cliff I had seen from the road loomed fierce and black. I hastily gave Don the end of the rope. He expected it thank goodness… It took Don two and a half hours to climb [the main] pitch. It must be the finest piece of rock climbing I have ever seen. I sang 'rock' to relieve the tension (mine as well as his). Don smoked incessantly in extraordinary resting positions. Two climbers passed the foot of the crag and the following ensued:

"What route's that?" (looks of disbelief from Don's overhanging positions);

"It aint… yet" (from above);

"Who are you?" (from below);

"Whillans" … pause as a big grass ledge narrowly misses the amazed ones below (premeditated?);

"Yer must be mad" (parting shot from those below, who were not seen again)."

Colin Mortlock, Entity, ***CC Journal 1961.***

"In the short space of six months this climb has already become a legend, and many are the tales told about it. Tales of the great dobbing match that took place the night before, how the star in a moment of terrible anger produced "the dob of all dobs, right from the floor it came". How at one point on the climb, leader and second were climbing together, 150 feet apart, the leader making desperate moves at the front end, and the second climbing Very Severe stuff at the rear. Although it was only the second day of the holiday they both packed up and went home – to recuperate. Of course I cannot personally vouch for these stories, but there's no smoke without fire…" Allan Austin, Lakeland Report, ***CC Journal 1961.***

1960 Apr 22 **Hrothgar** – NJ Soper, D McE Dixon, CD Curtis

Last pitch was added 29th May 1962, NJ Soper, LJ Griffin, O Woolcock. A sling was used for aid. The climb superseded H Drasdo's **Deflected Route**.

1960 May 29 **Drag** – P Ross, G Oliver

1960 May 29 **Eliminate Girdle** – G Oliver, P Ross (alt)

The ascent took only 1½ hours! Pitch 1 had been climbed previously by J Brown and DD Whillans.

1960 Jun 16 **Susan** – DW English, DH Beattie

1960 Jul **Birkett's View** – C Griffiths, J Siddle

1960 Sep **Pericles** – O Woolcock, MS Wild

	A combination of two earlier routes, **Peregrine Crack** and **Achilles Heel**.
1960 Sep	**Bar Sinister** – O Woolcock, MS Wild
1961 Easter	**Fiasco** – NJ Soper, D Dixon
1961 Easter	**Dandelion Wall** – NJ Soper, O Woolcock
1961 May 9	**Geronimo** – D Hutchinson, TH Robinson, JF Wadeson, F Smith
	Jude Said Yes, R Salm, G Scott, 17th May 1989. ***The Challenge Side Stepped,*** D Menadue, D Davey, 9th September 2004.
1961 Jun 19	**Domination** – AD Hallsworth, JF Wadeson
1961 Jun	**Girdle Traverse, Scrubby Crag** – O Woolcock, NJ Soper (alt)
1961 Jul 9	**Falcon Ridge** – JF Wadeson, D Hutchinson
1961 Jul 29	**Sundown Slab** – JF Wadeson, D Hutchinson
1961 Aug 10	**Burdock** – N Ross, GA Leaver (alt)
1961	**Rust** – K Wood, P Blamire
1962 May 25	**Girdle Traverse of Fang Buttress** – C Griffiths, RK Watson (var)
	Two pegs used for aid - now free.
1962 Jun 10	**Hiraeth** – B Ingle, P Crew (alt)
	"We called it Hiraeth because we were longing to get home to Wales" Peter Crew. Nevertheless he stopped around long enough to make the second ascents of both Dovedale Groove and Extol.
	Variation to pitch 3, C Read, J Adams, 10th June 1973.
1962 Aug 1	**Exhaustion** – AJ Maxfield, DF Price
1962 Oct 13	**Little Taff** – WF Dowlen, A Dowlen, GW Morrall
	Direct Start, S Howe, D Gerrish, 10th April 1984.
1962 Oct	**Sleep Walk** – I Roper, D Hall (var)
1963 Apr 1	**Kleine Rinne** – JJS Allison
1963 May	**Bantam** – M Burke, G Page
1963 Jun 6	**Entity** – E Metcalf, NJ Soper (alt)
1963 Jun 27	**The Shackle** – D Hall, I Roper, P Shackleton, JF Wadeson (alt)
	One peg used for aid - now free.
1963 Jul 4	**Nimbus** – I Roper, JF Wadeson
1963 Sep 21	**Merlin** – CD Curtis, JM Rogers
1964 Jul 4	**The Tippet** – NJ Soper, R Soper
1964 Jul	**The Ghost** – AG Cram, WA Barnes, W Young
	Climbed on a quick visit on the way home from the Alps. Originally finished up Rigor Mortis - present finish climbed by W Freelands, 1968. Reclimbed following the loss of the block by P Whillance, D Armstrong, 16th April 1977.
	The Loop, R Matheson, G Fleming, 24th September 1969.
1964 Jul	**The Minotaur** – I Roper, D Hall
1964 Jul	**Dandle Direct** – P Shackleton, I Roper, D Hall
1964 Aug 1	**Gambol Rib** – N Allinson, B Bullivant
1964 Aug 1	**Grisedale Slabs** – N Allinson, B Bullivant (alt)
1964 Aug 30	**High Girdle, Eagle Crag** – CD Curtiss, Jane Rogers (alt)

Pitches 1 – 3 only; Pitches 4 – 7 added by N Allinson, NJ Soper (alt) and M Elders, 12th June 1967. Incorporated the only new climbing on **Eagle** (VS) by MA James and O Woolcock, 12th August 1959.

1964 Sep 1 **The Medlar** – M Boysen, CJS Bonington (var), M Thompson
Three points of aid were used. *"As I remember, it was Martin who had spotted the line and then suggested to Chris and me that we go and take a look. There was a tree, somewhere near the start, that Martin, as a professional botanist, proclaimed to be a medlar (though I rather think he was wrong about that). There was a double meaning to the name, however, since Chris hand-placed a piton in a little hole as protection below the crux on the first pitch, at the same time jumping at my idea that, since no hammer was involved, it could be regarded as a rather odd-shaped nut!"*
Mike Thompson recalls halcyon new routeing days.
An outstanding climb and probably the fiercest undertaking in the Lakes at that time. Pete Whillance, 'A Short History of Lakeland Climbing (Part III)', *FRCC Journal 1986.*
First free ascent, C Jones, 1976.

1964 Sep 2 **Totalitarian** – CJS Bonington, M Thompson
One peg used for aid. Climbed free by E Grindley, JA Austin and R Valentine, 21st July 1974.

1964 Sep **Echo** – A Wright, RD Brown

Above: Chris Bonington about the time he did the first ascents of **The Medlar** and **Totalitarian**. **Photo:** Tony Greenbank

Above: Mike Thompson who partnered Chris Bonington on both **The Medlar** and **Totalitarian** in 1964. **Photo:** Chris Bonington

1964 Nov 8 **Ghoul** – RD Brown, JD Lovett (alt)

1965 Easter **Good Friday** – RJ Pawsey, RJ Moore
Two slings used for aid - now free.

1965 Jun 16 **Matheson Avenue** – K Woods, M Goff, M Biden
Climbed as part of a variation finish to the Eliminate Girdle.
Direct Finish, P Gomersall, Bonnie Masson, Easter 1977 - they also named the route.

1965 Jun 17 **The Last Laugh** – CJS Bonington, P Ross, B Henderson, K Mosley
Aid was used on the second pitch but the climb quickly acquired a reputation on the basis of its bold and serious first pitch. Pitch 3 had been climbed in 1953 by DD Whillans, D Roscoe. First free ascent, H Pasquill, D Hollows (alt).

1965 Jul 12 **The Final Giggle** – MA Toole, P Ross
One point of aid used - now free.

1965 Jul 18 **High Noon** – D Melling, A Kay

1965 Sep **Kneewrecker Wall** – N Allinson, B Bullivant

1966 Mar 20 **Left Edge** – C Griffiths, G Oliver

1966 May 18 **Gossamer** – N Allinson, J Howarth

1966 May 19 **The Whistler** – N Allinson, D Gregg

1966 May **Kneewrecker Direct** – N Allinson, R Eggleston

1966 Jun 13 **Microcosm** – N Allinson, NJ Soper

1966 Jun 20 **The Ramp** – NJ Soper, ND Curtis

1966 Jun 28 **The Wasp, Quail** – JA Austin, NJ Soper (alt)

1966 Jun **Girdle Traverse, Gowbarrow** – N Allinson, NJ Soper (alt)

1966 Jul 4 **The Lurcher** – NJ Soper, N Allinson (alt)
Sling used for aid - now free.

1966 Aug 15 **Thrangstone** – NJ Soper, N Allinson (alt)

1966 Aug 15 **Thrang Slab** – N Allinson, NJ Soper (alt)

1966 Aug 31 **The Nymph** – NJ Soper, N Allinson (alt)

1967 Jul 3 **The Apocrypha** – NJ Soper, N Allinson
One point of aid used - now free.

1967 Jul 23 **The Merger** – A Liddell, P Ross

Above: FRCC guidebook writers and climbing partners Jack Soper, left and Neil Allinson in 2007, many years after their numerous contributions to the Eastern Crags. **Photo:** Phil Rigby

1968 Jun 15 **Mordor** – AG Cram, JF Jones
Pitch 1 had been climbed by M Boysen, C Rowlands 1965.

1968 Jul 13 **The Mole** – J Workman, DA Elliott

1968 Nov 10 **Eilethgia** – AJ Maxfield, D Overton

1968 Nov 17 **Standing Slab** – D Chapman, JR Sutcliffe

Pre-1969 **Route 1, Ken's Wall, Kenny the Lad, Taurus, Route 3, Birkett's Arête, Route 4, Route 5, Calf Howe Slab, Kentmere Slab, Ancients' Crack, Route 8, Twilight Slab.** These and other routes in the vicinity of Calf Howe Crags were developed by various permutations of K Wood, M Goff, P Goff, D Marshall, F Booth, D Birkett, B Birkett, G Carradus and others of the "Kendal Lads" over several years, mainly 1963 to 1965, some of which were recorded in 1969. Kenny the Lad was claimed and named by D Craig in 1979. Taurus was claimed and named in 1988 by J and K Daly, who also claimed Twilight Slab as Spartan Slab, and Ancients' Crack as Crash Landing.

1969 May **Bomber Wall** – DW Hodgson, RJ Kenyon (alt)

1969 May **Southern Slab** – RJ Kenyon, DW Hodgson

1969 Jun 24 **Eliminator** – W Freeland, K Rudd
Two points of aid used - first free ascent, E Cleasby, April 1975.

1969 Oct 25 **Express Crack** – JA Austin, DG Roberts, JJS Allison
Previously climbed in 1958 with two points of aid.

1969 **North Buttress** – C Woodhall, R Clarke
Using aid from pegs and bolts. The aid was reduced to two points by M Berzins, C Hamper in 1977 and the present crux avoided by following what was to become Fear and Fascination. The two aid points were eliminated by M Berzins, A Manson, 22nd May 1988, and the route was finally free climbed following the original line in its entirety by S Meyers, 5th May 1991. The variation first pitch was climbed by R Graham, D Lyle, TW Birkett, 27th June 1981.

1970 Sep **Cribin** – S Patterson, DL Van Meerbecks

1971 Apr 8 **Gravy Booby** – G Rigby, N Stuart

1971 May 2 **Chicken** – JR Sutcliffe, PW Green, J Forder

1971 Oct 3 **Girdle Traverse, Dove Crag** – J Adams, C Read (alt)
Six points of aid used. The section as far as Hangover was climbed free by TW Birkett, R Graham (alt), 12th June 1983, but the route is not known to have had a complete second ascent.

1971 **Gazebo** – G Lee, C Downer

1972 Apr 15 **Diagonal Route** – RJ Kenyon

1972 Aug 19 **Phobos** – C Read, J Adams
One point of aid used - first free ascent P Long, R Valentine, Spring 1974.

1973 Aug 27 **Scabby Horse** – RJ Kenyon, A Greenhow

1973 Sep **Empire** – K Myhill, K Jones (var)

Above: Colin Read, left and John Adams. Their **Girdle Traverse of Dove Crag** (1971) still awaits a complete second ascent. **Photo:** Keith Wake

"As autumn approached another pair of invaders came to the Lake District from the Peak's climbing crucible – Keith Myhill and Ken Jones. Myhill had noticed a tempting line on Raven Crag, Thirlmere. He became so paranoid at the thought of the route being poached from him, that he gave out invitations to a mythical party in Sheffield on the critical weekend to ensure that any likely competitors would be absent from scene! Two points of aid were used to reduce the difficulties, which would have been quite acceptable in the climate of that time. Myhill and Jones however exaggerated its difficulties and insultingly referred to the local climbing atmosphere as 'the insular Lakeland scene'. Fortunately a strong man appeared to restore local dignity; within weeks Jeff Lamb repeated the route completely free."* TREVOR JONES, Cumbrian Rock *(Pic Publications, 1988)*

* KEN JONES had described the route as *"a major breakthrough … snatched from the insular Lakeland syndrome."*

1973 Oct 17 **Mike's Dilemma** – RJ KENYON

1973 **Responsibility** – R EVANS

The groove had previously been pegged, and called **Irresponsible**.

1974 May 1 **Heorot** – JW EARL, RG HUTCHINSON (alt)

1974 May 18 **Gowbarrow Bastion** – RJ KENYON, J KILDUFF

1974 Jun 13 **Zhivago Sassenach** – RJ KENYON, S WILSON

1974 Jun 13 **The Bone** – RJ KENYON

1974 Jul 7 **Fang Direct** – RM FLOOD, JR SUTCLIFFE

1974 Aug **Side of the Hill** – S MILLER, N ROBINSON

1974 Aug **Slab Start** – S MILLER

1975 May 4 **The Pillar** – RG HUTCHINSON, JW EARL (alt), SM PORTEUS

1975 Jun 21 **Soliloquy** – N ALLINSON, C GREENHOW

1975 Jun 21 **The Sting** – N Allinson, C Greenhow
Two points of aid used - first free ascent, JA Austin, 1976.

1975 Jul 5 **Anabasis** – M Berzins, R Berzins, GN Higginson

1975 **Tamarist** – A Beatty, P Rigby

1975 **Practice Wall** – Penrith Mountain Rescue Team.
The Beat Goes On added by M van Gullick, 20th May 1999.

1975 **West Tower, Ashlar** – FJ Grant
Not recorded at the time. Subsequently named and claimed by P Rainsley, S Rainsley, D Duncan, C Swindley in 1979.

1976 Apr 21 **Morning Slab** – RG Hutchinson, Christine Fuller

1976 Apr **Earlybirds** – RG Hutchinson, JW Earl, SM Porteus

1976 May 9 **Problem Child** (pitch 1 and part of pitch 2) – M Berzins, E Cleasby (alt)
Pitches 2 and 3 added by J Lamb, P Botterill (alt), June 1979.

1976 Jun 10 **Strider** – R Sagar, K Jones

1976 Jun 30 **Explosion** – P Botterill, P Whillance

1976 Jul 31 **Redex** – CW Brown, TW Birkett (alt)

1976 Aug 7 **The Gates of Delirium** – P Botterill, S Clegg (var)
A **Direct Start** was added by D Dinwoodie, C McLean, August 12 1985. It has since been incorporated into The Second Coming (2003).

1976 Summer **Hernia** – B Rogers, W Day

1976 Sep 5 **Creation** – P Botterill, S Clegg

1976 **Sam** – S Miller

1976 **Machicoulis, East Tower, Sallyport** – FJ Grant
Not recorded at the time. Subsequently named and claimed by P Rainsley, S Rainsley, D Duncan, C Swindley in 1979.

1977 Mar **Gabriel** – P Livesey

1977 Easter **Ted Cheasby** – P Gomersall
Direct Finish recorded by J McHaffie, C Downer, 15th April 1999, though almost certainly climbed before this date.

1977 May 15 **Close to the Edge** – S Clegg, P Botterill (alt)
Direct Start, D Dinwoodie, C Ord, 1985.

1977 May 15 **The First Circle** – M Berzins, R Berzins (var)

Above: Pete Botterill, **The Gates of Delirium** and **Creation** (1976) amongst many others. **Photo:** Phil Rigby

1977 Jun **Peels of Laughter** – P Livesey, P Gomersall (alt)
The route superseded **Decline and Fall** (E2 5c, 1977) which moved left from The Medlar.

1977 Jul 29 **Common Man** – E Cleasby, J Eastham, R Matheson (var)

1977 Jul **Blitzkrieg** – P Gomersall, P Livesey (alt)
"Remember when we tried to climb a free ascent of Blitzkrieg, and Livesey and Gomersall claimed to have climbed it just before we did it; well they claimed they were at the crag the same day we were there, and they did it that day, but the thing is they weren't there at all. On that day we tried the groove [the crux] it was wet, and it couldn't go free, we saw the chalk from those two and it stopped at the crux, then it re-started higher up by the easier crack and continued up the top pitch."
"Yes, and when I spoke to Gomersall afterwards, he said that the crux was so easy they didn't use chalk there!"
"Why would someone be so devious and Machiavellian to claim this why risk damaging their reputation to manufacture a claim?"
"You've got to remember there was lots of competitiveness and winding up of the other teams, lots of deviousness maybe they said this to put us off the scent to give them a chance to go back and climb it free?" Rob Matheson and Ed Cleasby recall the good old days in an interview with Al Phizacklea, April 2009.

Above: Pete "**Blitzkrieg**" Livesey.
Photo: John Cleare

Above: Ed Cleasby – numerous contributions in the Eastern Crags.
Photo: Bâton Wicks Collection

'70s New Routes on Dove Crag

Above: Dave Armstrong on the first ascent of **Aurora** (E3) in 1977. He and Whillance's search for a new climb was inspired by the huge blank wall in the background of the photo of Extol in 'Hard Rock'.
Photo: Pete Whillance

Right: Pete Botterill on the first ascent of **Ommadawn** (E5) in 1978 – his discovery of a crucial sling runner allowed the completion of the poorly protected crux pitch.
Photo: Jeff Lamb

Superseded **Blitz** climbed by R Matheson, J Poole, 1971.

1977 Aug 21 **Aurora** – D Armstrong, P Whillance (alt)

1977 Aug 29 **Dogleg Crack** – RJ Kenyon, S Howe
Probably done before.

1977 Sep 2 **Jude the Obscure** – RG Hutchinson, JW Earl (alt)

1977 Sep 18 **The Wilderness** – RG Hutchinson, JW Earl

1977 Sep 18 **Locusts** – JW Earl, RG Hutchinson (alt)

1977 **Juniper Crack Direct** – GN Higginson

1978 Mar 11 **Reward** – D Armstrong
Pitch 1 only. Pitch 2 had been climbed on 25th August 1977 as part of a route called **South Crag Eliminate**. The pitches were linked together and named by TW Birkett, N Robinson, 6th May 1981.

1978 Apr 22 **The Worm** – A Stephenson, J Lamb (var)

1978 Apr 30 **Vaccination** – JW Earl, RG Hutchinson

1978 May 5 **White Dwarf** – TW Birkett, KW Forsythe
The right side of the 'white cone' was climbed by T and R Barley, 15th May 1966. This was in mistake for Rigor Mortis and was probably an ascent of much of White Dwarf. Robin Barley suggested the name **'Yorkshire Dwarfs'** but the current name was retained.

1978 May 11 **Ommadawn** – J Lamb, P Botterill, J Taylor (alt)

1978 May 14 **Birkett's Direct** – RG Hutchinson, JW Earl

1978 May 25 **Polytruk** – E Cleasby, R Matheson (alt)

1978 May **Ecstasy** – E Cleasby, B Wright, R Matheson

1978 May **One Hang Low** – N Siddiqui, R Whittaker

1978 Jun 11 **Darth Vader** – C Read, B Wilson

1978 Jun 18 **Heat Wave** – RG Hutchinson, JW Earl (alt)

1978 Jun 18 **Summer Diversion** – JW Earl, RG Hutchinson (alt)

1978 Jul 2 **Bloodhound** – RG Hutchinson, JW Earl

1978 Summer **Das Kapital** – P Livesey, P Gomersall (var)
Required several attempts over a number of weeks.
The Cave Direct (pitches 1 and 2) had been climbed with much aid, at HVS and A3 by P Ross, B Henderson (alt), November 1966.

1978 **Above the Timberline** – R Whittaker, P Pickering

1978 **Pinnacle Wall, Wall Climb** – D Armstrong (solo)

1978 **Razorback** – R Whittaker, P Pickering
Alternative start added by N Thomas, April 2003.

1979 May 7 **Younger Days** – AJ Thornber, PW Thorber
Believed to have been climbed previously.

1979 May 20 **Curtain Call** – RJ Kenyon, S Wilson
Nut used for aid.

1979 May 20 **Chalk Walk** – M Lovatt, B Windsor

1979 Spring **The Ultimate Eliminate** – J Lamb, P Botterill

1979 Jun 9 **Relayer** – J Lamb, B Berzins, M Berzins, P Botterill

1979 Aug 25 **Cerberus** – S Howe, D Kay

1979 Aug **Wingnut** – J Peel, M Johnson

1980 May 5 **One Step Beyond** – I Williamson, J White
One Small Step variation added by S Howe, J Beveridge, 1985.

1980 May 5 **G.T.X.** – P Whillance, R Parker

1980 May 17 **Tinker, Tailor, Soldier, Spy** – RJ Kenyon, M Roper

1980 May 18 **Broken Arrow** – TW Birkett, R Graham (alt) 2 points of aid used.
"Absolutely at the limit and beyond, the peg was part pushed, part tapped in. No way would it take a fall but would it take dead weight? If it popped out so would I and the fall would be long and damaging." Bill Birkett, 'Dove Crag – North Buttress', *FRCC Journal 1983*.

1980 Jun 26 **Fear and Fascination** – R Graham, TW Birkett

1980 Jul 9 **Castration Crack** – P Whillance, P Botterill

1980 Jul 9 **Vasectomy** – P Botterill, P Whillance

1980 Jul 10 **Times of Stress** – P Whillance, P Botterill

1980 Summer **First Republic** – E Cleasby, R Matheson
The first pitch was climbed by TW Birkett, R Graham.

1980 Sep **Grand Prix** – P Whillance, R Berzins, P Botterill

1981 Mar 30 **Big Dick Lustrum** – RJ Kenyon, S Wilson

Above: Fear and Fascination – Bill Birkett (left) and Rick Graham (right) below the North Buttress, Dove Crag circa 1980. **Photo:** Bill Birkett Photo Library.

Above: Jeff Lamb: **Ommadawn**, **Relayer**, **High Performance**, **Boy Racer**, **Running on Empty** – the list goes on (and on). **Photo:** Ian Roper

1981 Apr 3 **Return of the Natives** – P Botterill, P Whillance
1981 Apr 4 **The Dynasts** – D Armstrong, P Whillance (alt)
1981 Apr 4 **Far from the Madding Crowd** – P Whillance, D Armstrong (alt)
1981 Apr 4 **Scabby Horse Direct** – E Cleasby, M Lynch, A Phizacklea, P McVey, I Williamson
1981 May 2 **High Performance** – P Botterill, J Lamb (alt)
1981 May 25 **Desperate Remedies** – P Whillance, D Armstrong
1981 May 29 **Asolo** – TW Birkett, R Graham (alt) D Lyle

The name of a popular range of Italian boots. *"On Dove Crag Bill Birkett had a novel idea. Other sports had sponsorship and money provided for top athletes so it seemed reasonable for him to do the same for climbing. He approached several equipment makers to see if they would like their products immortalised in the name of a new route… His bank balance did not have a great influx of lira…"* Trevor Jones, Cumbrian Rock *(Pic Publications, 1988).*

"I engineered it to cause controversy. I went to a firm that made rock boots and told them that if they gave us the gear, we would give their trade name to the route. There was nothing controversial about the climb itself – it's a good route and we did it free. But the manufacturer's name caused a lot of discussion. It was an attempt really, to shake up the manufacturers and get them to pump more money into the sport. And it worked. There's lots of sponsoring now." Bill Birkett quoted by Alan Hankinson, A Century on the Crags 1988.

1981 May 30 **Top Gear** – P Whillance, D Armstrong

Pete Whillance (**Left, photo:** Rob Matheson) and Dave Armstrong (**Right, photo:** Phil Rigby) who added **Top Gear** to Raven Crag, Threshthwaite Cove in 1981.

"Rick Graham and Ian (Squawk) Dunn went to try an unclimbed shield of rock which they had partially cleaned by abseil, when Whillance arrived looking displeased at an encroachment on his preserve. Graham set off but couldn't climb a groove which had not been cleaned. With the aid of a Friend he removed the detritus. Dunn took over, climbed twenty feet above the Friend but gave up, ever conscious of the restless Whillance at the foot of the crag. The ropes were passed to him, but by this time it was raining and eventually he came to a slab covered with oozing green slime, from which he fell a total of a hundred and twenty feet and hit the ground with his face on the extension of the rope. He had snapped the top nut runner, torn open two karabiners, pulled out several other pieces of protection and was finally stopped by the Friend put in by Graham despite the fact that it had a broken trigger. His face was badly lacerated. In almost complete darkness the whole party went to hospital, but when he was told his wounds would need many stitches, he discharged himself and went home for his tea. He returned to finish the route…"
TREVOR JONES, Cumbrian Rock *(Pic Publications, 1988).*

1981 May **Child in Time** – P CORNFORTH, J WHITE
1981 May **All the Way From America** – J WHITE, P CORNFORTH
1981 Jun 12 **Granolithic Groove** – P WHILLANCE, J LOXHAM
1981 Jun 12 **Solidarity** – P WHILLANCE, J LOXHAM
1981 Jun 21 **Boy Racer** – P BOTTERILL, J LAMB (alt)
1981 Jun 30 **Night of the Long Knives** – S HOWE, RJ KENYON
1981 Jul 9 **Overdrive, Running on Empty** – J LAMB, P BOTTERILL
1981 Jul 13 **Black Gold** – D ARMSTRONG, P WHILLANCE
1981 Jul 14 **Marble Staircase** – P WHILLANCE, D ARMSTRONG
1981 Jul 16 **Hiddenite** – D ARMSTRONG, P WHILLANCE
1981 Jul 18 **The Steel Band** – P WHILLANCE, D ARMSTRONG (alt)
1981 Jul 29 **Lap of Honour** – J LAMB, P BOTTERILL (alt)
1981 **Crack in the Woods** – E CLEASBY, M DANSON
An old aid route climbed free.
1982 Mar 13 **The Blunder** – S HUBBARD
1982 Mar 20 **Marshall Law** – R GRAHAM, C DOWNER
1982 Spring **Summit Crisis** – I WILLIAMSON, J WHITE
1982 Apr 17 **Kryptonite** – R GRAHAM, C DOWNER
1982 May 5 **The Snip** – A HEWISON, C ROBINSON

Above: Karin Magog: involved in several first ascents on Dove Crag's steep North Buttress. **Photo:** Steve Crowe

1982 May 14 **Poisoned Arrow** – J White, I Williamson

1982 May 15 **Ocelot** – D Craig, B Kenton-Smith

1982 May 30 **Fast and Furious** – R Graham, D Lyle, TW Birkett
The ***Flying Fissure Finish*** was added by N Foster, M Berzins, 11th August 1990. The ***Inside Out Link*** was made by S Crowe, A Wilson (both led), K Magog, 10th August 2003.

1982 Jun 11 **Stir Crazy** – R Graham, C Downer (alt) S Kysow

1982 Jul 6 **Midge Wall, Sunset, A Day at the Races, The Runs** – RJ Kenyon, Miss AC Eckersall

1982 Sep 9 **Premier** – R Smith, JW Earl

1982 Sep 19 **Interlude** – JW Earl, R Smith

1982 **Valicide** – A Bowman, R Bowman, F Cope

1983 Jun 22 **Frank** – D Bowen, RJ Kenyon, C King

1983 Jun 22 **Californian Weirdo** – RJ Kenyon, C King, D Bowen

1983 Jul 27 **The Committal Chamber** – R Graham, C Downer

1983 **Gill Crag Grooves** – NF Kelshaw, K Griffiths

1983 **First Cut** – D Bowen, J Beveridge

1984 Apr 3 **Walk Under Ladders** – S Howe, A Hewison

1984 Apr 15 **American Pie** – D Armstrong, P Whillance

1984 Apr 15 **Breakfast in America** – P Whillance, D Armstrong

1984 May 7 **Hot Dog** – D Armstrong

1984 May 7 **Burger** – D Armstrong

1984 May 23 **D.K.W.** – D Hellier

1984 Jun 17 **Siren** – M Lynch, A Hewison, D Kay

1984 Jun 26 **Brave Ulysses** – C Dale, A Hewison

1984 Jun 27 **Sticky Jim** – A Hewison, C Dale, D Kay, M Lynch

1984 Jun 27 **Sasquatch** – C Dale, A Hewison, D Kay, M Lynch

1984 Jun 27 **Yowie** – C Dale, A Hewison

1984 Jun 30 **First Blood** – R Cassidy, S Howe

1984 Jun 30 **Space Shuttle** – S Howe, R Cassidy

1984 Jul 1 **Gulag Tour** – K Rawlinson, D Kay, J Delamere, M Lynch

1984 Jul 1 **Disappointment** – D Kay, M Lynch

1984 Jul 3 **Chimp Dach** – D Armstrong, P Whillance

1984 Jul 4 **Parched Parakeet** – G Derbyshire, C Struters, P Excell

1984 Jul 5 **Pebble Dash** – P Whillance, D Armstrong

1984 Jul 5 **Stingray** – D Armstrong, P Whillance

1984 Jul 7 **Jungle Genocide** – G Derbyshire, C Struters, P Excell

1984 Jul 7 **Chocolate Frog** – J Barber, P Excell

1984 Aug 1 **Failed Romantic** – S Hubbard
Many claims have been made on this area of rock. This route takes the best line but was probably climbed earlier.
Romantically Direct was recorded by SJH Reid, A Lywood, 2002, but it too had probably been climbed before.

1984 Aug 11 **Jumblat** – D Green, I Barker

Pitch 1 had been climbed before by C Struters, P Donnelly, I Barker, 7th July 1984.

1984 Aug 13 **The Widowmaker** – G Derbyshire

1984 Aug 21 **Ghetto Blaster** – G Derbyshire, P Smith

1984 Aug **The First One** – J Beveridge, A Davis, I Walker

1984 Aug **C. C. Rider** – A Davis, J Beveridge

1984 Sep 2 **Liquid Engineering** – P Rigby, A Murray (alt) ***Pitch 1*** had been climbed earlier, 27th August 1984.

1984 Sep **The Thin Blue Line** – SJH Reid, I Clark

1984 **Gorilla** – D Armstrong (solo)

1985 Mar 24 **Climbs of Quality** – R Graham, A Phizacklea

Above: Phil Rigby who added **Liquid Engineering** to Raven Crag, Threshthwaite Cove in 1984. **Photo:** John Williams

1985 May 27 **The Filling** – SJH Reid, L Steer

1985 May 30 **Tight Fit** – T Longhorne

1985 Jun 15 **Simple Solution** – R Smith, J W Earl

1985 Jun 15 **Stern Test** – JW Earl, R Smith

1985 Jun 15 **Gouttes D'Eau** – R Smith, JW Earl

1985 Jun 29 **Baby Driver** – R Smith, JW Earl

1985 Jul 6 **Cabriolet** – R Smith, JW Earl (alt)

1985 Jul 7 **Chicane** – JW Earl, R Smith

1985 Jul 7 **Silverstone** – R Smith, JW Earl

1986 May 8 **Shaken Not Stirred** – A Mitchell, T Walkington

1986 May 8 **Dream Chaser** – D Bates, T Walkington

1986 May 28 **Grubby Mitts** – D Bates, N Monson

1986 May 29 **Smooth Operator, Pagan Life** – D Bates

1986 May 30 **The Old Aid Route** – T Walkington

1986 Jun 4 **Left-Hand Slab** – T Walkington, D Bates

1986 Jun 6 **Right-Hand Slab** – T Walkington (solo)

1986 Jun 8 **Blind Vision** – D Bates

1986 Jun 15 **Hope** – JW Earl, R Smith

1986 Jun 19 **Monkey Business** – D Armstrong, J Williams

1986 Jun 19 **Slanting Corner** – T Walkington, B Rogers

1986 Jun 21 **Internal Combustion** – R Smith, JW Earl

Above: Bob Smith, left and John Earl, new routers and Eastern Crags guidebook writers 1987. They made numerous journeys from their homes in Northumbria whilst compiling the guide. **Photo:** Andy Birtwistle

1986 Jun 22 **Dipstick** – JW Earl, R Smith
1986 Jun 26 **Ape Factor** – D Armstrong, J Williams
1986 Jun 26 **How Hard** – RA Smithson, H Beanland
1986 Jun 27 **Day of the Squid** – D Bates
1986 Jul 1 **Never Ending Story** – D Bates, T Walkington
1986 Jul 1 **Physical Test** – T Walkington, D Bates
1986 Jul 12 **The Soup Dragon** – R Smith, JW Earl
1986 Jul 12 **The Clangers** – JW Earl, R Smith
1986 Jul 12 **The Iron Chicken** – R Smith, JW Earl, I Kyle
1986 Jul 20 **Stigma** – RJ Kenyon, J Hughes, S Wilson
1986 Jul 22 **Thornhow Wall** – M Turner
1986 Jul 22 **The Groove** – M Turner, S Parker
1986 Aug 4 **Eastern Promise** – A Davis, C King, RJ Kenyon
1986 Aug 10 **Songs from the Woods** – RJ Kenyon, M Bradley, J Beveridge
1986 Aug 11 **Two Pockets** – TW Birkett, J Hargreaves
1986 Aug 30 **Dandle Chimney** – MA Griffiths, N Hinchliffe
Probably climbed before as part of a route called **Dandle Way**.
1986 Sep 4 **Caged** – R Smith, JW Earl
1986 Sep 11 **Pig Balls** – R Parker (solo)
1986 Sep 20 **Under Pressure** – A Greig, R Parker
1986 Sep 27 **Western Union** – D Hall
"Douggie Hall had reputedly stopped of there on the way to his brother's wedding! Whether or not this is true, the tale has subsequently grown in local folklore, where the latest version has him leading the route in top hat and tails!" Al Phizacklea, 'A History of Lake District Climbing (Part 5)', *FRCC Journal 2008.*

1986 Sep 29 **Clearpoint** – C Downer, F Halbert
1986 Oct 11 **The Vorpal Blade** – AH Greenbank, J Lockley
1986 Oct 15 **The Slicer, The Cutter** – J White, C Downer
1986 Oct 16 **The Cleaver** – J White, E Grindley, A Boston, AH Greenbank
1986 Oct 16 **The Keenest** – TW Birkett, J Hargreaves
1986 Oct 16 **Silhouette Arête** – AH Greenbank, J Lockley, A Boston, J White, E Grindley
1986 **Ted's Route** – E Rogers
1986 **Fish Fryer's Convention** – TW Birkett, J Hargreaves
1986 **Piglet's Wall, Dizzy** – J White, TW Birkett
1986 **Diamond Life** – I Williamson, K White
1987 Jan 3 **Two Sizes Too Big** – RJ Kenyon, J Beveridge
1987 Apr 27 **The Slasher** – TW Birkett, AH Greenbank
1987 May 4 **Serious Sleeping** – A Hewison, A Davis
1987 May 5 **The Grater** – I Williamson, J White
1987 May 7 **Where Monkeys Dare** – D Bates, T Walkington
1987 Jun 14 **The Quest** – R Smith, JW Earl, I Kyle
1987 Sep 28 **Rusty Fish** – A Phizacklea
1987 Sep 28 **Polish Pork** – A Phizacklea
1988 Mar 13 **Victory V** – J Daly, K Daly
1988 Mar 25 **Splashdown** – J Daly, K Daly
1988 Apr 3 **Eddie the Eagle** – J Daly, K Phizacklea
1988 Apr 3 **Resurrection** – K Phizacklea, J Daly
1988 Apr 6 **Bloodletting** – R Wightman, A Rowntree
The route incorporates the ***Left-Hand Finish to Bloodhound*** climbed in May 1985 by S Howe and I Walker.
1988 Apr 11 **The Bulger** – J Daly, K Daly
1988 Apr 14 **Howler** – RJ Kenyon, J Beveridge
1988 May 28 **Bucket City** – M Berzins, N Foster
"The first route to breach the steep North Wall since Rick Graham and Bill Birkett climbed Fast and Furious in 1982."
Al Phizacklea, 'A History of Lake District Climbing (Part 5)', *FRCC Journal 2008.*
1988 Jun 17 **Yorkshire Pudding** – R Graham, P Ingham
The name may just possibly reflect Cumbrian Rick Graham's reaction to Yorkshireman Berzins' raid on his home crag!
1988 Jun 29 **Kirkstone Corner** – SJH Reid, D Mitchell
1988 Aug 15 **The Fells! The Fells!** – SJH Reid, I Conway
1989 Apr 31 **Never, and Again** – M Wood, J Freeman

Right: Mark Radtke on the first ascent of **Phoenix in Obsidian** (E6), Iron Crag in 1989.
Photo: Jane Cooksey

Above: Martin Berzins, a 'determined assault' on Dove Crag in the late '80s and early '90s. **Photo:** Berzins Collection

1989 May 28 **Horse Power** – D Musgrave, G Arthur, D Musgrave (Jnr)
Incorporates as its first pitch, **Heavy Horses,** which was climbed by RJ Kenyon, L Shore, 9th August 1987.

1989 Jun 5 **Beyond the Pail** – M Berzins, A Manson

1989 Jul 2 **Phoenix in Obsidian** – M Radtke (unseconded)

1989 Jul 11 **Wild Wall** – T Walkington, P Bryant

1989 Jul **Mindscape** – P Cornforth, I Williamson

1989 Aug 2 **Midget's Slab** – T Furniss, K Irons

1989 Sep 3 **Blood Poisoning** – A Phizacklea, J Holden

1989 Nov 16 **Rub Up, Push Up** – M Miller, E Blaylock

1989 Nov 23 **Swirled not Shaken** – P Carling

1989 **Does Bob Smith Drink Shandy?** – A Moss, C Morly

1990 Jan 20 **Fringe Benefits** – J Daly, R Daly

1990 Mar 30 **Sun City** – J Daly, K Daly

1990 May 15 **The Watchtower** – S Miller, P Andrews

1990 May 21 **Mitchell's Route** – SJH Reid, AH Greenbank

1990 May 28 **Green Eggs and Ham** – I Williamson, A Hyslop

1990 May 28 **Eleven Hundred Miles** – A Hyslop, I Williamson

1990 May 28 **Resignation Route, Legless Pigeon** – SJH Reid, AH Greenbank

1990 May 30 **Miv, Willet, Won't It, Patterdale Chimney** – SJH Reid (solo)

1990 Jun 3 **The Great Game** – M Greenbank, P Hadfield

1990 Jun 3 **Crusty Wall** – M Greenbank (solo)

1990 Jun 17 **The Raven** – M Greenbank
Direct Start, M Greenbank, 26th August 1990.

1990 Jul 12 **While the Cat's Away** – P Hicks, M France

1990 Jul 20 **The Greybeards** – A Davis, S Ely

1990 Jul 22 **Waiting for Laura** – D Kay, J Campbell

1990 Aug 4 **Pail Face** – M Berzins, N Foster
Outside Edge finish climbed by N Foster, M Berzins, 4th August 1990.
The ***FFF Link*** was made by S Crowe, K Magog, 16th August 2003.

1990 Aug 25 **Late Back for Laura** – J Campbell, D Kay (alt)

1990 Aug 26 **Vlad the Impailer** – M Berzins, N Foster

1991 Jan 22 **Keep Left of the Crack** – A Cannon

1991 Mar 23 **Marine's Slab** – A Phizacklea, J Holden
Captain Pugwash variation added by P Figg, 27th May 1991.
1991 Mar 23 **Barrow Boys' Day Out** – A Phizacklea, J Holden
1991 Apr 14 **Seconds Away** – J Holden, A Phizacklea
1991 Apr 14 **St John's Ambulance, Vale of Secrecy, Coup d'État, Eastern Promise** – A Phizacklea, J Holden
1991 Apr 23 **Fingery Fun** – S Holmes, P Batey
1991 Apr 25 **Nappyrash** – RJ Kenyon, G Baum, P Figg
1991 Apr 28 **Time and a Word** – K Telfer, G Telfer
1991 Apr 28 **Fragile** – G Telfer, K Telfer
1991 May 14 **Lost World** – K Wilkinson, D Ferguson, S Holmes
1991 May 26 **Lemon Dixon** – P Cornforth, D Booth
1991 May 26 **Baptismal Vows, Bambino Bolero** – RJ Kenyon, G Baum, G Irvine
1991 May 27 **Bucket Dynasty** – M Berzins, N Foster
1991 Jun 5 **Life Begins at Forty** – RJ Kenyon, G Baum, A Davis, T Price
1991 Jun 20 **Relative Ease, Bloodline** – A Ross, P Ross
1991 Jun 24 **Family Affair, Genetic Edge, Like Father, Like Son** – A Ross, P Ross
1991 Jun 26 **Take It or Leave It** – RJ Kenyon, C King
1991 Jul 1 **Sorry, No Bolts** – S Miller
1991 Jul 3 **Jack's Chimbley, Drystone Gulch** – SJH Reid (solo)
1991 Jul 3 **Picnic Groove** – SJH Reid (solo)
Working Lunch added by D Hall, June 1994.
1991 Jul 7 **Josse F. Boyas** – M Miller, E Blaylock, T Peak
1991 Jul 14 **Carol's Delight** – PJ Kane, C Bainbridge
1991 Jul 16 **Marc One** – C Bainbridge, P J Kane
1991 Jul 20 **Heirloom** – R Graham, AH Greenbank, TW Birkett
1991 Jul 20 **Powder Monkey** – J Eastham, M Lynch
1991 Jul 20 **Doghouse** – M Lynch, J Eastham
1991 Jul 21 **Shundraw Slab** – PJ Kane, C Bainbridge
M Greenbank and A Bacon climbed a route called **Tottering Wall of Death** in this area. The description read 'somewhere on the left' and was impossible to follow.
1991 Jul 21 **Graping Aches** – A Slattery, R Davison
1991 Jul 28 **Friendly Fire, Citizen's Charter, Jungle Fever** – M Lynch, B McKinley, R Matheson, K Phizacklea
1991 Jul 28 **Lovely Boy** – B McKinley, R Matheson, K Phizacklea, M Lynch
1991 Jul **Short Circuit** – P Botterill, P Smith
1991 Aug 8 **Her Indoors, Tying the Knot, Under the Thumb** – P Ross, M Ross
1991 Aug 8 **Bold as Brass** – C Bainbridge, PJ Kane
1991 Aug 8 **Scallywag** – RJ Kenyon, SJH Reid
1991 Aug 18 **Gruesome Twosome** – PJ Kane, C Bainbridge
1991 Aug 18 **Snapshot** – C Bainbridge, PJ Kane

1991 Aug 25 **Glaslost** – S Barber, P Allder
1991 Aug 28 **Vulture's Crack, Vulture's Claws, Vulture's Flakes** – A Cannon
1991 Aug 30 **Reunion** – P Ross, P Lockey
1991 Aug **Lost in Space** – A Parry, S Coffey
1991 Oct 28 **Last on the List** – SJH Reid, J Campbell (alt)
1991 Dec 14 **On the Edge** – RJ Kenyon
1991 Dec 15 **"It's a good job the Vulture's got long wings"** – A Cannon, D Walker
1991 Dec 27 **Beyond the Fringe** – RJ Kenyon
1991 Dec 28 **Tyke's Teeter** – RJ Kenyon, A Davis
1991 **Blencathra Badger** – A Phizacklea, J Holden
1991 **Hit the Fan** – R Matheson, I Greenwood
1991 **Xoanan** – M Miller
1992 Feb 1 **Farewell to Adventure?** – RJ Kenyon, J Bardgett
1992 Jun 3 **Confidence** – SJH Reid, JE Reid
1992 Jun 7 **Brothers in Arms** – C Bainbridge, S Bainbridge
1992 Jun 7 **Starbug, Hologram** – J Shepherd, K Lunt
1992 Jun 7 **Desert Storm** – K Lunt, J Shepherd
1992 Jun 20 **Mega Drive** – J Shepherd, K Lunt
Some rests taken on the gear – climbed free after abseil inspection and practice, R Graham, 14th September 1996.
1992 Jun 20 **Histoplasmosis** – K Lunt, J Shepherd
1992 Jun 24 **Pandamania** – SJH Reid, JE Reid
1992 Jun 28 **Call to Arms, England Calling** – E Cleasby, J Eastham, M Lynch
1992 Jun 28 **Call-up, Call Girl** – J Eastham, M Lynch (varied leads) E Cleasby
1992 Jul **Crack of the Under-Table World, Golden Shot** – RJ Kenyon, M Golden
1992 Aug 16 **One Step Right** – B Davison, Penny Clay
1992 Aug 20 **If 6 was 9** – D Birkett
"The route climbs a big overhanging face, broken by a rather evilly placed ledge at 10 metres – finely placed to kill you if you fall from the redpoint crux another 15 metres above that. The climbing is high standard – F8a+

Above: Dave Birkett, his **If 6 was 9** (1992) remained unrepeated for fifteen years. **Photo:** Steve Crowe

but positive at least, so sport climbing fitness of 8c+ or 9a means at least you can just apply more power to get out of trouble, or reverse out of the death zone near the top if something goes wrong – the only way to justify an ascent so dangerous, for me at least. The gear can be more simply be described; crap. There are three pegs, the first two look reasonable – I'd lower off on them. It's irrelevant anyway. If you are good enough to actually lead the route, the only place you'd fall is the second last move, and onto the third and last peg. Naturally this is the worst one – a poor peg in crumbly rock. I tied into the ropes and briefed Claire "If I come off from the top move, the third peg will slow me down and I'll swing in. Then it will rip and I'll land on the ledge. Hopefully it'll slow me down enough so it won't hurt… erm… too much…?" Dave McLeod mulls things over prior to the second ascent.

1992 Sep 5 **Showtime** – RJ Kenyon, A Heron
1992 Sep 5 **Time Stops for No-one** – RJ Kenyon
1992 Oct 10 **Swirlaround** – P Botterill, P Smith
1992 Oct 17 **American Express** – P Botterill, P Smith
1993 Mar **Damp Powder** – M Walker, R Cassidy
1993 Apr 11 **Easter Bunny** – SJH Reid, RC Withers
Twin Chimney Variation added by SJH Reid, CAJ Reid, 13th April 1997.
1993 Apr 12 **Cottontail, Flopsy** – SJH Reid, RC Withers
1993 Apr 12 **Graveyard Gully** – SJH Reid (solo)
1993 Apr 12 **Roger Rabbit** – RC Withers, SJH Reid
1993 May 4 **Tyke's Teeter Direct** – C Bainbridge, PJ Kane
1993 May 4 **Swirl Pinnacle** – SJH Reid (solo)
1993 May 4 **Swirligig** – SJH Reid, RC Withers, A Scott
1993 May 7 **The Brunt** – A Slattery, R Davison
1993 May 17 **Shoulthwaite Crack** – D Birkett, P Cornforth
1993 May 17 **Better Than Disneyworld** – P Cornforth, D Birkett
Variation Finish, C Downer, A Prickett, 6 th July 1993.
1993 May 22 **Grand Larceny** – P Ross, P Lockey
1993 May 22 **Lost Era** – P Lockey, P Ross
1993 May 22 **The L.A. Way** – C Downer, P Ross, P Lockey, L Alderson
1993 May 23 **Remission** – P Ross, P Lockey, C Downer
1993 May 26 **Professor Challenger** – C Downer, J Holliday
1993 Jun 7 **Hidden Agenda** – C Downer, E Prickett
1993 Jun 13 **Roraima** – C Downer, E Prickett
1993 Jun 17 **GCSE Escape** – E Prickett, C Downer
1993 Jun 21 **New Age Traveller** – E Prickett, C Downer
1993 Jun 21 **Buffalo Girls** – C Downer, E Prickett, A Prickett
1993 Jun 25 **Jurassic Park** – C Downer, E Prickett, A Prickett
1993 Jun **Lovely Charter, Citizen's Fever** – S Scott, R Graham, T Rogers
1993 Jul 20 **Thunder Dragons** – C Downer, A Prickett, J Holliday
1993 Aug 16 **In Like Flynn** – C Downer, J Holliday, G Frazer

1993 Aug 18 **Pumping Iron** – G Sutcliffe, J Fletcher
1993 Aug 28 **The Gelding, A Snip in Time** – P Carling
1993 Aug 31 **A Crow Flies North** – S Miller, D Johnson
1993 **Stegasaurus** – T Greenbank, M Greenbank
1994 Jul 11 **The Fondue Party** – J Bumby, J Parkin
1994 Jul 22 **Crusader** – T Daley, D Bodecott, J Campbell, D Absalom, CJS Bonington
1994 Aug 7 **Tautalist** – J Robertson, J Beveridge
A similar line with a different start (***Boddycount***) and finish was climbed by M Charlton, A Cater, A Moist, 24th May 1997. Robertson and Beveridge lowered off from the Tamarist ledge at the end of the hard climbing. The route as described incorporates both climbs.
1994 Aug 31 **Deliverance** – T Marr, M Tooke
Pitch 3 only. Pitches 1 and 2 were climbed as part of an eliminate called ***One World, One Family*** by R Kenyon, C King, G Baum, J Grinbergs, August 1990. Pitch 2 Direct was climbed by C Downer, F Fowler, 7th August 1993.
1994 Sep 22 **Lost Left Sock, Broken Jinx** – I Healey, M Day
1994 Oct18 **Central Climb** – SJH Reid, J Campbell (alt)
1994 Oct18 **Central Rib Semi-Direct** – SJH Reid, J Campbell
1995 Jun 27 **Bobby Rascal** – RJ Kenyon, B Johnson, A Heron, M Golden
1995 Apr 9 **In Commemoration** – M Turner
1995 Jun 27 **Road Rage** – N Wharton, H Davies, P Clavey, D Donnini
1995 Jul 1 **The Crystal Maze** – K Lunt, L Sharman
1995 Aug 1 **Ken Rognon** – RJ Kenyon, SJH Reid
1995 Aug 1 **Crazy Horse** – K Lunt
1995 Sep 9 **Odile** – J Unsworth, D Blanden
1995 Sep 16 **Loaded Dice** – C King, RJ Kenyon
1995 **Route Twelve** – I Weetman, D Birkett
Direct Finish, R Graham, T Rogers, 16th August 1997.
1995 **Route Thirteen** – D Birkett, I Weetman
1996 Jul 14 **Lion Sheep, Morton's Boys, Gary's Crack, Armo's Slab, Cross Hands, Shake Hands** – D Armstrong, G Storey
1996 Jul 14 **Nanga Parbat Pilgrimage** – I Wilson, H Binns
1996 Aug 23 **No Picnic on Mt Kenya** – I Wilson
1996 **Divine Cross** – D Weatherley, I Grace, P Soulsby
1997 Mar 12 **Meltdown, The Necker** – M Lovatt, T Whiteley
1997 Mar 12 **Rampart Road** – M Lovatt
1997 Apr 12 **Punter's Rib** – T Whiteley, S Wilcock
1997 Apr 13 **Carrick's Climb** – SJH Reid, CAJ Reid (aged 6!)

Left: Pete Botterill on the first ascent of **Swirlround** (E3), Lower Swirl Crag in 1992.
Photo: Pete Smith

Above: Almost the first ascent of **Road Rage** (E7), – Nick Wharton. **Photo:** Dominic Donnini

1997 May 2 **Good-bye Mr Major!, Good Luck Mr Blair!** – P King, RJ Kenyon (var)

1997 May 7 **Last Dash** – C Bainbridge, PJ Kane

1997 May 11 **The Quarryman, Hound-dog, Twilight** – PJ Kane, C Bainbridge

1997 May 28 **Rabbit Run** – T Rogers, R Graham

1997 Jun 1 **Polecat** – R Graham, T Rogers, TW Birkett

1997 Jun 1 **Badger Wall** – T Rogers, R Graham, TW Birkett

1997 Jun 1 **Route Seventeen** – TW Birkett, T Rogers, R Graham

1997 Jun 8 **Route Fourteen** – R Graham, T Rogers

1997 Jun 10 **Gremlin Groove, Slab and Groove** – T Rogers, R Graham

1997 Jun 10 **Ride the Wild Turf** – R Graham, T Rogers

1997 Jul 5 **Grotto Crack** – T Rogers, R Graham

1997 Jul 6 **The American Cowboy** – A Hocking, J McHaffie

1997 Aug 2 **Slab in the Face** – D Douglas, K Whitaker

1997 Aug 10 **Bat Crack** – T Rogers, K Forsythe, TW Birkett

1997 Aug 15 **Horse and Farrier Special** – EVMC party

1997 Aug 16 **Chameleon** – T Rogers, R Graham

1997 Aug 16 **Diamond Wall** – R Graham, T Rogers

1997 Oct **Lucky Streaks** – M Bagness, S Wood

1998 Mar 15 **Please Release Me** – C Allen, Suzanne Allen, R Wright, Angela Wright

1998 May 4 **Shed Shifting for Beginners** – A Phizacklea, J Holden

1998 May 5 **Shed Shifters of the World Unite** – A Phizacklea, J Holden, A Towse

1998 May 23 **Sea of Knobs** – A Hyslop, S Wood
1998 May 23 **Minuteman** – R Graham, T Rogers
1998 May 25 **Langdale Lads** – D Birkett
1998 May **Too Baldly Go** – S Britt, S Pretty
1998 Jun 13 **The Dalesman** – R Patterson, A Scott
1998 Summer **Gritstone Dreamer** – S Stout, Mrs Jo Jones, SJH Reid
1999 May 20 **Mist Arête** – RJ Kenyon, C Rhodes, J Davis
1999 May 20 **Keep out of the Kennel** – RJ Kenyon, C Rhodes
1999 May 31 **Surgical Cut, Incision** – P Rigby, M Hetherington
1999 Jun 24 **Grand Day Out** – T Marr, M Tooke, F Fitzgerald
Frank Fitzgerald is involved in a first ascent on Eagle Crag 45 years after he put up Original Route on the same crag.
1999 Jul 8 **Nexus** – T Marr, M Tooke
1999 Jul 10 **Idle Vice** – SJH Reid, D Bodecott
1999 Jul 25 **Raptor, Thoroughbred** – T Marr, M Tooke
1999 Aug 5 **Groove Central** – N Dixon, S Ashworth, M Bond
1999 Aug 16 **Late Night Groove** – B Davison, P Clay
1999 Aug **Red Pit Crack** – A Swann, R Gordon
1999 Oct 17 **Two Bit Bombed Butty** – T Walkington, N Evans
2000 May 7 **President, Bossman** – T Walkington, N Evans
2000 May 24 **Bin Laden, Aristocrat** – T Walkington, J Campbell
2000 Jul 12 **V.I.P.** – T Walkington, E Barnes
2000 Jul 24 **Misplaced Trussed** – M Turner, A Blyth
2001 Aug 1 **Lords** – T Walkington, E Barnes
2000 Aug 5 **Nick's Brasher Boots** – J Cooper, N Evans
2001 Sep 1 **Meritocrat** – T Walkington (unseconded)
2001 Sep 16 **Monarch** – T Walkington, N Evans
2001 Sep 22 **Taliban** – C Read, GL Swainbank (alt), P Fleming
2002 May 5 **90 Years Young** – RJ Kenyon, D Jones
2002 Aug 10 **Fear of Failure** – J McHaffie
The first new route on Dove Crag for eleven years and the start of a new routeing boom.
2002 Sep 23 **Table de Roc** – BJ Clarke

Above: Duncan Booth, contributor of many fearsome lines in the Eastern Crags. **Photo:** Steve Crowe

Above and opposite page, from left to right: Dove Crag pioneers – Chris Hope, Al Wilson and Steve Crowe. **Photos:** Al Wilson and Steve Crowe

2002 Oct 18 **Lilith** – D Pomfret
Almost certainly climbed before.

2002 **Romantically Challenged** – SJH Reid, A Lywood
Almost certainly climbed before.

2003 Jun 11 **Hot Wheels of Steele** – A Phizacklea, AM Atkinson
Supercedes an earlier incomplete attempt by A Phizacklea, J Holden, November 1993.

2003 Jun 11 **Sadgit Wall** – A Phizacklea, AM Atkinson

2003 Jun 24 **Imminent Arrival** – D Booth, J Beveridge

2003 Jul 6 **Fetish for Fear** – C Hope, D Booth (both led), A Wilson, J Beveridge
"Chris Hope not only climbed the stunning Fetish for Fear at E8, he also inadvertantly took a massive 25 metre dive attempting to repeat another line, narrowly missing the deck. Apparently one team gearing up at the base of the crag was so horrified at this spectacle they packed up and left the scene!"
Al Phizacklea, 'A History of Lake District Climbing (Part 5)', *FRCC Journal 2008.*

2003 Jul 19 **Dusk Till Dawn** – A Wilson, C Hope (both led)
"The most out there route in the Lakes!" Al Wilson comments on his own superb creation.
Right-Hand Start added by A Wilson, 5th October 2003.

2003 Aug 9 **The Brasov Incident** – S Crowe, K Magog (both led)

2003 Aug 13 **The Whisperer, Dobby's Sock** – K Telfer, C Telfer

Above: Duncan Booth on first ascent of **Relentless Rage** (E7), Gouther Crag in 2003. **Photo:** Jimmy Beveridge

2003 Aug 13 **The Second Coming** – D Booth, M Weeks
The start had been climbed as a **Direct Start to The Gates of Delirium** by D Dinwoodie, C McLean, 12th August 1985.

2003 Aug 14 **The Whinger** – K Telfer, C Telfer

2003 Aug 16 **Fast City** – S Crowe, K Magog (both led), A Wilson
May have been done before.

2003 Aug 17 **The Doghouse** – R Wilkinson, B Peace

2003 Aug 23 **Infestation Finish** – D Booth, J Robertson, J Beveridge

2003 Sep 14 **Die Another Day** – K Telfer, P Morgan
Top roped and RPs pre-placed prior to ascent. Incorporates the best parts of two routes that were previously recorded up the pillar of the second pitch. These are **Snap Dragon**, JP Hotham, E Brown, 1993, and **Make Hay while the Sun Shines**, D Birkett, A Hyslop, 27th July 1997.

2003 Sep 27 **Relentless Rage** – D Booth, J Robertson, M Greenbank, J Beveridge

2004 May 20 **Appliance of Science** – SJH Reid, C King

2004 May 20 **The Stopper** – SJH Reid, C King (alt)

2004 Jul 31 **Liquid Wall** – A Mitchell

2004 Jul **Freddie Flintoff, Fred Dibnah** – M Bagness, D Duxbury

2004 Sep 23 **Cold Frontier** – G Uney

2004 Sep 29 **Ilex Slab, Two Step Buttress** – G Uney

2005 Jun 9 **The Darkest Hour** – D Birkett

2005 Aug 23 **Scrubs Up Nicely** – J Arnold, K Arnold, A Davis
2005 Aug 29 **Sursum Tuus** – GL Swainbank, C Read (alt)
2006 Feb 10 **Smearing on Sunshine** – BJ Clarke (solo)
The direct start, ***Happy Feet***, was added by BJ Clarke, Tanya Coates, 15th May 2007.
2006 May 10 **Short and Brutal** – J Arnold, K Arnold
2006 Sep 7 **Blade Buttress, Sine Nomine, Santiago, La Haye Sainte** – BJ Clarke (solo)
2006 Sep 22 **Sensor Slab** – BJ Clarke (solo)
2006 Sep 26 **Ahab's Slab, Moby Dick, Terpsichore, Flashdance** – BJ Clarke (solo)
2007 Mar **Nether Pillar, Never say Nether, Better late than Nether, Nether Never, First Knight** – S Brown, C Brown
2007 Mar **Netherlands, Last Knight, Second Knight, Pacemaker Special** – C Brown, S Brown
2007 Mar **Good Knight** – S Brown (solo)
2007 Apr 6 **Twenty Metre Slab** – BJ Clarke (solo)
2007 Apr 11 **Gazelle, Impala, Norwester, Grate Wall, Wildebeest, Mephisto, Pequod** – BJ Clarke (solo)
2007 Apr 16 **Sofa on Cofa, Yonder Slab** – BJ Clarke (solo)
2007 Apr 29 **It's Easily Done** – BJ Clarke (solo)
2007 Apr 30 **Eachan Trillvite, Slaberitif, Hearty Slab** – BJ Clarke (solo)
2007 May 4 **Pokketz Slab, Standing Room Only, Standing Joke, Exhibition Rib, One for the Road** – A Phizacklea
2007 May 29 **Goldrill Thrill, Beckstones Buttress, Goldrill Grooves, Old Bones Rib** – BJ Clarke (solo)
2007 Jul 8 **A Century on the Crags** – A Phizacklea, JL Holden
So called because the joint age of the Al Phizacklea/John Holden team had reached 100.
2007 Jul 9 **Ker-ching, Flossy** – BJ Clarke (solo)
2007 Aug 26 **Sippling Groove, Sippling Rivalry, Speeding for Fun** – A Phizacklea, JL Holden
2007 Sep 8 **Diamond Jubilee** – A Phizacklea, JL Holden
2008 May 31 **Dog On The Edge** – M Kenyon, RJ Kenyon, C Kenyon
2008 May **Ask Jim** – J Fotheringham, S Broatch, D Hayward
2008 May **Alfie** – S Broatch, J Fotheringham, D Hayward
2008 Jun 7 **Validation** – G Widdowson, S Broatch
2008 Jun 8 **Conundrum** – G Widdowson, S Broatch
2008 Jun 8 **Go Mamasike** – S Broatch, G Widdowson
2008 Jun 11 **The Iron Man** – A Wilson, M Johnston
2008 Jun 14 **Rudd** – G Widdowson, S Broatch
2008 Jul 23 **Hawkeye** – T Marr, M Tooke
2008 Jul 23 **Full Circle** – T Marr, M Tooke
2008 Aug 25 **Warbird** – T Marr, M Tooke (alt)
2009 May 24 **Recess Route Direct** – SJH Reid, Sarah Bailey

2009 May 30 **Bombay Bambino** – K Metcalfe, C Downer, M Nicholson
2009 May 30 **Lakeland Spice** – K Metcalfe, C Downe r, M Nicholson
2009 May 30 **Help the Aged** – C Downer, K Metcalfe, M Nicholson, G Lee
2009 May 30 **Grave Dodger, Age Concern** – C Downer, K Metcalfe, M Nicholson
2009 Jun 2 **Swoop** – T Marr, M Tooke
2009 Jun 3 **Ruby Tuesday** – M Nicholson, K Metcalfe, C Downer
2009 Jun 4 **Trill Groove, Hobblit** – BJ Clarke
2009 Jun 12 **Amabilite** – N Wharton, C Gore, T Whiteley

Above: Tony Marr on the first ascent of **Swoop** (E2), Eagle Crag, Grisedale in 2009. **Photo:** Mike Tooke

2009 Jun 13 **Peeping Tom, Shameless** – C Downer, K Metcalfe, M Nicholson, G Baxter
2009 Jun 29 **DJ Slate** – M Nicholson, C Downer, K Metcalfe
2009 Jul 6 **Sweepstake** – K Metcalfe, M Nicholson, C Downer
Sweepstake Corner was added by C Downer, K Metcalfe, M Nicholson the same day.
2009 Jul 10 **Yew Crag Pinnacle, *Offwidth Start*** – C Downer
2009 Jul 15 **Up Hellya** – D Birkett (unseconded)
"You have to pull hard with the fingers and push hard with the feet," Dave Birkett stating the obvious after the first ascent.
2009 Jul 21 **Bobby Dazzler** – C Downer, C Higgins, D Ferguson, C Fowler
2009 Jul 25 **Lady Driver** – M Greenbank, R Dicks
2009 Aug 2 **Forever Young** – A Davis, S Goodwin
2009 Sep 13 **Dapper Dan** – C Downer, G Proctor
2009 Sep 19 **Bon Courage** – C Downer, C Higgins, D Ferguson, C Fowler
2009 Sep 19 **Mr Angry, Bonne Chance** – C Downer, M Nicholson
2010 May 1 **Caterpillar Ridge** – S Caldwell, Miss C Elphick
2010 May 8 **The History Boys** – C Downer, G Lee, G Proctor
So named because the combined age of the team totalled 200 years!!
2010 Jun 12 **Michelangelo** – M Norbury
2010 Jun 14 **Bram Crag Wall** – M de Vaal
2010 Jun 14 **Middle Earth** – M Norbury
2010 Aug **Wai Lord** – M Greenbank
2010 Nov 6 **The Knacker's Yard** – M Scrowston, J Loxham

Details of the first ascents of the following routes are not known; any information or claims would be appreciated and can be recorded at www.frcc.co.uk.

Bramcrag Quarry: *Seconds Away Variation (1991), Moggy's Meander (1991).*
Castle Rock of Triemain: *Overhanging Bastion Direct Finish, Chapel Cracks Alternative Start, No Name.*
Upper Swirl Crag: *The Race (1991), La Habanera (1991), Ballet Mecanique (1991), Bimbo (1991).*
Snail Shell Crag: *Left Arête , The Scoop, The Gully, Slabs Left , Recess Route, Barker's Slab, Barker's Slab Direct, Right Crack.*
Slape Crags: *Bloodaxe.*
Gowbarrow: *Whistle Away, Shamrock Crack, Dave's Slab, Gowbarrow Corner, Gowbarrow Buttress, Bypass (1975).*
Arthur's Pike: *Left-Hand Crack, The Slab, Right-Hand Crack.*
Scrubby Crag: *Heorot Variation Finish.*
Gill Crag: *Right Ridge.*
Dove Crag: *South Gully.*
Gouther Crag: *Sostenuto Variation Start, Hindleg Crack Direct.*
Buckbarrow: *Cleft Ghyll Chimney.*
Iving Crag: *Pagan Life Easy Way.*

Right: Nick Wharton reaches the good slot on **Amabilite** (E4), Iron Crag on the first ascent in 2009. **Photo:** Tim Whiteley

Index

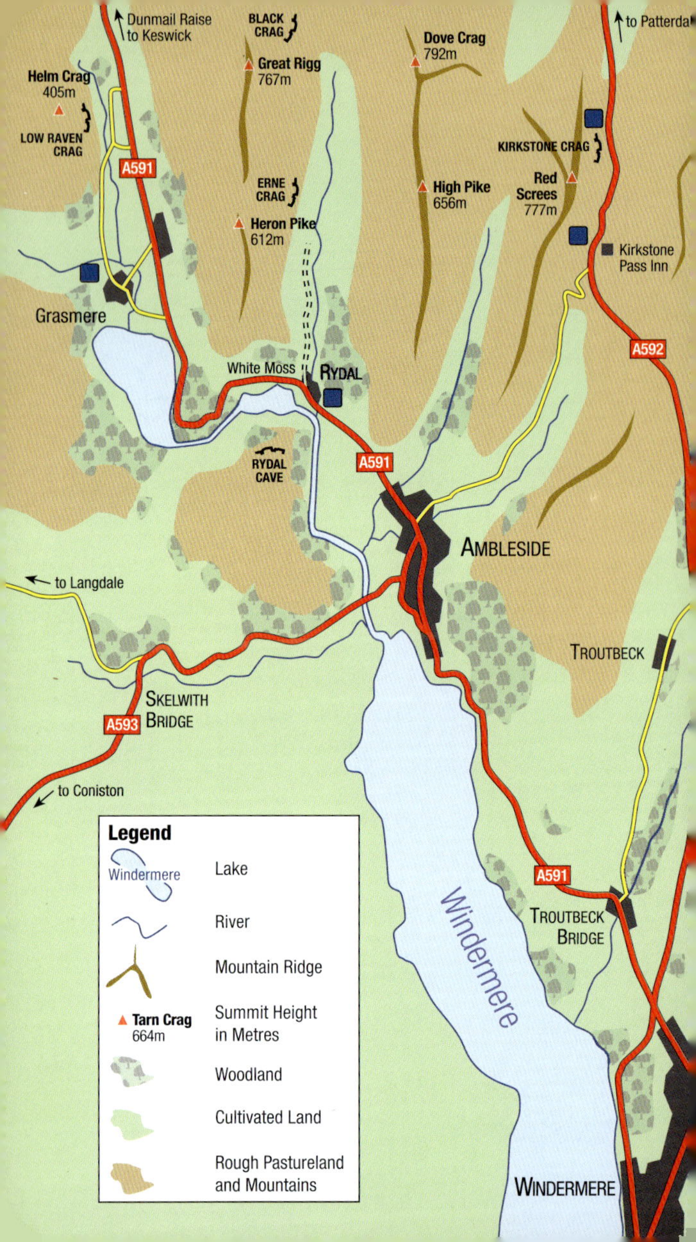

Dunmail Raise
to Keswick
BLACK CRAG
Great Rigg
767m
Dove Crag
792m
to Patterdale
Helm Crag
405m
LOW RAVEN CRAG
A591
ERNE CRAG
Heron Pike
612m
High Pike
656m
KIRKSTONE CRAG
Red Screes
777m
Kirkstone Pass Inn
Grasmere
White Moss
RYDAL
A592
RYDAL CAVE
A591
AMBLESIDE
to Langdale
TROUTBECK
SKELWITH BRIDGE
A593
to Coniston
Legend
Windermere
Lake
River
Mountain Ridge
Tarn Crag
664m
Summit Height in Metres
Woodland
Cultivated Land
Rough Pastureland and Mountains
Windermere
A591
TROUTBECK BRIDGE
WINDERMERE

0km
1
2
3
N
NAN BIELD PASS
GATESGARTH PASS
Harter Fell
778m
Froswick
720m
Ill Bell
757m
Kentmere Pike
730m
Tarn Crag
664m
BUCKBARROW CRAG
TONGUE SCAR
GOAT SCAR
RAINSBORROW CRAG
CALF HOWE CRAG
IRVING SCAR
SADGILL
GARBURN PASS
Garburn Pass Boulder
Badger Rock
KENTMERE
Kentmere
Longsleddale
to the A6
NETHER CRAG
Garnett Bridge
A591
INGS
STAVELEY
to Kendal

CHURCH CRAG
Dale Bottom
to Keswick
A591
SHAW BANK
St. John's in the Vale
BRAMCRAG QUARRY
SANDBED GHYLL CRAG
B5322
YEW CRAG
GOAT CRAG
SMAITHWAITE BANKS CRAG
SIPPLING CRAG
CASTLE ROCK
Stanah
IRON CRAG
Shoulthwaite Valley
RAVEN CRAG
Great Dodd
857m
Stybarrow Dodd
843m
Thirlspot
Raise
883m
Greenside
LOWER PIKETOE KNOT CRAG
Thirlmere Valley
Thirlmere
UPPER SWIRL CRAG
LOWER SWIRL CRAG
THACKMELL CRAG
BULL CRAG
Helvellyn
950m
EAGLE CRAG
Nethermost Pike
891m
STANDING CRAG
HARROP TARN CRAG
FALCON CRAG
TARN CRAG
COFA PIKE SLABS
NAB CRAGS
Steel End Farm
Ullscarf
726m
Wythburn Valley
Fairfield
873m
Steel Fell
553m
Dunmail Raise
Seat Sandal
736m
A591